The first role of the developed world is not to help, but to understand.

Xavier Gorostiaga S.J., 'The Function of Governments: a Third World View',
Ten Years of Action for Justice (Dublin: Trócaire, 1985).

Contents

Acknowledgements

DESC wishes to acknowledge the support of the Higher Education Development Committee (HEDCO) in funding this book.

The editors would like to thank Mary Riordan, librarian, the Development Studies Information Centre, University College, Dublin for assistance which went way beyond the call of duty.

The editors and publishers wish to thank the following who have kindly given permission for the use of copyright material:

John Toye and Basil Blackwell Limited for an extract from *Dilemmas of Development* (1987).

Amartya Sen and the International Labour Organisation for extracts from *Poverty and Famines. An Essay on Entitlement and Deprivation* (1982) Oxford University Press, pages vii and 11-17. Copyright 1981, International Labour Organisation, Geneva.

David Colman and Frederick Nixson and Philip Allan Publishers Limited for an extract from *Economics of Change in Less Developed Countries* (1986).

Nigel Harris and Penguin Books Ltd for two extracts from *The End of The Third World* (Harmondsworth: Penguin, 1986) pages 12-29 and 200-203. Copyright Nigel Harris. Reproduced by permission of Penguin Books Ltd.

Andrew Webster and Macmillan, London and Basingstoke for 'Modernisation Theory' from *Introduction to the Sociology of Development* (1984).

Ankie M. M. Hoogvelt and Macmillan, London and Basingstoke for two extracts from *The Third World in Global Development* (1982).

Geertje Lycklama à Nijeholt for an extract from 'The Fallacy of Integration: the UN strategy of integrating women into development revisited' from *Netherlands Review of Development Studies* Volume 1, 1987.

Michael Lofchie and Cambridge University Press for 'Political and Economic Origins of African Hunger' from *Journal of Modern African Studies* Volume 13 part 4 (1975).

Michael Lofchie and Lynne Riener Publishers for 'Africa's Agricultural Crisis' from Commins, Lofchie and Payne, eds., *Africa's Agrarian Crisis: The Roots of Famine*. Copyright 1986 by Lynne Rienner Publishers. Reprinted by permission of the Publisher.

William W. Murdoch and the Johns Hopkins University Press for extracts from *The Poverty of Nations* (1980).

The New Internationalist for extracts from the *State of the World's Women 1985* press kit.

Amartya Sen and Third World Foundation for 'The Food Problem: Theory and Policy' from *South-South Strategy* (1982) edited by Altaf Gauhar.

Amartya Sen and Basil Blackwell Limited for 'Family and Food: Sex Bias in Poverty' from *Resources, Values and Development* (1984).

Francis Green and Bob Sutcliffe and Penguin Books for extracts from *The Profit System* (Harmondsworth: Penguin 1987). Reproduced by permission of Penguin Books Ltd.

Diane Elson, Ruth Pearson and Routledge and Kegan Paul for an extract from *Of Marriage and the Market* (1981) edited by Kate Young, Carol Wolkowitz and Roslyn McCullagh.

'Multinationals and Foreign Investment' is reprinted from *Economic Development of a Small Planet* by Benjamin Higgins and Jean Downing Higgins, by permission of W. W. Norton & Company, Inc. Copyright © 1979 by W.W. Norton & Company, Inc.

Eoin O'Malley and Harcourt Brace Jovanovich Limited for 'The Problem of Late Industrialisation and the Experience of the Republic of Ireland' from *Cambridge Journal of Economics* 1985, 9.

Harold Lever and Christopher Huhne for the extract from *Debt and Danger* (1985). Reprinted by permission of A.D. Peters & Co. Ltd.

Keith Griffin and Macmillan, London and Basingstoke for 'The Debt Crisis and the Poor' from *World Hunger and the World Economy* (1987).

Introduction © Richard Quinn.

At the time of going to press, every effort had been made to obtain permission to reprint 'Why Poor People Stay Poor' by Michael Lipton from *Rural Development* edited by John Harriss (London: Century Hutchinson, 1982).

Introduction

Richard Quinn

Development studies are concerned with what used to be called progress. They consider the great issues that have agitated human beings since the beginning of time – issues such as justice, equality and inequality, and the nature of the good life.[1]

In practice, development studies deal mainly with Third World development. The subject had its origins in development economics, which specialised in the problems of economic growth and development in the non-industrialised countries of the Third World. Recognition of the complexities of the development process led in due course to a broader approach, calling on the insights of other disciplines besides economics, such as sociology, anthropology, geography and agronomy.

A third approach to development issues is that of development education, which, in common with development studies, seeks to analyse and understand processes of world development, but is also committed to an active approach towards changing social and economic structures in both developed and developing countries. This book is a general introduction to the main concepts and concerns of development studies: theories of development and underdevelopment, concepts of poverty, food and famine, rural stagnation, unequal trade relations, the subordination of women, the endless struggles imposed by poverty. The needs seem overwhelming and obvious: people must have food, clean water, incomes. How are economies and social structures to develop so that they can provide decent standards for their populations?

Development Economics

Development economics emerged in the early 1950s as one response to the problems of overwhelming poverty in the Third World. The western world had embarked on a long period of prosperity; problems of mass unemployment and recession had, it seemed, been solved for ever.[2] But the vast majority of the world's people lived on the edge of survival in countries that frequently lacked even the most basic infrastructure of road networks and piped water. It was argued that the experience and expertise of the West – which it seemed willing to share – would help the poorer countries to catch up. There was 'an implicit assumption that the ultimate goals would be European-style political institutions and levels of living within a capitalist system'.[3]

Development economics was intended to solve problems. Its practitioners attempted not only to analyse and gain understanding of economic development, but also were involved actively in framing policy and devising strategies for development. The plans adopted and the policies proposed, both by those who fall into the category of 'development economists' and by mainstream economists (who are often very critical of their development colleagues), derive from various theoretical constructs – there is no one generally accepted theory of development.

Three main strands in the economic aspect of development theory can be identified:

the classical school, which emphasises the importance of international trade and the free market mechanism.

the structuralists, who identify rigidities in economic structures requiring state intervention to promote development,

and

the dependency schools, which maintain that many poor countries are poor because they are integrated into the international economic system in a dependent, exploitative manner.

The three strands of thought shade into each other: structuralists draw on classical theory, and dependency theorists build on the insights of the structuralists. Dependency theorists also draw on Marxian thought, but have been attacked by neo-Marxists for certain methodological and analytical failures.

The classical approach has its origin in the classic writers on political economy of the eighteenth and nineteenth centuries. Their emphasis on international trade as the engine of economic growth represents an extension to the world as a whole of the important role of trade in nineteenth-century English economic development. Development is seen as almost exclusively a process of economic growth, measured quantitatively by such indices as the rate of increase of Gross National Product. Economic growth 'was the most effective way of eradicating poverty. It was on the growth of incomes, especially in modern, organised, large-scale industrial activity, that the hope for improvement in basic welfare was built . . . growth was not an end in itself (in spite of what is now often said in a caricature of past thinking) but merely a performance test or an indicator of development.'[4] Sociologists proposed corresponding theories of modernisation that postulated stages of growth and evolutionary processes through which, it was maintained, all societies must pass in order to become developed.

The emphasis on a country's economic growth as the principal performance test was justified in three ways: first, it was believed that the gains from economic growth would automatically 'trickle down' to the poor and would be spread throughout the society by market forces. Secondly, it was argued that democratic governments would necessarily be concerned about the fate of the poor. Thirdly, such writers believed that, in the early stages of economic development, the fate of the poor must not be a direct concern: the best way to help them was indirectly, by building up the economy's productive capacity.[5]

The second school of development theorists, the structuralists, tend to emphasise non-economic aspects of the measurement and analysis of causes of development. They point out that increased access to the markets of developed countries, or indeed high rates of GNP growth, do not automatically ensure better living standards for the most needy within the poorer countries. They argue that, by equating development with economic growth, the classicists ignore the problem of how to distribute any increase in wealth among the competing sectors within the developing country's economy. In addition, they claim that the classicists, by confining themselves to a strictly economic framework, fail to recognise that impediments to economic development often lie in the social structure.

In short, structuralists argue that the development process is dependent on the preparedness of various aspects of the developing society – social, political and demographic as well as economic. In addition, they maintain that the path to development will vary from nation to nation and that individual governments will find it necessary to regulate the market mechanism in line with its chosen path. Their policies therefore tend to be *ad hoc* and to demand a good deal of government intervention. Such interventionism, of course, is anathema to the classical advocates of free trade, who deplore what they would describe as interference with the market system. The structuralist argument is that, although free trade and the international division of labour theoretically may maximise gains to all concerned, practical experience has shown that most gains accrue to the already rich countries.

Dependency theorists, members of the third school of development theory, agree that free trade and the market mechanism have tended to benefit the richer countries. Their central theme – that the industrially advanced centre gains at the expense of the poor periphery – is in fact an elaboration of certain structuralist ideas. However, dependency theorists differ from structuralists in that they see these gains as the inevitable result of systematic exploitation of the periphery, the market system being the instrument of exploitation. Accordingly, they claim that the abolition of the present structure of the market system is a prerequisite for proper development and economic justice. Poorer nations are seen as dependent, in as much as growth occurs as a reflex of the expansion of the dominant economies not as a response to local needs. Many of these theorists are Latin American and for them the problem of Latin America's underdevelopment is not that it is pre-capitalist or feudal, but that from the beginning of its penetration by Europe it has been absorbed into the capitalist market as a supplier of raw materials.

Furthermore, since the pattern of development reflects foreign and not local realities, a whole infrastructure of dependency arises; for example, legal systems serve to maintain Western ideas of property rights and are not used to reform unjust structures. Similarly, the educational process is geared to notions of individual advancement, not community service or social change, and the whole process of industrialisation is oriented towards Western consumer demand, not domestic needs.

It should be remembered that theorists within the same schools of thought will often disagree as violently among themselves as they will with theorists from opposing schools; also that all the schools agree on the need for capital accumulation, structural change, industrialisation and the provision of employment opportunities. Other disciplines in the social sciences are also characterised by a lively debate about what constitutes development and how it may be achieved. Where the economist will talk about development, the sociologist, for instance, will tend to use the word modernisation and will see societies becoming modern by adopting the values, behaviours, institutions and structures which characterise modern, namely, western society. Thus will be created a modern society which will stress individualism, achievement, enterprise, the importance of the profit motive, of reading newspapers, of being on time, all of which are seen as characteristics of the kind of society which values, rewards and promotes economic growth. Those who disagree with the modernisation approach would stress the dependency explanation for the lack of economic growth and social progress in the developing countries.

Development Studies

During the international crises of the 1970s and 1980s, when the global economic system struggled with inflation, recession, oil price shocks, mass unemployment, and increasing financial instability (compounded by debt problems), the old certainties faded. Economic growth had been achieved in many Third World countries, but mass poverty had also increased. Many grandiose development projects had gone disastrously wrong or, succeeding in their own terms, had in the process brought unforeseen misery to vulnerable groups.

Increasingly, too, it was recognised that models of typical less developed countries and of universal paths to development ignored history, lumped diverse nations and cultures into one homogeneous category, assumed common goals and values (some of the power struggles within Third World countries dealt liberal illusions a fearful blow) and generally treated underdeveloped countries with lofty contempt. They 'were expected to perform like wind-up toys and to "lumber through" the various stages of development single-mindedly: their reactions to change were not to be nearly as traumatic or aberrant as those of the Europeans. . . these countries were perceived to have only *interests* and no *passions.*'[6]

Development economics (which roughly corresponds with the first two schools referred to above) has gone through a period of questioning. This is reflected in the literature in such titles as 'The Rise and Decline of Development Economics'[7], 'Development: Which Way Now?',[8] 'The Disparaging of Development Economics'[9] and the view that development economics had died, to be reincarnated as development studies.[10] This 'loss of faith in the large generalisations about economic development and policy that . . . dominated earlier post-war decades' led to two reactions.[11] One was a return to ancient verities in the form of a belief in the power of market forces. This approach is now in the ascendant in the centres of power. The other reaction was 'a retreat to theoretical fragmentation', away from the search for a unified general theory of development. This approach emphasises case studies and is 'respectful of evidence and of the complexities of human institutions', but it has little influence.[12] The danger for the poor is that, as market forces are given their head, so will the weak be crushed in the name of 'structural adjustment' or 'efficiency' or 'rationalisation'. Their needs, in the rich as well as in the poor countries, have slipped down the agendas of the powerful. Yet the interests of the poor remain at the heart of development studies.

Economics, too, remains at the core of development studies, although recognition of the complexity of the development process has led to an interdisciplinary approach to development problems. 'It is now a conventional wisdom of development studies that development problems are so multi-faceted and complex that no single discipline can hope to encompass them, let alone offer solutions.'[13] The subject matter of the discipline is also a matter for discussion, with 'a continuous process of questioning [its] boundaries.'[14]

Some definitons by implication exclude the industrialised, First and Second World countries from consideration: development studies is 'concerned with the development process in all the comparatively poor nations of the world. . . [with] such diverse issues as the nature and feasibility of industrialisation, the problem of small-scale agriculture and rural development in the Third World, the trade and other links between developed and developing countries and their effects on the development prospects of the poor, the nature and causes of poverty and inequality and the record and future prospects of development planning as a method of accelerating development.[15]

Development Education
Many of the insights gained from studying the intricacies of the development process in Third World countries are equally relevant in analysing development problems at home.[16]

Development education has been described as 'bringing development studies home'. It arose from several sources, including the views of some economists and sociologists that many of the problems of the developing countries originate in policies pursued by the developed world; concerns expressed by the churches, particularly about equality, justice, the nature of private property and the obligation to share not just the fruits of production but the factors of production with the needy; the approach to education exemplified by Paolo Freire[17] which defines the student as subject of his/her own learning and decries the banking system of education which treats students as objects to be filled with the teacher's knowledge.

This view of development education is at variance with the mainline or conventional view, which focuses on 'problems out there', i.e. in the low income countries. Such problems are legitimate subjects for study, but the cumulative effect of the preoccupation with conditions in the Third World has been to reinforce the superficial, yet widespread, belief in the rich countries that the root causes of the growing gap between rich and poor nations are to be found within the low income countries themselves. Attention is concentrated on militarism, corruption, inefficiency, 'bottlenecks', and dualistic societies.

Development education, on the other hand, takes the view that many, but not all, of the problems of the poor countries originate in and are sustained by factors and policies in the rich countries and many, but not all, of the governmental and voluntary aid efforts 'out there' are of little use, unless those root causes located within the high income countries are tackled simultaneously.[18] Development education, therefore, encompasses both a global awareness process and a process of 'conscientization'. It has many components: a comprehension of the conditions of the developing nations, an analysis of past and present relationships and interaction between the rich and poor countries, an understanding of the struggle for Third World liberation, and an exploration of how we as individuals and as nations can work to make international development possible.

While development studies may (and perhaps should) confine itself to intellectual and academic consideration, development education is concerned with action, with a methodology in which the process of education is not separate from the content. Development education is a student-centred, participative and experiential learning process in which both learner and teacher or facilitator work in dialogue with each other. The development educator is concerned to understand development issues, usually from a certain perspective, so that action can be encouraged and sponsored in the home countries; it has therefore both an intellectual component and a consciousness-raising element.

There is a growing interest in development studies in Ireland and increasing empathy with the problems of the developing world. We could speculate about the reasons for this growth. The importance of the missionary movement in shaping such consciousness should not be underestimated. We share a colonial past with many developing countries; and we have suffered the cataclysm of a famine which destroyed countless lives and subverted social structures. More recently we have had our own swift-slow experience of trying to develop our economy: we have followed policies suggested as panaceas to the developing countries – reliance on either agriculture or industry as an engine of growth, or of other frequently advised development paths such as de-linking or export-led growth. All these we have tried and, while economic growth has occurred, it has not invariably been accompanied by social progress nor by decreases in inequality. Ireland has been described as a non-poor, developing country: our own recent history teaches us that the path to development will not be easy and may lead to new problems every bit as intractable as the old, with 'development' as elusive as ever. Thus, when advising policy-makers in the developing world, if we ignore what our own history teaches us, we may be condemning them to repeat our mistakes.

Richard Quinn C.S.Sp.
Director, Development Studies Centre
Kimmage Manor.

NOTES

1. Gavin Kitching, *Development and Underdevelopment in Historical Perspective* (London and New York: Methuen, 1982), preface.
2. Michael Stewart, *Keynes and After* (Harmondsworth: Penguin, 1967), p. 254.
3. Dudley Seers, 'Back to the Ivory Tower? The Professionalization of Development Studies and their Extension to Europe' (European Association of Development Research and Training Institutes, Information Paper 2/77).
4. Paul Streeten, 'From Growth to Basic Needs', *Finance and Development,* September 1979.
5. To verify that this theory persists and that policies derived from it have adverse effects on poor people, see *IDS Bulletin,* January 1988.
6. Albert Hirschman, 'The Rise and Decline of Development Economics', *Development: Seeds of Change,* 1986:3.
7. ibid.
8. Amartya Sen, 'Development: Which Way Now?' in *Resources, Values and Development* (Oxford: Basil Blackwell, 1984).
9. John Toye, 'The Disparaging of Development Economics', *The Journal of Development Studies,* Volume 20, October 1983.
10. Dudley Seers, 'The Birth, Life and Death of Development Economics (Revisiting a Manchester Conference)', *Development and Change,* 10, 1979.
11. David Felix, in a review in *Economic Development and Cultural Change,* Vol. 36, No. 1, pp. 194-95.
12. ibid.
13. Ray Bromley and Gavin Kitching, *Development and Underdevelopment in Historical Perspective,* Series Editors' Preface.
14. John Toye, 'Development Studies and Change in Contemporary Britain' in Lalage Bown and Mike Veitch (eds), *The Relevance of Development Studies to the Study of Change in Contemporary Britain* (London: Economic and Social Research Council, 1986), pp. 22-23.
15. Bromley and Kitching, ibid.
16. See *The Relevance of Development Studies to the Study of Change in Contemporary Britain.*
17. Paolo Freire, *The Pedagogy of the Oppressed* (Harmondworth: Penguin, 1972) and *Pedagogy in Process.*
18. Jorgen Lissener, *The Politics of Altruism* (Geneva: Lutheran World Federation, 1977).

Section I
Thinking About Development

Thinking About Development

A country, or a village, or a community, cannot be developed; it can
only develop itself. For real development means the development, the
growth, of people. Every country in Africa can show examples of
modern facilities which have been provided for the people – and which
are now rotting unused. We have schools, irrigation works, expensive
markets, and so on – things by which someone came and tried to
'bring development to the people'. If real development is to take place,
the people have to be involved. . . . For the truth is that development
means the development of *people*. Roads, buildings, the increase of crop
output, and other things of this nature, are not development; they are
only tools of development. A new road extends a man's freedom only if
he travels upon it.

Julius Nyerere, *Freedom and Development*,
Dar es Salaam: Oxford University Press, 1973), pp. 25,59.

There are many competing interpretations of what development is or should be
about. Theories of development are shaped by personal values and beliefs about
people and the meaning of life. Given the diversity of political, economic and
religious ideologies, it is not surprising that there is no generally accepted theory
of development and little common ground among analysts and practitioners on
the type of development programmes that should be advanced in less developed
countries.

The readings are chosen, first, to clarify the terms of discussion and to bring
out the complexity in what initially may seem straightforward; and secondly, to
consider some of the development theories that influence policies and strategies.
The section opens with discussions of three key concepts in development studies
– the Third World, poverty, and development itself.

In 'Is the Third World Still There?' John Toye discusses the meaning of the
term 'Third World', which came into general use in the late 1960s. Often used
interchangeably with 'developing countries', 'less developed countries', 'the
South' and so on, the term has political and psychological, as well as economic
and geographical, connotations. Toye discusses the trauma of colonisation as it
was articulated by Frantz Fanon, and looks briefly at theories of modernisation
and dependency, theories examined at greater length in the papers by Andrew
Webster and Ankie Hoogvelt later in this section.

Poverty and the Third World seem inextricably linked. In 'Concepts of
Poverty', the notions of relative and absolute poverty are considered by Amartya
Sen. The question is whether poverty should be 'estimated with a cut-off line
that reflects a level below which people are – in some sense – "absolutely

3

impoverished" or a level that reflects standards of living "common to that country" in particular.' The relativity argument underlines the point that people who have adequate nutrition, shelter and clothing nonetheless may be excluded from participating in the usual activities of the community – for example, because they do not own what is considered to be socially acceptable dress. While agreeing that the concept of relative poverty has greatly advanced the general understanding of depivation, Sen concludes that 'there is an irreducible core of absolute deprivation in our idea of poverty', so that the notion of relative poverty 'supplements rather than supplants the analysis of poverty in terms of absolute dispossession.'

In 'The Concept and Measurement of Development', Colman and Nixson discuss the thorny question of what exactly development is and whether it can be measured. It can be seen either as 'a process of improvement with respect to a set of values' or as 'a comparative state of being with respect to such values', those values being desired conditions in society. This definition raises further questions, such as how the specific 'desired conditions' are decided upon. The authors note that, although there is little agreement about the causes of development and the relative importance that should be assigned to different goals, nonetheless there is consensus on the broad objectives to be pursued. These include adequate family incomes, improved access to education, and some form of democracy.

Efforts to measure development run into similar difficulties; instead of precise measures of states of development, various rather crude indicators are used, the best-known being average national income or Gross National Product per capita. Colman and Nixson discuss this measure's many shortcomings and some of the attempts made to devise indices that better reflect social and economic welfare.

In 'Development Economics: Schools of Thought', Nigel Harris looks at various theories which emerged to explain the nature and causes of economic underdevelopment and to help in the formulation of policies to overcome it. The idea that countries needed to go through various 'stages of growth' on the road to development was widely accepted during the 1960s. The question was how to speed up the rate of progress. Orthodox economics seemed to offer little help in this task since it did not apply to non-industrialised economies. Growth and development could not be left to international trade, which indeed often made the problems worse; nor could it be left to the operation of free markets; 'only governments could mobilize the resources, only governments possessed the political power to break through the bottlenecks, bend the inflexibilities and force the pace of growth.' Harris divides the variations within these broad assumptions into four schools of thought – conservative reformers, radicals, revolutionary nationalists, and revolutionary internationalists – and contrasts them with classical and Marxist theory and with mainstream or neo-classical economics.

For many writers, 'development' meant 'modernisation' and modernisation meant following the example of the West, specifically the USA of the 1950s. In

'Modernisation Theory', Andrew Webster discusses the model of development that dominated development thinking during the 1950s and 1960s. Western social, political, cultural, psychological and, above all, economic values were regarded as indispensable to development. What was needed was 'to make men modern' by instilling, through education and other means, 'modern' rational attributes such as the 'need for achievement'. Traditions that valued kinship ties, the extended family system, and other 'obstacles' to modernity were condemned. Modernisation theories, which ignored the impact of colonialism, could not explain or predict social change, and presented a false dichotomy of tradition versus modernity.

In 'Theories of Imperialism, Dependency and Underdevelopment', Ankie Hoogvelt considers perspectives radically opposed to the modernisation approach. Theorists of imperialism argue that, in the long term, the rate of profit in capitalist societies tends to decline. Capital is exported to areas abroad that offer profitable opportunities; political domination, to protect the investment, follows. The theories focused on the causes of imperialism, but gave little attention to its effects on the colonised. Dependency theories redressed the balance and, in their attack on the modernisation, liberal bourgeois approach, made a considerable impact on thinking about development: 'Underdevelopment – as distinct from undevelopment – it was claimed, is not due to some "original state of affairs", as bourgeois theory has it, but is the result of the same world historical process in which the now developed countries became developed . . . the advanced capitalist countries had become developed by expropriating economic surplus from those overseas countries with which they first traded and which they later colonised, while the overseas countries became underdeveloped by aiding the ascendancy of the West.'

On the whole, empirical economic research did not support the claims of the dependency schools and by the early 1970s the approach had run out of steam. Nonetheless, many of its insights have now been incorporated into the conventional wisdom. As Hoogvelt concludes: 'Having arisen as a criticism of bourgeois development theory, dependency theory has now itself become bourgeois.'

The final paper in this section, 'Women and Development: The Fallacy of Integration', presents a critique of another conventional wisdom: that of the necessity of integrating women into development. Geertje Lycklama à Nijeholt argues that women are and always have been, fully incorporated into economic and social life, but the form of that integration is unequal and exploitative because of the institutionalised domination of women by men. Women 'contribute to development by much hard work . . . the question is under what conditions are women participating in development and who benefits from the products of their work?' Much of women's work, particularly in food production, childcare and housework, is essential to society, yet it is undervalued and even ignored when compiling GNP statistics, for example. Nijeholt calls into question development policies drawn up by agencies and governments staffed mainly by men, who proceed often on the basis of wrong assumptions: for instance, that men are the providers for women and children.

This feminist perspective on development poses the fundamental question: what kind of development do women want? '. . . there exists no blueprint for a transformation of patriarchal societies. Women in their specific situation will have to develop a vision of . . . what kind of a society they want [and devise] strategies, methods and means for the transformation of development into a process which leads to a society where people, women and men, are no longer oppressed and exploited.'

Is the Third World Still There?

John Toye

This reading is from the opening chapter of the author's book, Dilemmas of Development *(1987).*

---

*The poor throughout the world, and even the poor countries as a whole, are thus emerging as the new dangerous classes. This is the idea which is suggested – whatever reservations may be made regarding this highly ideological division of our planet into three worlds – by the French expression 'Tiers-Monde', by association with the 'Tiers-État' of pre-revolutionary France. The poor of the world today, like the poor of Europe in previous centuries, come alive for us only if we see them through the eyes of the dominant classes; they are but the subject of writings and speeches, never their authors. They are only allowed to be interviewed, photographed, measured, weighed, analysed, and to give a factual account of their work, their daily lives, what they eat, drink and desire. Civil servants define their basic needs in terms of calories, proteins, and lengths of cloth. They are advised to have fewer children and to educate them according to our own standards; they are urged to become more enterprising.

Pierre Spitz, 'Silent Violence: famine and inequality'
Revue Internationale des Sciences Sociales, Vol XXX, (1978), No. 4.

The first lesson which great disasters like the Ethiopian famine should have taught is that, although disaster relief is the top priority in the short term, the long-term avoidance of vulnerability to disaster requires a successful development policy. Those who would transform their concern into more permanently constructive action will thus necessarily have to try to come to grips with development issues and the many debates which surround the question of devising a successful development policy. For a start, they will have to go back to their newspapers, weekly magazines and television programmes and discipline themselves to read and watch those boring bits. These should indeed become very much less boring, if one wrestles to make sense of them and fit them into an overall pattern. Not everything is going to fit in at the first, or even the second or third attempt. But many things do become clearer as one struggles to put different pieces of the development jigsaw together.

Widespread famine represents the most visible and most shocking distant disaster. But it is also a complex event, for which simple and obvious explanations will not always suffice. Famines can occur in the midst of plenty, when particular groups of people lose their accustomed means of access to the available food supply. Famine among pastoralists often occurs in a deteriorating natural environment. But it is difficult to sort out whether the deterioration has

*This quotation has been added by the Editors.

7

autonomous physical causes, or whether it results from population growth, or simple abuse of the habitat based on ignorance. And what role does politics play in causing famine? Cultivators who are moved on to new land for military reasons may be being put at risk, and governments may give or withhold relief supplies as a weapon in a political game.

A country will not suffer from famine just because its inhabitants are poor. India's per capita income lies in between those of Ethiopia and Sudan, but India has managed to avoid famines for all of the forty-odd years since she became independent.[1] There are many other poor countries which can make the same claim. Although at present famine and the threat of famine seem to haunt Africa, particularly sub-Saharan Africa, the contrast between Africa and Asia is not absolute. China experienced severe famine in the early 1960s, as did Bangladesh in the early 1970s. Clearly, the cause and the incidence of famine are not easy to unravel.

The reports from faraway places do not tell only of famine. Finance as well as food is currently a major issue of development policy. When the oil price rose by leaps and bounds in 1973 and again in 1979, its effect was to withdraw substantial amounts of purchasing power from oil-consuming economies, and to transfer these amounts in the first instance to oil producers who were unable all at once to spend their great increases in income. This was evidently a depressing influence on world economic activity and, in an attempt to lessen the impact of the depression, oil revenues (or petro-dollars) were 'recycled' by the private banking system. A large part of this recycling was done by lending petro-dollars to governments of poor countries, in the belief that this kind of lending ('sovereign debt') carried minimal risks of default. From 1973 to 1982, the governments of many countries took on more loans than they could possibly repay, given their ability to generate foreign exchange earnings. Their poor foreign exchange earning ability at the end of the borrowing spree indicated that many had borrowed more than they could invest in hard-currency-earning enterprises.

In the last few years, the media have carried many reports on this debt crisis, which was allowed to reach the point where the stability of some large private US banks began to be questioned, as well as where numerous governments of poor countries were pleading to have their debts re-scheduled. Bail-out plan has followed bail-out plan, bankers' revolts and debtors' revolts have come and gone, austerity packages have been devised, imposed, evaded and re-imposed. The crisis is far from over and its management shifts from tactic to tactic, trying to learn something along the way.[2]

Just as famine is said to be Africa's problem, so the debt crisis is said to be Latin America's. This is because it was Mexico and Brazil in 1982 who first indicated that their debt burden had become unsustainable. But no continent has exclusive proprietorship of particular development problems. Although ten of the fifteen countries which the IMF defines as heavily indebted are Latin American, three are African (Nigeria, Morocco and the Ivory Coast), one is Asian (Philippines) and one is European (Yugoslavia).

The examples of Mexico and Nigeria indicate that having indigenous supplies of oil was no guarantee of being able to avoid the debt crisis. Borrowing undertaken when the oil price was high quickly became unsustainable when the oil price softened and collapsed. The crux of the matter was never just the possession or non-possession of domestic oil supplies. It was the ability to manage resources well in the face of great turbulence in a key commodity price. India, though on balance hurt economically by the oil price rise, never took large commercial bank loans. As a result, she has escaped the worst traumas of the debt crisis.

In oil-exporting countries, the rapid growth of the 1970s has been followed by stagnation in the 1980s as the oil price has fallen. In addition to Mexico and Nigeria, it is the countries of the Middle East who have been the most seriously affected. In the 1980s, countries that rely on primary product exports have had somewhat faster growth than the Middle East, benefiting from the slight acceleration in economic activity in industrialized countries after the trough of the recession in 1982. But the only group of poor countries to have grown consistently fast in the 1970s and 1980s are those that export manufactures. These include the newly industrializing countries (NICs) whose growth performance has been held up as a model for the development of countries still caught up in the toils of famine or debt.

It is important not to confuse economic growth, the expansion of the measured output of goods and services, with development. One can imagine some forms of economic growth that would not seem much like development. For example, output can be produced by the severe exploitation of labour – the payment of mere subsistence wages, bad health and safety conditions and the unfair treatment of workers – with the resulting profits being channelled to private bank accounts in foreign tax havens. This would be the kind of development that few people would vote for, if they were allowed to vote. So would growth that was accompanied by environmental pollution and gross overcrowding. The process of very rapid industrialization, new or old, can create widespread social distress and conflict, as well as previously undreamt of levels of material wealth and technical advance.

These ambivalences of rapid industrialization are characteristic of what have become known to journalists as 'the four Asian tigers' – the two city-states of Hong Kong and Singapore, and the two larger political entities of South Korea and Taiwan. But these are not the only NICs. There is another important group in Eastern Europe (Romania, Yugoslavia and Hungary), plus the big, heavily populated, countries which have pursued industrialization by import-substitution, India and Brazil.

Trying to make sense of the information which reaches us about poor countries a long way away seems, then, to lead to the identification of a set of contemporary problems – famine and the related problems of the production and distribution of food; the financing of development through the private banking system and the related problems of debt, the oil price, inflation and the choice of productive investments; and the social costs of rapid industrialization.

Although at first glance, it might appear that these problems were to be found in different continents – famine in Africa, the debt crisis in Latin America and the agony and the ecstacy of rapid industrialization in Asia – a closer look showed that this was not entirely so. Although each problem was concentrated to a noticeable degree in one continent more than the others, a sharp geographical demarcation of problem locations was not warranted. Similar phenomena appeared to a lesser degree elsewhere.

The continents of Africa, Asia and Latin America are diverse, both geographically and historically. This diversity accounts for the tendency of particular development problems to concentrate in particular continents. Asia has much greater pressure of population on cultivable land than Latin America or Africa, but Africa has a much more unfavourable ratio of food availability from domestic supply and imports to its food requirements than does Latin America, or (to a lesser extent) Asia. Land is but one term in the agricultural equation and other historical and geographical factors have put Africa at a special disadvantage.[3]

Latin America (apart from Colombia and Venezuela) is much more diversified economically than Africa, where even the discovery of oil has hardly altered the pattern of relying on one or two sectors to generate most export revenue. But Latin America has also drawn much more heavily than either Africa or Asia on foreign sources for its direct investment. So its economies are much more influenced by decisions taken by multinational corporations (particularly US multinationals) than are those of Asia or Africa (notably excepting Liberia). Politically, Latin America and Africa are more prone to military *coups d'état*, while Asia has found greater political stability, although often by authoritarian means. Given these contrasts, it is explicable why Latin America has had less sustained rapid industrialization than parts of Asia and greater entanglement in the problems of international debt.

The Basis of the Third World: Politics and Psychology

These continental contrasts, combined with the evident differences between the most pressing problems of development in different places, naturally lead people to ask whether there really is 'a Third World'. Does it make sense to lump the problems and circumstances of Latin America, Africa and Asia together as those of 'the Third World', and talk of that world in a way which inevitably emphasizes similarities rather than differences? Might it not be better to confine discussion of development policy to a regional rather than a global perspective?

In the flood of comment on the dilemmas of development policy, an abrasive new approach has been heard increasingly in the 1980s. This new approach has been called a counter-revolution in the theory and practice of development . . . |which maintains| that the Third World only exists because it has been created. Further, the creative force was not history or geography, or economics. It was psychology and politics, namely 'Western guilt' and the politics of foreign aid, which between them conjured up 'the Third World'.

The Third World and its antecedents and synonyms, such as the underdeveloped world, the less developed world and the developing world (all still used) and now also the South, are for all practical purposes the collection of countries whose governments, with the odd exception, demand and receive official aid from the West. . . . The Third World is the creation of foreign aid: without foreign aid there is no Third World.

(Bauer 1981:87)

In turn, 'insistence on foreign aid is a major theme of the recent literature of Western guilt', which holds that the West is responsible for the poverty of most of Asia, Africa and Latin America. If there is no truth in this suggestion of 'responsibility' and no virtue in the policy of aid, as some development counter-revolutionaries believe, the Third World itself exists only as a kind of collective psychological delusion.

In responding to assertions of the kind just quoted, it is necessary to begin by examining the psychological and political aspects of the concept of a Third World. What truth is there in the suggestion that it denotes an association of countries dedicated to the moral blackmail of a guilt-afflicted West? Once the psychological and political influences on the identity of the Third World have been clarified, the further question of whether they share a common type of economy will be addressed.

It would be misleading to argue that being a Third World country is simply a matter of experiencing certain economic conditions and problems. There are also, and possibly even predominantly, psychological and political elements in 'Third Worldliness'. But they are of a distinctly different character than that alleged by the development counter-revolutionaries.

What then is the political significance of a Third World? The term has been traced to several different origins. In Europe in the 1920s, there was some talk in political circles of finding a 'third way', meaning a political programme that was neither explicitly capitalist nor explicitly socialist in orientation. The details of the programmes, clerical, fascist and business variants of social corporatism, are less important than the enduring idea that some third alternative was possible, and that the struggle between capitalism and socialism did not have to be all-engulfing. An alternative origin with a related connotation lies in the French term 'the third estate'. Just as, in the approach to the French Revolution, the third estate found its political opportunity in the quarrel between nobility and clergy, so at the end of the Second World War, the US-USSR conflict provided the political opportunity for independence in the less developed countries. The analogy here is with benefiting from the struggle between two superior forces, not merely surviving it.

This is not the political interpretation which the development counter-revolutionaries give to the idea of the Third World. They ignore the struggle between two superpowers with opposing ideologies and, therefore, Third Worldism is seen by them as a form of hostility to the West which is inspired by a positive (if covert) preference for socialism. Hence their constant criticism of developing countries for socialistic behaviour, or what is read as such. Third World countries as a group are blamed for over-extended public sectors – which are actually smaller proportionally than that of the US is to the size of its total economy – and excessive reliance on government controls, even when those controls are known to be easily circumvented by private enterprise firms, which are nowhere near to being centrally planned in Soviet style.

If the political thrust of Third Worldism were merely anti-Western, it would presumably find favour with those committed to socialism. But this presumption is wrong. On the contrary, 'radicals . . . are usually reluctant to posit a third world, for they see most, perhaps all, of these countries as underdeveloped capitalist ones, tied in subordinately to the first world. Thus, the main radical view is that there are only two worlds, one of capitalism and one of Marxian socialism' (Griffin and Gurley 1985:1090). The orthodox socialist position is thus that the Third World does not exist, because it is really subordinated to the first, capitalist world. This is uncannily similar to the position of the counter-revolution itself, that the Third World only exists to the extent that it is able, by exploiting Western guilt feelings, to be insubordinate and anti-Western. The second world (socialism) will not recognize the third, on the pretext that it is really part of the first. But the first will not do so either, on the pretext that the third is indistinguishable from the second.

The political interpretation which the development counter-revolution gives to the concept of the Third World is one which derives from its continuing political engagement with the struggle against socialism. By the same token, the orthodox socialist position on the Third World derives, although much more self-consciously and with much more open public acknowledgement, from the struggle against capitalism. Both are declaring, in effect, that there cannot be independents or non-combatants in their ideological confrontations. It is precisely this kind of doctrinaire exclusiveness which fuels the continuing search for a third way.

Moving on from political ideas to political practice, the origin of the Third World as an active group of cooperating countries was a desire to establish a strong group of neutrals during the US–USSR 'cold war'. Their aims were to avoid any entanglement with superpower rivalries and to safeguard their national sovereignty as (mainly) countries which had recently become independent of European colonial powers. In fact, the actual political coherence of the Third World nations as a group has been greater in relation to the politics of decolonization than in relation to the politics of US-USSR superpower rivalry. Ironically, the posture of non-alignment adopted by many Third World countries since 1961 has been adhered to less strictly than the posture of opposition to colonialism and imperialism (Willetts 1978). It is the latter, rather than the competition between capitalism and socialism as social systems and as power blocs, which holds the key to the politics of the Third World.

The advocates of a counter-revolution in development thinking place the emphasis the other way round from this. They stress the anti-West attitudes of Third Worldism, the West's irrational guilt that supposedly encourages these attitudes and the alleged crypto-socialist policies of Third World governments. For them, Third World politics is nothing if not part of a continuing cold war. That Third World politics is centrally about decolonization and the future security and prosperity of former colonial countries is thus denied and treated as an irrelevant distraction.

The basis for dismissing decolonization as the central Third World issue is the fact that some countries which are now generally recognized to be part of the Third World have been continuously independent of formal control by a foreign power at least since 1815. Paraguay, Saudi Arabia, Turkey and Nepal fall into this category (Crow and Thomas 1983: 11). There are a few other countries where either the period of colonization was relatively brief or relatively informal, such as Thailand, Iran and Ethiopia. The fact that colonial expansion was to this degree less than worldwide in its reach is taken as an argument against the political definition of the Third World in terms of the politics of decolonization. It is difficult to follow the logic of this. Some very inhospitable parts of the world are both relatively unattractive to foreign imperialists and relatively inaccessible for military conquest. But countries located there still share with their neighbours who have experienced colonization a common interest in avoiding it. There is no country so remote, so inaccessible and so well entrenched in its history of independence that it cannot become a battleground for foreign troops. The history of Afghanistan since 1979 should illustrate that proposition vividly. And the real experience of colonization has been overwhelmingly more commonplace than the untutored fear of it.

Decolonization
'Decolonization', like 'Third World' itself, is a modern term of mid-twentieth-century vintage. The modern politics of decolonization have not directly affected Latin America very much, with the exception of Guyana and Surinam and the 1982 conflict over the Falklands/Malvinas. Most Central and South American countries had freed themselves from Spanish and Portuguese colonialism in the nineteenth century, only to find themselves, from the Monroe Doctrine of 1842 onwards, coming under the growing hemispheric overlordship of a rapidly industrializing United States. Thus by the end of the Second World War, and the arrival of the modern episode of decolonization, any declaration of non-alignment by the Latin American states would have been construed by the United States as a hostile act. Latin America, therefore, occupied a special position within the Third World. It was the first continent to liberate itself from colonialism and, yet, it was not able to participate fully in the political construction of the Third World.

The psychology of Third Worldism is the psychology of decolonization. If decolonization wrongly implies the initiative for independence was always taken by the colonial powers, the psychology of Third Worldism can also be described as the psychology of national liberation (Chamberlain 1985: 1). The classic account of the psychology of national liberation was that of Fanon. According to Fanon, the social relationships of colonial societies denied the native populations a true human identity. True identity could only be achieved by a violent struggle against the colonialists who created and imposed a sub-human personality on the native. In turn, this historical necessity for redeeming violence created a dilemma for the supporters of decolonization in the colonial countries. Their support derives from a Western cultural humanism. But Western culture has to be rejected because it condemns violence and also because it is shot through with a racially biased hypocrisy. Its claim to universal values is said to be contradicted by the racism practised in the colonial situation.

Sartre paraphrased Fanon's essential message as follows: 'The rival blocks take opposite sides and hold each other in check; let us [i.e. the Third World] take advantage of this paralysis, let us burst into history, forcing it by our invasion into universality for the first time. Let us start fighting; and if we have no other arms, the waiting knife's enough' (Fanon 1967: 11). It was this message that led Sartre to conclude that 'the Third World finds itself and speaks to *itself* through [Fanon's] voice' (p. 9).

There is much to quarrel with in *The Wretched of the Earth*. The notion of redeeming violence is inexcusably romantic; the understanding of Western humanism is superficial; the politics of a national peasant revolution are wildly utopian. So one could go on. What it provides is neither an accurate description of colonialism, nor a useful prescription for how to overcome it. What it provides instead is an excellent intuitive account of the psycho-pathology caused by colonial wars and the deformations of values and vision caused by the acutely stressful conflicts of decolonization. How else than like Fanon could people feel, at the end of a long war of atrocity and counter-atrocity, such as that of Algerian liberation between 1954 and 1962?

Fanon usefully reminds Anglo-Saxon readers that decolonization has not just been a matter of the peaceful transfer of power by metropolitan countries benignly seeking the future welfare of colonial populations. Although in India the worst bloodshed was caused by communal violence within the newly independent country, Britain itself has conducted fierce military campaigns against 'terrorists' in countries soon to become independent, for example, in Palestine (1946-8), Kenya (1952-5), Malaya (1957-63), Cyprus (1956-60) and Aden in the 1960s. The war in Algeria, however, dwarfed all of these, with France committing an army of half a million men there by 1962. When decolonization intersected with superpower rivalry, as it did in Vietnam between 1965 and 1973, the scale of conflict was even larger. There the US committed over two million ground troops, of whom 55,000 were killed, while half a million Vietnamese were slaughtered in both ground and aerial bombing attacks.

The voices of the development counter-revolution speak of 'Western guilt' as the psychological force which gives coherence to the Third World. Western guilt is presented as an abstract neurosis, a subjective feeling detached from the objective circumstances of contemporary history. But objectively, colonial conflicts create intense brutalization and trauma on both sides. The effects do not cease when the conflict ceases. The intensification of racism and drug abuse in ex-colonial countries is directly connected to the brutalization of some participants and the trauma of others in the course of recent colonial wars. Anxiety about these self-inflicted social evils combines with the self-doubt of Western humanism described by Fanon to creat a psychological unease which is well grounded in fact and history.

The ex-colonies themselves do not escape unscarred. The counter-revolution in development thinking is quick to condemn the many instances of illiberalism to be found in countries of the Third World. But it does not pause to consider the social forces which make oppression and persecution so relatively simple to organize. One important force is the great power of the army, often with foreign training and technology, when political independence comes at the end of a long armed struggle, as in Mozambique and Zimbabwe. It takes immense political skill to keep the armed forces under civilian control in such circumstances. Too often that political skill is lacking.

The full trauma of the process of decolonization is not yet over. South Africa and Namibia remain as instances of white settler colonialism, with overtly racialist domestic policies distilled into the inhuman system of apartheid. The pressure towards violence; the unwillingness of liberals to support whole-heartedly the national liberation struggle; the dragon's teeth, to use the phrase of Kiernan (1982: 227) about armies, sown in the course of conflict and bringing forth their harvest once the political victory has been won – all are now set to be replayed one more time and perhaps more fiercely than ever before, in the years ahead.

The Third World is not, despite all that the development counter-revolution says, yet able to be dismissed from our minds. It is not a figment of our imagination ready to vanish when we blink. It is a result of our collective lack of imagination, our inability in our present difficult circumstances yet to see ourselves as belonging to one world, and not three.

The Basis of the Third World: Economics

The term 'Third World' when applied to a country is often taken to be synonomous with descriptions like underdeveloped, less developed and developing. But these terms have a different point of reference, the degree of economic and social backwardness. 'Underdeveloped' and 'less developed' imply relative backwardness, while 'developing' implies movement away from backwardness. That is, perhaps, clear enough. But what is 'backwardness'? Evidently, being at some remove from 'forwardness'. So what is 'forwardness'? Well, there can be more than one opinion about that, surely?

It is important to realize that an apparently neutral and scientific word like 'development' is no such thing. Definitions of the goals of development and of the process by which these goals should be striven for, unavoidably depend on the values of the person doing the defining, as well as on facts that are in principle falsifiable. Further, people's values are not identical, nor are they completely at variance, fortunately. Although all theories are to some extent contestable because of differences in values rather than problems of logic or observation, theories of development are particularly subject to disagreements arising out of value differences.

Modernization Theory

The original theory of socioeconomic development that accompanied the post-1945 decolonization of Asia and Africa rested on the idea of modern society as the goal of development. Modern society supposedly had typical social patterns of demography, urbanization and literacy; typical economic patterns of production and consumption, investment, trade and government finance; and typical psychological attributes of rationality, ascriptive identity and achievement motivation. The process of development consisted, on this theory, of moving from traditional society, which was taken as the polar opposite of the modern type, through a series of stages of development – derived essentially from the history of Europe, North America and Japan – to modernity, that is, approximately the United States of the 1950s.

It was the ideas of countries that were less developed (LDCs) according to the above modernization paradigm of development which was most closely linked in practice to the giving of foreign aid. Within this paradigm, Western experts have an extremely prominent and powerful position as guides and advisers in poor countries. Not only are their values being imported wholesale, usually without much awareness on anyone's part that this is what is happening, but Western technology is assumed to be appropriate and the embodied technology of Western machines and equipment is assumed to be transferrable with only modest difficulty. All of these assumptions are convenient to support large-scale capital aid programmes.

This theory and practice of development was bound to come into question before long. Leaving aside the social and psychological side of modernization theory and concentrating on the economic side, it had a conception of a typical less developed economy. This was predominantly agricultural, with small cultivators growing crops primarily for household subsistence needs. It had low rates of investment, low stock of capital employed per worker and low rates of economic growth. The foreign trade sector was small, and so was the share of national resources passing through the government budget. Infrastructure was poor as a result of low government investment. The typical less developed economy admittedly showed some variation from place to place, but the variations were essentially natural. Some were islands, some were landlocked; some were big and some were small; some were arid, some were flood-prone; some were mountainous and some were on the plain. But all were typical less developed economies.[4]

Criticism gradually focused on the part of this story that concerned trade. Two main reasons for this focus stand out. The idea of development as the passage through a series of predetermined stages assumes that *timing* of the development process, in relation to the development of other countries, is of no major consequence. Countries can embark on their journey and reach their desired destination without regard for the timetables that others have followed, or are about to follow. In other words, development is independent, national development and there are no 'late developers' whose prospects are damaged by their very lateness. Trade forms part of the network of international interdependence. It is, therefore, one of the key linkages that binds the national development process together – for better or worse.

The second reason why criticism of the idea of the typical LDC focused on trade was that the link did not appear, on inspection, to be of the negligible kind posited by modernization theory. Most LDCs seemed to have developed one or more major export sectors: specialized agricultural commodities like cocoa, bananas, sugar or tea; raw materials like rubber or jute; or minerals, particularly copper, tin or bauxite. Moreover, 'underdeveloped countries generally trade with advanced countries and not with each other. This pattern is clearly quite unlike that of an "untouched" pre-capitalist economy. . . .' (Brewer 1980:9). This raised the possibility not allowed for in modernization accounts of development that the typical LDC economy had already been shaped by its trade contacts with other countries into a distorted form, from which a 'normal' development process, through the usual stages of modernization, would not be possible.

This possibility was seized on as a certainty by some writers in the 1960s who believed that modernization theory was a way of denying the adverse economic effects of colonial rule and legitimizing foreign aid as an instrument to maintain former, colonial patterns of international relations. The nexus of international exchange, often referred to loosely as 'the capitalist system', was credited with the major role in creating the specific form of backwardness found in the Third World. This specific form was called 'underdevelopment': it was not a pristine condition of low productivity and poverty but an historical condition of blocked, distorted and dependent development.

It is this conception of underdevelopment created by the capitalist system which the counter-revolution in development rejects most vehemently. Rightly so, because it is an extreme position, the logical and empirical supports for which were never properly worked out by its own advocates. In adopting this position for the decade between 1965 and 1975, its partisans were allowing values, in this case strident anti-imperialism, to dominate almost completely their choice of theory.

The theory of underdevelopment implied a continuous polarization in income and welfare between developed and underdeveloped countries. However, the normal indicators of income and welfare did not show that such a polarization was taking place. The average rate of growth of income per head in both groups of countries was, between 1950 and 1975, just over 3 per cent a year. If anything (though recalling that these kinds of statistics are subject to large margins of error), the underdeveloped group grew more quickly, indicating a slight movement towards closing the relative income gap (Morawetz 1977: 26). A rate of growth of just over 3 per cent a year was also faster than that of today's developed countries during the second half of the nineteenth century.

Physical indicators told a story that was consistent with that of the group growth rates. Between 1950 and 1979, life expectancy rose on average in all developing countries from 43 to 58 years, while literacy rose from 33 to 56 persons in every hundred and the mortality rate in children between 1 and 4 years old fell from 28 to 12 per thousand. Again, these rates of improvement are faster than those experienced by today's developed countries during their period of fastest development. At the same time, there is still massive scope for further improvement before developing countries reach the levels of health and education currently enjoyed by today's developed countries (Killick 1986).

If the facts rule against the idea of a long-period process of polarization between rich countries and poor, there is no need to spend time discussing the causes of such a process. However, that does not mean that one must deny that colonialism produced negative economic effects. Certain pre-colonial forms of economic activity were destroyed, certain colonial investments were inappropriate except within the context of colonialism itself and liberation conflicts have often burdened countries after independence with costly and turbulent military establishments. Economies have been distorted by colonialism in a way which hampers their future action for development. But these negative effects are not insuperable; they can be struggled against successfully. In the end, whatever the extent of the economic damage of colonialism, countries which do nothing but persuade themselves that they are the victims of history will let slip such opportunities for development as they do have now.

The evident absence of a long-period process of polarization should lead us neither to deny the negative economic impacts of colonialism nor to deny short-period setbacks which developing countries have experienced as a group. Certainly, since about 1980, economic recession has badly affected all countries, developed and developing, by greatly slowing their growth of income per head. It has also affected the developing countries as a group more seriously than the developed countries. Any past tendency for the relative income gap to narrow has thus, since 1980, been put into reverse. The main causes of the present severe slackening in developing countries' growth have been falling commodity prices, rising real interest rates and the reduction in concessional and other financial flows (Singh 1986).

But looking at the economic performance of developing countries only as a group would conceal something that is highly relevant to the question of whether, from an economic perspective, the Third World is still with us. For within the average results for the whole Third World group, an increasing differentiation between regions and types of countries has been taking place. The growth that has been achieved has not been uniform and across the board. It has affected some countries and some regions very much more than others. As a result, the Third World in the last twenty years has lost some of its earlier economic homogeneity.

The relative position of Africa has worsened steadily in the last ten to fifteen years, with the continent as a whole seeing little growth in the 1970s and falls in output in the 1980s. Some African countries were not affected by stagnation (for example, Cameroon and Tunisia), but the general picture has been very bleak. More recently, economic retrogression has extended itself, via the debt crisis and falling oil prices, to Central and Latin America and the OPEC countries. Economies least affected by the recession of the 1980s were those already growing very fast. Important in this group were the East Asian economies achieving their growth through investment in industries that could produce manufactured exports, plus India and China, who have followed an inward-looking strategy of industrialization.

The differentiation within the Third World economies has resulted in two very different responses, one at each end of the economic spectrum. At the top, a debate has been begun on the issue of 'graduation', that is, the formal recognition that a developing country has developed sufficiently for it no longer to be regarded as a developing country. Rather little has been achieved except verbal sparring on the graduation issue. Whatever its degree of economic progress, a developing country is reluctant to graduate, because it thereby loses its access to certain privileged financial facilities, like concessional World Bank loans. There is also reluctance on the part of international organizations concerned with developing country interests to lose the participation of their more successful and powerful members. These institutional pressures obscure the degree of differentiation that has taken place at the top of the group.

At the bottom of the group, however, the inhibitions to recognition have been less powerful. Although UNCTAD was initially unhappy about doing so, a separate lower-end sub-group has been identified since 1979 among the members of the 'Group of 77' (which confusingly contains over 100 Third World countries). This sub-group is composed of 31 'least developed countries', also known as LLDCs. The LLDCs are defined as countries with an average income of less than $100 per head, an adult literacy rate of less than 20 per cent and a manufacturing sector which provides less than 10 per cent of gross domestic product. The Third World average for literacy was 56 per cent and for share of industry in output was about 20 per cent in 1980.

The emergence of LLDCs is a reflection of the particular development problem faced by small, underpopulated and often landlocked African states like Chad, Mali, Niger, Burkina Faso, Uganda, Malawi, Rwanda and Burundi. In all, Africa has two-thirds of all LLDCs. With a few exceptions like Nepal, Ethiopia and Afghanistan, the great majority of LLDCs are former European colonies.

What has happened then over the last thirty years has been neither the uncomplicated succession of economic take-offs which modernization theory predicted, nor the continuously growing gap in income and welfare between the rich countries and the poor countries prophesied by underdevelopment theorists. Instead, there has been a combination of some take-offs, mainly in East Asia, and some severe cases of economic retrogression, mainly in Africa. Thus the polarization that has taken place has done so *within* the Third World, but not between the Third World taken as a group and the developed economies of the non-socialist world.

Does this intra-Third World economic differentiation matter? The answer to this depends on one's values and viewpoint. Politically, it makes the cohesion of the Third World more difficult, as conflicts between different sub-groups increase. In the 1970s, such a conflict was always threatening between the oil exporters and the oil importers in the Third World. In the 1980s, with new commercial lending almost non-existent, a conflict threatens over the division of the remaining concessional finance between the least developed countries – whose need is greater – and the rest – whose ability to use the finance productively is probably greater. So to all who see the building up of the political unity of the Third World as a major task, economic differentiation does matter because it makes that task more difficult.

Economically, what most people would say mattered ultimately is the ending of large-scale poverty. It is the sickness, ignorance and premature death, not to mention the violence, ugliness and despair of daily life, which accompany poverty and underemployment, that revolt most people. Those things can be found in any Third World country on a scale that would never be tolerated elsewhere and they must be eliminated as quickly as humanly possible. Thus increasing inequality between countries is, in itself, a matter of indifference. What matters is whether mass poverty is expanding or contracting and whether the means are at hand for doing something effective to reduce it.

NOTES

1. See the discussion of India's experience with famine, in contrast with that of China, in Sen (1983: 757-60). (*Editor's note:* see page 170 in this volume).

2. A good, basic introduction to the current state of the world debt crisis is provided by Lever and Huhne (1985: 1-38). (*Editor's note:* see reading in Section III in this volume).

3. The varying characteristics of soils in tropical areas can be found in brief in Kamarck (1976: 22-29).

4. The failure of development economists to take some of these natural variations more seriously as discriminators of radically different modes of rural economy has been attacked by economic anthropologists, notably Polly Hill (see Grillo and Rew 1985: 117-30).

REFERENCES

Bauer, P.T. (1981), *Equality, the Third World and Economic Delusion*. London: Methuen.

Brewer, A. (1980), *Marxist Theories of Imperialism: A Critical Survey*. London: Routledge and Kegan Paul.

Chamberlain, M.E. (1985), *Colonization: The Fall of the European Empires*. Oxford: Basil Blackwell.

Crow, B. and A. Thomas (1983), *Third World Atlas*. Milton Keynes and Philadelphia: Open University Press.

Fanon, F. (1967), *The Wretched of the Earth*. Harmondsworth: Penguin.

Griffin, K. and J. Gurley (1985), 'Radical Analyses of Imperialism, the Third World and the Transition to Socialism: A Survey Article', *Journal of Economic Literature*, 23 (3) (September).

Grillo, R. and A. Rew. (eds)(1985), *Social Anthropology and Development Policy*. London and New York: Tavistock Publications, (ASA Monographs 23).

Kamarck, A.M. (1976), *The Tropics and Economic Development: A Provocative Inquiry into the Poverty of Nations*. Baltimore and London: Johns Hopkins University Press, for the World Bank.

Kiernan, V.G. (1982), *European Empires from Conquest to Collapse 1815-1960*. London: Fontana.

Killick, A. (1986), 'Twenty Five Years in Development: The Rise and Impending Decline of Market Solutions', *Development Policy Review*, 4 (2) (June).

Lever, H. and C. Huhne, (1985) *Debt and Danger: The World Financial Crisis*. Harmondsworth: Penguin.

Morawetz, D. (1977), *Twenty-five years of Economic Development 1950 to 1975*. Baltimore and London: Johns Hopkins University Press.

Sen, A.K. (1983), 'Development: Which Way Now?', *Economic Journal*, 93 (372) (December).

Singh, A. (1986), 'The Interrupted Industrial Revolution of the Third World: Prospects and Policies for Resumption,' *Industry and Development* (12).

Willetts, P. (1978), *The Non-Aligned Movement: The Origins of the Third World Alliance*. London: Frances Pinter.

Concepts of Poverty

Amartya Sen

This reading is from the Preface and Chapter 1 of the author's book,
Poverty and Famines: An Essay on Entitlement and Deprivation (*1982*).

---

*. . . poverty is a lack of choice. When you don't have choices, you are poor. And when the poor people have no land, have no education, have no health, have no housing, they don't have choice.

Xavier Gorostiaga S.J. 'The Function of Governments: a Third World View',
Ten Years of Action for Justice (Dublin: Trócaire, 1985).

Much about poverty is obvious enough. One does not need elaborate criteria, cunning measurement, or probing analysis, to recognize raw poverty and to understand its antecedents. It would be natural to be impatient with long-winded academic studies on 'poor naked wretches' with 'houseless heads and unfed sides' and 'loop'd and windowed raggedness', to use King Lear's graphic description. And furthermore it may also be the case, as Lear told the blind Gloucester, that 'a man may see how this world goes with no eyes'. There is indeed much that is transparent about poverty and misery.

But not everything about poverty is quite so simple. Even the identification of the poor and the diagnosis of poverty may be far from obvious when we move away from extreme and raw poverty. Different approaches can be used (e.g. biological inadequacy, relative deprivation), and there are technical issues to be resolved within each approach. Furthermore, to construct an overall picture of poverty, it is necessary to go well beyond identifying the poor. To provide an aggregate profile based on the characteristics of those who are identified as poor, problems of aggregation have to be squarely faced. Finally – and most importantly – the *causation* of poverty raises questions that are not easily answered. While the 'immediate' antecedents of poverty may be too obvious to need much analysis, and the 'ultimate' causation too vague and open-ended a question to be settled fully, there are various intermediate levels of useful answers that are worth exploring. The problem is of particular relevance in the context of recent discussions on the causation of hunger and starvation. . . .

In his famous study of poverty in York, Seebohm Rowntree (1901) defined families as being in 'primary poverty' if their 'total earnings are insufficient to obtain the minimum necessities for the maintenance of merely physical efficiency'. It is not surprising that biological considerations related to the requirements of survival or work efficiency have been often used in defining the poverty line. Starvation, clearly, is the most telling aspect of poverty.

The biological approach has come under rather intense fire recently.[1] There are indeed several problems with its use. First, there are significant variations related to physical features, climatic conditions and work habits.[2] In fact, even for a

---

This quotation has been added by the Editors.

specific group in a specific region, nutritional requirements are difficult to define precisely. People have been known to survive with incredibly little nutrition, and there seems to be a cumulative improvement of life expectation as the dietary limits are raised. In fact, physical opulence seems to go on increasing with nutrition over a very wide range; Americans, Europeans and Japanese have been growing measurably in stature as their diets have continued to improve. There is difficulty in drawing a line somewhere, and the so-called 'minimum nutritional requirements' have an inherent arbitrariness that goes well beyond variations between groups and regions.

Second, the translation of minimum *nutritional* requirements into minimum *food* requirements depends on the choice of commodities. While it may be easy to solve the programming exercise of a 'diet problem', choosing a minimum cost diet for meeting specified nutritional requirements from food items sold at specified costs, the relevance of such a minimum cost diet is not clear. Typically, it turns out to be very low-cost indeed,[3] but monumentally boring, and people's food habits are not, in fact, determined by such a cost minimization exercise. The actual incomes at which specified nutritional requirements are met will depend greatly on the consumption habits of the people in question.

Third, for non-food items such minimum requirements are not easy to specify, and the problem is usually solved by assuming that a specified proportion of total income will be spent on food. With this assumption, the minimum food costs can be used to derive minimum income requirements. But the proportion spent on food varies not merely with habits and culture, but also with relative prices and availability of goods and services. It is not surprising that the assumptions made often turn out to be contradicted by actual experience; for example, Lord Beveridge's estimate of subsistence requirements of income during the Second World War proved to be far from correct, since the British were spending a much lower proportion of their income on food than was assumed (see Townsend, 1974, p. 17).

In view of these problems, one may well agree with Martin Rein's (1971) assertion that 'almost every procedure in the subsistence-level definition of poverty can be reasonably challenged' (p. 61). But the question that does remain is this: after we have challenged every one of the procedures used under the biological approach, what do we do *then*? Do we simply ignore that approach,[4] or do we examine whether something remains in it to be salvaged? I would argue that there does remain something.

First, while the concept of nutritional requirements is a rather loose one, there is no particular reason to suppose that the concept of poverty must itself be clear-cut and sharp. In fact, a certain amount of vagueness is implicit in both the concepts, and the really interesting question is the extent to which the areas of vagueness of the two notions, as commonly interpreted, tend to coincide. The issue, thus, is not whether nutritional standards are vague, but whether the vagueness is of the required kind.

Second, to check whether someone is getting a specified bundle of nutrition, one need not necessarily go through the procedure of examining whether that person has the income level that would generate that bundle. One can simply examine whether the person is, in fact, meeting that nutritional requirement or not. Even in poor countries, direct nutritional information of this type can be collected through sample surveys of consumption bundles and can be extensively analysed (see, for example, Srinivasan and Bardhan, 1974, especially the paper by Chatterjee, Sarkar and Paul, and Panikar *et al.*, 1975); and the 'identification' exercise under the nutritional approach need not go through the intermediary of income at all.

Third, even when we do go through the intermediary of income, the translation of a set of nutritional norms (or of alternative sets of such norms) into a 'poverty-line' income (or poverty-line *incomes*) may be substantially simplified by the wide prevalence of particular patterns of consumption behaviour in the community in question. Proximity of *actual* habits and behaviour makes it possible to derive income levels at which the nutritional norms will be 'typically' met. . . .

Finally, while it can hardly be denied that malnutrition captures only one aspect of our idea of poverty, it is an important aspect, and one that is particularly important for many developing countries. It seems clear that malnutrition must have a central place in the conception of poverty. How exactly this place is to be specified remains to be explored, but the recent tendency to dismiss the whole approach seems to be a robust example of misplaced sophistication.

The Inequality Approach

The idea that the concept of poverty is essentially one of inequality has some immediate plausibility. After all, transfers from the rich to the poor can make a substantial dent on poverty in most societies. Even the poverty line to be used for identifying the poor has to be drawn with respect to contemporary standards in the community in question, so that poverty may look very like inequality between the poorest group and the rest of the community.

Arguments in favour of viewing poverty as inequality are presented powerfully by Miller and Roby, who conclude:

> Casting the issues of poverty in terms of stratification leads to regarding poverty as an issue of inequality. In this approach, we move away from efforts to measure poverty lines with pseudo-scientific accuracy. Instead, we look at the nature and size of the differences between the bottom 20 or 10 per cent and the rest of the society. Our concern becomes one of narrowing the differences between those at the bottom and the better-off in each stratification dimension.[5]

There is clearly quite a bit to be said in favour of this approach. But one can argue that inequality is fundamentally a different issue from poverty. To try to analyse poverty 'as an issue of inequality', or the other way round, would do little justice to either. Inequality and poverty are not, of course, unrelated. But neither concept subsumes the other. A transfer of income from a person in the top income group to one in the middle income range must *ceteris paribus* reduce inequality; but it may leave the perception of poverty quite unaffected. Similarly, a general decline in income that keeps the chosen measure of inequality unchanged may, in fact, lead to a sharp increase in starvation, malnutrition and obvious hardship; it will then be fantastic to claim that poverty is unchanged. To ignore such information as starvation and hunger is not, in fact, an abstinence from 'pseudo-scientific accuracy', but blindness to important parameters of the common understanding of poverty. Neither poverty nor inequality can really be included in the empire of the other.[6]

It is, of course, quite a different matter to recognize that inequality and poverty are *associated* with each other, and to note that a different distribution system may cure poverty even without an expansion of the country's productive capabilities. Recognizing the distinct nature of poverty as a concept permits one to treat it as a matter of interest and involvement in itself. The role of inequality in the prevalence of poverty can then figure in the analysis of poverty without making the two conceptually equivalent.

Relative Deprivation

The concept of 'relative deprivation' has been fruitfully used in the analysis of poverty,[7] especially in the sociological literature. Being poor has clearly much to do with being deprived, and it is natural that, for a social animal, the concept of deprivation will be a relative one. But within the uniformity of the term 'relative deprivation', there seem to exist some distinct and different notions.

One distinction concerns the contrast between '*feelings* of deprivation' and '*conditions* of deprivation'. Peter Townsend has argued that 'the latter would be a better usage'.[8] There is indeed much to be said for a set of criteria that can be based on concrete conditions, so that one could use 'relative deprivation' 'in an objective sense to describe situations where people possess less of some desired attribute, be it income, favourable employment conditions or power, than do others.'[9]

On the other hand, the choice of '*conditions* of deprivation' can not be independent of '*feelings* of deprivation'. Material objects cannot be evaluated in this context without reference to how people view them, and even if 'feelings' are not brought in explicitly, they must have an implicit role in the selection of 'attributes'. Townsend has rightly emphasized the importance of the 'endeavour to define the style of living which is generally shared or approved in each society and find whether there is . . . a point in the scale of the distribution of resources below which families find it increasingly difficult . . . to share in the customs, activities and diets comprising that style of living'.[10] One must, however, look also at the feelings of deprivation in deciding on the style and level of living the failure to share which is regarded as important. The dissociation of 'conditions' from 'feelings' is, therefore, not easy, and an objective diagnosis of 'conditions' requires an objective understanding of 'feelings'.

A second contrast concerns the choice of 'reference groups' for comparison.

Again, one has to look at the groups with which the people in question actually compare themselves, and this can be one of the most difficult aspects of the study of poverty based on relative deprivation. The horizon of comparison is not, of course, independent of political activity in the community in question,[11] since one's sense of deprivation is closely related to one's expectations as well as one's view of what is fair and who has the right to enjoy what.

These different issues related to the general notion of relative deprivation have considerable bearing on the social analysis of poverty. It is, however, worth noting that the approach of relative deprivation – even including all its variants – cannot really be the *only* basis for the concept of poverty. A famine, for example, will be readily accepted as a case of acute poverty no matter what the relative pattern within the society happens to be. Indeed, there is an irreducible core of *absolute* deprivation in our idea of poverty, which translates reports of starvation, malnutrition and visible hardship into a diagnosis of poverty without having to ascertain first the relative picture. Thus the approach of relative deprivation supplements rather than supplants the analysis of poverty in terms of absolute dispossession.

NOTES

1. See, for example, Townsend (1971, 1974) and Rein (1971).

2. See Rein (1971), Townsend (1974), Sukhatme (1977, 1978), and Srinivasan (1977a, 1979).

3. See, for example, Stigler's (1945) astonishing estimates of 'the cost of subsistence'. See also Rajaraman (1974).

4. Much depends on what the alternatives are. Rein (1971) himself recommends that 'other' conceptions 'deserve more attention and developments' (p.62). Since 'subsistence' is one of his three 'broad concepts' of poverty, we are left with 'externality' and 'inequality'. Inequality – though related to poverty in terms of both causation and evaluation – is, however, a *distinct* issue from poverty, as will be presently argued (see Section 2.3) . . . .

5. Miller and Roby (1971, p.143). Also Miller, Rein, Roby and Cross (1967). See Wedderburn (1974) for discussions of alternative approaches.

6. It is also worth noting that there are many measures of inequality, of which the gap 'between the bottom 20 or 10 per cent and the rest' is only one. See Atkinson (1970), Sen (1973a), Kolm (1976a, 1976b), and Blackorby and Donaldson (1978, 1980b). Also, inequality is not just a matter of the *size distribution* of income but one of investigating contrasts between different sections of the community from many different perspectives, e.g. in terms of *relations of production*, as done by Marx (1859, 1867).

7. See Runiciman (1966) and Townsend (1971), presenting two rather different approaches to the concept.

8. Townsend (1974), pp.25-6.

9. Wedderburn (1974), p.4.

10. Townsend (1974), p.36.

11. For example, Richard Scase (1974) notes that Swedish workers tend to choose rather wider reference groups than British workers, and relates this contrast to the differences in the nature of the two trade union movements and of political organization generally.

REFERENCES

Atkinson, A.B. (1970), 'On the Measurement of Inequality', *Journal of Economic Theory*, (2).

Blackorby, C. and D. Donaldson (1978), 'Measures of Relative Equity and their meaning in terms of Social Welfare', *Journal of Economic Theory*, (18).

Blackorby, C. and D. Donaldson (1980b), 'A Theoretical Treatment of Indices of Absolute Inequality', *International Economic Review*, (21).

Kolm, S.Ch. (1976a), 'Unequal Inequalities: I', *Journal of Economic Theory*, (12).

Kolm, S.Ch. (1976b), 'Unequal Inequalities: II', *Journal of Economic Theory*, (13).

Marx, Karl (1859), *A Contribution to the Critique of Political Economy*. London: Lawrence and Wishart, 1971.

Marx, Karl (1867), *Capital*. Vol I, London: Allen and Unwin, 1938.

Miller, S.M., M. Rein, P. Roby and B. Cross (1967), 'Poverty, Inequality and Conflict', *Annals of the American Academy of Political Science*.

Miller, S.M. and P. Roby (1971), 'Poverty: Changing Social Stratification', in Townsend (1971).

Rajaraman, Indira (1974) 'Constructing the Poverty Line: Rural Punjab, 1960-61', Discussion Paper No. 43. Research Program in Economic Development, Princeton University.

Rein, M. (1971), 'Problems in the Definition and Measurement of Poverty' in Townsend (1971).

Rowntree, S. (1901), *Poverty: A Study of Town Life*. London, Macmillan.

Runciman, W.G. (1966), *Relative Deprivation and Social Justice*. London: Routledge and Kegan Paul.

Scase, R. (1974), 'Relative Deprivation: A Comparison of English and Swedish Manual Workers', in Wedderburn (1974).

Sen, A.K. (1973a), *On Economic Inequality*. Oxford: Clarendon Press.

Srinivasan, T.N. (1977a), 'Poverty: Some Measurement Problems' in *Conference Proceedings*, 41st Seminar of the International Statistical Institute held at New Delhi.

Srinivasan, T.N. (1979), 'Malnutrition: Some Measurement and Policy Issues' mimeographed, World Bank, Washington, D.C.

Stigler, G.J. (1945), 'The Cost of Subsistence', *Journal of Farm Economics*, (27).

Sukhatme, P.V. (1977), *Nutrition and Poverty*. New Delhi: Indian Agricultural Research Institute.

Sukhatme, P.V. (1978), 'Assessment of Adequacy of Diets at Different Income Levels', *Economic and Political Weekly*, (13), Special Number.

Sukhatme, P.V. (1977), *Nutrition and Poverty*. New Delhi, Indian Agricultural Research Institute.

Sukhatme, P.V. (1978), 'Assessment of Adequacy of Diets at Different Income Levels', *Economic and Political Weekly*, (13), Special Number.

Townsend, Peter (1971), *The Concept of Poverty*. London: Heinemann.

Townsend, Peter (1974), 'Poverty as Relative Deprivation: Resources and Styles of Living' in Wedderburn (1974).

Townsend, Peter (1974), *Poverty in the United Kingdom*. Harmondsworth: Penguin.

Wedderburn, D. (1974), *Poverty, Inequality and Class Structure*. Cambridge: University Press.

The Concept and Measurement of Development

David Colman and Frederick Nixson

This extract is taken from the authors' study, Economics of Change in Less Developed Countries (*1986*).

---

*The questions to ask about a country's development are therefore: What has been happening to poverty? What has been happening to unemployment? What has been happening to inequality? If all three of these have declined from high levels then beyond doubt this has been a period of development for the country concerned. If one or two of these central problems have been growing worse, especially if all three have, it would be strange to call the result 'development' even if per capita income doubled.

Dudley Seers, 'The Meaning of Development', *Eleventh World Conference of the Society for International Development* (New Delhi, 1969).

At the outset it is necessary to clarify the meaning of 'development'. While this is by no means a simple matter, and involves a certain amount of controversy, there is a broad measure of agreement about it (see Section 1.1). Having defined development, the problem is the way in which it should be measured. As will become clear in Section 1.2, however, this is even more problematic. In fact the direct measurement of development turns out to be unmanageable and, instead, various rather crude indicators have to be used – indicators are measurable variables which are assumed to be directly correlated with development. As will be seen, there are doubts as to whether any available indicators are particularly highly correlated with development, but there is a (rather grudging) acceptance that national income per person is as useful as any; certainly it is the most widely used. This measure of agreement is important because it provides the essential requirement for the classification of countries according to their state, or rate, of development.

In classifying countries by their state of development a strict numerical ranking could be adopted, but more usually they are arbitrarily classified into groups. A commonly used device is to classify countries, other than the centrally planned ones, into two groups: those countries with the highest per capita incomes (almost exclusively the industrialised capitalist ones) are classified as developed countries; the larger number of countries which rank lower on this scale are classified as developing, less-developed, or underdeveloped (according to the preferred terminology). While at many points in the book we shall accept this crude division of countries into two groups, it is recognised that the groups are by no means homogeneous. In particular, there are differences between the less-developed countries; thus, where it is considered appropriate, further arbitrary

This quotation has been added by the Editors.

subdivisions can be made within the group of developing countries. This further subdivision may be made according to the per capita income criterion, as for example when employing the UN categories of low, middle, upper-middle, and high income developing countries. Alternatively, subdivision may be made according to some other characteristic, such as when distinguishing the oil-exporting developing countries from those without oil, or in separating developing countries with a high proportion of industrial exports from those almost wholly dependent upon primary commodity exports. While we recognise the arbitrariness of the distinction between developed and less-developed countries, and also between different categories of less-developed countries (LDCs), we accept the conventions about the usefulness of such a distinction. . . .

1.1. What is Development?

Development can be considered either as a process of improvement with respect to a set of values or, when comparing the relative levels of development of different countries, as a comparative state of being with respect to such values. The values in question relate to desired conditions in society. Self-evidently, there is no universal agreement about what these desired conditions should be; individuals certainly have different preferences regarding their lifestyle and relationships with the rest of society; and through their political manifestos and the policies operated by government, nations express different collective (majority or minority) views about the desired state of society – views which change through time. Inevitably, therefore, the rate or the relative level of a country's development are normative concepts whose definition and measurement depend upon the value judgements of the analysts involved.

The assertion that development is a normative concept which will be measured differently by different people constitutes a serious charge but is one which affects all areas of the social sciences and is not unique to development studies. For as Myrdal observed (1970, p. 42), the fact is 'that value premises are needed even in the theoretical stage of establishing facts and factual relations. Answers can only be given when questions have been asked. A view is impossible except from a viewpoint'. Not only are value judgements an inevitable part of deciding what concepts and relationships should be employed to answer questions such as 'what causes development?' or 'has development occurred in any specific instance?', but value judgements are also necessary in deciding how to represent concepts empirically. For example, in defining gross domestic product, should unpaid housewives' services be included, and if so, how should they be valued? Similarly, what procedures should be used to measure the volume and value of food produced for own consumption and not exchanged in the market? These questions can only be resolved judgementally, there being no uniquely appropriate procedures.

It has thus to be recognised that value judgements are inescapable elements of factual study in the social sciences. They are, however, especially prominent elements in development economics precisely because a central aspect of the subject is to formulate criteria for development, and also because many of the commonly chosen criteria are difficult to define and measure. Consequently, there would appear to be plenty of scope for judgemental disagreements about what development is, what are its most important goals, and what are the relationships between aims. Certainly there has recently been extensive debate about these issues in the literature (see below), but this, while demonstrating the existence of disagreements about how development is caused and what weights should be assigned to specific goals, nevertheless demonstrates a broad measure of agreement about the main categories to be achieved in development.

Possibly this measure of agreement is not surprising if, as Seers has said (in Baster 1972), 'Surely the values we need are staring us in the face, as soon as we ask ourselves: what are the necessary conditions for a universally accepted aim, the realisation of the potential of human personality?' Based on this premise, that the ultimate aim and yardstick of development is that implied by the question, Seers identifies a number of objectives for development in the poorest countries. These are: (1) that family incomes should be adequate to provide a subsistence package of food, shelter, clothing and footwear; (2) that jobs should be available to all family heads, not only because this will ensure a distribution of income such that subsistence consumption levels will be generally achieved but because a job is something without which personality cannot develop; (3) that access to education should be increased and literacy ratios raised; (4) that the populace should be given an opportunity to participate in government; and (5) that national independence should be achieved in 'the sense that the views of other governments do not largely predetermine one's own government's decisions'. As progress is made towards the economic goals, that is as 'undernourishment, unemployment and inequality dwindle', Seers argues that the 'educational and political aims become increasingly important objectives of development'.

Seers's list of development criteria or objectives is similar in basic respects to those suggested by others. Myrdal, for example, adopts as 'instrumental value premises' (i.e. criteria for assessing development) certain 'modernisation ideals' which are (1) rationality, (2) development and development planning, (3) rise of productivity, (4) rise of levels of living, (5) social and economic equalisation, (6) improved institutions and attitudes, (7) national consolidation, (8) national independence, (9) democracy at the grass roots, and (10) social discipline.

Similarly, to Streeten, who participated in the preparation of Myrdal's magnum opus *Asian Drama* (1968), 'development means modernisation, and modernisation means transformation of human beings. Development as an objective and development as a process both embrace a change in fundamental attitudes to life and work, and in social, cultural and political institutions' (Streeten 1972, p. 30). More specifically (p.15), Streeten sees the process of development in terms of progress in a number of inter-related dimensions: (1) output and incomes, (2) conditions of production, (3) levels of living (including nutrition, housing, health and education), (4) attitudes to work, (5) institutions, and (6) policies.[1] Streeten's concept has evolved into what is now known as 'the basic needs' approach to development (see, for example, Streeten *et al.* 1981 and Stewart 1985). According to this, development is to be measured or implemented with respect to the increased satisfaction of basic needs (as defined in terms of the various development values listed above). This automatically gives great weight to the interests of the poorer sections of society, since it is there that basic needs are least likely to be met. It is an influential concept which has attempted to steer the focus of development away from growth of GNP to the ways that the benefits of growth are distributed and to the ways that they contribute to desirable social and political change. . . .

---

* Brazil's president from 1969 to 1974 was once asked by a journalist what he thought of Brazil's 'economic miracle', a reference to GNP growth rates of over ten percent yearly between 1967 and 1971. With unaccustomed candour [the president] replied: 'The miracle is good for Brazil's economy, but bad for its people'.

Denis Goulet, 'Obstacles to World Development: an Ethical Reflection', *World Development*, Vol 11, No. 7, 1983.

Little purpose would be served by presenting yet other proposed lists of development criteria. They would inevitably include many of the components common to the lists above, and would tend to lend some support to Seers's assertion that the criteria of development are largely self-evident. Whether this is true or not, the lists of values presented do indicate the extent to which there is agreement about certain key criteria, and about development as a multi-dimensional process or set of objectives, in which the dimensions are economic, social, political and cultural in the widest sense of these terms. But the lists also indicate clearly that strong personal values intrude into conceptions of development. This is well borne out in Myrdal's approach; even his initial general characterisation of development in terms of 'modernisation ideals' amounts to a strong value judgement, namely that modern methods and attitudes (presumably as revealed in some of the wealthier nations) are preferable to more traditional approaches (as found in the poorer countries?). While a majority of people may agree with this value premise, there are undeniably others who would dispute it. The personal nature of the value judgements is even more evident in some of the individual criteria. 'Social discipline', which for Myrdal largely involves stamping out corruption in what he calls the 'soft state', is liable to widely differing interpretations. Similarly, 'national consolidation' and 'democracy at the grass roots' have different meanings to different people and political systems. Indeed, there may be an innate tendency for the development criteria proposed by private individuals, such as development economists, to diverge considerably from those of political authorities which make policy choices from the viewpoint of needing to promote the continuity and development of the nation state.

*This quotation has been added by the Editors.

It should also be reiterated that there is no agreement as to what weights to assign to each of the individual objectives for the operational purposes of policy formulation and measurement of development. This is partly due to the inevitable differences in personal values, but it is also due to the need for the weights to be changed with changes in the level of development. Whatever its causes, this problem of not being able readily to represent development as a single variable creates serious problems in the study of development. This emerges most clearly when we examine theories of development which . . . tend to circumvent the problem by analysing only selected subsets of development objectives. The problem also poses appreciable difficulties for measuring development – an issue taken up in the next section of this chapter.

One important conclusion which emerges from the attempt to define development is that as a process it is not synonymous with economic growth. It is conceivable that, in a particular country, average GNP per capita might have risen, while at the same time income inequality increased, the poor became poorer, and negative progress been made to other development goals. Such a situation might be classed as economic growth with negative development in that, although average incomes may have risen, the economic lot of the mass of the population would have deteriorated and negative or no progress would have been made in transforming personal attitudes and institutions in the manner required by the modernisation ideals. Conversely, it is possible to envisage development with negative growth. This might occur where a major restructuring occurs in attitudes, political institutions and production relations (by such means as land reform and/or collectivisation) which creates the conditions for future development, but at a short-run cost of reduced GNP due to disruption of the previous production and distribution system. In this context Streeten (1972, p. 31) has argued, 'Just as there can be economic growth without development, there can be development without economic growth'. Not everyone would agree with Streeten in this respect, however. Szentes (1971, p. 14), for example, argued tellingly that:

> Any distinction between the theories of 'development' and 'growth' can at best only be accepted for practical reasons . . . however by no means, as a scientific distinction. The terminological distinction on a semantic basis is unacceptable, because development always and everywhere involves and presupposes the dialectic of quantitative and qualitative changes, of evolution and revolution. And even if a purely quantitative 'growth' can be observed in a given place and at a given time within the framework of the existing structure or system, it is not only the consequences of a previous qualitative change but it also inevitably paves the way for a new one.

Development economists were perhaps rather slow in appreciating the full implication of this remark. It is only recently that a number of writers have begun to question the generally accepted distinction between growth and development (see, for example, Palma 1978; Bernstein 1979; Warren 1980; and Nixson 1986) and to pursue to their logical conclusion the implications of the concepts of normative development outlined, as above, for example, by Seers.

The recognition that economic growth, of and by itself, did not automatically lead to the wider, normatively defined goals of development was an important step in the evolution of the study of development in the postwar period. However, the increasingly abstract and utopian definitions of development popularised in the literature pose a number of theoretical problems and force upon us the need to reconsider the concept of development. Four points in particular require brief mention (for a fuller discussion, see Nixson 1986).

Firstly, the now popular concept of development refers to an ideal world or state of affairs that is both ahistorical and apolitical – ahistorical because it postulates an idealised structure that does not and never has existed, and apolitical because development is defined in an abstract sense and is not related to any particular political/social/institutional structure. The goals of development enumerated by Seers, Streeten, Myrdal, etc., *are* of great significance and importance, but we must raise the question as to which specific socio-political framework will best permit the achievement of such objectives. The undesirable features of economic growth and structural change are not the inevitable consequence of these forces as such but are, rather, the characteristic features of the specific process of capitalist development as it is unfolding in contemporary LDCs. This is not necessarily an argument for an alternative form of socio-political organisation or development ('socialist' development is not free from its own problems) but it is an argument for emphasising the fact that 'development' does not occur in a political vacuum.

Secondly, this idealised concept of development goes some way to explaining the current state of pessimism in development economics . . . . 'Development' in many LDCs has turned out to be very different from what was expected or hoped for by many development practitioners, but development economics as such can hardly be blamed for present conditions in LDCs, however misguided some of its early analyses and overoptimistic its policy pronouncements may have been (for a contrary view, see Lal 1983; Little 1982). Development theory may well have 'failed' in the sense that it gave overly simple or misleading explanations of the problems of development and underdevelopment, but it was/is *not* the cause of those problems.

Thirdly, there is a marked tendency in development economics, of both neoclassical and structuralist/dependency varieties, to confuse explanation (the historico-analytic) with policy prescription. Too often we find development specialists confusing what *ought* to be with what *is* (Lall 1976, p. 182). This is not to argue against policy prescription *per se*, for as Leeson (1983, p. 24) has argued: 'Certainly most development economists would reject the notion that policy advice is not a proper sphere for the involvement of the profession'. However, it is worth noting that much writing masquerading as analysis is in fact far more concerned with policy prescription, and we must avoid confusing the desire for a better world with the fuller understanding of the very imperfect reality. In this book the emphasis is firmly historico-analytic rather than policy prescriptive.

Fourthly, development economics all too often appears to assume that structural problems have somehow been 'solved' in the developed (capitalist) economies and that their problem is 'merely' one of ensuring self-sustaining and continuous growth (or, at its simplest level, that 'developed' economies have, by definition, overcome the problems of 'development'). This is clearly not the case. Problems of unemployment, inequality, deprivation and various kinds of structural disequilibria (relating to the balance of payments, deindustrialisation etc.) clearly exist in many of the developed capitalist economies. These major problems are rooted in the structure of those economies and they are not 'solved' by 'development'; indeed, they arise as a consequence of specific forms of development both within those economies and in the wider global economy.

What implications do the above arguments have for our concept of 'development'? The main point to emphasise is that development is not smooth, undirectional and non-problematic but is rather, to quote Joseph Schumpeter (who published his theory of economic development in 1911),[2] 'lopsided, discontinuous, disharmonious'. Development is a dialectical process in that every change in the economy brings with it new problems and adjustments – to paraphrase Streeten (1983), there are always problems to every solution. It is contradictory and complex, and these aspects of the development process are best highlighted by viewing development as an historical process which is not consciously willed by anyone (Arndt 1981, p. 460). The concept of economic development as an activity consciously engaged in mainly, but not solely, by governments, with the intention of approaching or reaching certain specific objectives (the normative definition of development outlined above), complements the alternative concept of development as an historical process. However, it must be recognised that once the abstract objectives of development have been defined, the concrete, specific socio-economic and socio-political structures *within which it is believed that such objectives can best be realised* must also be made explicit.

1.2. Measuring Development

Interest in measuring development is intense. Everyone who reads this book is likely to have accepted some statistical notion about the level of development of his/her own country in comparison with certain others, and will either feel satisfaction or concern about its relative position. At a national level such pride or concern has a central role in the political process and in engaging electoral support for the policies of political parties or governments. As in development studies, the focal point of concern is often the statistical evidence of a widening gap between the standards of living in the richer (so-called developed) countries and the poorer (less developed) ones (LDCs).

The fact, is, however, that it is extremely difficult to measure comparative levels of development. The statistical methods available may be thought fairly reliable for obtaining acceptable measures of rates of growth of living standards and of ordinal rankings as to whether one country is more developed than another, but they exhibit grave deficiencies when used as cardinal measures of by how much or how many times one country is more developed than any other.

The fundamental cause of the measurement difficulty lies with the definition of development. As identified in the previous section, many of the criteria or objectives by which development is to be judged or measured are qualitative ones. Such criteria as the standard of living, health levels, the educational level, and the extent of grass-roots participation in government are all qualitative ones which cannot be measured directly. They have to be measured indirectly using indicators which are directly measurable quantities. Thus among the many possible indicators of a 'nation's state of physical health' might be included the number of people per trained doctor, the rate of child mortality, or the average life expectancy; and for the standard of living one might use such indicators as average national income per person, the proportion of families with piped water for their living quarters, the proportion of households supplied with electricity, and so on.

This multiplicity of possible indicators for any given general dimension of development simply compounds the problems arising from the existence of several general dimensions.[3] Firstly, no quantitative indicator is capable of exactly measuring a qualitative criterion. Secondly, no one indicator can conceivably approximate the qualitative levels attained with respect to all the major dimensions of development, especially when it is remembered that these are economic, social, political and cultural. Thirdly, there are appreciable difficulties in deriving a method (weighting scheme) whereby various indicators for different qualities can be added together into a single index of a country's level of development.

Since the concept of development only acquires substance through a process of measurement, it is important (in the light of the foregoing statement of the problems of measurement) to examine briefly some of the major alternative proposals for development indicators, and some of the criticisms levelled at them. Most effort to date has been devoted to the development of economic indicators, and this is reflected by the fact that most of the rest of this section is devoted to economic indicators, and little to political indicators, social indicators or to combinations of these.

Economic Indicators of Development
It is natural that analysts should want to employ a single indicator of develop-ment rather than a set of separate ones. It is attractive not only because it simplifies (at least in a mechanical sense) the task of producing theoretical models of development but also because it facilitates communication and thought to consider a single series of numbers rather than several simultaneously.

In practice, one indicator has dominated all others, and that is national income or gross national product (GNP) per capita.[4] This is the name given to a series which can be calculated for any country, using a specific basic set of measurement rules which have been devised in the Western industrial countries to measure their overall level of income or production. It is important to note that the measurement rules used for adding together the values of different economic activities were not derived with any concept of development in mind, but to produce indicators of annual levels of production and income. Consequently, a love-hate relationship has developed over the use of GNP as a development indicator. In its favour (1) it is an indicator of a set of key activities, the provision of goods and services, an increase in which is almost[5] a necessary condition for development; (2) the measurement rules, which are complex, have evolved over time and are well known and understood; and (3) most member countries of the United Nations (UN) produce estimates of GNP for inclusion in UN official statistics.

Against GNP as a development indicator are the facts that (1) it is an indicator only of some economic aspects of development – it makes no allowance for changing income distribution – and it has no direct implications for the other non-economic criteria; (2) it is a heavily value-loaded indicator, and the subjective element is larger in countries with poor statistics and large subsistence sectors than in countries where a much smaller proportion of transactions bypass the market; and (3) irrespective of any deficiencies GNP may have as a measure of national economic activity, there are additional problems in using it for making international comparisons, Most of these points are perfectly obvious ones – but in view of the frequency with which GNP is encountered in international 'league tables' of development, they deserve a certain amount of amplification.

Regarding the first point, there is no way in which a simple total of the value of goods and services produced can reflect details of income distribution. It is, therefore, quite possible for any increase in average GNP per capita to be due to the increased incomes and consumption of only a relatively few richer members of society and to be accompanied by a worsening income distribution . . . . In this case, depending upon the weight that would be assigned to income inequality as a criterion for development, it is possible for an increase in GNP per capita apparently to signal an increase in social welfare when it has in fact diminished.

The question of the value-loaded nature of GNP as a development indicator is a somewhat broader one, but basically it revolves around the appropriateness of using market prices to value social welfare. Thus, returning to the question of income distribution, it is observed that the prices and quantities of goods and services consumed depend upon the prevailing income distribution. To the extent that the distribution may be highly unequal, increases in measured GNP may give a poor indication of the extent to which social need is increasingly satisfied; certainly, at any level of GNP the pattern of consumption might be markedly changed by altering the distribution of income. This consideration is amplified by major doubts arising in relation to the possibility that, because of market imperfections, the market prices used for valuing components of GNP are appreciably different from the appropriate social valuations. Not only may prices be distorted by the existence of monopolistic forces, by policy intervention, and by the possibility that the pricing of public goods may be to some extent arbitrary, but also 'many aspects of the quality of life and the environment fall outside the market calculus' (Baster 1972, p. 3) and therefore are assigned a zero price, which clearly undervalues their social worth. Thus there are a number of well-recognised sources of potential bias in GNP as a measure of the social value of national income.

In making international comparisons of development levels, the general procedure is to take each country's own estimate of GNP calculated in local currency units and then to convert these into some common currency unit, usually the US dollar, for comparative purposes. It has to be recognised that there are several sources of bias in this procedure. One of these is that the subjective elements in the measurement procedure may be resolved differently in different countries, resulting in a lack of standardisation between countries' estimates. In richer countries a high proportion of domestic services are purchased in the form of washing machines, vacuum cleaners and refrigerators; housing construction and repair costs are mainly in the form of purchased inputs; and food is largely purchased rather than home produced. Thus a high proportion of the consumption of these services is provided in the form of traded labour and consumer products which will be recorded by the normal national accounting procedures.

However, this is not so in poor countries where only a small proportion of such services will be purchased. This is particularly significant (because it constitutes a high proportion of total product) in the case of food, a high proportion of which is consumed directly by the producer and his family. But it is also true of house construction, household and other services, many of which are provided by family labour in LDCs. Hence in poor countries a high proportion of these important services is supplied without involving trade of a conventionally accountable type. If, as is often the case, due to lack of statistical evidence, national income accounts omit or inadequately allow for the consumption of such non-traded goods and services, the resultant GNP estimates will be biased in favour of the rich and against the poor countries precisely because a higher proportion of total economic activity takes a non-traded form in the latter. This is a serious problem, as Seers describes it (in Baster 1972, p. 23).

> But what are all the voluminous tables of national income accounts really worth? So far as the Third World is concerned, much of what they ought to cover is virtually outside the scope of official statistics. This applies above all to output of domestic foodstuffs, even the staples, let alone subsidiary crops which come under the general heading of 'market gardening' (American 'truck farming'), not to speak of fish, forest products, etc. Extremely rough methods of estimation are often used, much of the output being assumed to rise in proportion to the increase in rural population, an increase which is in turn assumed to be some

constant arbitrary rate in the absence of registration of births and deaths, or data on migration. Secondly, we know very little about construction in the countryside by the farming community itself; this apparently amounts to a good deal if one takes account not only of building houses but also clearing land, digging wells and ditches, constructing fences and hedges, etc. Thirdly, there are practically no basic data on domestic service and other personal services, even those which are remunerated.

Another bias arising from the use of national income accounting statistics as welfare measures is that some items which are in fact necessary and unavoidable costs of living are treated implicitly as benefits. This is true of the costs of travelling to work. To the extent that such costs may be a significant item in the accounts of rich countries and negligible in poor countries, comparison of GNP levels will exaggerate the extent of the gap between rich and poor.

There is also a major complex of biases for comparative use of national accounts statistics which arises from the choice of an exchange rate to convert from local currency units to (say) US dollars. In the first place, where a country operates a multiple exchange rate system it may be difficult to decide which rate to use. For example (Open University 1975, Table 2), Colombia apparently operated four separate and highly variable exchange rates for different classes of transaction, so that it may be necessary to impute an exchange rate for the sort of purpose being considered here.

More importantly, the choice of any exchange rate carries with it certain implications for the relative prices of non-traded goods and services which may be quite inappropriate and misleading. Consider, for example, an exchange rate between the pound sterling and US dollar of £1 = $1.40. A simplified interpretation of this is that (before allowing for transport costs) £1 will buy for a Briton a basket of traded American goods which would cost an American $1.40, and conversely $1.40 will buy a basket of British traded goods which would cost a Briton £1. Applying this exchange rate to an estimate of UK GNP to convert it to its dollar equivalent involves implicitly assuming that £1's worth of those British goods and services which are not traded would cost $1.40 in the USA. This is unlikely to be true. A pound's worth of car servicing in the UK may cost substantially more than $1.40 if carried out in the USA, and the same with house construction costs, electrical repairs and so forth. In that case comparing US national income per capita with the dollar equivalent (at £1 = $1.40) of UK national income per capita will overstate the margin by which the average American is better off than his British counterpart.

The magnitude of this class of bias is likely to be far larger when comparing income levels in the USA to those of the poorest countries. Indeed, the absurd results which would occur from a welfare interpretation of such comparisons are well demonstrated by Usher (1966). He reproduces UN data which indicate that for 1963 the USA has a GNP of $2,790 per capita and Ethiopia, toward the bottom of the league, only $40 per capita. As Usher asks, what conceivable meaning can be accorded to the notion that the average Ethiopian lived on 11 cents a day? A person would have starved in the USA unless he had far more than that, and yet most Ethiopians survived. The only possible conclusion is that Ethiopian prices for basic commodities were much lower relative to those in the USA than implied by the exchange rate, that the dollar cost of subsistence was much lower in Ethiopia than the USA, and that the implied ratio of American to Ethiopian living standards of 70 to 1 was a sizeable exaggeration. It is obvious that if Ethiopia's output of goods and services were valued at local prices and then converted at the dollar exchange rate, then its national income would appear substantially larger than one-seventieth of the USA's. By the same token valuing the USA's output of goods and services at Ethiopian prices would appreciably reduce the estimate of their value to Ethiopian output.

Table 1. Comparison of National GDP per Capita at Local and International (USA) Prices, 1970

	GDP per Capita					
	Valued at local prices			Valued at internatioal prices		Exchange rate deviation index
Country	National currency	$ US	% of US level	$ US	% of US level	
Colombia	6,113	329	6.9	763	15.9	2.32
France	16.118	2,902	60.5	3,599	75.0	1.24
Germany FR	11,272	3,080	64.2	3,585	74.7	1.16
Hungary	31,116	1,037	21.6	1,935	40.3	1.87
India	736	98	2.0	342	7.1	3.49
Italy	1,062	1,699	35.4	2,198	45.8	1.29
Japan	721	2,003	41.7	2,952	61.5	1.47
Kenya	1,027	144	3.0	275	5.7	1.91
UK	893	2,143	44.6	2,895	60.3	1.35
USA	4,801	3,984	100.0	4,801	100.0	1.00

Source: Kravis *et al.* (1976), Tables 1.1 and 1.3.

These observations are the *raison d'être* of the so-called 'binary' comparison method for adjusting GNP measures. This method has been applied by Usher (1966), and more recently by Kravis *et al.* (1975 and 1978) as part of the UN International Comparison Project, to compare the value of gross domestic product (GDP) of various countries to that of the USA. It involves first obtaining what might be called the 'conventional' estimates of GDP by converting GDP in local currency (with all components of output valued at local prices) to US dollar values at the prevailing currency exchange rates. These are then compared to estimates of GDP obtained directly in dollar terms by valuing the outputs of each country at the prices of comparable outputs in the USA.[6] While the explanation of the method by Kravis *et al.* (1975) clearly indicates that this is by no means as simple as it sounds (and many complex statistical adjustments are needed), this alternative measure does grapple with the fundamental weakness of the conventional measure, which is that it makes no correction for the fact that at any given exchange rate the relative prices (expressed in either currency) of goods and services in any pair of countries may diverge widely, especially between a DC and an LDC.[7]

From Table 1 it can be seen that the estimated ratio of the 1970 GDP per capita of individual countries to that of the USA under the conventional pricing rule was significantly different from that obtained by pricing all national output at US (i.e. international) prices. The measure of the difference for each country is shown by the exchange rate deviation index. For example, Kenyan GDP per capita in 1970 was conventionally estimated at only 6.9% of the USA level, whereas valuing all outputs at international prices raised this 2.32 times to 15.9%. For India the effect was even more marked, suggesting GDP per capita was 7.1% of the US level in 1970, rather than only 2%. Even the relative GDP of industrialised countries can be seen to be higher when valued at international prices. Thus Table 1 highlights one of the most important inadequacies about the conventional national income comparison, namely that it exaggerates the gap between rich and poor countries. Having said this, however, it should be emphasised that there is no way of equating a halving of the ratio between NI per capita in two countries (from, say, 20:1 to 10:1) with a halving of our degree of concern for the poorer country. There is no definable correspondence between 'units of concern' and ratios or gaps between NI per capita, although presumably most people would accept that there is some direct correlation between them. Thus it is not a matter of indifference whether the ratio is 20:1 or 10:1. One of these values will be a better indicator of relative welfare than the other, but how much better is not assessable.

What the preceding illustration and calculations show is that it is possible, by repricing methods, to adjust the conventional national income estimates so that their performance as relative welfare indicators is improved. However, these methods cannot overcome all the problems, and in any case the binary pricing approach is laborious and involves the statistician in a whole new set of subjective judgements. Naturally, therefore, consideration has been given to alternative economic indicators of development, some of which appear to represent a shortcut to the common pricing approach. Usher (1966) mentions two of these: (1) the social adequacy method; and (2) the related, direct attempt to measure levels of living. In the social adequacy method, for 'each country, income per head in local currency is divided by an estimate of the bare cost of subsistence; ratios arrived at in this way are then treated as measures of real income. The one attempt to compare incomes by this method, a comparison of Japan and the United States, raised the ratio of Japanese to American income almost 600 per cent over what it appears to be when national incomes are compared through the foreign exchange rate' (Usher 1966, p. 37). The main obvious difficulty with this procedure is in defining the cost of subsistence in each country. The concept of subsistence may be defined (not without difficulty) as a purely physiological level, but is often defined to include a psychological component for consumption thought to be socially necessary, e.g. the minimum quality of housing demanded by the average European is far higher than that expected in poor African countries. But this sort of judgemental hurdle is found with all measurement procedures, including Usher's second class of method. In this, following Clark and Haswell (1964, Ch.4), an attempt might be made to 'measure' living standards in terms of a key welfare indicator such as 'grain equivalent'. In this the value of all goods and services would be divided by the local price of a standard measure of grain so that national income for countries could be expressed and compared in terms of so many grain equivalents. Interesting though this is, none of the proposed alternatives has yet supplanted national income as the main economic indicator of development. . . .

All the alternative indices encounter the same basic difficulties in construction. The main ones are: (1) that all components need to be transformed to a common unit of measurement so that, for example, such disparate indicators as expectation of life at birth, radio receivers per 1,000 of the population, and the vocational enrolment ratio can be added together with others to produce a single index; and (2) that in the absence of any natural weights, a weighting scheme has to be devised to determine what importance should be ascribed to one indicator as opposed to another.[8]

This is not the place to consider in detail the ingenious procedures which have been created to normalise and weight various lists of separate indicators and to combine them into a single measure. These are helpfully and briefly sketched out in Open University (1975), and the UNRISD method is presented in detail by McGranahan *et al.* (1972). However, as the Open University publication states (p. 37), none of the alternatively proposed procedures has made much progress in supplanting GNP (or GDP) per capita which,

> . . . remains the most comprehensive and widely used indicator of development levels. While recognising its inherent weaknesses, it is still the most convenient measure of the level of development. Many studies show that economic and social indicators are highly correlated with the level of GDP per capita, and therefore a ranking based on their combinations is relatively close to a ranking based on per capita GDP alone.

Hicks and Streeten (1979) arrive at a similar conclusion when they state (p. 577):

> The search for a composite index of social welfare, analagous to GNP as an index of production, has been a fruitless one so far, since it has proven virtually impossible to translate every aspect of social progress into money values or some other readily accepted common denominator.

They do, however, argue, from a basic needs perspective, that information on how much is produced (GNP) should be supplemented by attention to what is produced, by what means, for whom and with what impact. To do this they advocate that 'what is required . . . are some indicators of the composition and beneficiaries of GNP, which would supplement the GNP data, not replace them'.

Since it is now the practice of UN agencies, and the World Bank's annual World Development Report, to present values for a large number of indicators for all countries, the means are readily to hand to respond to this last injunction . . .

NOTES

1. For those who are interested, Streeten provides a detailed breakdown of the criteria which should be considered within each of these six groups.

2. The book was entitled *Theorie der Wirtschaftlichen Entwicklung*. It was translated into English in 1934.

3. For a full discussion of proposed development indicators and of the problems associated with them, see the various contributions to Baster (ed.) (1972).

4. It should be observed that the national income measure most commonly used is in effect gross national income (GNI). This has to be distinguished from net national income (NNI), which equals GNI minus the allowance for capital depreciation. Thus, while GNI measures the income equivalent to the total value of production in society, NNI indicates the value of the product available for consumption and net new investment, and is therefore probably a better welfare indicator. These two income measures have their exact value equivalents in gross national product (GNP) and net national product (NNP). All of the four measures referred to so far include within them any net property income from abroad, the value of which does not reflect local productive activity – in the LDCs this flow is typically negative as a reflection of repatriated profits by companies and capital export by wealthy individuals. By subtracting net property income from GNP a measure is obtained of gross domestic product (GDP). If the difference between GNP and GDP is large, in so far as the latter is a measure of the total goods and services produced within the economy (before allowing for capital depreciation) it is the better indicator of the productive capacity of the economy and its employment potential.

5. As has already been said, if as GNP increases negative progress is made towards other development goals, such as equality or political participation, negative development might be judged to occur.

6. This definition of the binary method describes that applied by Kravis *et al.* in obtaining the results presented here in Table 1.1. Usher (1966) actually adopted a somewhat different version of the procedure. His method assumes that the 'true' ratio of two countries' living standards lies in between the values of the two ratios obtained by first valuing both countries' GDP at the prices of one country and then at those of the other, and that it is approximated by the geometric average of these two ratios.

7. This is well illustrated by Table 1 in Kravis *et al.* (1978) which indicates that not only do the prices of non-traded goods in 1970 vary greatly between countries, as expected, but that the prices of traded goods also differed significantly, even between DCs.

8. Note: In deriving an index for national income, all the various goods and services are measured in common units of money, and the weighting scheme is provided by their prices.

REFERENCES

Arndt, H.W. (1981) 'Economic Development: A Semantic History', *Economic Development and Cultural Change*, Vol. 29, No. 3, April.

Baster, N. (ed.) (1972) *Measuring Development*, Frank Cass.

Bernstein, H. (1979) 'Sociology of underdevelopment vs. sociology of development?', in D. Lehrman (ed.), *Development Theory: Four Critical Studies*, Frank Cass.

Clark, C. and M.R. Haswell (1964) *The Economics of Subsistence Agriculture*, Macmillan.

Drenowski, J. and W. Scott (1966) *The Level of Living Index*, UNRISD, Report No. 4, Geneva.

Hicks, N. and P. Streeten (1979) 'Indicators of development: the search for a basic needs yardstick', *World Development*, Vol. 57, 567-80.

Kravis, I.B., A.W. Heston, and R. Summers (1978) 'Real GDP per capita for more than one hundred countries', *Economic Journal*, Vol. 88, No. 350, 215-42.

Kravis, I.B., Z. Kenessy, A. Heston, and R. Summers (1976) *A System of International Comparisons of Gross Product and Purchasing Power*, Johns Hopkins Press.

Lal, D. (1983) *The Poverty of Development Economics*, Institute of Economic Affairs.

Lall, S. (1976) 'Conflicts of concepts: welfare economics and developing countries', *World Development*, Vol. 4, No. 3, March.

Leeson, P.F. (1983) 'Development economics and its companions', *Manchester Discussion Papers in Development Studies*, 8304, Mimeo.

Little, I.M.D. (1982) *Economic Development: Theory, Policy, and International Relations*, Basic Books Inc.

McGranahan, D.V., C. Richard-Proust, N.V. Sovani, and M. Subramanian (1972) *Contents and Measurement of Socioeconomic Development*, Praeger.

Myrdal, G. (1968) *Asian Drama: An Inquiry into the Poverty of Nations*, Allen Lane (London), Pantheon (New York).

Myrdal, G. (1970) *The Challenge of World Poverty*, Penguin Books.

Nixson, F.I. (1986) 'Economic development: a suitable case for treatment?', in B. Ingham and C. Simmons (eds.), *The Historical Dimensions of Economic Development*, Frank Cass.

Open University (1975) *International Comparisons of Levels of Development*, Statistical Sources Unit 15, Open University Press.

Palma, G. (1978) 'Dependency: a formal theory of underdevelopment or a methodology for the analysis of concrete situations of underdevelopment?', *World Development*, Vol. 6, Nos. 7/8.

Schumpeter, J.A. (1934; 1961) *The Theory of Economic Development*, Oxford University Press.

Stewart, F. (1985) *Planning to Meet Basic Needs*, Macmillan.

Streeten, P. (1972) *The Frontiers of Development Studies*, Macmillan (especially Ch. 3).

Streeten, P. *et al.* (1981) *First Things First: Meeting Basic Human Needs in Deveoping Countries*, Oxford University Press for World Bank.

Streeten, P. (1983) 'Development dichotomies', *World Development*, Vol. 11, No. 10, October.

Szentes, T. (1971) *The Political Economy of Underdevelopment*, Akademiai Kiado, Budapest.

Usher, D. (1966) *Rich and Poor Countries*, Eaton Paper 9, Institute of Economic Affairs.

Warren, B. (1980) *Imperialism: Pioneer of Capitalism*, Verso.

Development Economics:
Schools of Thought

Nigel Harris

This reading is from Chapter 1 of the author's The End of the Third World (*1986*).

[In 1985 the Bandung Conference] marked a major change in the world order, the entry to international politics of a new group of countries that came to be known as the Third World . . . . A new perception of the world and of the role within it of the new states was created. Around that perception developed a body of theories which we have called here Third Worldism. By now, of course, many of the proposals of this ideology have become absorbed into the political 'common sense' of the world, and it is difficult to identify them today.

The idea of the Third World was a radical critique of the order of world power that had governed international affairs. . . . At the heart of the new ideology was a series of propositions about the possibility of national economic development in the countries of the Third World. Why were those countries so poor when the Europeans and North Americans were so rich? How far could markets be shaped or superseded to force the pace of national economic growth? What should be the role of government in that process? The preoccupations of analysis, explanation and prescriptions for government action came to constitute a new branch of economics, 'development economics'. In fact, the theorization began much earlier than the 1950s and took up themes that emerged after the Great Depression following 1929. It seemed then as if capitalism had exhausted its potential, and new alternatives were needed for all countries. Economists from countries which exported in the main raw materials – Latin America and Eastern Europe – were particularly concerned to formulate methods by which their countries could escape slump. The earlier and later concerns merged, as we see in the evolution of one strand of thought in Latin America.

The Origins of Development Economics
The new states recognized early that maintaining political independence required economic power; rewarding those who had thrown off foreign domination required rising incomes. Many different routes led to the problem of 'economic development'. What did it mean? In Europe and North America, countries had gone through a process, lasting in some cases more than a century, in which most workers had left agriculture (and rural areas) and become industrial (or at least urban) employees. In economese, a declining share of national output was being created in sectors with a low productivity of labour

44

(traditional agriculture) and a rising share generated in high-productivity sectors (particularly industry, and within industry, manufacturing). This structural change was seen as the key element in rising incomes and national power.

The structure of an economy was changed by disproportionate investment in the high-productivity sectors. If manufacturing were expanded more swiftly than the rest over a period of years, then the change could be accomplished. There was a set of problems that flowed from this diagnosis – how to mobilize the resources for a programme of sustained investment, how to acquire the imported equipment for the growth of manufacturing, the infrastructure and power supplies, and the technically skilled workforce. In the late 1940s, it seemed that all these tasks should be undertaken by the state. The new governments undertook the deliberate transformation of their societies.

In so far as economists had concerned themselves with these questions earlier, it had been assumed most often that growth in the world trading system would in time overcome the problems of poverty and backwardness. In a world market, if there were no restrictions and competition determined prices, then each country would become specialized in those forms of production which it was most efficient for it to undertake. And this would allow the 'comparative advantage' of each country ultimately to produce an equalization of incomes (a case formally demonstrated under special assumptions by a leading contemporary economist, Paul Samuelson, in the late 1940s).[1]

For those confronting what seemed to be the endemic poverty of the majority of countries, this theory appeared to be no more than an excuse for complacency and a rationalization of the wealth of the richest people and countries. Poverty was not inevitable, nor could the problem of poverty safely be left to the normal working of the world market. All around was the evidence that the governments of the rich countries had not merely relied on the market; armies, prison camps, legal systems, investment and tax policies – not to mention straight robbery – had all played a role in their capture of a disproportionate share of the world's wealth. The group of poor countries, identified as 'underdeveloped' in the late forties, could not afford to await the possible long-term effects of free trade.

The dispute was not simply about different means to the same end. There were two different conceptions of economic development. On the one hand, the orthodox economists, known as 'neoclassical', envisaged a world economy in which different countries played specialized roles, and were therefore economically interdependent. To them, economic development could only mean working towards a given level of income, since each national economy would be different, depending upon its specialization. The radicals, on the other hand, saw national economic development as a structural change in the *national* economy rather than a relationship to a world economy, and a change such that each country produced most of what it needed at home; thus, each country would be, to a greater or lesser extent, a microcosm of the world, not a specialized contributor (indeed, the specialized economy, the 'monocultural' agricultural exporter, for example, was seen as peculiarly subject to endemic poverty). With a fully diversified home economy, it was thought, self-generating growth was possible on the basis of an expanding home market, regardless of what happened in the world at large.

The starting-point for these preoccupations was the attempt to explain why the orthodox theory of world trade did not work for the poor countries – why for them, it apparently produced impoverishment. In Latin America, one of the most famous founders of development economics, Raúl Prebisch, began his work at this point; his conclusions became the inspiration of the United Nations Economic Commission for Latin America (ECLA, or CEPAL in Spanish).[2] He argued that, although the theory was not working in the twentieth century, it had worked in the nineteenth. Then, Britain and other European powers had depended on imported raw materials in order to expand domestic manufacturing. Imports from Latin America (made possible by European investment there) had in turn expanded the economies of Latin America, making it possible for them to service their borrowings from Europe and to import manufactured goods as well. The division of labour, an exchange of agricultural for industrial goods, had been mutually beneficial.

However, in the twentieth century, a changed structure of relationships turned the beneficial relationship into a malign one – 'reality is undermining the outdated scheme of the international division of labour', as Prebisch expressed it.[3] The United States, a much larger and much more self-sufficient economy, replaced Britain. Its need for imports from Latin America was low; Latin America could no longer earn the means to purchase vital manufactured imports, and must therefore cover its purchases with its limited gold reserves. The hoard at Fort Knox grew while Latin America became increasingly unable to expand; its failure to be able to import then contracted the world market, to the disadvantage of the exporters of manufactured goods. By 1944, Prebisch was warning of a long-term disequilibrium in the world economy as the result of the 'inner-directed development' of the United States, a problem revealed in the growing shortage of US dollars available to Latin America for the purchase of vital imports (a case subsequently applied to Europe as the 'dollar problem').[4]

Parallel to this argument, Prebisch developed another and more far-reaching one. In the Great Depression, he noted, the prices of agricultural exports declined much more than those of manufactured goods. Countries specializing in one or the other therefore faced very different effects of slump. With further work, Prebisch concluded that the phenomenon was not simply the result of slump but reflected a long-term trend, a growing inequality of exchange. Why might this arise? Because, Prebisch suggested, the exporters of manufactured goods (what he now called the 'centre' or 'centres' of the world system) had a monopoly of the supply of such goods and could therefore control their prices. Exporters of agricultural goods (the 'periphery') were many, and thus competition drove down prices.

This argument explained slump, short-term movements. Prebisch then went on to propose that the explanation of long-term deterioration lay in the faster pace of technical development in manufacturing: monopoly controls of the prices of manufactured exports ensured that declining costs of production (as the result of technical innovations) benefited only the sellers of manufactured goods, not the buyers, whereas the reverse was true for the growers of agricultural goods – 'while the centres kept the whole benefit of the technical development of their industries, the peripheral countries transferred to them a share of the fruits of their own technical progress'. A later revision shifted the emphasis from a monopoly of the supply of manufactured goods to a monopoly of the supply of labour; trade-union controls in Europe and North America prevented wages falling in a slump and ensured their steady long-term growth, forcing the prices of manufactured goods to remain high; for the cultivators of the soil, the reverse was true, producing a growing inequality: 'the less that income can contract at the centre, the more it must do so at the periphery'.[5] Later, empirical work on long-term price movements in international trade seemed to confirm the Prebisch thesis of continuing deterioration,[6] and other writers gave new explanations; Hans Singer related the issue to a declining demand for raw-material inputs in manufacturing output as the result of technical advances making economies possible.[7]

By the late forties, the United States had acquired an unprecedented domination of the world economy. It had become the 'cyclical centre' of the system, according to Prebisch, able to determine the world business cycle and ensure domestic full employment, and oblige the periphery to conform to the interests of Washington.

However, there was a way out. The centre's domination arose from its monopoly of manufacturing. Industrialization of the periphery could begin to restore the equilibrium – it would reduce the dependence of Latin America on imports and so reduce its need to export; it would increase domestic employment and incomes, so expanding the domestic market, and thus the demand for a further round of industrialization. The benefits of technical progress in manufacturing would now be retained in the country concerned. However, it would be impossible to industrialize if manufactured goods could be freely imported from the centre; competition from more advanced and larger-scale industries at the centre would stifle the new industries of the periphery. This was the basis of the strategy of controlling imports in order to force the pace of growth of domestic manufacturing industry in a poor country – what became known as 'import-substitution industrialization'.

Such a strategy paid no heed to the theory of comparative advantage and the concept of an international division of labour with national specializations. Industrialization would proceed according to the selection of industries to be protected from imports; general protection would stimulate general industrialization, regardless of the costs of local production. The state had the power, it seemed, to determine the shape of the domestic economy.

Prebisch and his immediate followers were not revolutionaries. They were not opposed to foreign capital nor to international trade. Theirs was not a recipe for autarky, but for what Prebisch called 'healthy protectionism'. Nor did they feel any industry should be pursued at any price – the 'measurable well-being of the masses' was more important than national self-sufficiency.[8] Others who came afterwards spoke of the exploitation and robbery of the periphery, of the need for a violent break in international trade and domestic organization.

Prebisch's case was also not as novel as it seemed at the time. Indeed, it could have been identified as no more than a rationalization of what had already happened. In the late forties, protectionism was the norm for all countries. In the case of Latin America, the world slump of 1929-33 cut the purchasing power of the continent's exports by 60 per cent, and ended the possibility of much borrowing abroad. Most countries were obliged to suspend the convertibility of their currencies, cut imports radically and take measures to stimulate the production of domestic substitutes. The results were impressive – whereas the annual rate of growth of manufacturing output in the United States in the ten years after 1929 was negative (−0.6), Colombia's was 8.8, Brazil's 6.4, Mexico's 4.3 and Chile's 3.3 per cent.

The results were, however, the accidental byproduct of government efforts to save foreign exchange, not the product of a deliberate policy of industrialization. After 1945, efforts became more deliberate, particularly since they were now supported by industrial beneficiaries – as Macario puts it, 'Originally dictated by external factors, industrialization became, especially under the pressure of vested interests, a fundamental objective of the economic policy of the governments concerned.'[9] Furthermore, the process was doubly protected, for the demand for Latin America's raw-material exports now revived; there was therefore no shortage of foreign exchange to purchase the imports which were still needed, and, indeed, exports could be taxed by maintaining a value for the local currency which was artificially high – and therefore made imports cheaper.

Rationalization or not, the prescriptions of CEPAL and Prebisch exercised a powerful influence among Latin American intellectuals and a rising generation of social scientists. The effect on governments was more limited, except in the sense that policy agreed on other grounds acquired a CEPAL vindication. But there was no causal 'model' at work.

Even without the CEPAL philosophy, in the 1950s a multitude of other poor countries outside Latin America adopted programmes of industrialization which depended on limiting imports. For the newly independent powers, it became the norm, as much an emotional and moral principle of new nationalism as an economic tactic. The intervention of the state to determine which industries or sectors whould grow and which should not, became direct participation in these countries too. It seemed as if state capitalism, in part or whole, was the norm for the 'peripheries', even when described as one or other form of socialism – the royal Buddhist socialism of Cambodia, the Arab, African, Indian, Burmese, Indonesian forms of socialism, and many more. The frequency with which new governments defined a nationally specific socialism suggested some elements in common other than past subjection – similarities of culture, social structure and aspiration, factors greeted with acclaim at Bandung in 1955.

It took more time to find the right term. Alfred Sauvy claimed he invented the term, the 'Third World', modelled on the Third Estate of the 1789 French Revolution. That was in 1952. In 1956, a Paris journal, *Tiers Monde*, adopted the term. But this was advanced intellectual opinion. It took another ten years for the phrase to become used more generally, but then only by radicals. It identified not just a group of new states (joined later by the older states of Latin America), nor the majority of the world's poor, but a political alternative other than that presented by Washington and Moscow (the first and second worlds).

The Schools of Thought

By the late 1960s, the analysis of the nature and causes of economic backwardness, and the formulation of proposals to overcome it, had become very substantial. It is as if the world's attention had suddenly become focussed on the question, producing a veritable flood of books, journals, reports and documents, whole libraries of scholarship. From the first identification of the crude economic equations, study had spread into subtle appraisals of history, culture and psyche. Most of the work was, however, critical of the inherited wisdom of the West, and to a greater or lesser degree radical; it was a new perspective on what seemed a newly discovered world.

Nonetheless, the economic formulations remained fundamental. International trade, it was assumed, could not develop the backward countries; on the contrary, trade made the problems of backwardness worse. Countries, it was said, were the basic units of the system (not sectors, industries or companies), and each national economy needed to go through a series of clearcut historical phases as the process of cumulative investment continued, in order to arrive at a 'developed' destination (a theory famously formulated in Rostow's *The Stages of Economic Growth: a Non-Communist Manifesto*, 1960). However, raising levels of investment was difficult, since each backward national economy was characterized by a set of rigidities; the structure of the economy inhibited change, and made it virtually impossible for domestic capitalism to support continued and healthy growth ('healthy' usually implied the production of a desirable set of goods). It followed that orthodox economics, founded upon the analysis of the market and private capitalism, was of little help in moving a backward economy forward. Only governments could mobilize the resources, only governments possessed the political power to break through the bottlenecks, bend the inflexibilities and force the pace of growth.

However, within these broad assumptions, there were many variations in the theory of development economics that spanned the political spectrum. Four variations are identified here, with inevitable arbitrariness. Two others, the first and the last, which fall outside the terms of reference of 'development studies', are included to highlight their contrast with the four.

1. Classical and Marxist

In so far as economists in the past concerned themselves with 'economic development', it was as a movement 'towards opulence and improvement', as Adam Smith expressed it,[10] rather than structural change in a national economy. It was assumed that the operation of a free market would ultimately lead to general prosperity for all countries participating (a position taken over by the neoclassical economists of the 1970s). The market evoked the resources required for development; structural relationships were created, sustained and dissolved by changing market prices; there were no long-term inhibiting factors that prevented development.

Marx was the economist who added history to this picture, with a major emphasis upon the historical process of the growth of capital and its successive self-transformations. But he also assumed that as capital spread its influence geographically, the more backward areas would increasingly be transformed in the same way as the more advanced – the market forced all into development. Bukharin and Lenin qualified this, since in their time it seemed the European empires invariably allied with the pre-capitalist ruling orders (as, for example, the Indian princes) and the process of creating capitalism was inhibited. However, in his most famous work on the subject of the 'backward countries'[11], Lenin envisaged their industrialization;[12] the imperial 'centres' were increasingly restricted to financing the rest of the world, to *'rentier'* and 'bond-holding' states, while the future proletariat was being created in the colonies. There was one element, none the less, which recurred later: the population of advanced countries was becoming parasitic on the labour of the workers in the colonies, a proposition half echoed in the argument that the trade unions of the 'centres' forced the impoverishment of the 'peripheries'.

2. *The conservative reformers*

The conservative reformers were the main leadership in the field of development economics. Directly influential with a number of governments – particularly in Latin America and India in the fifties, in Africa in the sixties – they provided much of the intellectual inspiration for the activity of many international agencies (particularly the United Nations Conference on Trade and Development and the International Labour Organization, as well as the idea of a new international economic order, the 'basic needs' programme, and the content of the Brandt Commission Report).[13]

At its simplest, the problem of development was identified as raising resources on a scale sufficient to achieve a level of investment that would change the structure of the economy. In very poor societies, incomes seemed to be too low to support a level of national savings which would be adequate to the task. On the other hand, it was assumed that resources would not be available from abroad – from borrowing, aid or through trade – on a sufficient scale. Indeed, external support of this kind was thought to jeopardize fatally a government's attempt to develop – international trade was subject to long-term deterioration in the exchange between raw materials and industrial goods; it was highly unstable; it diverted the economy away from feeding the domestic poor to supplying rich foreigners; it weakened the national government's autonomy, its capacity to pursue long-term plans; and sooner or later, the advanced countries would close their markets to imports as they had done in the early thirties.

The central problem, then, was the mobilization of resources from the domestic economy. The formulation – between investment and growth –

received proper theoretical expression in what was known as the Harrod-Domar model, and became the inspiration of fledgling planning commissions. There was dispute about whether investment should be 'balanced'; moving all sectors together at once (so preserving complementarities and proportionalities), or should concentrate on the 'big push' (Rosenstein-Rodan), on unbalanced growth (Hirschmann). But the central idea, a gathering together of efforts which would achieve what W. W. Rostow named, with singular but misleading vividness, 'economic take-off' remained dominant.

It was thought that increased savings, directed by the government to industry, with protection against industrial imports, was the recipe for development; major changes were not required either in the domestic social structure (although these might also be desirable) or in international economic relations.

3. The radicals

The radicals challenged this position. There had been sustained investment, they said, but society had not been transformed. Not only did the poor remain exactly as before, but the structure of the economy had scarcely changed and, above all, in Latin America imports remained decisive despite many years of import substitution and the economy was still highly vulnerable to external changes. The Chilean economist, Osvaldo Sunkel, writing in the late sixties, concluded:

> The import of capital and intermediate goods necessary to produce consumer goods has been substituted for the import of consumer goods themselves. The structure of manufacturing production is now organized basically to produce for the consumer and the traditional export sector has been left to 'produce' the investment goods. This seems to me the fundamental reason why our economies have become more dependent, more vulnerable and more unstable.[14]

The failure, it was argued, arose because the existing social structure inhibited the effect of investment. A severely unequal distribution of income cut the size of the domestic market and also skewed it towards upper-income consumption goods. Unequal land distribution severely reduced the capacity of the rural majority to sustain market demand and also reduced the incentives to cultivate more. Import barriers forced foreign companies to make the minimum manufacture legally required in the country (to escape the restrictions on imports), but, because the market was so small, their costs were very high, the product inferior, and increased profits were drained out of the country instead of going to domestic investment. For most countries, the domestic market was too small to support the development of efficient heavy and intermediate industries; for these economic federations were needed – the Latin American Free Trade Area (as also the Andean Pact, the Central American Common Market, etc.)

This line of argument merged with that of the next group. Paul Singer criticized the CEPAL philosophy for ignoring the way in which the external trade and capital relationships (now identified as 'economic dependency') not only produced a particular type of economy on the periphery, but also a particular type of social structure, which was no less inhibiting for growth. The exploitation of the periphery by the centre was part and parcel of the exploitation of the Latin American working class in each country.

4. The revolutionary nationalists

Revolutionary nationalists started here. Not only was it impossible to break the external links of the economy, but it was also impossible to promote domestic development of the right kind (that would help the mass of the population), because the existing class structure blocked all change. The 'structural rigidities' now included precisely those people and classes CEPAL relied upon to transform the domestic economy. The old ruling class rendered domestic reform and development and economic independence impossible. The world system was dominated by imperialism, a group of great powers with the largest share of the world's capital, companies, banks and armed forces, and they operated through a close alliance with the classes that ruled Latin America. There was no way that this pattern could be changed through the existing ruling classes, for their very power depended on retaining and strengthening subordination to imperialism. All the talk of import-substitution industrialization, with or without national planning and large public sectors, was thus irrelevant to the central task of breaking the domestic social order. That was impossible without revolution and the use of popular armed power to destroy the old order by force.

It was a case explored in detail by Paul Baran, Samir Amin, Andre Gunder Frank[15] and a host of others. In conjunction with a political tradition derived from the experience of revolution in Cuba, Fidelismo, and to a lesser extent, in China, it became the inspiration in the 1960s for a host of guerrilla groups in Latin America, which became known as national liberation movements. And so it was in much of the rest of the developing countries also. Each continent produced its models of the total domestic transformation – China and Vietnam in Asia; Algeria, Mozambique, Angola and Guinea-Bissau in Africa; Cuba and Nicaragua in Latin America.

5. Revolutionary internationalists

There was a further development, which was neither widely known nor influential, but which nevertheless completed the spectrum of estimates of the difficulties in pursuing economic development. For now it was argued that the structure of world capitalism made national economic development impossible, even if there were domestic revolution in a backward country. Removing the old ruling class, nationalizing the means of production (and expropriating foreign capital), redistributing income and land, forced accumulation, would not suffice to overcome the paralysis imposed by the changed structure of world capitalism.[16]

In Michael Kidron's *Western Capitalism since the War*,[17] advanced states and their associated national capitals had become so powerful that it was impossible for the backward nations to begin to compete. The minimum size for the economies of scale of modern industry ruled out development for a majority of countries (one estimate suggested a population of ten to fifteen millions was the bare minimum, but that most advantage accrued to countries with fifty million or more inhabitants.):[18]

> They [the weaker powers] are compelled to make huge single-shot expenditures in facilities for which the minimum sizes are set by the immense capitals of the north [the developed countries] in terms of their own huge absolute sizes, gained after decades of concentrating the world's surpluses in their hands. The minima have now become so large that no country in the south can hope to attain them on its own. None can hope to bring together what it takes to exchange equal values with the advanced capitals or to exchange equal clout.[19]

Once this became apparent, there could be no geographical spread of the system from its more to its less advanced areas – 'The extension of the system in the strict sense of capital replication, or in a looser sense, of proletarianizing a growing proportion of the world's population, ended.'[20]

Development economists examined the symptoms of this growing problem – increasingly uncompetitive exports from the developing countries, saleable only with heavy subsidies which constituted yet again a net transfer from poor sellers to rich buyers. Political instability flowed from the collapse of hopes of development, which in turn produced military instability, a further drain of resources out of development investment. Only a revolutionary change in the centres of the system, the more developed countries, could change the context for the economic development of the periphery.

6. The neoclassical school

There had been critics of the received theses of development economics from the beginning,[21] but it had been very much a minority view, a pre-Keynesian trend of thought. From the late sixties, however, this school expanded with astonishing speed, to become in the seventies a new dominant orthodoxy in the industrialized countries. The neoclassical critics argued that there was great doubt about any long-term deterioration in the terms of trade between agricultural and industrial goods; that there was no peculiar merit in industrialization; that the 'rigidities' and bottlenecks which supposedly vindicated the intervention of the state were in fact the result of earlier public interventions or distorted prices. There were, they affirmed, no long-term problems which could not be overcome through the free operation of unrestricted markets. Governments were needed both to provide the framework for production, and to move towards efficient prices, but not to seek to direct the national economy towards predetermined ends; if they did that, perverse results would either defeat the public purpose or have negative effects elsewhere in the economy. The most important task of government was systematic reform in all sectors – labour, financial, business, capital markets, and government itself – in order to ensure that prices accurately reflected real scarcities in the world. We shall return to the practical effects of these arguments later.

In sum then, the development economists – those whose views have been listed above (2–5) tended to agree that capitalism had become transformed to the point where it could no longer repeat the process of the dispersal of development that had occurred in the nineteenth century. 'The capitalist system,' wrote Baran in the mid fifties, 'once a mighty engine of economic development, has turned into a no less formidable hurdle to human advancement'.[22] It was an argument that echoed those who had seen in the Great Depression of the thirties the sign that capitalism had finally exhausted its potential for growth. Yet others later went further, to deny that in the earlier period capitalism had produced growth in the periphery – from the beginning. Europe had imposed and sustained what was now seen as underdevelopment on the periphery; there had always been an inexorable asymmetry.

There were different reasons why this was said to be so, but they frequently amounted to some idea of 'unequal exchange' – whether this was seen as virtual robbery,[23] as an accident of the structure, or as a systematic phenomenon whereby the exports of the periphery were undervalued while their imports were overvalued.[24] Free trade always favoured the more developed power, so where such conditions prevailed, they always increased inequality between the trading countries. Different reasons were proposed for this (as we saw in discussing the thesis of the long-term deterioration in the terms of trade between agricultural and industrial exports). For example, it was said that the low income level of the backward made it impossible to establish industries of the most efficient size; imports would always be cheaper. Paul Baran, like Prebisch, identified monopoly as the source of unequal exchange; the industrial countries had a monopoly of the supply of industrial goods and could hold up their prices when producers of agricultural goods could not. Amin linked the high prices of industrial exports not to a monopoly by the industrialized countries, but to a monopoly of the supply of labour by the trade unions of the industrialized countries – 'It was monopoly that made possible the rise of wages' (in the more developed countries), producing 'an unequal specialization which always expressed a mechanism of primitive accumulation to the advantage of the centre . . . the "development of underdevelopment".'[25] Furtado argued that the class struggle in the centre pushed wages up and obliged the state to maintain full employment, which in turn sustained an expanding domestic market; on the periphery, weak trade unions had the reverse effect.

Whatever the reasons, conservatives and radicals agreed that 'the outside world was public enemy number one'.[26] But almost as important at various times were the internal obstacles to development. In the early fifties, Baran identified these as the old ruling orders – 'a political and social coalition of wealthy *compradors*, powerful monopolists, and large landowners, dedicated to the defence of the existing feudal, mercantile order . . . this coalition has nothing to hope for from the rise of industrial capitalism, which would dislodge it from its position of privilege and power'.[27] It was a case which emerged in different forms in many arguments, particularly those concerning what came to be known as 'dependency' (the dependence of the backward on the advanced).[28] Indeed, in the period of disillusion with import substitution in Latin America in the early sixties, it was to the social obstacles to growth that Prebisch reverted in seeking to explain why the process had failed – the upper income groups remained preoccupied with luxury consumption,[29] which was one of the factors distorting the pattern of investment and limiting the general growth of the market. Later, his gloom intensified – the small surplus generated on the periphery seemed always to be expropriated by the centres, by the rich and by the state (especially where the military were powerful); trade-union action might check the rich and the state, but only at the cost of high rates of inflation; 'in the advanced course of peripheral development', he concluded pessimistically, 'the process of democratization tends to become incompatible with the regular functioning of the system'.[30]

Such gloom was far from the high hopes of the early fifties. Then the world market might be an obstacle, but at home, if power could be won, there was nothing to stop growth. What had hitherto been squandered or hoarded by the rich would become available to fuel growth; at the time of the second Indian Five Year Plan (1955), Baran boldly asserted that 'there can hardly be any doubt' that 15 per cent of India's national income could be invested without cutting mass consumption, since 25 per cent was already absorbed by the 'unproductive strata'. But it required bold political action; without it, 'The injection of planning into a society living in the twilight between feudalism and capitalism cannot but result in additional corruption, larger and more artful evasion of the law, and more brazen abuses of authority.'[31]

Others saw potential in the vast mass of very poorly paid workers. Low incomes narrowed the market, but it meant also that there could be an immense growth in the labour force at relatively low cost. One of the leaders of the new movement offered a simple model to prove the efficacy of this paradox.[32] From the opposite corner came those who saw as the only hope the limitation of population growth, a case that became increasingly popular as the difficulties of development became more apparent.

The experience of the Soviet Union played a particularly important role in shaping the perceptions of some of the new governments. For there, it was said, industrialization had been autarkic and particularly swift; the process had telescoped the historical stages of development – from light to heavy industrial development – by beginning with the stimulation of heavy industry. Planners in many backward countries were fascinated by heavy industry; it was always the key, it was thought, to economic independence, to full development. Elements of the first Russian Five Year Plan were emulated in the first Chinese plan, with its emphasis on the growth of steel output, and in the model which was the inspiration for the second Indian Five Year Plan.[33]

The heavy industrial emphasis of the Stalinist model of planning conflicted with the views of those who believed that economic development should be directed at increasing employment. The development of heavy industry was notoriously profligate in the use of scarce capital, and produced very few jobs. One of the first economic rejections of the Stalinist model led to a whole school of thought, crystallized in a long-term research programme by the International Labour Organization, concerned with increasing employment, particularly through more labour-intensive forms of production. This in turn led on to the United Nations' 'basic needs' programme to identify and meet a minimum level of consumption among the poor of the less developed countries.

In practice, heavy industrial programmes proved very burdensome. Understanding why giant public-sector enterprises were so often a drain on, rather than a contribution to, the savings for future development was one contributory thread in the radical change of opinion in the seventies. If the Third Worldists were right and their views were revolutionary, the seventies saw an astonishing victory for counter-revolutionary thought. The neoclassical economists (at least some of whom had formerly been ardent Third Worldists) attacked the entire system of thought – the idea of the economy as a rigid structure; of the government as a benevolent, strong and rational agent; of industry in general, and heavy industry in particular, having some peculiar merit; of the domestic market being superior to exports, domestic capital to foreign, of self-sufficiency to interdependence. The very idea of conscious long-term direction of the economy by the government was questioned.

Import substitution came to be identified as the very source of the problems of backwardness – high-cost, low-quality industrial output, neglect of agriculture and popular consumption, worsening income distribution, an entrenched position of foreign capital inside the economy, a bias to capital-intensive manufacture: in all respects, it was said, industrialization through import controls robbed the masses, inflated the profits of a minority and increased the power of the state. The remedies had come to be seen as the cause of the illness.

By the end of the 1970s the 'less developed countries', as they were now known, were exporting more manufactured goods than raw materials, a change producing 'a spiritual revolution as great as that experienced by economists over the age of thirty who were converted to Keynesianism in 1936'.[34] By 1980, the more developed countries exported 36 per cent more primary commodities than did the less developed. From the perception of the 1950s, the world had been turned topsy-turvy.

Ideologies, and their substructures of economic theory, are no better than the prejudices of the age and the classes from which they derive, but it is rare for such a complete transformation to take place in such a short time. It is a mark of how unconscious most participants are that the change received little systematic attention – it seems that, pragmatically, one thing led to another, even though the 'another' contradicted the 'one'. The truth was less simple . . . [the] reality . . . fitted neither side in the dispute.

NOTES AND REFERENCES

1. Paul Samuelson, 'International trade and the equalization of factor prices', *Economic Journal*, 58, June 1948, pp. 163-84.

2. See in particular: Economic Commission for Latin America (ECLA), *The Economic Development of Latin America and its Principal Problems*, New York, United Nations, 1950; *Economic Survey of Latin America, 1949*, Part 1, New York, United Nations, 1951, reproduced in *Economic Bulletin for Latin America*, 7, 1, Santiago, February 1962; *Problemas teóricos y prácticos del crecimiento económico*, New York, United Nations, 1952; *International cooperation in a Latin American development policy*, New York, United Nations, 1954 (especially Chapter 4).
   For a most useful account of Prebisch's intellectual development, see Joseph L. Love, 'Raúl Prebisch and the origins of the doctrine of unequal exchange', *Latin American Research Review*, 15, 3, 1980, pp.47-72.

3. *The Economic Development of Latin America*, op. cit., p.1.

4. See Thomas Balogh, *Dollar Crisis: Causes and Cure*, Oxford, Blackwell, 1949, and G.D.A. MacDougall, *The World Dollar Problem*, London, Macmillan, 1957.

5. *The Economic Development of Latin America*, op. cit., p.65.

6. See Hollis Chenery, 'Interactions between industrialization and exports', *American Economic Review* (Papers and Proceedings, 92nd Annual Meeting, 1979), 70, 2, May 1980, p. 281; and United Nations, *Relative Price of Exports and Imports of Underdeveloped Countries*, Department of Economic Affairs, Lake Success, New York, 1949, p. 7.

7. Hans Singer, 'The distribution of gains between investing and borrowing countries', *American Economic Review* (Papers and Proceedings), 40, May 1950, pp. 473-85. See also his 'Problems of the industrialization of underdeveloped countries', *International Social Science Bulletin*, 6, 2, 1954. The role of trade in the nineteenth and twentieth centuries is examined by Ragnar Nurkse in *Equilibrium and Growth in the World Economy*, edited by Gottfried Haberler and Robert M. Stern (Harvard Economic Studies 118), Cambridge, Mass., Harvard University Press, 1961; see also Irving B. Kravis, 'Trade as a handmaiden of growth', *Economic Journal*, December 1970, pp. 850-72.

8. *Economic Survey of Latin America*, op. cit., p.3.

9. Santiago Macario, 'Protectionism and industrialization in Latin America', *Economic Bulletin for Latin America*, 9, New York, ECLA, United Nations, 1964, p. 63.

10. *The Wealth of Nations*, vol. 1, edited by E. Cannon, London, Methuen, 1950, p. 367.

11. *Imperialism, the Highest Stage of Capitalism*, in *Selected Works*, vol. 5, London, Lawrence & Wishart, 1936.

12. A case which combined a thesis of Rudolf Hilferding, in *Finance Capital, A Study of the Latest Phase of Capitalist Development*, edited and introduced by Tom Bottomore, London, Routledge, 1981 (original edition 1910), and M. N. Roy – see his *Memoirs*, Bombay, Allied Publishers, 1964, and *Documents of the History of the Communist Party of India*, vol. 1, edited by G. Adhikari, New Delhi, People's Publishing House, 1971.

13. *North-South, A Programme for Survival* (Brandt Commission Report), Report of the Independent Commission in International Development Issues, London, Pan, 1980.

14. 'National development policy and external dependence in Latin America', *Journal of Development Studies*, 6/1, October 1969, p. 37.

15. See, for example, Paul Baran, *The Political Economy of Growth*, New York, Monthly Review Press, 1957; A. Emmanuel, *Unequal Exchange: A Study of the Imperialism of Free Trade*, New York, Monthly Review Press, 1972; Samir Amin, *Accumulation on the World Scale: a Critique of the Theory of Underdevelopment*, New York, Monthly Review Press, 2 vols., 1974; A. Gunder Frank, *Dependent Accumulation and Underdevelopment*, New York, Monthly Review Press, 1979, and numerous other works; see also F. M. Cardoso and L. Faletto, *Dependency and Development in Latin America*, Los Angeles, University of California Press, 1979.

16. Thus, the relatively slight differences in long-term growth performance between India and China up to the mid seventies suggested that the underlying material constraints were similar despite different political systems – cf. Chapter 10 in my *India-China: Underdevelopment and Revolution*, Delhi, Vikas, 1974.

17. London, Weidenfeld & Nicolson, 1968.

18. In E. A. G. Robinson, ed., *Economic Consequences of the Size of Nations*, London, International Economic Association/Macmillan, 1960.

19. Michael Kidron, *Capitalism and Theory*, London, Pluto, 1974, pp. 108-9.

20. Ibid. See also his 'Memories of development', republished in ibid. For a summary of the contingent factors at stake, see my *The Crisis of Development* (World University Service Symposium, Ibadan, Nigeria), mimeo, Geneva, 1972.

21. For example, see P. T. Bauer and B. S. Yamey, *The Economics of Underdeveloped Countries*, Chicago, Chicago University Press, 1957; Jacob Viner, *International Trade and Economic Development*, Oxford, Clarendon Press, 1953; and Gottfried Haberler, *Terms of Trade and Economic Development*, Cairo, National Bank of Egypt, 1959. The neoclassical case was developed in: I. M. D. Little, T. Skitovsky and M. Scott, *Industry and Trade in Some Developing Countries*, Development Centre, London OECD/Oxford University Press, 1970 (with associated studies of Brazil by Bergson; Mexico by Kingl; India by Bhagwati and Desai; Pakistan by Lewis; Taiwan and the Philippines by Hsing, Power and Sicat); Anne O. Kreuger, *Foreign Trade Regimes and Economic Development:Liberalization Attempts and Consequences*, Cambridge, Mass., National Bureau of Economic Research/Ballinger, 1978, and in the same series, Jagdish Bhagwati, *Foreign Trade Regimes and Economic Development: Anatomy and Consequences of Exchange Control Regimes*, 1978; B. Balassa, and others, *The Structure of Protection in Developing Countries*, Baltimore, Johns Hopkins University Press, 1971, and *Development Strategies in Semi-industrial Economies*, Baltimore, Johns Hopkins University Press, 1982; I. M. D. Little, *Economic Development: Theory, Policy and International Relations*, New York, Twentieth Century Fund/Basic Books, 1982. For a polemical summary, see Deepak Lal, *The Poverty of 'Development Economics'* (Hobart Papers) London, Institute of Economic Affairs, 1983.

22. *Political Economy of Growth*, op. cit., p. 249.

23. See, for example, Pierre Jalée, *The Pillage of the Third World*, 1968, and *The Third World in World Economy*, 1969, both Monthly Review Press, New York.

24. Most elaborately explored in Emmanuel's *Unequal Exchange*, op. cit.; cf. also Christian Palloix, *L'Economie mondiale capitaliste*, Paris, Maspero, 1971; and Emmanuel and others, *Imperialismo comercio internacional: el intercambio desigual*, Cordoba (Argentina), Pasado y Presente, 1971.

25. *Accumulation on a World Scale*, op. cit., pp. 83-4 and pp. 89-90.

26. Fernando H. Cardoso, 'The originality of a copy: CEPAL and the idea of development', *CEPAL Review*, second half, 1977, p. 26.

27. *Political Economy of Growth*, op. cit., pp. 194-5.

28. The literature is voluminous, but among the best examples and discussions might be included: Colin Leys, *Underdevelopment in Kenya*, London, Heinemann, 1975; Anibal Quijano, *Nationalism and Capitalism in Peru: a Study in Neo-imperialism*, New York, Monthly Review Press, 1971; Thomas Biersteker, *Distortion or Development? Contending Perspectives on the Multinational Corporations*, Cambridge, Mass., MIT Press, 1979.

29. Among other factors enumerated in *Towards a Dynamic Development Policy for Latin America*, New York, United Nations, 1963, p. 71. See his much later, *Capitalismo periférico: crisis y transformación*, Mexico City, Fondo de Cultura Económica, 1981.

30. Prebisch, in Gerald H. Meier and Dudley Seers, eds., *Pioneers in Development*, Washington, World Bank/Oxford University Press, 1984, p. 189.

31. *Political Economy of Growth*, op. cit., p. 225. See also his 'On the political economy of

backwardness', *The Manchester School*, January 1952, republished in A. N. Agarwala and S. P. Singh, *The Economics of Underdevelopment*, New York, Galaxy Books, 1963, pp. 75-92.

32. Arthur Lewis, 'Economic development with unlimited supplies of labour', *The Manchester School*, May 1954.

33. By P. C. Mahalanobis; see his 'Some observations on the process of growth of national income', *Sankya*, 12 (Indian Statistical Institute, Calcutta), September 1953, pp. 307-12.

34. Sir Arthur Lewis, in Meier and Seers, *Pioneers*, op. cit., p. 129.

Modernisation Theory

Andrew Webster

This reading is from the author's Introduction to the Sociology of
Development (*1984*).

In the 1950s and early 1960s modernisation theory was developed by a number
of social scientists, particularly a group of American scholars the most prominent
of whom was Talcott Parsons. . . . much of this interest in modernisation was
prompted by the decline of the old colonial empires. The Third World became a
focus of attention by politicians who were keen to show countries pushing for
independence that sustained development was possible under the western wing
(rather than that of the Soviet Union). Academics reflected this interest by
examining the socio-economic conditions conducive to modernisation.

Tradition versus Modernity

In constructing their accounts of development, theorists drew on the tradition-
modernity distinction of classical sociologists. Like Durkheim and Weber, these
theorists placed most emphasis on the values and norms that operate in these
two types of society and their economic systems. Like Durkheim, most argued
that the transition from the limited economic relationships of traditional society
to the innovative, complex economic associations of modernity depended on a
prior change in the values, attitudes and norms of people. Bauer (1976, p. 41)
for example argues that:

> Economic achievement and progress depend largely on human aptitudes
> and attitudes, on social and political institutions and arrangements which
> derive from these, on historical experience, and to a lesser extent on
> external contacts, market opportunities and on natural resources.

Development then depends on 'traditional', 'primitive' values being displaced
by modern ones.

In a 'traditional' society, three crucial features are noted:

(a) The value of traditionalism itself is dominant: that is, people are oriented
to the past and they lack the cultural ability to adjust to new
circumstances;

(b) The kinship system is the decisive reference point for all social practices,
being the primary means through which economic, political and legal
relationships are controlled. One's position in the kinship system and
hence in the society is ascribed, not achieved – that is, is a reflection of
the status or standing of the family, clan or tribe into which one is born;
one's position only changes as one moves up the family hierarchy. Status
is then, not earned or achieved, but conferred by virtue of kin
relationships;

(c) Members of the traditional society have an emotional, superstitious and fatalistic approach to the world: 'what will be will be'; 'things have always been this way'.

In contrast, 'modern' society is made up of completely opposite characteristics:

(a) People may still have traditions but they are not slaves to them and will challenge any that seem unnecessary or get in the way of continued cultural progress (that is they do not suffer from 'traditionalism');

(b) Kinship has a very much less important role in all areas of society (even within the family) because of the need for geographical and social mobility which weakens family ties; moreover, one's position in the economy, polity etc., is earned through hard work and high achievement-motivation and not determined by kinship;

(c) Members of the modern society are not fatalistic but forward-looking and innovative, ready to overcome the obstacles they find in their way, particularly in business affairs, reflecting a strong entrepreneurial spirit and rational, scientific approach to the world.

It is evident that various ideas from classical sociology are incorporated in these profiles of the two types of society. For example, the description of the modern society includes reference to the splitting off or 'differentiation' of kinship from the economy, stresses individual freedom from constraint especially in business and points to the rational, calculating character of innovative entrepreneur. Parsons (1951) develops this model in considerable detail elaborating on the choice of actions or behavioural orientations that tend to typify the two types of society. For example he argues that in modern society an achievement orientation is the likely choice of action for people particularly within the economic sphere since it is a much more rational criterion for deciding who should be given what sort of jobs with what level of reward, than are ascriptive criteria. In the achievement oriented society jobs are allocated and rewarded on the basis of achieved skills and hard work: it is what one can do, not who one is that gets rewarded.

The necessity of developing an 'achievement' orientation in the values system has not merely been regarded as part of a wider process of development. For some theorists of social change the desire to achieve has been seen as the crucial or determinant factor of development. For example, McClelland (1961) and Hagen (1962) claim that the level of achievement in a society is expressed in terms of the level of innovation and entrepreneurship. In traditional cultures both are at an exceptionally low level. Economic constraints or limitations can be overcome given a sufficiently high motivation to do well by the individual entrepreneur. As McClelland (1961, p. 105) argues,

Men with high achievement will find a way to economic achievement given fairly wide variations in opportunity and social structure. . . These results serve to direct our attention as social scientists away from an exclusive concern with the external events in history to the internal psychological concerns that in the long run determine what happens in history.

The stress on ideas and psychological factors in shaping history and the rate of development is clearly evident.

Lerner (1964) adopts a similarly socio-psychological approach to explain the transition from traditional to modern society. There is in fact, he believes, a 'transitional' society, a society which has, through the process of cultural diffusion from more advanced sectors of the world, been exposed to modernity. For Lerner, the 'transitional society' is the 'empathetic society'. The society is defined by what it *wants* to become: the transitional man 'wants really to see the things he has hitherto "seen" only in his mind's eye, really to live in the world he has "lived" only vicariously'. (p. 72). Empathy involves the ability to 'rearrange the self-esteem on short notice', the capacity to 'incorporate new roles', and to have a publicly minded orientation that encourages participation. Lerner's description of traditional society is similar to that offered by Durkheim's notice of mechanical solidarity: Lerner (1964, p. 50) says that:

> Traditional society is non-participant − it deploys people by kinship into communities isolated from each other and from a center . . . [it lacks] the bands of interdependence, people's horizons are limited by locale.

In general, then, for Lerner, the more a society exhibits empathy the more it will be engaged in the process of modernisation and the more likely is it to be modern. As McClelland's measurement of achievement orientation in society, Lerner's empathetic criterion of modernity has quantifiable dimensions:

> The latent statistical assertion involved here is this: In modern society *more* individuals exhibit *higher* empathetic capacity than in any previous society. (1964, p. 51).

Lerner's account of modernisation is somewhat different from the simple model of two societies, traditional and modern, seen so far, since he tries to identify an *intervening* stage, the 'transitional society'. A more elaborate 'stage' model has been provided by the development economist W. W. Rostow. In his *Stages of Economic Growth: A Non-Communist Manifesto* (1960, p. 4) he claims that,

> It is possible to identify all societies, in their economic dimensions, as lying within one of five categories; the traditional society, the preconditions for take-off, take off, the drive to maturity, and the age of high mass-consumption.

These five stages are derived from an analysis of the British industrial revolution, and take-off he defined as the 'great watershed in the life of modern societies' when obstacles to economic growth are removed, particularly by the onset of an adequate rate of capital investment so that growth becomes a normal condition. It seems clear that entrepreneurial ambition combined with sustained capital accumulation and investment are seen by most modernisation theorists as two of the principal forces of development. As Roxborough (1979, p. 16) says,

> This emphasis on entrepreneurship and capital accumulation is the single most pervasive theme in the literature on economic growth. It always appears as *the* lesson to be learnt from Western experience and to be mechanically applied to the rest of the world so that they can repeat the transition.

Let us briefly summarise some of the basic themes of modernisation theory and draw out their implications particularly for development policy in the Third World.

Summary of Modernisation Theory and its Implications

By way of summary the following points seem most important:

(a) there is a clear mixture of sociological, psychological and economic features to modernisation theory including, for example, reference to values systems, individual motivation, and capital accumulation;

(b) most accounts give greatest priority to the role played by the values, norms and beliefs of people in determining the sort of society – traditional or modern – that they create, and thus value changes are the most important conditions for social change;

(c) the history of the development of industrialisation in the West is no longer regarded as something unique as Weber thought, but as the blueprint for development throughout the world. As one of the contributors to modernisation theory, Eisenstadt (1966, p. 1) claimed:

> Historically, modernisation is the process of change towards those types of social, economic and political systems that have developed in Western Europe and North America from the seventeenth to the nineteenth centuries.

(d) the evolution of societies occurs as traditional behaviour patterns give way under the pressures of modernisation. While these pressures built up gradually *within* Western societies, the 'developing' countries of the Third World can be *exposed* to them from outside. That is, they can be helped along the road to modernity with the assistance of the developed countries whose ideas and technologies can be introduced and diffused throughout these poorer countries;

(e) this process of 'modernisation by diffusion' should encourage the development of a number of features in the Third World, including urbanisation based on nuclear family households, educational growth for literacy and training, the development of mass media to disseminate ideas and encourage increased awareness about society, heightened political awareness and participation in a democratic system, increased business opportunities through providing capital for investment, the replacement of patterns of authority based on traditional loyalties (for example monarchies, local chiefdoms) with a rational system of law coupled with representative national government;

(f)   different societies are at different stages of development because they have been more or less successful in introducing the features of modernity highlighted above in (e).

These, then, are the major tenets of modernisation theory. What theoretical implications do they have for an understanding of development?

(1) Lack of development is seen as a condition prior to development: that is, that present day Third World societies are underdeveloped countries gradually moving towards modernity. This may seem self-evident: however . . . this lack of development may *not* reflect obstacles apparent from the internal history of these countries but be instead a result of the relationship they have had over the past few centuries with outside countries.

(2) Lack of development is the 'fault' of Third World countries' socio-economic systems that create obstacles to modernisation and encourage little ambition or incentive among individuals, particularly in their work: they tend to have little interest in commercial production and rationally planned long-term enterprise being content to work only as long as they need to satisfy their immediate (limited) demands.

(3) Development is presented as a relatively straightfoward process of efficient social adaptation to periods of strain (for example one brought about by increasing population); there is little debate about the possibility of fundamental *conflict* between social groups.

(4) Development occurs not only along Western lines for Third World societies but also for those countries which are now socialist states (for example the Soviet Union, China), whose future paths will, because of the forces of industrialisation, converge with the road beaten out by the pioneering West.

(5) The Western economies will continue to grow and develop so that, in Rostow's (1960) terms, they enjoy the prosperity of the period of 'high mass consumption'. There is no sign given of the possible collapse or steady decline in the fortunes of these economies.

The social scientists who developed these arguments in their professional capacity as academics were co-opted to work with the development agencies, particularly of the United States and the UN. Given that their diffusionist thesis explicitly argued that the developed countries could have nothing other than a benign influence in the 'developing' countries their ideas were a great source of justification for the activities of the development agencies. A whole range of policies were fostered by modernisation theory. . . . They have included the injection of capital to aid both industrial 'take-off' and the commercialisation of agriculture, the training of an entrepreneurial élite in the values and motivations most likely to promote free enterprise, the expansion of educational programmes, and only assisting 'democratic' (or notionally democratic) countries.

This policy role for modernisation theory and its evident support of the economic strategies of the development agencies gave it a virtually impregnable position in academic circles, particularly in the United States. Parsons' work came to be regarded as having a significance of classical proportions and his fellow contributors provided further credibility for the whole theoretical edifice. It remained intact for almost twenty years, but, by the late 1960s and early 1970s a number of criticisms began to appear that developed into an out and out attack on its central assumptions and propositions. The main and most devastating attack came from those working within radical, Marxian sociology, till then very much on the margins of academic social science . . . .. Here we can examine a range of general criticisms made by sociologists, anthropologists and economists that initiated the attack on the foundations of modernisation theory.

The Critique of Modernisation Theory

Modernisation theory claims to identify those factors crucial for economic development such as achievement motivation and a decline in the significance of extended family relationships. While it may be the case that substantial economic growth cannot occur without changes in, say, technology, the level of capital investment and market demand, it need *not* be the case that such growth requires major alterations to value systems and social institutions as modernisation theory claims. Indeed, there is a good deal of evidence to the contrary. The following section illustrates this through presenting a number of important empirical and theoretical criticisms that have appeared in the literature since the late 1960s.

First, many critics have pointed out that the principal terms of the theory – the 'traditional' and the 'modern' – are much too vague to be of much use as classifications of distinct societies. The two terms do not give any indication of the great variety of societies that have and do exist; instead, the 'traditional' label is offered as a blanket term to cover a range of pre-industrial societies that have exceedingly different socio-economic and political structures such as feudal, tribal and bureaucratic empires. A much more careful historical analysis is required of these distinct pre-industrial forms in order to have any hope of understanding the subsequent processes of social change they undergo. Eisenstadt, one of the more historically sensitive of the modernisation school, recognised the force of this criticism, and in a later contribution (1970, p.25) wrote:

The process of modernisation may take off from tribal groups, from caste societies, from different types of peasant societies, and from societies with different degrees and types of prior orientation. These groups may vary greatly in the extent to which they have the resources, and abilities, necessary for modernisation.

Secondly, although the theory is supposed to be about the way society develops there is little explanation offered for this process. This is a serious weakness. Apart from reference to the need for forward looking attitudes and healthy economic motivation we have no idea which mechanism it is that brings about the process of social differentiation of which so much is made.

Thirdly, even if, for the sake of the discussion, one were to accept the use of the terms 'traditional' and 'modern' societies is it the case that they are so mutually exclusive as the theory states? Remember, the claim is that, as societies develop, the 'traditional' world gets squeezed out by the force of modern values and attitudes. Yet there is a wealth of evidence to indicate that economic growth and the advent of modernity does *not* necessarily mean the abandonment of so-called 'traditional' patterns of action, values or beliefs. For example, Gusfield (1973) points out that the 'traditional' religion of Islam has been *reinforced* by the diffusion of modern technology, particularly transport, that makes the visit to the shrine of Mecca a much more practicable proposition for many more people than had been true in the past. Or again, Salisbury (1962) shows that in the Highlands of New Guinea when steel axes replaced the old stone ones the villagers found that they could complete their farm tasks much more speedily to leave extra time for the traditional ceremonies and rituals which were thereby *enhanced* not undermined. There is also evidence to show that in 'modern' industrial society 'traditional' values not only persist but actually play an important role in keeping it going. Frank (1969, p.26) shows how the norm of ascription (judging people according to their family background, age or sex for example) plays an important role in allocating reward in Japanese industry, a paragon of 'modernity' if ever there was one. Frank shows that, although recruitment to Japanese companies is based on achievement criteria – the skills and qualifications applicants have – once they are employed their level of pay and promotion prospects depend very much on the age, background and family responsibilities of the workers, highly ascriptive considerations. Frank in fact offers considerable evidence of the persistence of so-called 'traditional' values in many modern industrial societies, including Japan, Britain and the United States. At the same time, we can find evidence that modern industrial society does not necessarily encourage achievement by motivation among all its members, but in fact the very opposite, a lack of ambition: thus, gender relations in modern capitalist society whether expressed in the family, schools, the mass media or in employment discourage equal levels of achievement between the sexes resulting typically in male dominance and female subordination; or again, there have been many sociological studies of the educational system in advanced economies and some suggest that for many working class youth the experience of schooling is to dampen down their ambitions, being socialised into *low* achievement motivation (for example, Willis, 1977), rather than high, as McClelland would assume.

Fourthly, one should question the proposition that as industrialisation and its attendant urbanisation develop the wider kinship system is weakened as people become primarily concerned with their own nuclear family. As Long (1977, p.37) says,

> Several studies have concluded that certain extended family systems not only survive in a modern economic context but that they often function positively to enable individuals to mobilise capital and other resources essential for modern capitalist enterprises.

Moreover, for urban poor as well as the middle class, and for those who move to towns in search of work, extended family kin are an important source of support as British studies by Anderson (1971) of nineteenth century Preston and studies of London by Willmott and Young (1971) have shown. While it would be foolish to suggest that urbanisation does not change kinship relationships it would be wrong to claim that it completely undermines the value of extended family ties; rather, these are modified or sustained in a manner different from that which prevailed prior to urbanisation. Yet again, the essential weakness of the tradition-modernity thesis is revealed here, namely, its persistent recourse to generalisations that such and such will happen without inspection of the historical or current evidence.

Fifthly, much use is made of Weber's ideas by McClelland in his analysis of 'achievement motivation' which he believes lies at the heart of economic growth. But Weber's thesis is distorted by McClelland's theoretical handiwork. As we saw at the beginning of this Chapter, Weber saw the activity that derived from the concern for salvation among Protestants as an important contributory factor in the rise of rational capitalism. McClelland effectively ignores the importance Weber gives to this religious anxiety by reducing it to a latent psychological drive for success which can be found not only in post sixteenth-century Western Europe but also in a wide range of societies that experienced economic growth later. This does an injustice to Weber not only in terms of an abuse of his particular thesis about Protestantism but also in terms of its failure to respect Weber's general approach which was much more sensitive to the sociologically distinct patterns of change that have occurred in history.

Sixthly, as already hinted at above in our fourth criticism, it seems that people may be able to use their 'traditional' roles and expectations (such as those associated with kinship) as *resources* that can be drawn on to serve their social and material needs. A good example of this is provided by Ortiz (1970) who examined the impact of a Mexican government development scheme on a northern community, Tzintzuntzan, whose villagers produced pottery. The government wanted the potters to develop higher quality items for sale on a wider market but, after the failure of initial attempts to do this through the installation of more sophisticated kilns, the project was abandoned. Subsequently, however, pottery production and sales increased dramatically. Ortiz argues that this was due to the growth of the local urban maket for domestic cooking pots and the construction of a much better road for the potters to take their wares to town. What is of interest here is that this expanded business enterprise relied on the *traditional personal ties* of friends, kinship and immediate family, so, rather than being an obstacle to commercial growth, these ties were harnessed in such a way as to promote entrepreneurial productivity and success. Commenting on this survey, Long (1977, p.50), in an excellent summary of many similar case studies, writes:

> It is difficult in the light of this example to accept the view that peasant culture is a major brake on change. On the contrary, once a viable set of opportunities presented themselves the peasants showed every willingness to increase production and become more involved in the market economy.

The notion, therefore, that 'traditional' peasant culture is necessarily contrary to the development of economic growth must be subject to serious question. But surely, one *does* find evidence for peasant conservatism and fatalism? After all, studies of rural development programmes in Africa have suggested that many problems were associated with the lack of peasant motivation: as DeWilde (1967, p.176-7) argued, 'the conservatism of the peasants, unless closely supervised, is a major problem'. However, while such conservatism may exist it is more likely that it reflects the *insecurity* of the rural producer, who is more vulnerable than the higher social classes to disease, death, adverse weather, fluctuating income from produce, and last but not least, exploitation by the political and social system that ultimately makes the peasants' land holding so uncertain. In many ways, then, peasants are *more* likely to be exposed to socio-economic change than other social groups. Conservatism may represent the attempt to establish some continuity and order in these precarious circumstances. When opportunties are more favourable, however, many case studies show that the peasantry will respond in an innovative and commercial manner. As Moore (1969, p.387) says,

> They will not change simply because someone has told them to do so. That has been going on for some time. It is necessary to change the situation confronting the people on the land if they are going to alter their behaviour. And if this has not yet happened, as by and large it has not, there are likely to be good political reasons.

The final and in many ways most forceful criticism of modernisation theory, is that it entirely ignores the impact of colonialism and imperialism on Third World countries. This is a staggering omission. It is also a failure to acknowledge that economic growth is as much if not more about the *power* to control resources as it is about the 'ambition' to do so. With this in mind, Hoogvelt's (1976, p.18) sarcasm is deadly:

In Parsons' approach one gets the impression that the history of mankind has been one happy, relaxed and peaceful exchange of ideas, stimulating progress here, there and everywhere where contact between societies was made. Cultural diffusion appears as a friendly merchant traveller, a timeless Marco Polo, innocently roaming the world, gently picking up a few ideas in one place and harmlessly depositing them in another. Incredulously, the 'domination', 'exploitation', 'imperialism', and 'colonialism' are *not* discussed in any of Parsons' works on evolution.

This is perhaps not as surprising as it might first appear, since, in basing much of his analysis on Durkheimian evolutionary theory Parsons was merely repeating the omissions of Durkheim's original work. The latter too had little to offer by way of an analysis of power in general and nothing about the specific impact of the imperialism at work in the Third World at the very time Durkheim published his first text on the division of labour. His thesis on the division of labour itself lacks an adequate conception of power. It implies that the differentiation of roles and institutions occurs as a process of harmonious adaptation in which people choose roles appropriate to the needs of modernisation. Clearly the division of labour in the economy *has* occurred but it might be the case that certain groups in society, élites or upper classes, have the power to *impose* this division on subordinates, determining the reward for and control over the work task . . . . choice relies on an exercise of power that is unlikely to be equally shared by all people . . . .

Conclusion
In conclusion, two general remarks can be made. First, modernisation theory is clearly an oversimplified model of development that lacks two essential ingredients: an adequate historical input and a structural perspective. Historically, it ignores a wealth of evidence, some of which has been presented above, which indicates that the process of economic growth cannot be encapsulated in simplistic notions about the displacement of 'traditional' values systems and institutions by 'modern' ones. Structurally, the theory is insensitive to the specific ways in which factors for economic growth such as the introduction of new technology or markets may be interpreted, or modified or accommodated within *existing* social relationships. In addition, the inequalities of power and social class that structure these relationships are virtually ignored.

Secondly, despite the weakness of its thesis, modernisation theory is right to focus our attention on the role of values and attitudes in affecting people's behaviour and thereby their response to and fashioning of social change. It may be the case that economic opportunities existed for many entrepreneurs in Western European modernisation who could thereby give full rein to their innovative, calculative spirit. Yet it may well be the case that such opportunities do not exist in the Third World (nor for that matter in some of today's advanced states) . . . . Thus, the values and attitudes that people in the Third World draw on do not necessarily express the ambitions of an 'achievement' drive since this would be unrealistic where economic opportunities are heavily influenced by the presence of large multi-national corporations. Instead people may well draw on 'traditional' values of repositories of some security and, at the same time, the values of 'nationalism', 'socialism' and perhaps 'self-reliance' as resources for social change.

The relationship betwen values and the economic context is, therefore, a complex and dynamic process inadequately conceived by the traditional values/traditional economy-modern values/modern economy dualism of modernisation theory.

REFERENCES

M. Anderson (1971) *Family Structure in Nineteenth Century Lancashire* (Cambridge: Cambridge University Press).

P. Bauer (1976) *Dissent on Development* (London: Weidenfeld & Nicolson).

J. C. De Wilde (1967) *Experience with Agricultural Development in Tropical Africa* (Baltimore: Johns Hopkins Press).

M. Dobb (1963) *Studies in the Development of Capitalism* (London: Routledge).

E. Durkheim (1984) *The Division of Labour in Society* (translated by W. D. Halls) (London: Macmillan and New York: The Free Press).

S. N. Eisenstadt (1966) *Modernisation: Protest and Change* (Englewood Cliffs, NJ: Prentice-Hall).

S. N. Eisenstadt (ed) (1970) *Readings in Social Evolution and Development* (Oxford: Pergamon Press).

A. G. Frank (1969) *Latin America: Underdevelopment or Revolution* (New York: Monthly Review).

J. Gusfield (1973) 'Tradition and Modernity', in A. Etzioni and E. Etzioni-Halevy (eds), *Social Change* (New York: Basic Books).

E. E. Hagen (1962) *On the Theory of Social Change* (Homewood, Ill: Dorsey).

A. M. Hoogvelt (1976) *The Sociology of Developing Societies* (London: Macmillan).

D. Lerner (1964) *The Passing of Traditional Society* (New York: The Free Press)

N. Long (1977) *An Introduction to the Sociology of Rural Development* (London: Tavistock).

G. Marshall (1982) *In Search of the Spirit of Capitalism* (London: Hutchinson).

B. Moore (1969) *Social Origins of Dictatorship and Democracy* (Harmondsworth: Peregrine).

D. McClelland (1961) *The Achieving Society* (New York: Van Nostrand).

S. Ortiz (1970) 'The Human Factor in Social Planning in Latin America', in R. Apthorpe, *People, Planning and Development Studies* (London: Frank Cass).

T. Parsons (1951) *The Social System* (London: Routledge).

K. Polanyi (1944) *The Great Transformation: The Political and Economic Origins of Our Time* (New York).

W. W. Rostow (1960) *The Stages of Economic Growth* (Cambridge: Cambridge University Press).

I. Roxborough (1979) *Theories of Underdevelopment* (London: Macmillan).

R. F. Salisbury (1962) *From Stone to Steel* (Cambridge: Cambridge University Press).

M. Weber (1971) *The Protestant Ethic and the Spirit of Capitalism* (London: Unwin University Books).

P. Willis (1977) *Learning to Labour* (Westmead: Saxon House).

P. Willmott and M. Young (1971) *Family and Class in a London Suburb* (London: New English Library).

Theories of Imperialism, Dependency and Underdevelopment

Ankie M. M. Hoogvelt

This reading is from the author's study, The Third World in Global Development, *(1982).*

It is as well to make the point at the outset that theories of imperialism are not exclusively the product of the Marxist tradition. In the nineteenth century the concern with 'empire' and with 'making the empire bigger' had encouraged the formulation of apologetic bourgeois theories of imperialism as well as critical Marxist ones.[1] 'Imperialism' then was not the dirty word that it is now. In the minds of classical, liberal economists an aggressive colonial policy was a necessary complement to the creation of a perfect international division of labour in which each area of the globe, each region or country, would specialise in what it was good at and would thus cash in on Ricardo's theory of comparative advantage. The classical model saw colonisation as a means of imposing on underdeveloped countries a specialisation of production that would eventually benefit them. Since the classical economic theorists were at the same time staunch supporters of 'free trade', the *continuation* of colonial rule with all its petty restrictions and protectionist devices presented them with a real dilemma. As there was no way they could defend the phenomenon on theoretical economic grounds, they soon developed *political* and even *demographic* explanations, e.g. national rivalries between the European powers, excess population in Europe, etc.[2] Over time, when the direct political subjugation of overseas peoples ('colonialism') was no longer seen to serve any useful purpose in the continuation of existing world economic relations, liberal economic thinkers preferred to regard imperialism as a thing of the past, and they filed away the concept in historical archives.

Marxist writers on imperialism, on the other hand, have experienced no such intellectual difficulty, as to them the essence of imperialism had always been *economic* domination and subordination, while 'colonialism' was only regarded as a historically specific political complement of imperialism.

Marxist theories of imperialism, moreover, are theories of *capitalist* imperialism because essentially they regard imperialism as a necessary expansive phase of capitalism. Marxists, since Lenin, exclusively reserve the concept of imperialism to denote a necessary stage in the development of capitalism, and only of capitalism. However, it would not be correct to say that Marxists were the only writers to connect imperialism with the dynamic development of capitalism. Paradoxically, the foundation of the theory of capitalist imperialism is equally credited to two writers, V. I. Lenin and J. A. Hobson,[3] the latter of whom was not a Marxist but a liberal. The argument which both developed and which may be considered the centrepiece of the theory of capitalist imperialism is that the rate of profit in capitalist societies over a long period tends to decline because the very process of capitalist accumulation increases the amount of fixed capital per

71

worker and increases productivity. The declining rate of profit leads to crises of overproduction and underconsumption. To counter the declining rate of profit at home entrepreneurs will export capital abroad, and colonial expansion, defined as direct political domination over areas where capital is invested, will follow. Thus the essence of imperialism is the export of capital rather than of commodities. Since the need to export capital, by the logic of capitalist development, occurs when a certain degree of capitalist accumulation and concentration has been achieved, imperialism as a necessary expansive stage of capitalism coincides with the monopoly stage of capitalism. Although both Hobson and Lenin attributed the exodus of capital to declining investment opportunities at home, Hobson's remedy was to improve living standards at home, especially of the rural population, who had lost out in the uneven distribution of the benefits of capitalist progress. This remained the favourite prescription of liberals and of various shades of West European social democrats for decades to come. By contrast, its impossibility under capitalism became one of the leading tenets of Marxism.

The very emphasis of classical theorists of imperialism such as Lenin, Hilferding and Bukharin on the dynamics of capitalist development in the advanced countries as the *source* of imperialism made them neglect the study of the *effects* of imperialism in the overseas territories to which capital was being exported. If they expressed any thoughts about the colonies at all, these displayed a naive conception of the uniformity of the overseas experiences and of the synonymity of capital with capitalism. It was taken for granted that the penetration of capital would inevitably work up the same social-structural forces and tensions as the emergence of capitalism had already done at home. It was assumed that under imperialism capitalism would spread across the globe, and that in so doing it would turn the whole world capitalistic, and hence ripe for world-wide socialist revolutions. The only notable exception was Rosa Luxemburg, who – much before her time – made the point that the capitalist mode of production depends precisely for the production of surplus-value on an exchange with non-capitalist modes of production.[4]

Theories of Dependency and Underdevelopment
If modernisation theories were the bourgeois theorists' answer to the plight of the underdeveloped countries, dependency theory was the product of the application of Marxist theories of imperialism. From about the late 1950s theories of imperialism began to address popularly the *effects* of imperialism on the overseas territories in an attempt to explain the roots of backwardness. The dependency theory that emerged from this exercise thus became a counterpart to Marxist theories of imperialism. Imperialism is seen from the standpoint of the subordinate nations.[5] It has been observed by several commentators, critical and sympathetic, that 'theory' is probably not an apt description of the type of work carried out under the name. What surfaced was more of a 'perspective', a 'paradigm', or a 'school' of thinking which brought a wide variety of Marxist and non-Marxist radicals together under one banner.[6] The dependency perspective

which these thinkers, and development strategists – for many were employed as policy-makers/advisers to international organisations and governments – came to share was sufficiently potent to act as a classificatory principle, distinguishing the dependency theorists from the bourgeois modernisation theorists. Indeed, the genesis of dependency thinking and its continuing qualifying essence was its criticism of bourgeois modernisation theory.[7]

The original version of 'dependency and underdevelopment' theory, as outlined by first Paul Baran,[8] and next more popularly and grandly by André Gunder Frank,[9] concentrated on locating the cause of backwardness of Third World countries, more especially of Latin America, within the dynamic growth of the world capitalist system. Underdevelopment – as distinct from *un*development – it was claimed, is not due to some 'original state of affairs', as bourgeois theory has it, but is the result of the same world historical process in which the now developed capitalist countries became developed. Thus, from the very beginning, the dependency approach has been a *world-system* approach, explicitly rejecting the concept of the unified state as actor and the notion of the global system as a collection of nation-states.[10]

Baran was the first to make the point that 'development and underdevelopment' is a two-way street: the advanced capitalist countries had become developed by expropriating economic surplus from those overseas countries with which they first traded and which they later colonised, while the overseas countries became underdeveloped by aiding the ascendancy of the West. For their intense economic interaction with the industrialising capitalist states left the overseas countries with a narrowly specialised, export-oriented primary production structure which found its handmaiden in a frozen internal class structure dominated by a small, landed and mercantile ('comprador') élite whose economic interests became increasingly intertwined with those of the advanced capitalist states, and whose cultural life-styles and tastes were a faithful imitation of the same. This is the essence of 'dependency'. The imposed specialisation of production and the continued coincidence of interests between the imperialist states and the ex-colonial élites even after *in*dependence blocked any attempt at industrialisation and internal social transformation (e.g. a bourgeois revolution). Overall economic stagnation and extreme pauperisation of the masses was the result. Thus, in contrast to Marx's own optimism regarding the historically progressive role of capitalism everywhere, Baran demonstrated the impotence of the imported variety.[11]

André Gunder Frank expanded and formalised this substantive theme into a theory of underdevelopment, postulating three 'laws' of motion of the process of development and underdevelopment and coining the twin concept 'metropolis–satellite' to characterise the nature of imperialist economic relations.[12] He went little beyond Baran's masterpiece when he traced the metropolis–satellite contradiction beyond the international into the national-local sphere. The ties of dominance and dependency, he said, run in chain-like fashion throughout the global capitalist system, with metropolitan states appropriating the surplus from the satellites, their towns removing the surplus from their hinterland, their landlords from the peasants, their merchants from shopkeepers, and finally, the shopkeepers from the customers. Frank's mixing of spatial with social metaphors gave his image of the chain of metropolis–satellite contradictions rather more ideological than scientific value. At any rate it was soon criticised for being un-Marxist because of its identification of the mechanism of economic surplus extraction with the capitalist market.[13] Thus it located 'exploitation' in the sphere of exchange rather than production. Nor was it made quite clear how exactly this exchange led to exploitation.[14]

Now, the structural link between the development and underdevelopment of different world regions had already been postulated before by others, more especially by the scholars from the Economic Commission for Latin America. The notion of dependent external-structural relationships particularly was associated with the name of Raoul Prebisch, one-time founder and president of UNCTAD, whose centre–periphery model antedated Frank's metropolis-satellite model of world capitalist relationships by over a decade.[15] Where Paul Baran and André Gunder Frank transcended the ECLA analysis was in defining this structural link in *politico*-economic terms, rather than in strictly economic terms. Prebisch and ECLA had put the underdevelopment of Latin America down to its unequal trade with the industrial world arising from two historical distortions of the world *market* system. The first was the international division of labour which had reduced colonial countries to being specialist producers and exporters of raw materials and foodstuffs, while encouraging the industrialised world to produce and sell manufactures. ECLA presented the by now well-worn technical economic arguments why such a pattern of international trade tends to favour the industrial over the primary producers in both the distribution of the benefits arising from such trade and in the general developmental impetus generated by it. The second historical distortion of the international market was that factor and commodity markets at the centre of the world capitalist system had become more monopolistic and oligopolistic than at the periphery. In the long run this affected the terms of trade for the periphery unfavourably.[16]

Thus the ECLA and Prebisch formulations had sought to establish the cause of underdevelopment in *external*, global, structures and dependent relationships, and their development strategies derived directly from this analysis. They prescribed a policy of inward-directed development for Latin America based on the twin principles of state-protected industrialisation and import substitution under the aegis of foreign investment. Such a policy, it was believed, would at one and the same time stimulate economic growth in Latin America and reduce Latin America's dependence on the advanced world.

At the time this analysis was thought to be extremely progressive, and it was even accused of being Marxist, no doubt because its emphasis on industrialisation indirectly threatened the traditional imperialist–feudal alliance. The irony was, however, that the imperialist–feudal alliance was never directly and openly attacked. Had that been the case, it would have alerted the ECLA intellectuals to the notion of class alliance itself and through it to the *dynamic* interaction between external and internal structural factors affecting Latin American development processes.

It is only when the ECLA policies failed in their objectives, that is, when the balance-of-payments problems were not eased but in fact worsened as a result of 'import substitution', when real wages did not rise sufficiently quickly to stimulate domestic demand, when unemployment grew more acute and income distributions more unequal, and when, as a result, industrial production became increasingly concentrated in products typically consumed by the élites, it was only then that the intellectual climate finally ripened for class analysis.

Both Baran and Frank helped this process by emphasising the complicity of local élites in the transfer of economic surplus from subordinate to imperialist countries. Frank, moreover, in a later work, was now able to 'explain' the failure of ECLA's policies by pointing to the same external/internal dynamic link: industrialisation, which was to have been a panacea of all dependency ills, itself had become increasingly dependent on the capitalist metropoles for financing, marketing, for capital goods, technology design, patents, trademarks, licences, etc. The very process of industrialisation had led to a deepening of dependence and to further underdevelopment.[17] Why was this so? Frank's argument is that the previous, colonially imposed, class structure had rendered a highly *unequal income distribution*. This unequal income distribution severely limits the internal domestic market. And this, in turn, has two correlate effects: on the one hand, it ushers in the process of industrialisation by way of production of luxury/consumer durables, and such a pattern of production, by its very own nature, involves a heavy reliance on imported producer goods, spare parts, technology, etc. On the other hand, the increasingly severe balance-of-payments problems resulting from this pattern of industrialisation leads to the pursuit of even greater dependency: foreign firms are now invited to invest their producer-goods/technology locally. Now, the combination of a limited domestic market and the presence of foreign industrial subsidiaries encourages a grotesquely inefficient system of production and a net outflow of resources: the Latin American subsidiaries have become the dumping-ground for either obsolete foreign equipment or foreign plants and have obsolescence deliberately built into them;[18] their capacity is grossly underutilised, and their labour absorption rate minimal. Over time remitted returns on foreign investment have come to exceed by several times the net inflow.[19]

By emphasising how external dependency interfaces with the internal structure of extreme income inequality, which in its turn distorts the industrialisation process, Frank has invited criticisms to the effect that his is a 'mechanical', economistic deterministic explanation of dependency and underdevelopment.[20] The national bourgeoisie is seen as a rather passive instrument of foreign domination unable to disentangle the national economic good from its own interests, which are solidly locked in with foreign capital (e.g. as partners/-managers of foreign firms, as subcontractors and distributors and as consumers of the luxuries). 'Dependence,' Frank claims, 'is indivisible and makes the bourgeoisie itself dependent.'[21] And this is why his solution to Latin America's problems is a radical break with the world capitalist system. Replying to his critics, Frank has also stressed the *active* role of the national bourgeoisie in its articulation of government policies that facilitate dependency and underdevelopment – government policies such as the liberalisation of import controls for capital and intermediate goods, repeated currency devaluations, a halt to agrarian reforms, and fiscal policies. 'In this manner, he says, ' "lumpendevelopment" is promoted by a "lumpenbourgeoisie".'[22]

It seems to me that Frank continues to miss the point made by his critics. The critical issue surely is *not* whether local elites consciously or unconsciously collaborate with foreign interests, but whether or not 'social classes are seen as completely derivative of economic forces, and whether these economic forces appear to be having a "necessary logic", thus denying the possibilities of struggles against imperialism'.[23] This is the critical point made by Colin Leys in a summary review of dependency theories generally. Remedies like a radical break deny such revolutionary potential, he continues, adding somewhat cynically that such denial is not just theoretical, it is also political, for both dependency theories and dependency theorists have been nicely 'co-opted' by the central institutions of global capitalism, notably the World Bank and the various UN organisations.[24] Having arisen as a criticism of bourgeois development theory, dependency theory has now itself become bourgeois: it is no longer radical because it fails to appeal to the masses of peasants and workers.

NOTES AND REFERENCES

1. Cf. D. K. Fieldhouse, *The Theory of Capitalist Imperialism* (London: Longman, 1967) Introduction.

2. See, for example, J. A. Schumpeter, 'The Sociology of Imperialism', in *Imperialism and Social Classes: Two Essays* (New York: Meridian Books, 1958)

3. V. I. Lenin, *Imperialism, the Highest Stage of Capitalism* (London: Lawrence & Wishart, 1916); and J. A. Hobson, *Imperialism: A Study* (London: Allen & Unwin, 1902).

4. Rosa Luxemburg, *The Accumulation of Capital* (New York: Monthly Reeview Press, 1968).

5. Of all writers on dependency and the dependency debate, Gabriel Palma most clearly places the debate within the Marxist tradition of writings on imperialism: Gabriel Palma, 'Dependency: A Formal Theory of Underdevelopment or a Methodology for the Analysis of Concrete Situations of Underdevelopment?', *World Development*, vol. 6, 1978, pp. 881-924.

6. See, for instance, Colin Leys, 'Underdevelopment and Development: Critical Notes', *Journal of Contemporary Asia*, vol. 7, no. 1, 1977, pp. 82-115; Alejandro Portes, 'On the Sociology of National Development: Theories and Issues', *American Journal of Sociology*, vol. 82, no. 1, 1976-7, pp. 55-63; Adrian Foster Carter, 'From Rostow to Gunder Frank: Conflicting Paradigms in the Analysis of Underdevelopment', *World Development*, vol. 4, no. 3, 1976;. and J. Samuel Valenzuela and Arturo Valenzuela, 'Modernization and Dependence: Alternative Perspectives in the Study of Latin American Underdevelopment', in J. Villamil (ed.), *Transnational Corporations and Transnational Culture* (Brighton: Harvester Press, 1979).

7. This was the central point made by André Gunder Frank in his original formulation of dependency in *The Sociology of Development and the Underdevelopment of Sociology* (London: Pluto Press, 1967).

8. Paul Baran, *The Political Economy of Growth* (New York: Monthly Review Press, 1967). (Originally published in Spanish in 1957.)

9. A. G. Frank, *Capitalism and Underdevelopment in Latin America* (New York: Monthly Review Press, 1967).

10. James A. Caporoso, 'Dependence and Dependency in the Global System', *International Organization*, vol. 32, no. 1, January 1978, p. 2.

11. Probably the best review and methodological critique of the Baran–Frank dependency theory is Palma, 'Dependency'. Useful criticisms of dependency theory from the point of view of the 'empirical' usability of the concept can be found in Christopher Case-Dunn, 'The Effects of International Economic Dependence on Development and Inequality: a Cross-National Study', *American Sociological Review*, December 1975; and the contribution by P. J. McGowan and D. L. Smith, 'Economic Dependency in Black Africa', *International Organization*, vol. 32, no. 1, 1978, pp. 179-235. This whole issue of *International Organization* was devoted to a critical assessment of 'Dependence and Dependency in the Global System'.

12. Frank, *Capitalism and Underdevelopment in Latin America*, Introduction.

13. Cf. E. Laclau, 'Feudalism and Capitalism in Latin America', *New Left Review,* May 1971.

14. David Booth, 'Andre' Gundar Frank: An Introduction and Appreciation' in I. Oxaal *et al., Beyond the Sociology of Development* (London: Routledge and Kegan Paul, 1976).

15. I am referring here to R. Prebisch's seminal paper, *The Economic Development of Latin America and its Principal Problems* (New York: Economic Commission for Latin America, 1950).

16. For good summaries of the ECLA–Prebisch–Frank connection, see Palma, 'Dependency', and Philip J. O'Brien, 'A Critique of Latin American Theories of Dependency' in Oxaal *et al Beyond the Sociology of Development.*

17. A. G. Frank, *Lumpenbourgeoisie, Lumpendevelopment* (New York: Monthly Review Press, 1972).

18. Ibid, p. 109.

19. Ibid, p. 94.

20. Leys, 'Underdevelopment and Development: Critical Notes', p. 95.

21. Frank, *Lumpenbourgeoisie, Lumpendevelopment*, p. 4.

22. Ibid, Introduction.

23. Leys, 'Underdevelopment and Development: Critical Notes', p. 95.

24. Ibid, pp. 99-100.

FURTHER READING (suggested by the editors)

Gavin Kitching, *Development and Underdevelopment in Historical Perspective* (London: Methuen, 1982).

Harry Magdoff, 'Imperialism; a Historical Survey' in H. Alavi and T. Shanin (eds), *Introduction to the Sociology of 'Developing Scoieties'* (London: Macmillan, 1982), pp. 11-28.

Vicky Randall and Robin Theobald, *Political Change and Underdevelopment, A Critical Introduction to Third World Politics* (London: Macmillan, 1985).

Women and Development: The Fallacy of Integration

Geertje Lycklama à Nijeholt

This reading is from a paper published in Netherlands Review of Development Studies (*1987*).

The Integration Strategy criticised

In studying the United Nations documents which relate to the integration of women into development, one is struck by the fact that hardly any attention is given to an analysis of male/female relations with respect to development processes. As a consequence of the a-historic approach no insight emerges on how patriarchy has been created over time and how control of women'ssexuality and procreativity has been one of its central features (Lerner, 1986). This dimension and the power struggles it involves, is neglected. There is no lack of documents which demand equality between women and men and present policy recommendations to reach that goal, but without a thorough analysis of all aspects of patriarchy these recommendations are questionable. Such analytical documents which link women's experience by analysis with theory and vice versa, are prepared by feminist activists and researchers, often women working in women's centres or in women's studies groups, so far not by the United Nations.

On the surface it sounds positive: integration of women into development, but what is the actual meaning of such integration? Is the term not giving a misleading picture of women's reality, for do not historical analysis, anthropological research and archaeological findings show that women always have been integrated into and always have contributed substantially to the society in which they live? Also in present day societies women make essential contributions. Early in the [UN] Decade [for Women 1975-85], Pala had already indicated that African women are well integrated into their societies. She argues that historically African women have always been active in providing for their families and this is what they do today. Not the integration of women into development, but the question of the dependency of the African economies is important in understanding the problems of women in the African context (Pala, 1977). Also Papanek had pointed out the curious ambiguity in the concept of integrating women, as women are always full participants in all processes of social change (Papanek, 1977: 15). Actually much of so-called 'development' can only take place because of women's work, domestic work and subsistence production. This work, however, is often not recognised as work and certainly it is not considered important work, because it is not paid, it is not production for exchange value. Yet it is this work that makes the 'real' work, the 'important-for-development' work possible. This women's work includes the production and upbringing of children, the daily maintenance of the labour force and a number of subsistence activities: food production, food processing, production and maintenance of clothing, of household goods, etc. In fact women in Third World countries are already fully integrated in the development of their societies, but often in a position that gives them little say over the products of their labour.[1] 'A woman should know her place in society', female guerilla fighters in Zimbabwe were told by their comrades-in-arms and they were then shunted aside.[2] This happens to many women and in many societies high percentages of women bear the complete responsibility for their households. This is demonstrated by the research of among others Buvinić et al., Risseeuw and Safilios who found figures of twenty to thirty per cent of women who carried the full burden of providing for the livelihood of themselves and their children. This percentage rises to sixty per cent in regions with a high migration of men.[3]

What actually happens to women in development processes that have been forced upon the countries of the South since colonial and post-colonial times, has been extensively documented in the pioneering study by Boserup: *Women's Role in Economic Development* (1970). How development agencies and their experts contribute further to the deterioration of women's position is analysed in Rogers' study, *Domestication of Women. Discrimination in Developing Societies* (1980). For those who hope that the situation of women has improved since the United Nations and most donor agencies have been implementing the strategy of integrating women into development, disappointment is waiting. For example, Dey's study, 'Women in African Rice Farming Systems' (1983) states:

> The basic problem is that as land is improved and its value increases there is a move from traditional communal use rights to a more individualised system of landownership. Men by virtue of their position of household head, tend to extend personal control over the land, squeezing out women. Inheritance practices, whereby land passes from father to son, reinforce male control of land, often depriving even widows with young children of rights of access to adequate land. (1983; para. 59).

Referring to examples of new rice technology, in particular irrigation, whereby more land is taken into production and more than one crop becomes possible, she points out that women are increasingly in demand as seasonal workers and she demonstrates that women's wages are lower than men's while overall the wages are already quite low. This according to Dey 'raises a fundamental question about women's inability to protect their interests and resist exploitation' (Ibid., para. 66). She emphasizes that 'planners and scientists also need to bear continually in mind the fact that men and women often have conflicting interests over control of resources and incomes within the household and that women generally have less economic power and socio-political support to protect their interests.' (Ibid. para. 47b). Schrijvers in her analysis of a large-scale resettlement and irrigation scheme in Sri Lanka demonstrates that the planning of the scheme turned out to be a blueprint for undernutrition. 'The chronic undernutrition in the Mahaweli H-area is a direct result of planning that cuts women off from their productive resources' (1985:77). And by using as the smallest unit of analysis the household, Schrijvers argues, inequalities which lead to undernutrition are obscured (Ibid.). Sen and Grown in 1985 further document on a worldwide scale how women's situation is deteriorating, by in particular focussing on the various world crises like the balance of payments and debt crises, the food-fuel-water crisis, increasing militarization and violence, the crisis of culture, and the impact these have on women. There is no doubt that women are fully part of these processes and they often suffer doubly from these crises. So the question is not whether women are integrated in development – they are, and they contribute to development by much hard work. Rather the question is under what conditions are women participating in development and who benefits from the products of their work? This requires in particular an analysis of the patriarchal nature of society, or in other words the way in which the domination of women by men is institutionalised in society (Ehrlich 1981;110). Thus demanding attention for the struggles of power between women and men and for women's (organized) efforts to replace men's control over women's sexuality, procreativity and labour power by women's independence and self-determination.

This leads to a *second* point of criticism that has been levelled against integration strategy: it is assumed that the existing development planning bureaucracy, the instruments, methods, means, the whole institutionalised fabric for development, both at the national and the international level, is of such a nature that it can contribute to women's development and liberation. As Rogers' study on international agencies (1980) shows, such agencies will need a thorough transformation of approach and ideology and a substantial increase in the number of women at all levels, before these agencies are able to serve women in development processes. One of the persistent wrong assumptions of both international agencies and national governments is for example, that men are the providers for women and children. Due to this assumption, it is taken as fact that women's employment is only 'supplemental' to that of men (Papanek 1977:15, Schrijvers 1985:73-77). Indeed, the 'terms of reference' for the integration of women into development are decided by men, women are hardly present in the decision-making bodies. In the context of development strategies, integration of women means integration with conditions set by men, as for example, Roberts shows in her discussion of some conceptual problems in relation to the integration of women into development processes in Niger (1979:63). In addition it should be mentioned that the arguments used by the development establishment are often quite instrumental in nature. The World Bank for example uses the argument that the Bank will assist member governments to extend the benefits of development also to women, 'thus to ensure that so large a proportion of the world's human resources is not under-utilized,' (1975:29) which shows that the Bank vastly underestimates women's contribution to development and in fact has a false picture of reality. Dubel analyses the approach of several international agencies with respect to poor rural women and shows that overall the approach is instrumental, the focus is on. '. . .turning women into more efficient food producers, water carriers, cooks and nutritionists and childbearers.' (Dubel, 1983:31). It is furthermore the international concern about the growth of the world population, in particular in countries of the South, which focussed the attention of development planners on women. Women's employment and education are considered to be important factors for a decline in fertility rates (Salas, 1984:23). It is therefore no surprise that the United Nations Fund for Population Activities (UNFPA) fully endorses the strategy of integrating women into development (Ibid.:22). The established development bureaucracy's instrumental approach to women in processes of development is fully part and parcel of the patriarchal nature of the societies from which it emerged and as such is not at all suitable to contribute to women's emancipation and liberation.

We therefore arrive at a *third* point of criticism of the integration strategy, a point, or rather a question which precedes the two earlier points: is development as it takes place the kind of development women want?

'Integration into what?' Boulding is asking herself in a study on women and technological change in Third World countries: 'What kind of a world do women want? That is the question to be asking, not How can women be integrated into development?' (1981:25). She continues: 'Women have only very recently been asking what they want, because they have been so busy adapting to what men want.' (Ibid.). Like many other women, Boulding is increasingly concerned about the direction in which technological developments will lead us, in particular with respect to armament. She points out that it is true that women have been marginal in all power structures in history but it is also true that they have the potential to create new social formations. 'Cooptation into existing power structures continually mutes their potential contribution to the future.' (Ibid.: 27). For this reason Boulding considers it important that women get together on a global level to seriously discuss what kind of future they want and how to realise it. An important contribution to such a discussion was given by the participants at the Forum, the meeting of non-governmental groups and organizations, in Nairobi in 1985. Boulding's view and the worldwide discussions in Nairobi imply a rejection of the integration strategy in favour of a strategy which aims at creating space for women to define the kind of changes they want and to realise a world which is better for human beings to live in than the present one. This is a perspective on development which at the same time heavily banks on women's capabilities to realise such a better world. Summarising, it can be concluded that the objective of IWY (International Women's Year) was to define a society in which women participate in a real and full sense in economic, social and political life and to devise strategies whereby such societies could develop . . .

The mainstream strategy chosen by the United Nations, donor agencies and national governments was the integration of women into development. The analysis of women's changing situation in processes of development indicates, however, that 'real and full' participation of women requires a transformation of the existing patriarchal nature of society and it is at this point that the integration strategy demonstrates its fallacy, it is just adding women to the existing structures and institutions rather than pursuing their transformation. It is a strategy based on a superficial understanding of the position of women in society, as defined in the political, socio-economic, cultural and legal domain. Due to its a-historic approach the complex process of the creation of patriarchy is neglected and as a consequence the conflicts of power between women and men are not analysed. Most UN documents are proof of this lack of understanding of the woman question. Over the years, however, in particular since 1980, out of the women's movement has emerged a much deeper understanding of women's oppression within the context of development and this has led to women's demand for more autonomy, for the right to define their own reality, their own needs and interests and to develop strategies with which to pursue their own objectives in transforming society.

Autonomy and Transformation

Analysis and the building of theory by feminist scholars like Jayawardena, Hartmann, Leacock, Lerner, Mies, Rubin and many others have led to the understanding that there exists no simple unidimensional explanation of women's oppression. Patriarchy has been created in a historic process and women are part of that process (Lerner, 1986:212). As a consequence every society has its specific historic form of patriarchy. Increasingly Third World feminists are analysing the specific forms patriarchy has taken in their society and they highlight the impact of colonialism and the penetration of western capitalism in the creation of patriarchal structures. Due to this they increasingly question the integration strategy and plead for a feminist analysis of women's oppression and for strategies of change which are based on such an analysis. Already in 1980 in Copenhagen Antrobus expressed her ideas as follows: 'In Mexico, the issue of integrating women in development seemed clear. Now after five years, I'm not so certain as I was (because) as far as I'm concerned there are very few 'developed' countries. . . . Do women want to be integrated into patriarchal development? The goal of a feminist development strategy would be . . . to allow women to make decisions and to shape the societies in which they lived. . . .' (*Forum*, 16 July, 1980). Since 1980 the emergence of a new women's movement can be observed in many Third World countries, a movement which takes a feminist perspective on development, emphasizing the need for autonomous organization by women and for transformation of their societies in the direction of feminist ideals. It was at the Nairobi Forum in 1985 that women from all over the world had the opportunity to discuss their alternative visions on development in view of the various existing world crises.[4]

Due to the complex history of women's subordination, it is quite clear that there exists no blueprint for a transformation of patriarchal societies. Women in their specific situation will have to develop a vision on what kind of development, what kind of a society they want, and on the basis of their understanding of their present situation devise strategies for change and methods to work towards that vision. It became very clear during the discussions in Nairobi that the formation of autonomous women's organizations is an important element in such strategies (See Sen and Grown, Ch. 3, 1985). Indeed, also in the official documents recognition is given to the importance of women's organizations in realising change (UN, 1984, Overview, A/Conf. 116/5*, para. 55).

Autonomy is a complex concept, it has different meanings in different political perspectives, for example in a socialist perspective the emphasis is on more or less autonomous organization by women with a common political framework and in a liberal perspective the emphasis is on individual freedom and equal rights. It is also a concept which operates at different levels. Wieringa (forthcoming) distinguishes three levels: the personal, the theoretical and the organizational level. In the context of development, the level of theory and analysis and the level of organization seem to be the most important. Unfortunately, in discussing autonomous organization by women with development planners and experts, the concept is often misunderstood as referring to a kind of separatist movement or a de-linking from the rest of society. At these two levels it should be understood, however, that autonomy is a method rather than a goal in itself. This is not the case at the personal level, here autonomy is a goal in itself. It refers to having a say over one's own life, body and sexuality vis à vis men and the institutions of society. (See for a further discussion of autonomy also G. Lycklama à Nijeholt (ed.), *Beyond the Decade*, a forthcoming publication of the Institute of Social Studies, The Hague, chapters one and six; see also RAWOO 1986). Autonomy implies the creation of space for realising women's own ideas about themselves, humankind and society. In practice, everywhere women are creating such spaces. Increasingly feminist signals from the Third World indicate that development can no longer be left to men and the state. Relevant in this context is the observation made by Muntemba, a Zambian researcher, who studied the deteriorating situation of women in food production: 'We identified three problem areas – land, labour and, connected with the latter, the sexual division of labour. Women themselves identified two major responsible factors – the state and men, whether husbands, headmen, or male kin members.' (1982:48). The development literature on women shows that in the seventies and early eighties a lot of energy has been spent on describing and analysing the deterioration of women's life and work conditions in processes of development. These years represent as it were an extensive period of 'problem identification'. It seems that the time has come for more energy to be spent on devising visions, strategies, methods and means of transformation of development into a process which leads to a society where people, women and men, are no longer oppressed and exploited. I am referring here to development in a broad sense as indicated by Antrobus (see p. 11). Within such strategies with a focus on autonomy and transformation, at least three major issues are of crucial importance:

(1.) A first issue is the need to take into account the many conflicts of interest which exist between women from different races, different classes, and different positions within the global economy. It is important to spend energy on methods and means which will help in bridging these gaps in a specific historic situation in, for example, a given country, city or village. It is important first to recognise the differences and then work towards overcoming them.

(2.) A second issue of importance is the identification of allies among men. As there are many women, so there are many men committed to promoting human emancipation and the transformation of society in such a way that people are no longer oppressed and exploited. To realise such a society and with that, women's liberation, demands not only changes in the structures and institutions of society, but also changes both within and between women and men. It is therefore important that women build alliances with men in order to work together towards realising a better society.

(3.) A third issue of importance relates to the fact that a feminist perspective on development aims at transforming the existing patriarchal nature of society, in other words feminism is a political prespective on society and human development. This not only implies that women will have to organize politically to realize change, it also implies that women need to consider in their strategies the specific socio-political context of their oppression. As was indicated earlier, there exists no blueprint for women's liberation. Women in countries of the South will need different strategies from those in countries of the North, and women in capitalist countries will need strategies which differ from those used by women in socialist countries. In the latter, women have the advantage that the official state ideology is committed to women's emancipation by stimulating their participation in social production. That this in itself is an insufficient condition for transforming the patriarchal nature of socialist societies and thus realising women's liberation, has been documented extensively by feminist scholars such as Croll, Hartmann, Molyneux and others.

I am making a distinction between emancipation and liberation. Emancipation in my view refers to the realisation of equal rights and equal opportunities for women and men in society (liberal perspective) and the entry of women into social production (the marxist perspective). Liberation on the other hand refers to destroying the patriarchal nature of society by transforming society at all levels including the micro level of family and household and the very personal level of realising one's sexuality, thus freeing women from all forms of oppression. It is the particular historic development of patriarchy within a given context of political ideology which women need to take into account when devising strategies for change.

Conclusion
When devising strategies to realise a feminist perspective on development,

women everywhere will need to consider the issues just mentioned in response to the specific situations they face; the strategies, methods and means which are designed may differ considerably. Depending on the specific socio-political situation, the strategy of integration of women into the existing processes of development may lead to women's emancipation. In most cases, however, to realise women's liberation will require special efforts to destroy the persistent patriarchal nature of society. In such situations the strategy of integrating women into development is a fallacious blueprint which will not lead to women's liberation. The challenge for the years to come is to work towards women's autonomy in very specific situations, as a means to transform the patriarchal nature of that situation. The DAWN document and the process it generated, in particular at the Forum in Nairobi, is a good starting-point for a true feminist perspective on development

NOTES

This article is a further elaboration of a farewell address delivered at the Agricultural University in Wageningen in March 1984. I would like to thank my friends and colleagues Reneé Pittin and Saskia Wieringa for the most useful comments made on an earlier draft of this article.

1. Since my focus is in the first place on the strategy of integrating women into development, I am emphasizing the 'integrated position' of women in the South. However, as far as recognition of women's work is concerned the situation of women in the North is more or less the same.

2. Comment made to the author during a visit to Zimbabwe in April 1981.

3. Constantina Safilios-Rothschild refers to percentages of female-headed rural households in Lesotho which are as high as 60-70 per cent (Safilios-Rothschild, 1982:8). Overall percentages of 20-30 per cent are mentioned by Buvinić et al. (1978) and Risseeuw (1980).

4. A series of panels and workshops was organised at the Nairobi Forum by the DAWN Advisory Committee Members, a group of 22 women, most of them from the South. In preparation for the Forum the group had prepared a document (basically written by Gita Sen and Caren Grown): *Development, Crises, and Alternative Visions: Third World Women's Perspectives* (Sen and Grown, 1985). A large number of Forum participants contributed to the discussion on this document.

REFERENCES

Barrett, Michèle (1980) *Women's Oppression Today: Problems in Marxist Feminist Analysis*. London: Verso Editions.

Boserup, Esther (1970) *Woman's Role in Economic Development*. New York: St Martin's Press.

Boulding, Elise (1981) 'Integration into what? Reflections on Development Planning for Women', pp. 9-32 in R. Dauber and M. L. Kain (eds) *Women and Technological Change in Developing Countries*. Boulder, Coloradoz: Westview Press.

Buvinić, Mayra (1983) 'Women's Issues in Third World Poverty: a Policy Analysis', pp. 14-31 in Buvinić, Mayra et al. *Women and Poverty in the Third World*. Baltimore: Johns Hopkins University Press.

Buvinić, Mayra et al. (1978) 'Women-Headed Households: The Ignored Factor in Development Planning'. Report submitted to AID/WID, Grant AID/otr-G-1593. Washington D.C.: International Center for Research on Women.

Croll, Elisabeth J. (forthcoming) 'Reflections on Chinese Strategies to Redefine Gender Roles' in G. Lycklama à Nijeholt (ed.) *Beyond the Decade*. The Hague: Institute of Social Studies.

Dey, Jennifer (1983) 'Women in African Rice Farming', Part I. Paper presented at the 'Women in Rice Farming Systems' conference of the International Rice Research Institute, Philippines, 26-30 September.

Dubel, Ireen (1983) 'Women and Development: To integrate or to disintegrate?' Thesis political science International Relations, University of Amsterdam, October.

Ehrlich, Carol (1981) 'The Unhappy Marriage of Marxism and Feminism: can it be saved?', pp. 109-33 in Lydia Sargent (ed.), *Women and Revolution, a Discussion of the Unhappy Marriage of Marxism and Feminism.* Boston: South End Press.

Forum (1980) quotation of Peggy Antrobus, Copenhagen, 16 July.

Hartmann, Heidi (1981) 'The Unhappy Marriage of Marxism and Feminism: Towards a more progressive Union', pp. 1-41 in Lydia Sargent (ed.), *Women and Revolution, a Discussion of the Unhappy Marriage of Marxism and Feminism.* Boston: South End Press.

Jayawardena, Kumari (1982) *Feminism and Nationalism in the Third World in the 19th and Early 20th Centuries.* History of the Women's Movement: A Lecture Series. Part II. The Hague: Institute of Social Studies.

_____ (1986) 'Feminism in Sri Lanka in the Decade, 1975 to 1985', *ISIS International Women's Journal,* 6, 22-31.

Leacock, E. (1981) *Myths of Male Dominance.* New York: Monthly Review Press.

Lerner, Gerda (1986) *The Creation of Patriarchy.* New York/Oxford: Oxford University Press.

Maguire, Patricia (1984) *'Women in Development: An Alternative Analysis'.* Amherst: Center for International Education, University of Massachusetts.

McIntosh, Mary (1978) 'The state and the oppression of women' in Annette Kuhn and Ann Marie Wolpe (eds) *Feminism and Materialism. Women and Modes of Production.* London, etc.: Routledge and Kegan Paul.

Mies, Maria (1986) *Patriarchy and Accumulation on a World Scale: Women in the International Division of Labour.* London: Zed Books Ltd.

Molyneux, Maxine (1981) 'Women in Socialist Societies: Problems of Theory and Practice', pp. 167-202 in Kate Young et al. (eds), *Of Marriage and the Market: Women's Subordination in International Perspective.* London: CSE Books.

_____ (1985) 'Mobilization without Emancipation?: Women's Interests, the State, and Revolution in Nicaragua', *Feminist Studies,* 11 (2), 227-54.

Muntemba, Shimwaayi (1982) 'Women as Food Producers and Suppliers in the Twentieth Century: The Case of Zambia', *Development Dialogue,* 1-2, 29-50.

Omvedt, Gail (1986) 'Women in Popular Movements: India and Thailand during the Decade of Women'. Geneva: United Nations Research Institute for Social Development.

Pala, Achola O. (1977) 'Definitions of Women and Development: an African Perspective', pp. 9-13 in the Wellesley Editorial Committee (ed.), *Women and National Development: The Complexitites of Change.* Chicago and London: The University of Chicago Press.

Papanek, Hanna (1977) 'Development Planning for Women', pp. 14-21 in The Wellesley Editorial Committee (ed.), *Women and National Development: The Complexities of Change.* Chicago and London: The University of Chicago Press.

RAWOO, Advisory Council for Scientific Research in Development Problems (1986), *'Towards Autonomy for Women: Research and Action to support a Development Process'.* Working Paper 1, The Hague: RAWOO.

Risseeuw, Carla (1980) *The Wrong End of the Rope. Women Coir Workers in Sri Lanka,* Colombo/Leiden: Research and Documentation Centre Women and Development.

Roberts, Pepe (1979) 'The Integration of Women into the Development Process: Some Conceptual Problems', *IDS Bulletin,* April, 60-6.

Rogers, Barbara (1980) *The Domestication of Women: Discrimination in Developing Societies*, London: Kogan Page.

Rubin, Gayle (1975) 'The Traffic in Women: Notes on the 'Political Economy' of Sex', pp. 157-210 in R. R. Reiter (ed.), *Toward an Anthropology of Women*. New York: Monthly Review Press.

Safilios-Rothschild, Constantina (1982) 'The Persistence of Women's Invisibility in Agriculture: Theoretical and Policy Lessons from Lesotho and Sierra Leone'. Centre for Policy Studies, Working Paper No. 88, New York: The Population Council.

Salas, Rafael M. (1984) *Reflections on Population*, New York, etc.: Pergamon Press.

Schrijvers, Joke (1985) *Mothers for life: Motherhood and Marginalization in the North Central Province of Sri Lanka*, Delft: Eburon.

Sen, Gita and Caren Grown (1985) *Development, Crisis, and Alternative Visions: Third World Women's Perspectives*. Printed in Norway. Reprinted by Monthly Review Press, New York, 1987.

United Nations (1970) General Assembly Resolution 2626 (XXV) of 24 October.

_____ (1972) General Assembly Resolution 3010 (XXVII) of 18 December.

_____ (1974) Economic and Social Council Resolution 1851 (LVI) of 16 May.

_____ (1975) Declaration of Mexico, Plans of Action, World Conference of the International Women's Year, 19 June-2 July, Centre for Economic and Social Information/OPI, CESI.E29.

_____ (1979) Convention on the Elimination of All Forms of Discrimination Against Women, General Assembly Resolution 180 (XXXIV) of 18 December.

_____ (1980) 'Programme of Action for the Second Half of the United Nations Decade for Women: Equality, Development and Peace. World Conference of the United Nations Decade for Women: Equality, Development and Peace', Copenhagen, Denmark 14-30 July, A/CONF.94/30, 13 August.

_____ (1980) 'Worsening situation of women will be main issue confronting Commission on the Status of Women,' Division for Economic and Social Information, DPI/DESI NOTE IWD/22, 13 February.

_____(1984) 'Review and Appraisal of Progress Achieved and Obstacles Encountered at the National Level in the Realization of the Goals and Objectives of the United Nations Decade for Women: Equality, Development and Peace,' World conference to Review and Appraise the Achievements of the United Nations Decade for Women: Equality, Development and Peace, Nairobi, Kenya, 15-26 July. Report of the Secretary-General: 'Overview', A/CONF.116/5, 5 December. Report of the Secretary-General: 'Part One, General Trends in Equality, Development and Peace,' A/CONF.116/8/Add 1. Report of the Secretary-General: 'Part Two, Development in Sectoral Areas III. Replies to Part II of the United Nations Questionnaire to Governments,' A/CONF.116/5/Add.2-14, 5 December.

United Nations Economic Commission for Africa and Organisation of African Unity (1984): 'Women in Africa to the Year 2000'. Regional Intergovernmental Preparatory Meeting for the World Conference to Review and Appraise the Achievements of the United Nations Decade for Women: Equality, Development and Peace. Third Regional Conference on the Integration of Women in Development, Arusha, United Republic of Tanzania, 8 to 12 October 1984, E/ECA/RCIWD/-OAU/10, 10 August.

Vargas, Virginia (1986) 'Women, Vote for Yourselves! Reflections on a Feminist Election Campaign', *ISIS International Women's Journal*, 5, 28-33.

Werlhof, Claudia von (1985) 'Zum Verhältnis von "Staat" und "Kapital" und "Patriarchat",' *Beiträge zur Feministischen Theorie und Praxis*, 13, 63-78.

Wieringa, Saskia (forthcoming 1987) *Women's Struggles and Strategies*, London: Gower Press.

World Bank (1975) 'Integrating Women into Development'. Washington D.C.

Section II
Food, Famine and Population

Food, Famine and Population

The failure of current political and economic systems to guarantee minimum living standards to all the world's people is starkly demonstrated by the recurrence of famines. The global economic crisis of the 1980s is poignantly represented by images of starving children – the most vulnerable, the least blameworthy.

The misery is acute in sub-Saharan Africa. Decades of neglect of the rural sector, an international economic system inimical to the needs of the poorest, policy mistakes making bad situations worse, the horrendous effects of war and civil disturbance – all have contributed to the downward spiral considered in the first two readings in this section, both by Michael Lofchie. 'Political and Economic Origins of African Hunger', although written more than a decade ago, remains relevant in its focus on the dualistic structures at the root of the problem of hunger. Policies that favour export crops against food crops for local consumption helped pave the way for disastrous declines in food production: '. . .countries where massive starvation was imminent in the early 1970s were, at the same time, exporting tens, if not hundreds, of thousands of tons of agricultural commodities to European and American markets.' However, the relative success of the export sector was not sustained. In the second reading, 'Africa's Agricultural Crisis: An Overview', Lofchie notes that by the mid-1980s export crop production was stagnant, while food production had declined still further.

According to Lofchie, the causes adduced by the many observers of the crisis fit into two broad categories: (1) internal factors for which governments can be held responsible, such as faulty price structures, currency overvaluation and inappropriate development strategies, and (2) external factors beyond the control of individual governments, such as declining terms of trade for primary products, protectionism by the industrialised countries, high interest rates compounding debt problems, and so on. In Lofchie's view, the additional effects of actions by donors such as the UN agencies and the World Bank are too often neglected in the analyses: '. . . in the rural sector . . . the influence of donor agencies is sometimes so strong that it can have a determinative effect on agricultural trends. It is clear that certain policies pursued by members of the donor community have played an important part in worsening Africa's agricultural crisis.' His conclusion is pessimistic: anti-statist free market solutions are now in favour with donors, but if future aid programmes contribute as little as those of the past, then the prospect for Africa's people is 'unspeakably dim'.

In the next paper, 'Why Poor People Stay Poor', Michael Lipton argues that the concept of urban bias helps to explain the persistent poverty of the rural majority. The balance of power in a system where politicians bow to urban populations who are demanding cheap food and where alliances are made between rural and urban élites is weighted against the isolated, unorganised rural poor. In most poorer countries resources are channelled disproportionately to urban areas. Agriculture, with 75 per cent of the population, contributes 45 per cent of GNP but receives only 20 per cent of investment; larger farmers are favoured against small farmers. This is not only inequitable, says Lipton, it is also inefficient, for small farmers have been shown to be more efficient than large farmers.

Many of these small farmers are women. Yet the bias against women, in this as in so many other facets of life, is pervasive. 'Women and Agriculture', a United Nations paper from the Nairobi conference on the Decade for Women, summarises some of the evidence on women and agriculture. It is estimated that over fifty per cent of the world's food is produced by women, but if there is a bias against the rural poor, there is an even stronger bias against rural women. The Food and Agriculture Organisation (FAO) points out: 'Despite the well-documented, crucial role that women play in food production in [Africa], agricultural modernization efforts have excluded them, leading to negative consequences for food production and the perpetuation of rural poverty.'

Food production, hunger, poverty and population growth are interconnected, but in popular discussions the exact nature of the linkages and causal relationships are often obscured. This question is taken up in William Murdoch's 'Population and Poverty'. His thesis is that 'the same political, economic, and social machinery both drives rapid population growth and constrains food production.' In other words, rapid population growth is not the *cause* of hunger; rather, both are caused by 'the structural poverty of rural populations in the underdeveloped world. This single phenomenon is the cause of both rapid population growth and inadequate food supplies.'

The last two extracts in this section are by Amartya Sen, who has contributed greatly to our understanding of recent famines, as well as those of the distant past. His 'entitlement approach' identifies the missing link between the existence of food (or other commodities) and people's access to it. It focuses on what a person owns, or may exchange, what is given free and what is taken away. In his book, *Poverty and Famines*, Sen gives the example of a barber 'who owns his labour power and some specialized skill, neither of which he can eat, and he has to sell his hairdressing service to earn an income to buy food. His entitlement to food may collapse even without any change in food availability if for any reason the demand for hairdressing collapses and if he fails to find another job or any social security benefit.'[1]

Sen argues that the entitlement approach is 'quite inescapable in analysing starvation and poverty. If, nevertheless, it appears odd and unusual, this can be because of the hold of the tradition of thinking in terms of what *exists* rather than in terms of who can *command* what. The mesmerising simplicity of focusing on the ratio of food to population has persistently played an obscuring role over centuries, and continues to plague policy discussions today much as it has deranged anti-famine policies in the past.'[2]

The entitlement approach is as helpful in explaining the export of food from Ireland at the height of the Great Famine in the 1840s, as it is in showing why food left the Wollo region of Ethiopia in 1974 while hundreds of thousands of people were starving. The paper included here, 'The Food Problem: Theory and Policy', does not downplay the importance of adequate food production, storage and transportation, but the problem of hunger, Sen concludes, ultimately belongs 'to political economy and political science. There is, indeed, no such thing as an apolitical food problem.'

Furthermore, as Sen points out in 'Family and Food: Sex Bias in Poverty', policy-makers should not neglect the fact that gender and age may be important factors influencing the pattern of deprivation: 'There is a good deal of evidence from all over the world that food is often distributed very unequally within the family – with a distinct sex bias (against the female) and also an age bias (against the children)' and 'there is no escape from the grave tragedy of the disproportionate undernourishment of children (or sharper undernourishment of the *female* children in distress situations. . .) or the unusual morbidity of women. . . .'

Thus we return inexorably to the image with which we started: that of starving children. It should be clear from the readings presented below that there is nothing inevitable or natural about this scandal: political and economic structures are shaped by people with power. These structures can be changed.

NOTES

1. Amartya Sen, *Poverty and Famines: An Essay on Entitlement and Deprivation* (Oxford: Oxford University Press, 1982), p. 155.

2. op. cit., p.8.

Political and Economic Origins
of African Hunger

Michael F. Lofchie

This article first appeared in Journal of Modern African Studies,
Volume 13, part 4 (1975).

Drought and famine have become so inextricably linked in both popular and academic analyses of Africa's food problems in the 1970s that the relationship between the two is now taken almost axiomatically as cause and effect. The logic is simple and persuasive. Drought produces crop failure and crop failure, just as inevitably, leads to human starvation. This reasoning and the colour photography of starving children in the world press have proved so irresistible that social scientists have had surprisingly little role in scholarly discussions of the causes of the recent African famine. The subject has been left almost entirely to climatologists, physical geographers, water experts and agronomists. Social scientists have so taken it for granted that the causes of African famine are natural and climatic that most of their literature on the subject falls into the genre of 'impact' studies which omit the issue of causality and deal almost entirely with the social and political after-effects.

There is a substantial literature, for example, which deals with the consequences of famine on the social fabric of Sahelian societies, and an abundance of material is also available on the prospects of post-drought social, economic and ecological reconstruction.[1] The various disciplines have aligned themselves in fairly predictable ways. Political scientists have generally been preoccupied with international aid efforts, and with assessments of the varying strategies adopted by different donor countries and agencies. A common theme in much of this analysis has been the familiar refrain of 'too little, too late', as if any amount of assistance could ever have been enough and on time. There has also been speculation about whether Sahelian nation-states can survive any further attrition of their economic base. Sociologists, on the other hand, have treated the famine largely in terms of its internal demographic consequences, and have focused, in particular, on the drastically accelerated process of rural-urban migration. The depopulation of the countryside has been so great that some sociologists are now doubtful whether food production can be fully restored once the drought has passed.

Anthropologists have largely centred their attention on the deterioration of traditional institutions and cultural practices among Sahelian peoples, and there is a strong implication that the impact of the drought has been nothing less than the permanent destruction of the institutional bases of these historic societies. Some anthropologists have added a macabre note to the discussion. At a recent meeting of the African Studies Association in the United States, there was an intense debate about the ethical pros and cons of 'salvage anthropology', an

94

enterprise which, if pursued, would despatch researchers armed with tape recorders scurrying to transcribe for posterity the essential lineaments of dying cultures.

Radically inclined scholars have also tended to accept the presumption that the famine in the Sahel is a product of natural causes. Even the most conspiratorially minded find it difficult to associate rainfall patterns with the global capitalist conspiracy. Instead of focusing on the origins of famine, radical analysis has called attention to the possibility of profiteering inherent in a basically fortuitous situation. Thus, for example, Claude Meillassoux tends to treat the famine as a kind of instant enclosure movement.[2] Famine drives the Sahel peasantry off the land, much as sheep grazing did in a different place at an earlier time. This, in his view, paves the way for a more fully commercialised development of the agricultural sector on the basis of large-scale capital-intensive farming, using expensive systems of irrigation. The prospect of lucrative investment opportunities in lands swept clear of peasant cultivators, Meillassoux believes, gives capitalist nations a vital economic stake in maximising the social effects of the famine, and, thus, largely accounts for the western world's complicity in widespread starvation and human dislocation.

The purpose of this article is not to criticise any of these approaches, but to call attention to one area of analysis which all, to some extent, overlook. Despite their wide range of disciplinary and ideological viewpoints, the preceding perspectives on African hunger share one basic premise. They treat the issue of diminishing food supply primarily in terms of natural calamity. In so doing, they have foregone an opportunity to broaden their understanding of the causes of the current predicament to include political and economic factors. This is a matter of no minor importance. Policies of development for the food-starved areas of Africa could only be improved by an enlarged understanding of the political roots of the crisis.

This point can be put even more strongly. Policy prescriptions which are informed by a predominantly non-political view of the world, tend, generally, to consist of technical and administrative recommendations. They stress, for example, the need for irrigation programmes, for more modern and weather-resistant agricultural practices and for the introduction of the newer high-yield varieties of seed. Aiding countries have been urged to create grain banks, and to set aside a certain proportion of the produce to be sold to poorer nations at below world market prices. However desirable and worthwhile such policies might be, they in no way reflect upon the political and economic arrangements, which, far more than changes in climate and rainfall, are at the base of human suffering and deprivation.

The point of departure for a political understanding of African hunger is so obvious it is almost always overlooked: the distinction between drought and famine. Drought is a natural climatic phenomenon involving the absence of rainfall over an extended period of time. Famine is a matter of human beings suffering from the lack of food and, often in growing numbers, imperilled by starvation. Not only is there no automatic or direct link between the two, but any analysis which assumes this misses a major political point. To the extent that there is a connection between drought and famine, it is mediated by the political and economic arrangements of a society. These can either minimise the human consequences of drought, or accentuate its effects. In Africa, political and economic arrangements have converted a problem of climatic unpredictability into an immense human catastrophe.

Nothing better underscores the analytical weakness of explanations which link famine to drought than the fact that African food production has been in perilous difficulty since long before the beginning of a climatic problem.[3] Food production in the vast majority of African countries has been inadequate since the late 1950s and probably earlier. Throughout the decade from 1960 to 1970 the productivity of the food-producing sector of most African agricultural economies was virtually stagnant, both in terms of output per worker and per unit of land. The rate of increase in food production for this period was so low, about 2.5 per cent a year, that it barely kept pace with the increase in population. Indeed as the rate of population growth increased towards the end of the decade and reached a figure upwards of 3 per cent a year, there was every indication that the rate of food production had fallen measurably behind the increase in population. As a result, a continent in which malnutrition and undernourishment were endemic in 1960, remained so a decade later, with considerable reason to believe that, even before the drought began, the situation had become worse rather than better. Africa was forced to become a net importer of food-stuffs to ward off starvation years before the emergency food shipments of the early 1970s.

Viewed in historical perspective, then, the drought intruded upon the African scene during a period when food production was already exhibiting all the symptoms of serious breakdown. In a certain number of countries, perhaps six or eight in all, it made a critical situation considerably worse, transforming perilous food shortages into the deepest human tragedy. The drought may have had its greatest effect, however, in obscuring the fact that Africa's food supply problem is continent-wide and has deep political and economic roots. These factors are not confined to any particular region of the continent, and, as a result, the tendencies towards a collapse of food production continue to unfold not only in drought areas, but in countries only marginally affected by the climatic problem.

Thus, the apparent end of the drought leaves Africa still in a position of great uncertainty as far as its agricultural future is concerned. The United Nations continues to predict that Africa's food production will fall shorter of supplying the needs of its population than that of any other continent. This will necessitate a continuation of heavy dependence upon food imports, a policy that will drain off funds that might have been used for more basic development purposes.

If independent Africa's recent agricultural record has been one of consistent failure in food production, it has also been one of booming success in the cultivation of export crops. These two aspects of African agricultural performance stand in utter contrast to one another and, for want of a better term, can be identified as Africa's agrarian paradox: a continent unable to produce sufficient foods to provide the majority of its citizens with even a barely minimal diet has been able to record sharp increases in its annual production of agricultural goods destined for external markets. During the second half of the last decade, when food production was already beginning to lag behind the rate of population increase, the production of export crops was rising by about 4 per cent a year.[4] Although this figure does not seem terribly large, its meaning, translated into human terms, is that countries where massive starvation was imminent in the early 1970s were, at the same time, exporting tens, if not hundreds, of thousands of tons of agricultural commodities to European and American markets.

The agrarian paradox can be discerned not only in the Sahel drought area, but in Eastern Africa where the effects of climatic irregularity are not so severe. The most dramatic example, however, is Mali, one of the Sahel countries most affected by drought conditions and a principal recipient of emergency shipments of food. Here the production of food crops for local consumption had fallen precipitously by the early 1970s. Corn production, for example, fell by more than one-third between 1969 and 1971, and millet, desperately needed to take up the slack, showed no increases whatsoever. During the same period, Mali's export crops had attained bumper levels. During the crop year 1971-72, cotton-seed production reached a record high of 68,000 metric tons, a figure which reflected more than a 400 per cent increase during a six-year period. Groundnut production totalled more than 150,000 tons that year, an increase of nearly 70 per cent during a four-year period. Rice production, also largely for export, reached a record high in 1972, amounting to about 174,000 tons.[5] The agrarian paradox assumes a particularly cruel form when one or more of the crops being exported is a basic food item which could be consumed locally.

Tanzania has found itself in a strikingly similar position. Food production for local consumption began to plummet disastrously during the early 1970s, a problem which the Government was inclined to attribute to climatic conditions, but which, it can be argued, was – to a far greater extent – a consequence of peasant resistance to an unwanted programme of socialist villages. By 1974, food production had fallen so low that the Government exhausted its entire reserve of foreign exchange to purchase food from overseas.[6] Additional shipments were being sent on an emergency relief basis, placing Tanzania in common category in this respect with Mali and other Sahelian nations. At the same time, however, the export sector of the Tanzanian agricultural economy was flourishing, and the total level of production of export crops was approaching record highs. During crop year 1972-73, just before the massive importation of emergency food supplies, Tanzania exported over 120,000 tons of cotton, more than 100,000 tons of coffee, about 235,000 tons of sisal, and nearly 280,000 tons of cashew nuts.[7] Thus Tanzania could be likened to Mali not only with respect to its dependence upon foreign supplies of food but, as well, in the impressively successful accomplishments of its export-oriented agricultural economy.

These figures, like any others, should be viewed with the utmost caution. The proposition that statistics can be made to tell virtually any story is, somehow, even more true when applied to the rural sector of agrarian societies. As Barrington Moore has admonished us, statistics often miss the major qualitative dimensions of socio-economic change.[8] There is an enormous range of variation in the agricultural performance of modern African societies, and the assiduous researcher could find solid basis to doubt the validity of an agrarian paradox involving great failure as regards food production and considerable success in the cultivation of exportable commodities. Some countries, Malawi for example, are enjoying prodigious success in both spheres. The figures of Mali and Tanzania are meant only to indicate a rough order of magnitude of a problem characteristic of innumerable other African societies: the paradox of a gross discrepancy in performance between two separate spheres of the agricultural economy. This occurs both in countries where drought has exposed the weakness of the food-producing sector by forcing famine on the attention of the world, and in other countries, undoubtedly a majority, where food production – even in the best of times – hovers precipitously between stagnation and disaster.

The agrarian paradox is central to a political analysis of the problem of African hunger. Authors who have failed to identify it as such, like those of the expensive MIT study cited earlier, have generally adopted a purely idiosyncratic mode of explanation, relying upon drought as the primary causal ingredient. Idiosyncratic explanations generally have only limited utility, and the problems inherent in this particular case are glaring. If drought is the explanation, why has it not affected export crops as well as food crops? And why are there food shortages almost as acute in countries where rainfall has not been a major difficulty? The answer, of course, is that Africa's problems of food production are not reducible to a matter of rainfall levels. They have to do fundamentally with the dualistic structure of Africa's agricultural economies.

Dualistic Agricultural Economies

The concept of a dualistic agricultural economy generally refers to one in which there is a conspicuous division between large-scale, relatively capital-intensive production of a narrow range of export crops, and a labour-intensive peasant sector which provides the bulk of the population's food requirements.[9] This concept has come into some prominence in discussions of the impact of colonial rule on the structure of African economies. The economic interests of the European powers led them to structure agricultural production so as to maximise their colonies' foreign-exchange earning capacity. Only in this way could they assure European investors a satisfactory return on their capital, and guarantee that the colonial territory would be able to become involved in European trade on a self-financing basis.

There are other economic interests as well. The colonial powers usually assumed, for example, that the costs of overseas administration should be borne entirely by the colonised territory and not become a burden on the home treasury. Export agriculture furnished a relatively easy way to ensure this degree of self-sufficiency. It is also worth noting that the foreign earnings of colonial territories were often deposited in European banks where they could be used to finance European development. All these factors can be shown to have contributed in varying degrees to an over-emphasis, during the colonial era, on export agriculture.

The idea of a dualistic agricultural sector also figures prominently in most discussions of Africa's continuing economic dependence upon Europe and the West. An African society's export crops contribute a vast proportion of its foreign exchange earnings and, in many cases, a substantial portion of its governmental revenues as well. Senegal is an excellent example. The groundnut crop, which takes up about one half of the total cultivated area, annually accounts for about three-fourths of the country's export earnings and approximately one-third of its budgetary revenues.[10] Other examples of this sort of dependence in modern Africa are almost endless. The Ivory Coast obtains well over half its export earnings from cocoa and coffee; Ghana, nearly three-fifths from cocoa alone; and Chad, more than four-fifths from raw cotton. In Eastern Africa, Uganda obtains about three-fourths of its export earnings, from coffee and cotton; Malawi, about three-fifths from tobacco and tea; and Kenya, nearly half from coffee and tea.[11] These figures illustrate the extent to which the development of a dualistic agricultural economy, which places great emphasis on the export sector, causes African societies to remain in a state of continuing economic dependence upon Europe.

Agricultural dualism can also be held directly accountable for Africa's contemporary problem of inadequate food production. For the success of export production has been achieved almost entirely at the expense of an economically impoverished peasant, food-producing sector. Decades of over-concentration on export cultivation have left the continent's food-producing regions badly under-supplied with infrastructure, deprived of government services, desperately short of capital for development, and technologically pre-feudal. As a result, any attempt to improve Africa's food-producing capability will need to concern itself with a fundamental structural transformation of the rural economy. Efforts to achieve this may well encounter considerable political difficulty. Policies which have the potential to undermine the established economic primacy of the export sector would run directly counter to the large and powerful array of social groups which have a stake in the profitability of the export economy. No small part of the difficulty will lie in the fact that some of those who profit from the present situation are in key positions of political power in their societies.

Strong political support for the export sector has been one of the major common denominators linking the policies of the colonial governments to those of independent African regimes. The political influence wielded by exporting interests is so strong that it helps account for some of the enormous differences between the plantation and peasant sectors, as well as the over-emphasis on export production. It may, for example, explain why African governments have, with very few exceptions, been so consistently supportive of the institution of private ownership in the export sector, regardless of whether this has involved expatriate corporations, foreign nationals, or local citizens, while the condition of communal tenure in the food-producing areas has been left virtually intact. In addition, the strong political position of the exporting interests almost certainly accounts for the fact that their farms nearly always occupy the best arable areas, a matter of immeasurably greater importance than the proportion of a country's land in their possession.

The political influence of the exporting regions can also be held directly accountable for the fact that they benefit from the whole array of government supports. The infrastructures of African nations, their road and railway systems in particular, are – time and time again – patterned in such a way as to facilitate the transportation of exportable agricultural commodities from the interior to the principal ports, rather than to improve the internal distribution of food items. The agricultural extension services of most African governments are also directed primarily towards the exporting areas and, as a result, the farms which grow cash crops benefit from a wide range of scientific inputs, including fertilisers, pesticides, and new varieties of high-yield seeds.

Perhaps most importantly, government-sponsored irrigation schemes are almost always built to deliver an assured supply of water to export crop areas, with food-producing regions eligible only for the remainder after the needs of the large-scale cotton, rice, or groundnut farms have been provided for. It is pertinent to note, for example, that Mali's record-high crop of rice in 1972-3 was made possible by irrigation schemes in the Segou and Mopti areas. One of the reasons this rice had to be considered, to a large extent, an export crop, was that it was necessary to defray the cost of imported equipment and supplies used in construction. In a nutshell, then, African governments have provided an impressive variety of supports and services to the export sector, and have, in this way, undoubtedly furnished export agriculture with a substantial indirect subsidy.

The peasant food-producing sector has benefitted from few, if any, of these supports or subsidies and, as a result, stands out as a model of agricultural backwardness. The technological life style of African peasant food-growers, an assorted grouping which probably comprises about 90 per cent of the population, can only be described as little advanced beyond the iron age. By far the most common implement is the hand-held hoe, a tool which disappeared millennia ago from most of European and North American agriculture. In contrast to the diesel tractors which perform much of the basic work in the plantation sector, the use even of animal-drawn ploughs is rare among African peasant farmers. The technological contrast between African export-crop production and food-crop cultivation could not be greater. The former involves the most advanced scientific inputs available; the latter uses techniques which are not much advanced over those employed when human societies first abandoned a hunter-forager livelihood in favour of sedentary agricultural production. If any explanation were necessary of the utter stagnation of productivity among African peasant food-producers, it lies here, in the almost complete absence of technological and scientific inputs of the modern age.

Africa's food-producers are also conspicuously unsupported by the whole range of governmental services available to the export sector. The most conspicuous difference in this respect has to do with infrastructural services. Whereas the exporting regions normally benefit from the ready availability of road and railroad networks, Africa's food-producing regions continue to be badly deficient, even with respect to a minimal system of feeder roads. Even the most casual visitor to a food-producing area of an African countryside cannot fail to notice the extent to which the basic means of transportation usually consists of heavily loaded bicycles being pushed, not pedalled, sometimes for miles, along narrow, winding paths.

In many countries the difficulties of transporting basic food items from the countryside to the major cities are so great that large amounts of these crops often languish and spoil in rural markets, where they can be purchased for absurdly low prices, while urban demand, though sufficiently strong to encourage greater production at a more reasonable price level, goes unsatisfied. Often, there are not even the most elemental facilities for the storage of perishable food items, with the result that any given country's supply of basic staples tends to go through an extreme cycle which ranges from high availability during harvest season, to severe scarcity or utter non-availability during the agricultural off-season. Food items which could easily be stored and processed locally are, instead, imported from abroad at great cost in foreign exchange, while local food producers lack sufficient capital to improve their land or purchase more up-to-date equipment.

This situation is also related to the absence of marketing agencies to assist in the transportation and sale of food produce. Whereas farmers who grow such items as cocoa, coffee, tea and other staples of the export trade can depend upon the assistance of governmental marketing boards with nation-wide bureaucracies, the marketing of food crops normally proceeds on an almost anarchic laissez-faire basis. The entire system of food distribution and sale has an extraordinarily haphazard quality. Demand-prediction, price-stabilisation, and quality-monitoring, all of which are now routine in the export sector, are virtually unheard of so far as local food items are concerned. After 75 years of colonial rule and about 15 years of independent government, the establishment of a state-supervised marketing system for basic food items is not even a remote possibility in most nations. To the extent that institutional involvement is a barometer of concern, African governments exhibit more interest in the satisfaction of European coffee and tea drinkers than they do in the food consumption patterns of their own populations.

The same sort of situation often prevails with respect to agricultural extension services. Whereas export crops benefit from the whole range of modern agro-scientific inputs, food production is carried on without even the most elemental level of support. A 1970 survey by the Food and Agricultural Organisation, for example, showed that the use of fertiliser per unit of arable land in Africa was lower than in any other continent and, in fact, only about one-third of that in Asia, the second lowest continent in fertiliser utilisation.[12] While this can to some extent be accounted for by the greater availability of land per person in Africa, and by the greater unpredictability of other factors of production including rainfall, the figure for Africa (7 kg. per hectare) is nevertheless indicative of the extent to which peasant producers are deprived of inputs which would enable them to boost their level of production. Indeed, when it is taken into account that export-crop producing areas in Africa make extensive use of fertilisers along with other scientific inputs, the non-availability of modern supports for food production becomes all the more dramatic by comparison.

The impoverishment of the peasant food-producing sector in African agriculture is not the accidental by-product of benign neglect, the un-intended consequence of a mere misplaced over-emphasis on export production. The reasoning behind this assertion borrows heavily from Rodolfo Stavenhagen's recent study of the impact of plantation production in both Africa and Latin America.[13] In addition to a high level of governmental support, and a continuous infusion of modern agro-scientific inputs, the exporting plantations had one additional major requirement as a pre-condition of their economic success – an abundant and readily available supply of low-wage agricultural workers. In order for the large-scale plantation to thrive, the African peasantry had to be forced to make itself available, at least during peak harvesting periods, as a pool of migratory workers. The only way to achieve this objective was to lower the living standards of nearby peasants to the point where their material survival was, at least partially, dependent upon rural wage income. Thus, Meillassoux is completely correct in viewing the modern fate of the African peasantry as a variant on the classic enclosure phenomenon. The error in his article lies in identifying this process only with the social consequences of the recent drought. Africa's enclosure movements, in fact, began almost a century ago, and can be dated from the earliest beginnings of the plantation system of production for export crops.

Historians of the period have pointed to a whole variety of methods whereby the colonial administrations in Africa attempted to compel the rural population to make itself available as a labour-supply for the cash-crop estates. These included various systems of taxation, such as the head tax, poll tax, and graduated taxes with minimum per person requirements, the imposition of certain work requirements as part of an individual's obligation to colonial authority and, on occasion, out-and-out recourse to forced labour. These, however, are but the most obvious manifestations of a policy which sought to transform peasant cultivators into rural proletarians. Significantly less visible, but immeasurably more consequential, was the rural policy which so starved the peasant food-producing areas of governmental services, supports and agro-scientific inputs that production faltered to a point where wage labour became an imperative of survival. Long before the drought, this process had proceeded to the point where the very notion of an African peasantry as a class, which survives by cultivating and selling its own crops, had become something of a misnomer. Rare indeed is the African family which does not survive, at least partially, on the basis of remittances from one or more of its members engaged in wage labour, either in the city or in cash-crop areas of the countryside.

The impoverishment of peasant production has had one additional consequence relevant to the economic prosperity and profitability of the cash-crop plantations. It prevents the small-scale peasant producer from entering into economic competition with the larger estates. Peasant farmers, given a modicum of opportunity, can better the large plantations not only in terms of output per unit of land but, more importantly, in terms of cost per unit produced. In Kenya, for example, peasant families who were resettled on the farms of former European settlers made impressive gains, in some cases nearly doubling the level of output.[14] The economic potential of efficient peasant production poses an immense threat to capital which has been invested in large-scale plantation enterprises. This, perhaps, explains why it is so rare to find any African country which, during either colonial or independence periods, has encouraged peasant production of cash crops which are also being grown under extensive farming conditions. In addition to the danger of economic competition, there is, of course, also the prospect that peasants who can survive economically on the basis of their own production are under less pressure to offer their labour cheaply on the larger farms.

In general, then, the essential contours of rural development in modern Africa can be summarised as follows. Peasant production of food items for local consumption has, by and large, been sacrificed to the production of export crops. These are frequently grown on the basis of large-scale units in which capital can be invested. A considerable amount of peasant production of export crops, however, has been allowed, indeed, sometimes encouraged, but almost never in areas where this would pose any sort of threat to the economies of plantation-style production, either in the form of direct competition, or in the more hidden form of labour shortages. The agricultural policies of African states, during both colonial and independence periods, have been part and parcel of this bias in favour of export crop production, and against the production of food crops. The one indispensable ingredient in the entire pattern is the need to convert a significant proportion of the peasantry into a labour supply for cash-crop areas.

The most visible manifestation of this overall pattern has been in the area of agricultural pricing policies. By and large, the pricing policies of African nations offer rural producers a high return for the cultivation of exportable commodities whether these are grown on a plantation or small-holder basis. This has, over time, encouraged a shift in land-use patterns away from food crops to export items, a tendency which further reinforces and exacerbates the discrepancy between food crop production and export crop yields. Although governments do skim off a certain proportion of the world market price of export crops as tax revenue, usually through national marketing boards, this policy is not often pressed to the point where it interferes with the affluence and prosperity of cash-crop farmers. This group has, as a result, emerged increasingly in numerous

African societies as a wealthy capital-accumulating class. The emergent rural gentry is not always of rural origin. Sometimes urban élites – politicians, civil servants, and professionals – are attracted by the prospect of high returns from export crop production, and so invest in farms in cash-cropping areas. This pattern is characteristic, for example, of the Ivory Coast and Kenya. In other nations, prosperous cash-crop farmers use their profits to invest in urban enterprises such as hotels, bars, restaurants, rental property, and taxis. This pattern was prevalent among Uganda coffee-growers before the military coup and is characteristic, today, of Ghanian cocoa farmers and Senegalese groundnut farmers. Whichever pattern occurs, the phenomenon is a reflection of pricing policies which make cash-crop production a lucrative enterprise, and which, by the same token, discourage the more entrepreneurial elements in a society from engaging in food production.

Market prices for food items, on the other hand, have consistently been maintained at relatively low levels. This can be viewed as but one ingredient, albeit an important one, in the overall policy of minimising the income of food producers in order to convert them into a labour supply for the export sector. It is also connected to other economic purposes less immediately germane to this article – for example, the provision of a low-cost urban labour force for commercial and industrial enterprises. A cheap food supply is also connected with the attempt to lessen the likelihood of urban unrest by making it possible for the unemployed and underemployed to survive on minimal levels of cash income. One need only add that urban dwellers generally, even including high-income strata, are interested in paying as little as possible for their food requirements. The irony here, of course, is that shrinking food production in the African countryside, attributable in no small part to the inadequate returns from cultivation, has now forced the townspeople to pay much higher prices for imported food items purchased at world market price levels.

A far less visible manifestation of the policy bias in favour of export cultivation is the willingness of African governments to preserve communal patterns of land ownership in food-raising areas. Communal landholding has taken on something of a sacrosanct quality, both among observers of the African scene and among African governments. Academic fondness for the institution arises, in part, because it seems to symbolise a pure and pristine past, unsullied by colonial or capitalist influences and, in part, because it seems also to betoken a collective spirit which some would hope to see as Africa's future. The nostalgia for traditional collectivism is most boldly articulated by Julius Nyerere in his essay on 'Socialism and Rural Development'.[15] Doubtless, some scholars accept the concept out of admiration for the President of Tanzania. Whatever the origin of the sentiment, it represents nothing more than a crude form of academic populism, and like other political viewpoints which romanticise the past, it provides a convenient protective colouration for repressive economic policies.

The political fact of the matter is that communal land tenure in food-crop areas fits most conveniently into the policies of governments which are disinclined to develop or modernise their food-producing areas. For communal ownership is, to use a somewhat loaded term, a fetter on production. So long as rural land is legally held on a collective basis and no individual has clear title, it is impossible for any person to use this as collateral to obtain a development loan. If there is a single message to be inferred here concerning the politico-economic basis of Africa's contemporary difficulties concerning food production, it has to do with under-capitalisation of the food-producing sector, and with the fact that vested political forces have an interest in perpetuating this situation. Communal landholding serves precisely this purpose in preventing an inflow of development funds into food-growing areas. Unless this pattern of land ownership can be dismantled and replaced with a system of clear title deeds, African food producers will continue to be at a major disadvantage vis-à-vis their counterparts in cash-crop areas who have enjoyed the benefits of freehold tenure for several decades.

Future Implications

The implications of the foregoing analysis are probably already clear but, because of their gravity, may merit brief re-emphasis. Africa's greatest need is to redress the imbalance between food and export crop production. Two immediate steps would help achieve this objective. First, there must be a change in agricultural pricing policies in order to create added incentive for food crop production.[16] Significantly, some countries have already begun to move in this direction. Tanzania, for example, has raised the internal market prices for certain grains by 25 to 50 per cent; it is indicative of the extent to which these had been under-priced previously that the new prices are only about two-thirds of world market levels. A second step is the introduction of freehold tenure in food-crop areas. Since the purpose of such a measure is to facilitate the capitalisation of food-producing regions, this would be most efficient if combined with a lending programme to make funds available for land improvement. An integral feature of any scheme of conferring land titles is the principle that individual parcels of land cannot be sub-divided into smaller and smaller units. Such a process would be self-defeating since it would inhibit the introduction of capital-intensive methods of production. It is also integral to such a policy that the more successful farmers be enabled to add to their holdings by purchasing the land of others who may wish to sell.

The establishment of freehold land tenure is a less abrupt departure than might initially appear to be the case. For all of its collectivist symbolism, communal landholding in fact harbours a system of production which, in most cases, is already highly individualistic. Communal tenure generally means nothing more than that no individual possesses the right to alienate land from the community by selling it on the open market. This in no way mitigates against a system of use and appropriation that is already essentially privatised. A doctrine more closely analogous to the legal principle of usufruct governs these activities. An individual or family has the right to hold and cultivate a piece of land, so long as it is used productively, and in ways which do not harm the interests of the community as a whole. While some tasks – for example, the clearing of virgin fields – are done collectively, and parcels of land are sometimes reallocated between families, collective farming as such is exceptional. The basic system of African food production is, even now, one of separate family farms, with each family cultivating its own fields and, aside from specified obligations to the community, appropriating what is grown for its own use. The only missing ingredient is a system of individualised titles which would allow for greater inputs of capital.

Other badly needed measures are more fundamental and, therefore, of a long-range character. These include, for example, the development of a more adequate infrastructure for food-producing regions, and especially, such services as feeder roads, storage facilities, and institutional services to assist in distribution and marketing. the development of an agricultural extension network, which would introduce more technological and scientific methods of cultivation, is also a matter of desperate urgency. Implementation of these suggestions, however, presumes the capacity to confront the economic primacy of the export sector, and the political primacy of the vested interests which support it. Since these are often one and the same with any given country's most eminent politicians, the reform enterprise seems doomed from the start. It is not often in history that social classes act against their own economic interests. . . .

NOTES

1. See, for example, John N. Paden, Lois Godiksen, Hugh H. Smyth, et al., *A Framework for Evaluating Long Term Development Strategies for the Sahel-Sudan Region: socio-political factors in ecological reconstruction.* (Boston, 1974), Sahel-Sudan Project, Center for Policy Alternatives, Massachusetts Institute of Technology.

2. Claude Meillassoux, 'The Sahel Famine', in *Review of African Political Economy* (London), 1974, pp. 27-33.

3. Alan Rake, 'Collapse of African Agriculture', in *African Development* (London), February 1975, pp. 17-19.

4. UN Economic Commission for Africa, *Survey of Economic Conditions in Africa, 1972* (New York, 1973), ch. IV, 'Agriculture', especially pp. 103-05.

5. Edith Hodgkinson, 'Economy' (of Mali), in *Africa South of the Sahara, 1974* (London, 1974), pp. 516-17.

6. *Tanzania Sunday News* (Dar es Salaam), 17 November 1974.

7. *Daily News of Tanzania* (Dar es Salaam), 30 June 1974.

8. Barrington Moore, Jr., *Social Origins of Dictatorship and Democracy* (Boston, 1966).

9. A useful analysis of economic dualism can be found in H. Myint, *The Economics of the Developing Countries* London, 1973), pp. 18-66. For an outstanding discussion of the dual economy in Uganda, Kenya, and Tanzania, see Ann Seidman, *Comparative Development Strategies in East Africa* (Nairobi, 1972), pp. 13-32.

10. Edith Hodgkinson, 'Economy' (of Senegal), in *Africa South of the Sahara, 1974*, p. 681.

11. Ian Livingstone, 'Agriculture in African Economic Development', ibid., pp. 30-32.

12. Ibid., p. 33.

13. Rodolfo Stavenhagen, *Social Classes in Agrarian Societies* (Garden City, 1975).

14. Hans Ruthenberg, *African Agricultural Production Development Policy in Kenya, 1952-1965*, pp. 79-80.

15. Julius K. Nyerere, *Ujamaa: Essays on Socialism* (London, 1968), pp. 106-44.

16. The importance of pricing policy in inducing rural change is emphasised by G. K. Helleiner, 'Agricultural Export Pricing Strategy in Tanzania', in *East African Journal of Rural Development* (Nairobi), 1, 1, January 1968, pp. 1-18.

Africa's Agricultural Crisis: An Overview

Michael F. Lofchie

This paper is from Lofchie et al (eds), Africa's Agrarian Crisis:
The Roots of Famine (*1986*).

An increasing number of African countries cannot feed themselves. In many, domestic food production is inadequate to supply even the minimal needs of growing populations, and earnings from exports are insufficient to permit enough food imports to make up the difference. As a result, starving children have become a universal symbol of deepening economic deterioration. As television documentaries portray a human tragedy of unutterable anguish, World Bank reports provide cold statistical confirmation of the underlying phenomenon, an agricultural breakdown that is now continent-wide and has taken on ever-deepening proportions. Many African countries have suffered a precipitous decline in per capita food production since the 1970s, and, as a result, Africa now imports approximately 10 million tons of grain per year, an amount roughly equivalent to the needs of its entire urban population.[1] With a population growth rate of approximately 3.5 per cent per year (the highest in the developing world), Africa has been able to manage an increase in food production of only about 1.5 per cent per year. In 1980, per capita food production was only about four-fifths of its 1970 level. Africa is the only one of the world's developing areas to have suffered such a decline and skyrocketing food imports during the past five years; this suggests that the problem of agrarian failure may be worsening.

It is impossible to calculate the extent of chronic malnutrition and hunger-related deaths with any precision because there are no continent-wide surveys: most estimates are based on rough calculations within individual countries. But the World Bank estimates that by the end of 1984 as much as 20 per cent of the total population of sub-Saharan Africa was receiving less than the minimum amount of food necessary to sustain health. If correct, this would mean that the total number of severely hungry or malnourished persons may now have reached 100 million.[2]

Because export-oriented agriculture has also been subject to stagnating production, Africa does not produce a sufficient volume of agricultural exports to finance the purchase of minimal food requirements. The gross figures for export agriculture are at least as alarming as those for the food sector. By the end of the 1970s, Africa's marketed volumes of key agricultural exports were no higher than they had been 20 years earlier. This resulted in a sharp drop in the continent's share of the world market for such vital commodities as coffee, tea, cotton, bananas, and oilseeds. Today, it appears extremely unlikely that Africa will be able to recapture its former share of the agricultural world market. There is no indication whatsoever of a significant reversal in production trends. As a result, food aid, once considered a short-term response to momentary episodic events such as drought or political turbulence, has now taken on permanent status as the long-term moral imperative of the world's donor nations.

Human starvation on an appalling scale is only the most visible and dramatic outcome of agrarian decline. Africa has also become a continent of convulsive social and political turbulence that functions as both cause and effect of the agricultural breakdown. As a measure of its extreme instability, Africa, though it has only about 10 per cent of the world's total population, now accounts for at least 25 per cent of its refugee population. Approximately 2.5 million Africans are refugees, and this figure would be even higher if refugees remaining within their own countries were included.

There is a very real sense in which the human toll of agrarian breakdown extends to the entire population of most African countries. African governments, hard-presssed to find currency to sustain food imports, have often been compelled to cut back drastically on public services. The usual result of these cutbacks has been a drastic deterioration in the quality and availability of these services. In some countries, the educational and medical systems are so deprived of vital inputs that they function in name only.

In the political sphere, such endemic phenomena as corruption and repression also appear to be a direct outgrowth of economic decline. Political leaders, intent on maintaining their status and material perquisites in a context of diminishing overall resources, have used any means available to do so. Corruption in Africa also has its structural roots in the financial predicament of middle and upper class élites whose real incomes have been severely eroded by the inflationary process that has accompanied agrarian stagnation. This is most apparent in African societies such as Ghana, Tanzania, and Uganda, where the processes of economic decline are most advanced. In these countries, a civil servant's monthly salary is often inadequate even to finance a family's food requirements, let alone its other expenses, and corruption becomes the only alternative to white collar destitution. But these countries are simply the most extreme examples of economic trends that are, in fact, continent-wide. Political instability is compounded by the fact that corruption and repression inevitably give rise to a larger process of social and political demoralization.

To this degree, Africa's agrarian collapse is at the basis of a widespread breakdown of political legitimacy and a loss of social trust. Governments that cannot provide an adequate supply of reasonably priced foodstuffs to their urban populations have experienced sharp increases in public opposition, manifested most dramatically in the high incidence of food riots in many capital cities. Political demonstrations triggered by food scarcity have occurred, for example, in Cairo, Tunis, Monrovia, Lusaka, Khartoum, and Nairobi. The collapse of at least two of these governments, Liberia and Sudan, was rooted partially in sudden price increases for food staples. The collapse of the imperial government of Ethiopia in 1974 also grew from an agricultural crisis: the regime of Emperor Haile Selassie lost both domestic and international credibility because it could not resolve the problem of food scarcity in drought-stricken regions. Although the widespread loss of public trust in African governments is the outcome of a complex assortment of political and economic factors, none has as direct a bearing on popular attitudes toward government as the effectiveness of national political leaders in managing their countries' food systems.

The deterioration of the agricultural sector has had reverberations that extend to other important economic spheres such as industry and commerce. Africa's industrial sector was built largely on the principle of import substitution and is thus almost wholly dependent upon the foreign exchange earned by agricultural exports to finance the import of raw materials, capital goods, and energy supplies. As agricultural export earnings have sunk, so has the availability of these essential industrial items. In countries that are most seriously affected, the industrial sector is now operating at approximately 25 per cent capacity or less, and, given the numerous other pressures on foreign exchange reserves, it appears that the rate of capacity utilization in industry will only drop further in the foreseeable future. This creates a rapid increase in urban unemployment. In addition, the rapid proliferation of squatter settlements and peri-urban slums has been abetted by the massive influx of rural dwellers who are no longer able to sustain a livelihood in the countryside.

As a result, Africa's cities are increasingly unable to provide economic opportunity for an economically displaced peasantry. With the decline of industrial activity, the rate of urban unemployment has shot upward, and unemployment rates of 40 per cent or more are by no means uncommon. Even countries not so economically distressed, already confront a situation in which the number of school-leavers annually far exceeds the number of new job opportunities. In those countries where agricultural decline is more acute, annual job creation in the modern sector is a negative number. Such economic opportunities as are now available seem almost wholly confined to the informal sector where they provide barely enough income to sustain survival. Thus, the inexorable decline of Africa's agricultural base has also produced a steady widening of the gap between the poor and the well-to-do. Under these conditions, it is difficult to forsee any future other than a continued high incidence of military coups and other forms of political instability coupled with more serious manifestations of urban discontent such as food riots, political demonstrations, and anomic violence.

There is little basis for optimism that these trends can be reversed. Major economic indicators point in the direction of a further worsening of the present situation. During the past decade or so, Africa has become one of the world's major debtor regions, a status that, in itself, seriously complicates the process of economic recovery because of the burden of debt repayment. As late as 1974, the annual cost of debt repayment for the low-income countries of independent sub-Saharan Africa was less than $500 million. By 1984, that figure had climbed to almost $1.4 billion and was rising steadily. During this period, the average debt service ratio (debt repayments as a percentage of foreign exchange earnings from exports and services) for this group of countries increased from approximately 7 per cent to more than 30 per cent, and this figure will grow higher as borrowing from the International Monetary Fund (IMF) expands.[3] In the more serious cases, the debt service ratio is substantially higher, and for Sudan, Africa's most extreme example of debt problems, annual debt service actually exceeds total foreign exchange earnings.[4] Though unique, the predicament of Sudan may actually portend the future since other African countries have already had to reschedule their debt, and many have fallen far behind in their payments on foreign trade accounts.

A large proportion of Africa's foreign exchange earnings are now allotted to non-productive economic purposes. Debt-servicing is high among these but others include the cost of imported food and consumer goods, and energy supplies for nonindustrial or nonagricultural purposes (e.g., gasoline for private automobiles). There is almost no prospect whatsoever that foreign capital inflows will compensate for Africa's inability to invest in itself. For although foreign aid has continued to flow to Africa in generous amounts, it is clear that the continent's economic decline has had a chilling effect on foreign private investment which, outside the Republic of South Africa, has diminished drastically during the past five years. Africa may now have become a net exporter of capital. If the expatriation of capital by political elites interested in securing their personal resources abroad is added to other categories of capital outflow, the total could well exceed the net amount of capital entering the continent.

Contending Explanations

Africa's economic decline has given rise to a burgeoning academic and professional literature that seeks to establish the causes and potential remedies for this decline. Much of this literature ranges along an intellectual continuum that can roughly be described as externalist-internalist in character. Such broad categorization inevitably involves an unfortunate element of oversimplification, since no serious author falls unambiguously into a single analytic position, and the particular mix of causal factors may vary considerably from one country to the next. It does provide, however, a useful point of departure for establishing the enormous range of analytic opinion that currently exists. Broadly speaking, externalists are inclined to place primary emphasis on causal factors outside Africa and, therefore, beyond the jurisdiction of its political systems, while internalists place greater emphasis on the policy failures of African governments.

External factors

Among externalists, there is a tendency to assign primary responsibility for the crisis to salient features of the international economic system including the declining terms of trade for primary agricultural exporters. There is a general consensus among observers of Africa's present economic crisis that the continent has suffered badly because of adverse changes in the international terms of trade and that its current parlous state can be traced in large measure to the fact that the costs of the goods African countries need to import have risen far more rapidly than the price of exported commodities. The most recent research on Africa's terms of trade shows an especially sharp downward trend beginning in 1979. It assesses this decline in the following stark terms:

Between 1980 and 1982, prices of nonoil primary commodities declined by 27 per cent in current dollar terms. The loss of income due to deterioration in the terms of trade was 1.2 per cent of GDP for sub-Saharan Africa; middle-income oil importers suffered the biggest loss (3 per cent of GDP) . . . and low-income countries a loss of 2.4 per cent of GDP.[5]

This trend helps account for the critical scarcity of foreign exchange currently experienced by the overwhelming majority of African states.

For some countries, the potential benefits of increased production have been completely eroded by decreasing prices for their products. Sudan, for example, was able to increase cotton production by about 50 per cent in 1981 and 1982, but, due to a sharp drop in the world market price for this product, its foreign exchange position continued to deteriorate badly. World Bank economists now anticipate a continued fall in the terms of trade throughout the 1980s with price levels for Africa's key exports at least 15–25 per cent lower than those that prevailed in the 1960s.[6] Price declines of this magnitude make it extremely difficult for governments to implement policy reforms, such as price increases, to improve production. An increase in domestic producer prices could result easily in enormous budget deficits if the world market price of that particular commodity were to drop further. Externalists believe that the critics of African governments generally fail to distinguish between poor pricing policies and the depressed levels of primary agricultural commodities on world markets. They argue, as well, that the drop in foreign exchange reserves resulting from falling prices has constrained the implementation of infrastructural improvements intended to facilitate increased exports.

The scarcity of foreign exchange is compounded by another salient feature of the international economic system; namely, the markedly low demand elasticities for Africa's key agricultural commodities. World demand for such critically important agricultural exports as coffee and cocoa has been virtually static for the past decade or more and is generally expected to remain so for the remainder of this century. The World Bank's study of anticipated demand for Africa's principal agricultural exports over the next decade presents a particularly gloomy picture, suggesting that world consumption of the majority of these products will increase by only about 3 per cent or less for the foreseeable future.[7] For such critical commodities as coffee, tea, and cocoa, overproduction combined with sluggish demand growth could well result in a further downward trend of commodity prices, thus accentuating the already severe foreign exchange constraint. Of all Africa's agricultural exports, only palm oil is expected to benefit from a growth in international demand approaching 5 per cent per year. Ironically, due to the collapse of Nigerian palm oil production, most of this increase in demand will probably be satisfied by non-African producers.

These trends would appear to rule out almost entirely the feasibility of a development process based on the strategy of export-led growth. As agricultural exporters, African countries do not have the option of stimulating world demand for their products by cutting prices. In sharp contrast to world demand for industrial goods or manufactured consumer products, world consumption of Africa's most important agricultural commodities rises very sluggishly in response to falling prices. This means that African countries as a whole cannot compensate for low price levels by increasing the volume of agricultural goods they market. Although any given agricultural exporter could potentially expand its market share by lowering prices, its increased volume of exports would necessarily occur at the expense of other countries dealing in the same commodity. Export-led growth is not a development strategy available to African nations in general; it is a competitive market tactic available to individual producers.

Recent adverse trends in the international terms of trade give every indication of being long-term in character. The downward pressure on price levels for African agricultural goods has been further reinforced by the introduction of a number of synthetic products that substitute cheaply for natural items and, thereby, compete with them in the international marketplace: synthetic rubber for natural, soft drinks for coffee and tea, artificial chocolate for cocoa, non-caloric sweeteners for natural sugar, dacron and polyester fabric for cotton, etc. The impact of multinational corporations on Africa's agricultural trade is also a topic much deserving of further exploration. It seems clear that the companies that buy and sell agricultural commodities in world markets are in a far stronger position to take advantage of the potential profitability of these products than the producer countries, and that their interest in profit maximization is also a significant factor exerting downward pressure on producer prices.[8]

The economic future of African countries will be a direct function of their earnings from agricultural exports. As small nations with limited internal markets, they have almost no prospect of developing diversified and internally self-sufficient economic systems. The harsh reality of today's international economic system is such that there is almost no prospect whatsoever that their foreign earnings from agricultural exports will increase appreciably. Instead, there is far greater likelihood that the majority of countries will be compelled by circumstances beyond their control to make do with lower and lower levels of export revenues.

African countries have also been buffeted by a host of other external shocks. These include, for example, the precipitous increase since 1973 in the price of petroleum, an escalation that has drastically increased the cost of agricultural production since so many agricultural inputs are petroleum derivatives. A rapidly growing tendency toward administered protectionism by the world's advanced industrial societies also has been harmful. This policy discourages incipient efforts toward industrialization based on export-processing.[9] Adding to the list of external factors that have suppressed African economic growth is the overvaluation of the US dollar, which has created innumerable economic difficulties. It has severely compounded the difficulty of debt repayment, for example, since international loans are typically denominated in US dollars and has contributed indirectly to the steep increases in petroleum costs since trade in this commodity is also conducted in US dollars. Overvaluation has also increased the cost of a host of critically important consumer goods such as educational and medical supplies as well as vital agricultural and industrial inputs.

This inventory of adverse international circumstances could be compounded still further by taking into account the effects of the current global recession and high interest rates on hard currencies. Economic recession in industrial nations, for example, has contributed directly to sluggish demand for Africa's agricultural exports. High interest rates have not only driven up production costs but put still further pressure on foreign exchange reserves by adding to the cost of loan repayments. The major point, however, seems well established and not in need of additional argument. Taken together, these external factors add up to a strong case that African countries have had to confront a deeply inhospitable international environment, one that would have created critical economic difficulties even under the best internal management conditions.

Internal factors

Authors who emphasize the internal sources of agricultural decay are inclined to attach greater importance to the economic policies pursued since independence by African states. Chief among these is the continent-wide tendency to control and suppress agricultural producer prices. . . . Robert Bates has made this policy central to his analysis of Africa's agricultural crisis. In his classic study, *Markets and States in Tropical Africa*, for example, Bates notes that 'the producers of cash crops for export . . . have been subject to a pricing policy that reduces the prices they receive to a level well below world market prices.'[10] John C. de Wilde has commented as well on the extent to which African farmers have been burdened by governmental interventions in agricultural markets.

> The prices that farmers receive for their produce or that they pay for necessary production inputs and consumer goods have been significantly affected, not only by direct and deliberate price fixing but also indirectly by the cost and efficiency of parastatal organizations charged with the promotion of production, . . . by direct and indirect taxation of farm income, by differential exchange rates and by the maintenance of unrealistically high foreign exchange rates. Increasingly, too, the inflation engendered by government deficits . . . has impaired the ability to maintain adequate farm prices in real terms and caused serious delays in paying farmers for their products.[11]

Africa's agricultural crisis is continent-wide, but it occurs within individual countries and takes place on a country-by-country basis. Within any given African country, faltering agricultural production can be explained in large part by government policies that significantly reduce the incentives to agricultural producers.

The policy of price suppression is rooted in a variety of objectives including the desire to maintain a low-cost food supply for the cities and the belief that agricultural exports should generate an economic surplus adequate to finance the development of an industrial sector and the growth of important public services. It now seems clear that this policy has had effects that are precisely the opposite from those intended. It has become a major factor in accounting for the stagnation of Africa's agricultural exports. The disincentive posed by low food prices has severely constrained the available supplies of marketed food staples. Indeed, suppression of agricultural producer prices may well be the single most important factor in accounting for the sharp decline of Africa's share of world trade in agricultural commodities relative to other developing areas and for the skyrocketing increase of food imports.

A second major policy with adverse effects on agricultural productivity has been the ubiquitous tendency toward currency overvaluation.[12] The effects of this policy have been more severe in Africa's anglophone countries whose currencies are not tied directly to that of a major European power, but it occurs even in the francophone nations whose currency is tied officially and directly to the French franc. Currency overvaluation operates as a hidden tax on the financial return to the producers of export goods and thus has precisely the same effect on agricultural exports as the suppression of producer prices. It also depresses the availability of marketed food staples for local consumption. By artificially cheapening the cost of importing foods, it sets up an unfair competition with domestic food producers. The broad impact of currency overvaluation is to subsidize the cost of living of urban consumers at the expense of rural dwellers.

The widespread use of parastatal corporations also has had a substantial and deleterious effect on Africa's agricultural sector. Africa's parastatals are characterized almost everywhere by destructive levels of corruption, inefficiency, and mismanagement. In some cases, the expenses of the parastatal corporations are actually higher than their returns from crop sales, leaving no margin whatsoever with which to pay the producers. The result has been a consistent and growing tendency toward nonpayment, late payment, or partial payment of farmers, a major disincentive in and of itself to the production of marketed agricultural surpluses. In a number of African countries, agricultural parastatals also are given responsibility for the implementation of key agricultural services such as the provision of fertilizers and pesticides, and here, too, the record of parastatal performance is, with rare exceptions, a uniformly poor one.

A poor choice of development strategies has also contributed to the present crisis. Some observers feel that the decision to pursue a policy of industrialization through import substitution, for example, may be held at least partially accountable for the continent's deteriorating agricultural performance. This policy has sapped away capital and other resources that might otherwise have gone into financing needed agricultural improvements. Michael Roemer, for example, has criticized import-substitution strategies in Africa because 'they focus development efforts on industrialization although it is agriculture that remains the base of the economy and that employs the great majority of workers.'[13] One of the factors that has undermined Africa's position in world agricultural trade has been its inability to respond flexibly to changing market conditions by introducing new, high demand crops or more productive varieties of old ones. This rigidity seems rooted largely in the scarcity of capital for agricultural reinvestment, and this scarcity is fundamentally the product of an industrial policy that is not oriented toward the generation of its own sources of foreign exchange.

Industrialization by import substitution has also required high levels of tariff protection for the new industries, and this, in turn, has meant that Africa's farmers have been confronted with extremely high prices for consumer goods and for the agricultural inputs manufactured in the new industries.[14] Moreover, in many cases Africa's new industries have been marked by inefficient management, and this has sometimes resulted in severe scarcities of essential agricultural inputs. Urban industries also affect agricultural performance by competing in the same labor market; by bidding up the wage levels, they can contribute to a labor bottleneck in the countryside.

The Donor Impact
In the broad dialogue between externalists and internalists, the impact of donor policies often is omitted, for the donor community operates in the interstices between the international economic system and the agricultural policies of host governments. The omission is regrettable since the international donor community is a vitally important actor in Africa's economic affairs, and donor policies often have an extremely significant effect on the process of African development. This is nowhere more conspicuous than in the rural sector where the influence of donor agencies is sometimes so strong that it can have a determinative effect on agricultural trends. It is clear that certain policies pursued by members of the donor community have played an important part in worsening Africa's agricultural crisis.

Tempting as it has been to some to conceptualize the international dimension of development in Manichean terms that define the key actors in relation to good and evil, this viewpoint adds little to an understanding of the complexity of the African rual sector. Although it might be morally comforting to believe that the process of agricultural decline could be arrested by removing the villains from the scene, this view has little basis in political reality. In the real world of African development, the rural policies of donor-actors are generally well-intentioned, and no small part of Africa's current tragedy lies in the fact that well-intentioned policies may generate unexpectedly negative effects. The discovery of workable solutions to Africa's agricultural crisis involves far more than a change of heart on the part of the donor agencies.

The rural policies of Africa's international donor community can be viewed usefully in historical terms. They arise as a response to the problem of development as it is construed at a particular moment. The projects that are set in place by donor-actors then quickly become an integral part of the rural landscape which is then transformed because of their presence. This injects an almost dialectical quality into the process of rural development. Thus, as donor policies trigger a process of rural transformation, the problem of rural development is altered and takes on a new configuration. The new set of conditions then calls for a different set of policies and programs. It may be useful to illustrate this highly abstract formulation by referring specifically to donor policies in postindependence Africa. This would help to place the question of donor policy in broader perspective and, thereby, illuminate the ever-changing nature of the interaction over time between donor agencies and the African milieu in which they operate. More specifically, it may help to show how donor policies that are intended to help promote rural development can become part of the problem of the agricultural sector.

Although Africa's agricultural crisis has reached epochal proportions only during the last dozen or so years, its initial symptoms were clearly visible in the decade immediately following independence. Africa had become a net food importer as early as the 1960s, but, at that time, the problem was not identified as one of major structural weaknesses in the agricultural sector. Not only were Africa's key agricultural exports still enjoying a robust performance in the wake of the post-Korean War commodities boom, but the volume of food imports was relatively low and did not pose a serious financial burden. Since grain prices on world markets were both cheap and stable, and since it was increasingly possible to obtain food assistance on concessional terms, the need for food imports appeared to be an easily manageable problem, one well within the financial capacity of the countries concerned. Even though the volume of food imports had doubled by the end of the decade, the most intensely debated questions about development did not focus on agriculture at all but rather on the best means of achieving urban industrial growth.

From the standpoint of international donors interested in rural development, the critical problem was how to improve the productivity of the food-producing sector so that food imports would not continue to be a drain on financial reserves needed for industrialization. The principal constraint on this improvement as identified by these agencies was the absence of agronomic or technological development among peasant food-producers. In the economic argot of the era, food production was a 'backward' sector. It is not at all difficult to understand why development experts adopted this point of view. Africa's colonial governments had generally pursued a set of agricultural policies that were designed to promote the production of exportable crops and that often did so at the expense of the food-producing regions. In many instances, export agriculture was assigned the best quality arable land, often on highly favourable terms, and was generously subsidized with physical infrastructure, extension services, and marketing assistance. Colonial governments also employed a variety of tax, trade, and labor policies to maximize the growth of the export sector.

Food production, by contrast, had generally been neglected during the colonial era. In contrast with export agriculture, for example, the food-producing areas had been systematically deprived of vital inputs such as extension services or improved infrastructural facilities. Food staples were generally produced on small-scale peasant farms that had changed little, if at all, during colonialism. The dominant technology was the hand-held hoe, and even animal-drawn cultivation was relatively rare. Land tenure was typically communal in character, and this, too, was used by colonial administrations to constrain development since land that was held in this fashion was considered unacceptable as collateral for loans to finance farm improvements. Indeed, the very same policies that had contributed to the prosperity of the export farms were often the source of backwardness among food-producing farmers. Producer prices for staple foods, for example, were set often at unrealistically low levels so that peasant food-growers would have to make their labor available in the export sector. As a result of these policies, the most conspicuous feature of African agriculture when independence occurred was the glaring discrepancy between the modernity of export agriculture and the almost completely undeveloped state of the food-growing regions.

The challenge of rural development, as perceived by innumerable professional experts and academic observers, was to complete the diffusion of modern agricultural practices throughout the countryside so that food production could keep pace with rising national needs. The policy chosen to achieve this goal was the creation of large-scale farms that could demonstrate scientific agriculture and the beneficial cost/benefit equations associated with advanced agricultural practices. This strategy for rural development has generally been called the 'project approach,' and its hallmark characteristic is intensive research in such areas as new methods of husbandry, the development of new high yielding seed varieties, and the most economic methods of implementing these improvements at the level of the individual producer.[15] The operative idea underlying this strategy was that once peasant farmers had been made aware of the benefits to be derived from agricultural innovation, their traditional resistance to change would be overcome, and sweeping improvements in the process of food production would take place.

The project approach did achieve a few dramatic successes.[16] But as a general policy, it not only failed by a wide margin to attain the ambitious goals its proponents had claimed, it may even have contributed measurably to a worsening of economic conditions in the countryside. It is clear, for example, that the project approach rested on a highly questionable assumption about the nature of the African peasantry; namely that peasant cultural conservatism was the principal obstacle to agrarian innovation. Today, observers of the African rural scene are virtually unanimous in their conviction that African peasants are not bound by cultural constraints; that they respond with alacrity to economic opportunity; and that when financial incentives are present, their production for the marketplace increases accordingly.

The project approach failed to diffuse improved agricultural methods for reasons that had little, if anything, to do with peasant cultural proclivities for traditional agricultural methods. Basically, it did not address inherited systems of producer pricing that left the vast majority of farm families with only the most meager cash incomes. As a result of these pricing systems, Africa's peasant farmers were simply in no position to take advantage of higher cost agricultural methods. The only real beneficiaries **were governmental** elites who were in a position to invest in large-scale farms and to take advantage of the opportunities for patronage and corruption that the projects made available.

The project strategy not only failed to diffuse new methods of production to the food-producing areas, it may even have contributed to the problem of declining per capita food production. Food crops grown on heavily subsidized demonstration farms sometimes competed on the market with those grown by peasant producers, and this probably contributed to low price levels that drove marginal producers off the land. In addition, the demonstration projects were so expensive to maintain that, once donor support was withdrawn, African governments were almost invariably forced to abandon them, though not before some had expended invaluable personnel and financial resources in vain efforts to maintain donor goodwill by keeping the projects alive. By the early 1970s, the African countryside was littered with the debris of failed agricultural projects. The costs of this policy, in financial and human terms, have never been fully calculated. But Africa's donor community in the aggregate must certainly have spent hundreds of millions of dollars on projects that had little realistic prospect of success and in so doing, diverted comparable amounts of scarce local resources into failed ventures.

Large-scale, capital-intensive projects are also vulnerable to criticism on ecological grounds. There is serious concern about the environmental impact of temperate zone agricultural technologies when these are transferred to tropical regions. Systems of cultivation which require that large areas of land be cleared of their original cover of forest and perennial grasses and which replace indigenous farming systems that involved mixed cropping and long fallow periods are highly destructive of tropical ecosystems. The annual harvesting of large areas of land leaves the harvested acreage exposed to the elements during the off-season and, thereby, contributes directly to the degradation of the soil base, making it progressively less suitable for agricultural purposes. This point was put most succinctly by Erik Eckholm in his study of global environmental problems:

> [In the tropical regions] the soil is less a nutrient source than a mechanical support for plant life which constitutes an almost closed cycle of growth and decay. When the land is stripped of its dense cover, the soil temperature soars under the intense equatorial sun, hastening biological activity and the deterioration of remaining organic matter. Torrential downpours, sometimes bringing six to eight inches of rain in a single day, wash away the thin topsoil and leach the scant nutrients it holds downward, beyond the reach of crop roots.[17]

This description of the human origins of desertification has direct relevance to vast regions of western Africa, where, it is now estimated, the Sahara Desert may be moving southwards at a rate of several miles per year. Indications of the same problem can also be identified in eastern and southern Africa where such processes as soil erosion, nutrient-leaching, and laterization can be traced to the introduction of environmentally inappropriate cropping systems. There is also reason to believe that drought itself partly originates in changing patterns of human land use, particularly in areas where new forms of agricultural production have involved the massive stripping away of the earth's green cover.

Despite its shortcomings, the project approach has remained extremely popular with the donor community, and even today it remains a cornerstone of donor strategy for developing the African countryside. The donor nations' reluctance to abandon the project orientation may be explained partially by the fact that it retains a certain amount of popularity among African governments that welcome the vast inpouring of resources it makes available and the opportunities for patronage it creates at the local level. The donors' preference for large projects may also reflect the bureaucratic character of some of the donor agencies. Like other large-scale governmental bureaucracies, the donor organizations are often committed by their budget cycles to the expenditure of very large sums of money within very short periods of time, and they therefore frequently find it administratively impractical to fund numerous small-scale projects. There is clearly a continuing belief among many donor experts that the principal reason for the failure of the project strategy lies not in its intrinsic unsuitability, but, rather, in the cultural and educational inadequacy of the African peasantry.

It is clear that a decade of post-1974 famine development efforts based on the project model have done little, if anything, to prepare West Africa's agricultural systems for the effects of a period of climatic irregularity. Neither the innumerable large-scale projects that have been set in place nor the extensive programs of agricultural training and extension services that were developed to go along with them provided any cushioning whatsoever in the region's food producing capacity. As a result, when drought occurred, only massive programs of grain relief were able to limit the extent of human starvation. The famine of the 1980s is a watershed in the history of western approaches to African agricultural development. It has provided dramatic and incontrovertible evidence of the failure of the project approach. Indeed, if any single event could be said to have initiated a rethinking of the process of agrarian improvement and the possible contribution of western donors to that process, that event must surely be this famine. It also has altered substantially the present policy environment as it affects the African rural sector.

Conclusion: The Policy Environment in the 1980s
The single most influential example of the new research has been the World Bank report entitled *Accelerated Development in Sub-Saharan Africa: An Agenda for Action*, sometimes referred to as the 'Berg Report' after its principal author, Professor Elliot Berg. This report represents a fundamental shift away from the project approach that dominated donor approaches to rural development throughout the 1960s and 1970s. It explicitly rejects the notion that improved agricultural productivity can be achieved through the diffusion of practices and

techniques developed on large-scale, capital-intensive government farms. Whereas the project orientation was undergirded by a set of attitudes toward the African peasantry that bordered on the contemptuous, the Berg Report sees the African smallholder class in deeply admiring terms as the essential basis for any workable strategy of agricultural recovery. It states, for example, that 'all the evidence points to the fact that smallholders are outstanding managers of their own resources – their land and capital, fertilizer and water.'[18] The Report is unqualified in its insistence that African farmers already possess the requisite knowledge and agronomic skills to achieve both greater food output and a larger volume of agricultural production for export.

The most important feature of the Berg Report, however, is its unremitting antistatist position. Whereas the project orientation was based on the premise that African governments would have to play a major role in the dissemination of innovative agricultural practices, as well as in providing the proper climate for overall economic growth, the Berg Report is fundamentally committed to the proposition that the free market provides the most efficient stimulus to economic progress. Its analysis of the root causes of Africa's agricultural decline is decidedly internalist in character and its key arguments are strikingly similar, in many essential respects, to those of Robert Bates, noted above. The core argument, in a nutshell, is that African governments have pursued a set of policies that, taken cumulatively, represent a systematic bias against the agricultural sector. The effect of these policies has been to lower drastically the incentives for agricultural producers, and, thereby, to contribute directly to stagnating agricultural production, both of domestic food items and of export crops. The solution to Africa's agricultural conundrum is to constrain the role of the state as much as possible and to allow the free market to allocate resources and to set agricultural prices.

The importance of the Berg Report lies not so much in its content as in its impact on Africa's donor community. Its intellectual influence has been astonishing and now extends far beyond the World Bank to encompass a very large proportion of the national and international donor organizations that operate within African countries. Within the brief space of a few years, nearly all of Africa's major donors have sought ways to introduce approaches to rural development that combine the project orientation with the forces of the free market and the potential for greater productivity of the individual peasant farmer. A large number of donor governments and agencies now insist that African governments shift their own policies to allow greater scope for market forces as a condition of further assistance.

The donor community's heightened reliance on the market mechanism is nowhere clearer than in the conditionality practiced by the International Monerary Fund (IMF): it tends to insist that policy reforms of the sort advocated by Berg be implemented as a condition of financial assistance. Supporters of the IMF defend its conditionality on the basis that it is not a development organization but, rather, a lending institution whose principal interest is economic stabilization. Its role as a provider of capital to low-income

African countries has today become so great, however, that this distinction is difficult, if not impossible, to sustain. The policy reforms it attaches to its loans have a vital and direct bearing on the patterns of development that are occurring in a number of African countries.

One example of the IMF's impact is treated in detail in . . . Biswapriya Sanyal's essay 'Rural Development and Economic Stabilization: Can They Be Attained Simultaneously?'[19] . . . . Sanyal's findings [show] that the free market reforms insisted upon by the IMF did not generally produce the results intended: the evidence tends to show that the socioeconomic changes that took place were adverse to increased productivity on the part of smallholder farmers. IMF conditionality did not promote an increase of national investment in agriculture but, rather, led to a continuation of past investment policies that had concentrated the nation's capital in the mining industry. Nor did implementation of IMF reforms shift the internal terms of trade back toward the countryside and against the urban areas. Indeed, Sanyal's evidence shows unmistakably that the more distant smallholders were in substantially poorer circumstances after the implementation of the economic reforms than they had been previously. Although it might be premature to reach broad conclusions on the basis of a single case study, Sanyal's essay suggests strongly that the free market approach to African rural development merits more intensive scrutiny before its unbridled imposition on the African countryside.

In medical circles, there is an aphorism to the effect that a doctor who is not absolutely certain that the available cures will improve the patient ought to refrain from prescribing any treatment whatsoever. This advice, however sound in doctor-patient relations, does not seem at all realistic when applied to the interactions between donor and recipient nations in Africa. For twenty-five years, western and African nations have been mutually involved in a variety of aid relationships. These relationships seem destined to continue in one form or another for the foreseeable future. On the basis of past performance, however, there is little evidence to suggest that these relationships hold any significant promise of helping the continent to solve its agrarian crisis or the all-pervasive human starvation that this crisis entails. If future aid programs contribute as little to solving Africa's agricultural crisis as those that have been in place since independence, then the prognosis for Africa's human future is so unspeakably dim that it may be appropriate after all to consider the wisdom of the medical metaphor.

NOTES AND REFERENCES

1. The figures here are taken from the World Bank report, *Toward Sustained Development in Sub-Saharan Africa: A Joint Program of Action* (Washington, D.C.: World Bank, 1984). See esp. pp. 1-3, 9-14, and 21-22.

2. ibid., p. 9.

3. *Coping With External Debt in the 1980s* (Washington, D.C.: World Bank, 1985), pp. 6-7.

4. *Towards Sustained Development*, p. 13.

5. ibid., pp. 11-12.

6. *Sub-Saharan Africa: Progress Report on Development Prospects and Programs* (Washington, D.C.: World Bank, 1983), pp. 3-4.

7. *Coping With External Debt*, p. 8.

8. For a full account of this issue, see Barbara Dinham and Colin Hines, *Agribusiness in Africa* (London: Earth Resources Research Ltd., 1983). Also, Mohamed S. Halfani and Jonathan Barker, 'Agribusiness and Agrarian Change,' in Jonathan Barker, (ed.), *The Politics of Agriculture in Tropical Africa* (Beverly Hills: Sage, 1984), chapter 3.

9. For a full account, see *The Political Structure of the New Protectionism* (Washington, D.C.: World Bank Staff Working Paper No. 471, 1981).

10. Robert Bates, *Markets and States in Tropical Africa* (Berkeley and Los Angeles: University of California, 1981), p. 28.

11. John C. de Wilde, *Agriculture, Marketing and Pricing in Sub-Saharan Africa* (Los Angeles: African Studies Center and Crossroads Press, 1984), p. 118.

12. For an excellent survey of the relationship between currency exchange rates and performance of the agricultural sector in Africa, see Delphin G. Rwegasira, 'Exchange Rates and the Management of the External Sector,' *The Journal of Modern African Studies*, vol. 22 (September 1984), pp. 451-467.

13. Michael Roemer, 'Economic Development in Africa: Performance Since Independence, and a Strategy for the Future,' in *Daedalus* (Spring 1982), p. 132.

14. For an excellent discussion of the burden of industrial policy on Africa's agricultural sector, see chapter 4 in Bates, *Markets and States*, pp. 62-77.

15. For a discussion of the project strategy, see de Wilde, *Agriculture, Marketing and Pricing*, pp. 1-3.

16. The most widely cited of these is the case of hybrid maize in Kenya that during the late 1960s and early 1970s was widely adopted by peasant farmers and resulted in a production increase of between 50 and 100 per cent, enough to keep pace with that country's population increase for approximately a decade.

17. Erik P. Eckholm, *Losing Ground: Environmental Stress and World Food Prospects* (New York: Norton, 1976), p. 137. See also Antoon de Vos, *Africa: The Devastated Continent* (The Hague: Dr. W. Junk, 1975).

18. World Bank, *Accelerated Development in Sub-Saharan Africa: An Agenda for Action* (Washington D.C.: IBRD, 1981), p. 35.

19. Biswapriya Sanyal, 'Rural Development and Economic Stabilization: Can They Be Attained Simultaneously?' in Lofchie et al (eds), *Africa's Agrarian Crisis: The Roots of Famine* (Boulder, Colorado: Lynne Riener, 1986).

FURTHER READING

Andrew Storey, 'Food Crops vs Cash Crops in Africa', *Development Review* (Dublin: Trócaire, 1986), pp. 44-57.

Lloyd Timberlake, *Africa in Crisis: The Causes, the Cures of Environmental Bankruptcy*, (International Institute for Environment and Development, 1985). London and Washington D.C.: Earthscan.

Why Poor People Stay Poor

Michael Lipton

This paper appears in John Harris (ed.), Rural Development (1982).

Feed the people! Who then has taken it upon himself to feed the people? It is we, the civil servants, who have taken it upon ourselves to feed the very men who have always fed us and who go on feeding us every day . . . . It can be said that bread, not to mention all other forms of wealth, is produced directly by the people . . . How is it then that this bread is to be found, not in the possession of the people, but in our hands, and that, by a peculiar and artificial process, we have to return it to the people, calculating so much for each person? . . . Must we delude ourselves by saying that the people are poor merely because they have not yet had time to adjust to our civilization, but that, come tomorrow, we shall set about imparting all our knowledge to them, concealing nothing, and that then they will doubtless cease to be poor. . . . Do not all enlightened folk continue to live in the towns – for what they claim to be a very exalted purpose – and to eat in the towns the sustenance which is brought there and for want of which the people are dying? And these are the circumstances in which we have suddenly started to assure ourselves and everyone else that we are very sorry for the people and that we want to save them from their wretched plight, a plight for which we ourselves are responsible and which is indeed necessary to us. Here is the cause of the futility of the efforts made by those who, without changing their relationship with the people, wish to come to their help by distributing the riches which have been taken from them.

> Leo Tolstoy in a booklet on the famine in Russia in 1893.
> Quoted in Pienne Spitz, 'Silent violence: famine and inequality',
> *Revue Internationale des Sciences Sociales*, Vol. XXX (1978), No. 4.

Introduction: The Urban Bias Argument

In essence, the urban bias hypothesis is that the main reason why poor people stay poor in developing countries is as follows. Small, interlocking urban élites – comprising mainly businessmen, politicians, bureaucrats, trade-union leaders and a supporting staff of professionals, academics and intellectuals – can in a modern state substantially control the distribution of resources. In the great majority of developing countries, such urban élites spearheaded the fight against the colonizing power. Partly for this reason the urban élites formed, and have since dominated, the institutions of independence – government, political parties, law, civil service, trade unions, education, business organizations, and

*This quotation has been added by the Editors.

124

many more. But the power of the urban élite, in a modern state, is determined, not by its economic role alone, but by its capacity to organize, centralize and control. Hence urban power in developing countries – by comparison with early modern development in England in 1740-1820, or somewhat later in continental Europe – has been out of all proportion to the urban share in either population or production. Rural people, while much more numerous than urban people, are also much more dispersed, poor, inarticulate and unorganized. That does not make them quiescent, but it does diffuse their conflicts. On the whole, rural groups fight each other locally; nationally they seek to join or to use urban power and income, not to seize that power and income for the rural sector.

Consequently, the natural operation of personal and group self-interest has led in almost all developing countries to far wider disparities between urban living standards – themselves highly unequal – and rural living standards than prevailed in Northwest Europe, Japan, or the USA during their periods of early modern development. Resources – investment, doctors, teachers, clean water – are allocated between city and country in ways not merely inequitable but also inefficient. Not only could large amounts of resources, typically distributed, do much more to help poor people if shifted from city to village, because the city starts much less poor and more internally unequal: the equity point; but in most poor countries it is also demonstrable that such a shift – of doctors, public investment, cash – actually generates more results (more saved lives, more returns to investment) in rural than in urban areas: the efficiency point.

So it is not a case of efficiency versus equity, but of both versus power. The actions of the powerful, in almost all developing countries, have shifted income-per-person – inefficiencies and inequities notwithstanding – from rural to urban areas. Agriculture, with 70 per cent of workers and 40-45 per cent of GNP, has in most poor countries received barely 20 per cent of investment – but has, directly and indirectly, been induced or forced to contribute considerably more to saving. Public action renders farm products cheaper and farm purchases dearer, in domestic markets, than they would have been if such action were neutral. Education, while geared towards urban needs, transfers bright rural children to urban areas. (On the whole, however, the scope for rural-urban migration to correct gross rural-urban income disparities has proved very small in Africa and Asia, outside the Middle East.) The urban élite, for all the well-meaning talk of rural development, is in practice driven to concentrate the action heavily on the cities.

This has disappointing effects on employment, growth and poverty – partly because urban growth is increasingly costly and not very employment-intensive; partly because, with capital and skills scarce, urban bias means that largely rural, high-yielding, labour-intensive alternatives and the supporting administration and institutions especially are under-financed or overlooked; and partly because of the limited scope for successful townward migration. Cumulative *public* action to improve urban infrastructure, incentives and institutions – action itself responsive to *private* organization and voice, both far better developed in the towns – renders the movement townwards of yet more *private* capital, skills, and capacities to generate income disparity and to apply political pressure for yet more urban advance relatively to the rural areas.

But the struggle is not hopeless. Fortunately, the internal inconsistencies of urban-biased growth – and its rising cost, intensified by growing scarcities of both energy and aid – strengthen the forces, within state machines as well as among popular protest movements, seeking to reverse urban bias. However, as I will argue shortly, there is no evidence of the required massive switch to rural emphases in the past decade or so.

Before completing this compressed account of how urban bias keeps poor people poor, I must sketch another, equally important, side of the argument. Inequalities *within* rural areas also owe much to the urban-biased nature of development policy. The cities want to receive, preferably cheap, surpluses from the rural areas: surpluses of food; surpluses of savings over rural investment; surpluses of exportables over imports, to provide foreign exchange for industrial development; surpluses of 'human capital', in the shape of rural-born doctors, teachers, engineers and administrators, as children brought up largely at rural expense, but as adults serving largely urban needs. Who, in the rural areas, can provide such surpluses? Clearly, the better-off, especially the big farmers. Provide a small farmer, meeting only half his family food needs, with the extra irrigation, or the improved health, or the educated knowledge, to grow more food, and his family will consume the gains themselves. Provide similar inputs to a large farmer, and the resulting output will be sold – and the receipts, very probably, saved for reinvestment in urban activities. This, too, is inefficient (as well as inequitable), because it is the *small* farmer who saturates each acre, each kilogram of fertilizer, with more effort, and thus grows more output per acre-year than the large farmer.[1] But it is the large farmer who gets most of the goodies. That's the 'urban alliance'. The towns get their cheap surpluses, food, exportables, etc., even if not made very efficiently and equitably. The rural better-off get most of what is going by way of rural investment, price support, subsidies, etc., even if not much of these. The rural poor, though efficient, get mainly pious words, though often sincere ones.

Let me stress that there is no conspiracy afoot. Most of the time, the process and its results involve neither corruption nor dishonesty. The politicians (and the businessmen, labour leaders and academics) who proclaim their attachment to, say, minor irrigation investment and land reform to help the rural poor, but who then somehow end up spending much more on urban roads than pumpsets, while permitting massive evasion of land reform – these people are not being dishonest. They are responding to pressures; and urban pressures (for good roads and cheap food from big farmers) are stronger than rural pressures.

Counter Arguments: Prices and Subsidies

That account is of course oversimplified. Those who wish to decide whether it is right will, I hope, look at the evidence in my book,[2] and judge for themselves. Three sorts of argument have been advanced against the urban bias hypothesis:

that it is wrong; that it is old; and that it has been outdated by corrective, pro-rural pressures and actions.

I can't do justice here to the interesting arguments advanced against the existence of urban bias, but would say only that those who have argued against the hypothesis have some explaining to do. Why, if there is no urban bias, has growth in poor countries since 1945 – very fast growth by historical standards – been consistent with *both* widespread rural-agricultural stagnation (in terms of output-per-person), *and* the failure of prices to move dramatically in favour of agriculture?[3] Why, if there's no urban bias, have the much higher rates of return in many areas on agricultural investment and its rural support in the wake of the 'green revolution', not induced bigger or more massive flows of public and private funds, both into investment in 'green revolution' areas, and into research to make 'green revolutions' possible elsewhere? I shall not, therefore, say more about the view – rather rare and frankly a bit odd – that urban bias as an explanation of persistent poverty, is just wrong or unimportant.

I fully accept, however, a second sort of criticism of the urban bias hypothesis: that it is not new. This I have never claimed for it; indeed I have been at pains to stress its ancestry, including thinkers as diverse as Mahatma Gandhi, Mao Tse-tung, Karl Kautsky, Alfred Marshall, Frantz Fanon, Theodore Schultz – and Alexander Chayanov, whose central contributions I have not, in the past, given their deserved place.

What is worrying – or rather, a sort of temptation to premature relaxation – is the third sort of criticism: that urban bias has been recognized and largely eliminated. I wish this were true. Unfortunately the evidence does not support such a hopeful view. Two examples will suffice: agriculture's share in investment; and the movement of the inter-sectoral terms of trade.

India is unusual, in that the 1970s have seen a rise in the share of agriculture (in the broad sense) in investible resources to about 23–25 per cent, from the 18–20 per cent prevailing in the 1960s. Even in India, such a small change hardly matches the dramatic rise in the relative profitability of agricultural investment in the wake of the high-yielding varieties – let alone the much greater impact on *non*-agricultural costs of higher fossil-fuel prices. These should mean a big shift in India to farm investment, because fossil-fuel forms a much smaller part of Indian farm costs (including fertilizer) than (a) of costs of non-farm production in India, or (b) of the costs of farm production in much more energy-intensive countries from which India buys cotton – or grain, when grain imports again become necessary.

One major reason why India's agricultural investment share has risen so slowly is the decision to use extra food output only to replace imported foodgrains and to build up stocks, rather than to add significantly to the inadequate intake of large sections of the population. The other side of the same coin – to which I return later – is the concentration of access to, and subsidies for, agricultural innovation upon larger farmers. These deliver the extra food for urban consumption, but do not provide much extra demand to encourage much further investment in food-growing: neither direct demand for their family consumption (because, as they already eat enough, they spend the extra 'green revolution' incomes not on extra food, but mainly on urban products, thus increasing urban sales, selling prices, and incomes); nor even, to any great extent, indirect demand by farm employees. Large farmers, after as before the introduction of HYVs [high yielding varieties], put in much less labour-per-acre (which is why they produce rather less output-per-acre than do small farmers). True enough, large farmers hire a larger proportion of the labour they do use, whereas small farmers rely to a greater extent on family labour. But this is cancelled out by the bigger farmer's lower use of total labour – of all sorts – per acre. Especially since much of the bigger farmer's urban efforts go into seeing that politicians divert such resources as do go to rural areas into subsidies for his own labour-replacing innovations – in weedicides, reaper-binders, modern rice mills, the impact on employment, and hence even indirectly on demand for food, of a large-farm-based 'green revolution' has been disappointingly small. So, therefore, is the very modest rise in the farm sector's share of investment.

But India has done better, in correcting the urban-rural balance, than most developing countries. There, as I showed in my book, agriculture's share of total investment lagged far behind its share in output and employment during the 1950s and 1960s and did not show any uptrend. The FAO's *State of Food and Agriculture* (1978 and 1979 vols) showed that no significant increase in agriculture's share of total investment had taken place in the late 1960s or middle 1970s, either, in the great majority of poor countries with available data. (Investment in fertilizer plant, however desirable, is not – unlike irrigation – investment in agriculture, but in industrial production, for import avoidance or replacement.)

What, then of relative prices? In analysing urban bias, we must not claim that it is proved by movements of the terms of trade against farm products – or disproved by the opposite tendency. The movement of the farm-nonfarm terms of trade depends on three things: supply, demand, and changes (publicly or privately induced) in market power and market structure. Much the most important of these three is the movement of agricultural supply, in part due to medium-term trends such as the expansion of output in the wake of HYVs, but in much greater part due to fluctuations. Whether or not (as Irving Fisher believed) the US business cycle was a money-supply-based 'dance of the dollar', most of the year-to-year movement in the terms of trade in South Asia is certainly a rainfall-supply-based dance of the monsoons. Second, and less important, are changes in the demand for farm products: less important as a cause of changes in the far-nonfarm terms of trade, especially in a developing country where farming is dominated by cereal production and consumption, because the demand for food changes much more slowly (either in trends in fluctuation) than does income-per-person, which itself changes much more slowly than does agricultural supply.

The third cause of changes in the terms of trade between agriculture and the rest of the economy lies in changes in actions by government or by private monopoly power, to alter the structure, or size, of supply or demand for farm products. Only such action is relevant to urban bias. Changes in terms of trade between agriculture and non-agriculture could suggest changing urban bias *only* to the extent that they are due to changes in government (or cartel) actions affecting those terms of trade – for example, changing tariffs on non-farm inputs – rather than to exogenous change in demand or supply alone.

The careful recent analysis by Kahlon and Tyagi[4] shows that, since the mid 1960s and right through the 1970s the terms of trade of India's farm sector have usually been worsening. But this tells us little about urban bias. The only way to link terms of trade to urban bias directly is not by looking at 'movement' in those terms – which on its own (apart from depending heavily on the choice of base-year and the type of index-number) is likelier to reflect rainfall-induced components of supply than is government action. Rather it is by asking: if we take a three- or four-year average, and suppose that farmers – instead of exchanging their marketed surplus for non-farm goods at prices affected by non-neutral actions (of the state, and of private monopolies and cartels which are incomparably more important in industry than in agriculture) – were able to exchange at *world prices* the typical bundle of their products, for a typical bundle of their purchases of non-farm products: how much more, or less, of the latter would they have obtained, as compared with transactions actually taking place at national prices?[5] In the late 1960s, S. P. Lewis found that in Pakistan the farmers could have bought about 50 per cent more at border prices than at actual prices. In other words, non-neutral actions to affect the terms of trade were robbing the Pakistani farmer of about one-third of the value of his surplus. I have not seen similar calculations for India, but I should imagine that the degree of surplus extraction from farmers through prices alone was rather more for rice, and rather less for wheat. Probably the depression of farm prices hurts the whole rural sector, including deficit farmers and landless labourers, whose job prospects (and wage rates) suffer when price disincentives depress farm production: in the case of *food* prices, labourers paid in cash (not in food) gain, but it is hard to believe that any substantial rural group can long benefit from the artificial extraction, via price manipulation, of resources out of the farm sector.

We need to be careful about data suggesting that government action is changing farmers' share of the cake. For example, subsidies on fertilizers may be 'subsidies' on a price initially raised by protective tariff, to cover the high costs of domestic production. Or they may be far below comparable subsidies to non-farm inputs. Or they may leak to import licencees, contractors, or other urban middlemen. The usual impact, if the subsidized fertilizer is scarce, is to steer it to bigger farmers, who can more easily run the bureaucratic obstacle course to the subsidized prize. That makes the fertilizer not cheaper, but even scarcer and dearer, for small farmers, while it increases the share of the fertilizers going to surplus farmers, who use it to grow more food, exportables, and raw materials for delivery to the urban sector.

Another example, of the non-obvious impact of government action apparently helpful to farmers, is the large increase in the flow of credit to Indian agriculture, consequent on the shift from co-operative credit to nationalized commercial bank credit. First, this increase must be discounted to allow for inflation, and for the much greater cash input-costs (per acre and per unit of output) implicit in the new seed-fertilizer packages. Second, the increase has gone mainly to better-off farmers, and the share that has reached small farmers may (we do not know) merely have replaced, not supplemented, non-institutional credit. Third, and above all, *deposits* in the Indian banks *by* rural people exceed, and have increased faster than, *loans* by the Indian banks *to* rural people. So the shift of responsibility for Indian rural credit from co-operatives to banks has, on balance, taken credit out of the rural sector, not put credit in.

There have been major improvements in public policy towards Indian agriculture since the mid 1960s, especially in research. Foodgrain self-sufficiency, even if so far only in good years and at low caloric levels, is a big achievement. But we should not be too hasty in assuming that urban bias is dying. Certainly it is alive and well and living in Africa. All the old discredited anti-rural myths of South Asia two decades ago are rampant still in Africa, especially among European 'advisers': the myth of the irrational conservatism of peasants, as opposed to the fact of their rational, income-seeking, risk-averse, but innovative behaviour; the myth of the greater efficiency of large farmers, as opposed to the fact that yields, and returns to capital, are higher on smaller farms with most crops and most technologies; the myth that it is scientific to apply 'Western' and capital-intensive methods to increasingly land-scarce, maintenance-skill-starved, and possibly labour-surplus rural environments; the myth that purely technical agronomic or water or engineering research, conducted in field stations conveniently near the capital city, can yield useful results without economic experimentation in the farmer's field and without feedback from the farmer himself. Small wonder that output-per-worker on the farm, about 75 per cent of the output-per-worker off the farm in Europe during its early development and about 35 per cent now in Asia and Latin America, is only some 20 per cent in Africa now; that farm investment and research in Africa are exceptionally small relative to investment in other sectors, especially in lavish urban infrastructure; and that, unaffected by much serious application of research that really pays the small farmer, African food output per person has fallen quite sharply in the 1970s, contrary to the more hopeful trends in several of the rather less urban-biased environments of Asia.

Four Paths to Reduced Poverty
I have given a brief outline of the urban bias argument, and some reasons for scepticism that the supply of urban bias has decreased. On the other hand, the demand for its major modification is becoming more urgent. There are four possible paths to reduced rural poverty – and rural poverty is the origin of urban poverty, both because the growing army of rural poor seek (at least temporarily) to enter urban life but tend to increase the misery and congestion and excess labour supply on the semi-jobless urban fringe: and because the under-use of the human resources of small farmers and landless labourers prevents the rural sector from generating a lasting, soundly based, efficiently (because labour-intensively)

produced, farm surplus for exchange on fair terms with urban products, and permits only a big-farm surplus, costly because intensive in its use of capital and energy, but (due to inadequate, urban-biased incentives) too small and too unreliable to serve as a firm base for urban growth.

The four paths to reduced rural poverty are: rapid growth plus 'trickle-down'; intra-rural redistribution; urban-to-rural redistribution; or forms of growth specific to the rural poor. As for the first path, *very* rapid growth does trickle down to the *quite* poor. Abundant evidence shows that in several partial 'success stories' of the past two decades, really fast growth has sharply cut the proportion of people below a (constant) poverty line, as workers and small farmers seized their chances. This has happened in big countries – Brazil (after 1970), Nigeria, Kenya, Mexico, Indonesia and Thailand – apart from the 'Gang of Four' (Taiwan, South Korea, Hong Kong, Singapore) so often presented, rather ignorantly, to justify independent free-market capitalism.[6] Also *regions* of rapid growth, such as India's Punjab, Bangladesh's Comilla, and Sri Lanka's Jaffna, show real rural 'trickle-down'. But even rapid growth probably doesn't reach the *very* poor – the 15-20 per cent of South Asians in absolute caloric need. These are landless, assetless, uneducated people; overwhelmingly rural (or rural-based); often ill; often younger siblings in big families with only one earner. They usually can't respond by *working* harder for the crumbs, as they 'trickle-down' from the rapid growth on the rich man's table. Moreover, very rapid growth – the sort that trickles down – is not likely in the oil-less 'NOPEC countries' of Asia and Africa. They are squeezed three ways. OPEC imposes spiralling energy prices; the West's leaders, largely dogmatic monetarists 'high' on redemption by recession, are unlikely to expand imports or aid substantially; and the Soviet bloc, far from poor in wealth or oil, is persistently mean about aid and (in effect) protectionist about Third World exports. 'NOPEC' will do well to achieve even a modest growth in real income-per-person in the next decade.

So abysmal rural poverty is unlikely to be relieved by the first of the four paths, 'trickle-down' from rapid overall growth. What of the second path, redistribution from the rural rich to the rural poor? I remain convinced of the case for radical redistribution of rights in land, and/or individual or joint ownership by the rural poorest of new non-farm assets. However, first, it is not the unnatural wickedness of the kulaks that stops land reform, but the reluctance of the urban, and international, community to finance the compensation loan (to enable the beneficiaries to compensate the landowners), and to forgo the urbanized surpluses that big farmers provide. Second, why should these so-called big farmers – in Asia not mainly the few really rich landowners of Bihar and Hambantota and the Pakistan Punjab, but mainly poor 'kulaks' with four or five acres in Bangladesh or Java or Sri Lanka's Wet Zone – be singled out to have their aspirations reduced? Why should a five-acre farmer be told that he may not aspire to own a radio, but must give his alleged 'excess land' to the rural poor, by a desk-wallah in Delhi, Sussex or Washington, whose annual increment far exceeds the farmer's annual income, and who lives, works or even researches in a complex containing a significant area of sprinkler-irrigated lawn or garden? In any event population growth – and in some cases sales and transfers in anticipation of land reform – are already breaking down some of the large landholdings. I don't want to talk land reform down. It is efficient, because it transfers land to those who use it more labour-intensively, and produce more crops per year, of higher unit value, and with higher yield-per-acre. It is equitable, and in a few places in South Asia (and many in Latin America) it is hard to envisage a cure for rural poverty that does *not* involve the subdivision, among poor labourers and handkerchief-farmers, of large parts of presently underfarmed giant holdings. However, it is really unpersuasive for very wealthy urban people, like us, to lecture five-acre 'kulaks' about their duty to give land to the poor. We had better pay for that transfer ourselves, and not obstruct it (in the interests of maintaining the short-run food and savings surplus that big farmers supply, albeit less efficiently than small farmers could eventually do, to the cities) by laws that are at once evasive and easily evaded.

So, of the four paths to reduce rural poverty, the first two share rather limited prospects, and the trends of the 1980s seem set against them. Economic growth looks unlikely to be fast enough to 'trickle down' very far. Population growth is subdividing rural land and assets, leaving – at least in South Asia – few obvious large concentrations of wealth for redistribution to the poorest; anyway, with urban wealth (and internal inequality) so much greater than rural, and with increasing rural aspirations to the services and treatment that urban people take for granted, I think there will be growing resistance to paternalist *urban* proposals for selective, purely intra-*rural*, redistribution. The landless, the one-acre man and the five-acre man have their conflicts of interest, of course. But I sense, in the air, a feeling that they are beginning to recognize that these conflicts are enormously outweighed by their *shared* interest – in getting better prices, more productive investment, more security, and a larger share of doctors, good teachers, waterproof houses, administrators, and scientific research, out of an urban élite whose wealth and income (and whose advantages over the poor around them) far outweigh, for urban capital and labour and bureaucracy alike, those of most 'big' farmers.

HYVs and the Case for Rural-to-urban Redistribution
So the first two paths won't do. The fourth path – growth via techniques offering special gains to the rural poor – might seem, to us urbanites, an attractive way to avoid the rigours of the third, urban-rural redistribution. One such set of techniques, indeed, may appear to make irrelevant many of these conflicts, intra-rural and rural-urban alike. It is the spread, potential and impact of the high-yielding cereal varieties (HYVs). In ever more areas and crops, the HYVs are transforming rural Asia and much of Latin America (though they remain relatively neglected in most parts of Africa, at least at the level of research in farmers' fields).

Contrary to the published fears of many technologically illiterate social scientists – including me, before I did some overdue homework on the subject – the agronomic features of HYVs render them a potentially ideal innovation for the rural poor.[7] First, these seeds tend to produce what the poor – landless workers and deficit farmers – consume, buy and grow: coarse grains, not very tasty but cheap, and yielding many calories per acre. Second, HYVs attain their high levels of production mainly via extra human effort-per-acre, both directly in harvesting and threshing, and indirectly by raising the attractiveness of water-control and fertilizer application; all this increases both employment and wage rates, yet HYVs do not require costly items of fixed capital that only wealthy farmers can afford. Third, contrary to prevailing mythology, most HYVs – certainly most of those introduced in the last ten years or so – *reduce* risk, because they are better able to thrive despite inadequate or badly-timed water or sunlight, more responsive even to low levels of management and inputs, and better designed to resist (or to tolerate) insect and disease attack. This reduction in risk, too, should be specially helpful to the poorest farmers, because poor people are least able to take risks – and therefore least able to incur costs for seeds and fertilizers if the returns are at all doubtful.

So HYVs look like an ideal example of our 'fourth path': a technology particularly good for the rural poor. Yet it has not worked out quite like that. HYVs, by their contribution to food output, *have* saved many lives, almost all belonging to poor people (the rich eat too much anyway). But all the features of HYVs, listed above as specially favourable to the rural poor, have been somehow frustrated; bigger farmers gained most. In exploring why, we learn how the fourth path to the prevention of rural poverty – the path of poor-specific innovation – is very unlikely to lead to the destination unless the third path, of urban-to-rural resource redistribution, is taken first.

How has each of the three 'pro-poor' features of HYV innovation fared in practice? First, HYVs have indeed raised food output, especially of poor people's foods: coarser varieties of wheat and rice.[8] But, due to the actions of urban-biased nation-states, not much of the extra food has gone to increase poor people's caloric intakes. Instead the extra food has been used mainly to achieve food self-sufficiency – to replace food imports (or even to permit exports), so as to provide foreign exchange for non-food imports, especially imports of oil to nourish the endless 'energy sink' of modern capital-intensive industrial growth. Extra food output has also been used to build up large public stocks; stocks are a sensible but mainly town-orientated precaution against later shortages, and a less 'townish' policy would have helped farmers to store the grain by big advance purchases – thereby (since on-farm stored grain losses are in fact very small) reducing the huge food losses, and saving the huge transport and fuel costs involved in sudden seasonal and 'good year' upsurges of grain flows from farms to centralized grain stores. Moreover, misguided research emphases on cereal varieties with 'high protein' (when what the poor desperately need is calories), and on taste and cooking qualities (sought after mainly by richer consumers and the farmers who sell to them), have directed some research efforts away from the crucial search for high, safe yields of calories-per-acre at fairly low production cost.

What of the second 'pro-poor' feature inherent in HYV technology: the production benefits via extra employment income? Again, urban priorities, and their alliance with surplus farmers' interests, have diverted many of the benefits, this time from owners of labour to owners and hirers of equipment. How splendid it was, in the rural Punjab in the early 1970s to hear the bigger farmers' complaints of 'labour shortage' in the wake of HYVs! This complaint meant that, to get their harvesting and threshing done in time, these farmers had to hire many extra workers – usually poor migrants, often from Eastern UP [Uttar Pradesh] – and to bid up their wages. For a few seasons, the gains from HYVs were substantially shared by the rural poorest, as per the blueprint. But the migrants were not enough; wages, for a while, went really high, and the bigger farmers successfully pressed the urban State for subsidies on labour-replacing equipment – tractors, threshing machines, reaper-binders, even sometimes combine-harvesters: equipment that does little or nothing to raise output but cuts labour-costs and hence employment. Such subsidies were (and are) often hidden – as cheap credit, as special access to foreign exchange, as subsidized fuel or electricity – but their effect remains the same. Today, the rural poor face new threats, of subsidies (or consciously loss-making State provision) for combine-harvesters once more, and for modern rice mills – neither of which, as a rule, is commercially viable in South Asia without such open or concealed help. If governments find it too hard to resist the pressures from big farmers against higher labour-costs, and the linked pressure (for food for big farmers) coming from trade unionists and urban employers – or if States are actually part of these pressures! – then it's surely far better to 'cut labour costs' by supporting or subsidizing extra migration to, or employment in, the affected rural areas, rather than by spending the same money to create a bogus viability for 'unemployment machines'.[9] In any event, urban bias has greatly reduced the employment benefits of HYVs, because labour-replacing forms of irrigation, draught-power, and post-harvest technology – embodied in devices often produced or installed by city people – have been subsidized.

What of the third 'pro-poor' feature of the more recent HYVs: their risk-reducing benefits? If all farmers know about that feature, then the poor (being the most risk-averse) can expect the biggest proportionate gain from it. But education, agricultural extension, and seed and fertilizer distribution are all urban-managed institutions. All are grossly under-financed in most of rural Asia and Africa. Hence it is the better-off rural people who get hold of the few resources available. It is well known that access to education extension and inputs is heavily skewed to the better-off. With these benefits comes the information that alone can inform the farmer about the features and requirements of a new variety. Lacking such information, the small farmer faces very high *subjectively assessed* risks in innovating with a new HYV, even if its objective risk, to those 'in the know', is much lower than that of older varieties. But access to information is planned in the towns, and scarce – and therefore seldom found among poor farmers – in the villages. Of course, once poor farmers see how better-off farmers cut their risks and raise their output with a new variety of (say) wheat, the poor can follow the innovation; but by that time the extra supply of output, due to the better-off early adopters, has glutted local markets and greatly reduced the benefits to the later and poorer innovators.

It looks, then, as if the path to reduced poverty via 'trickle-down' from rapid growth is almost closed to most poor countries in the early 1980s; the path through redistribution of *rural* resources to the rural poor has limited access; and the path through pro-poor technology, as indicated by the experience of the HYVs, can lead to reduced rural poverty only if the path of urban-to-rural redistribution is taken first. Otherwise urban incomes, interests and power are likely to prevent even 'approporiate' techniques from reaching the rural poor.

How can rural-to-urban redistribution of income, assets, or power be achieved? Efficiency and equity both favour it; the existing balance of forces does not. Among factors that can help are the political organization of the rural poor; their capacity to perceive the *main* source of exploitation in the urban sector rather than in, say, landlordism and moneylending; their success in foreign alliances with the rural less-poor to get more and better investments, doctors, schools, etc. for all rural people; the existence even inside the urban-orientated bureaucracies of both public-sector and private-sector organization, of groups (such as the formal MFAL in India) whose career interests are helped by showing substantial benefit to the rural poor; and the growing *internal* inconsistency – in an environment of worsening urban congestion, rising oil prices, and a growing pool of overtly jobless – of a policy that encourages the diversion of outlay to relatively capital-intensive activities located in, or organized from, urban areas.

NOTES*

1. For conclusive recent evidence, see Berry and Cline (1979).

2. Lipton (1977).

3. For recent evidence on India, see Kahlon and Tyagi (1980).

4. ibid.

5. Raisuddin Ahmed, in a recent paper for the International Food Policy Research Institute, argues roughly as follows: in Bangladesh, when rice prices rise 10 per cent, output responds at best by rising 4 per cent; to this, employment responds at best by rising 2 per cent; therefore a 'pure', landless employee – who may well spend 70 per cent of his income on rice – must lose more by the price rise, than he gains from the extra farm employment. While logically correct, this argument rests on doubtful assumptions of partial equilibrium: can urban-rural income transfers, and their secondary (rural) spending, really harm the rural poor in the long term? See Ahmed (1979).

6. All four are in fact highly interventionist and relatively egalitarian, and have been or are heavily protectionist and aid-financed.

7. The abundant evidence for the statements in this paragraph is set out in Lipton (1979). (Readers should note, however, that some of Michael Lipton's assertions here remain controversial. For different interpretations, see Pearse, 1980; Byres, 1981.)

8. Despite recent efforts, the impact on the *poorest* people's foods – root crops, millets, sorghum, maize – remains disappointing. See Lipton (1975).

9. In other words, it is better for income-distribution, if 'the State' insists on alleviating a 'labour shortage', to do so by (say) subsidizing migration – to keep the wage *bill* up, even at the cost of artificially raising labour supply and hence of cutting the wage *rate* – than to encourage replacement of labour (and thus cutting both the wage rate and employment) by subsidizing equipment that saves labour.

*The notes are by John Harriss, editor, *Rural Development*, 1982.

REFERENCES

Ahmed, R. (1979), 'Foodgrain supply, distribution and consumption policies with a dual pricing mechanism: a case study of Bangladesh', IFPRI Research Report 8, May.

Berry, A. and W. Cline (1979), *Agrarian Structure and Productivity in Developing Countries*, Baltimore, Md: Johns Hopkins University Press.

Byres, T. J. (1981), 'The new technology, class formation, and class action in the Indian countryside', *Journal of Peasant Studies*, 8, 4, pp. 405-54.

Kahlon, A. S. and D. Tyagi (1980), 'Inter-sectoral terms of trade', *Economic and Political Weekly*, XV, 52, Review of Agriculture, December.

Lipton, M. (1975), 'Food policy and urban bias', *Food Policy*, 1, 1, November.

Lipton, M. (1977), *Why Poor People Stay Poor: Urban Bias in World Development*, London: Temple-Smith.

Lipton, M. (1979), 'The technology, the system and the poor: the case of the high-yielding varieties', in Institute of Social Studies, *Development of Societies: The Next Twenty-Five Years*, The Hague: Martinus Nijhoff.

Pearse, A. (1980), *Seeds of Plenty, Seeds of Want*, London: Oxford University Press.

Population and Poverty

William W. Murdoch

This reading is from the Introduction and Chapter 1 of the author's The Poverty
of Nations *(1980)*

---

* It has been said that one has only to step into the hordes on Calcutta's
streets to know there is a population problem. But, asked Mamdani,
would one also conclude there was a population problem from
encountering crowds just as large in London? Or, if you prefer, at the
Kennedy Center in Washington? Isn't it mass *poverty*, rather than masses
of people, that strikes with such sickening force in the streets of
Calcutta?

William W. Murdoch, *The Poverty of Nations*,
(Baltimore: The Johns Hopkins University Press, 1980).

[The] modern population explosion is almost entirely a phenomenon of the less
developed countries (LDCs). Their rate of increase *tripled* in thirty years,
reaching 2.4 per cent a year and yielding a doubling time of only twenty-nine
years by 1970. Their population growth in the 1970s was more than three times
faster than that of the rich nations, where population growth rates have declined
in the past thirty years. At present there are roughly 1 billion people in the rich
countries and 3 billion in the poor. Unless dramatic changes occur, by the year
2000 there will be some 6 billion people in the world, of whom about 80 per
cent, or almost 5 billion, will be in the underdeveloped countries – and
population will still be expanding.

Table 1. Demography of rich and poor countries in 1975

	Crude birth rate	Crude death rate	Annual rate of population growth (%)	Population in billions
Developed countries	16.1	9.6	0.7	1.1
Less developed countries (LDCs)	35.9	13.4	2.3	3.0
LDCs excluding China	39.7	15.1	2.5	2.0

Source: U.S. Bureau of the Census, *Current Population Reports,* Special Studies Series P-23, no. 79
(Washington, D.C.: U.S. Bureau of the Census, 1979).

It should not be thought from this account that world population size has
increased smoothly. It has been at times stationary. For example, although
world population doubled in the 1,600 years after Christ, it probably changed
little from A.D. 1 to 1000. At times world population has even declined. . . .

*This quotation has been added by the Editors.

In the face of the modern explosive acceleration in population growth, world food production on average has not only kept up with but surpassed the growth of population. Even in the poor countries, growth in food production has on average equaled or exceeded growth in people.

Unfortunately, the key phrase here is 'on average.' Thus, while food supply in the poor countries during the first half of this century kept pace with population, on average, food production per head in India declined throughout the last five decades of British rule.[1] Although, on average, food production in the developing nations has increased slightly faster than population since 1960, it has lagged behind population in some fifty to sixty of these nations; as a result, huge numbers of people have inadequate and dwindling food supplies. Some estimates have put the number of malnourished people at over 1 billion in 1970, although the most widely accepted estimate is about 460 million. . . .

Table 2. World population growth and doubling times

Date	Population size	Annual growth rate (%)	Doubling time (years)	Factor of increase per century*
8000 B.C.	5-10 million	0.035	2000	—
1650 A.D.	600 million	0.35	200	1.4
1750 A.D.	800 million	0.40	170	1.5
1850 A.D.	1.3 billion	0.50	130	1.7
1950 A.D.	2.5 billion	0.80	87	2.2
1975 A.D.	4.0 billion	1.90	36	6.7
		Other doubling times		
		1.0	69	2.7
		2.0	35	7.4
		2.5	28	12.0
		3.0	23	20.0

*For example, at an annual exponential growth rate of 3 percent a population would increase by twentyfold in 100 years.

Sources: Ansley J. Coale, 'The History of the Human Population,' *Scientific American* 231 (1974): 40-51: John D. Durand, 'Historical Estimates of World Population: An Evaluation,' *Population and Development Review* 3 (1977): 253-96; United Nations, Department of Economic and Social Affairs, *World Population Trends and Policies: 1977 Monitoring Report,* vol. 1 (ST/ESA/SER. A/62), 1979.

The notion of food and population as a race has characterized the public debate and much of the writing on the problem, and it has probably become the standard way in which most of us think about it.[2] Typically, population 'outruns' or 'outstrips' food supply, or food supply 'lags behind' population. Two quotations, from among the myriad available, will serve to illustrate this:

> It is abundantly clear to anybody who has looked at the statistics of
> human population growth and who knows the problems of agriculture
> and what is happening to the environment of our planet, that the race

between population growth and food production has been lost. World food production cannot keep pace with the galloping growth of population.[3]

The way we conceptualize the problem is important because it determines the kind of explanations we seek and the sort of solutions we propose. Thus the idea of a race, which arises quite naturally from a comparison of exponential growth rates, leads us just as naturally to consider food and population as two separate, independent variables, *with separate mechanisms governing the growth of each*. And, while one variable clearly influences the other, we are led nevertheless to think of two different sets of procedures: one demographic, for slowing down population, the other agricultural, for speeding up food production. This separation can be seen clearly in recent analyses of the problem:

> We are being misled by those who say there is a serious food shortage. This is not true; world food production this decade is the greatest in history. *The problem is too many people.*
>
> Our main focus here is on world agriculture. . . . But we consider that the primary issue for the longer-term future is reduction in the rate of growth of world population.[4]

James Echols, recent president of the Population Reference Bureau, suggests that 'without drastic population control measures, high fertility in the less developed countries will overtake food production.'[5]

Agriculturalists striving to increase food production through the development of new strains and other techniques see themselves as providing time during which population experts, using *their* techniques, can struggle to control fertility. Lester Brown views the Green Revolution in cereals as 'a means of buying time, perhaps an additional fifteen years, during which some way might be found to apply the brakes to population growth.'[6]

Pursuit of the race analogy has also led to devastatingly callous recommendations for a solution to the population and food problem. Several observers have concluded that population must win, which is to say that people will lose, because 'We have reached, or nearly reached, the limit of the world's ability to feed even our present numbers adequately.'[7]

Given such a foregone conclusion to the race, it is but a small step of logic to give up on those who are stumbling hopelessly even further behind and to help only those who have some hope of success. Hence we have 'lifeboat ethics,' which seek to make neglect of the poor a moral virtue, and 'triage' policies that help us decide which developing nations do not need help, which we should help, and which we should leave to rot on the battlefield of the fight for survival.[8] And if the connection between the two variables of food and population is extremely simple – 'more food means more babies'[9] – then there is all the more justification for the malign neglect of those who are faltering. According to this view, the problem will be best solved by our withdrawing food and other aid, or at most by giving it selectively to those developing countries that have some hope of solving their population problem.

In my view, the concept of the problem as a race, and the consequent separation of the two variables of population and food, are serious impediments both to understanding the issues and to developing an appropriate solution. On the contrary, it is essential to realize that rapid population growth and inadequate food supply have a *common* origin and a *joint* explanation. . . . the same political, economic, and social machinery both drives rapid population growth and constrains food production. That machinery has created and maintained the *structural poverty of rural populations* in the underdeveloped world. This single phenomenon is the cause of both rapid population growth and inadequate food supplies.

The emphasis on rural poverty is crucial because the rural population is the heart of the problem. In most developing countries, this segment of the population is the largest, the poorest, and has the highest birth rates, so it is the dynamo that drives population growth. Inadequate food supply is obviously an agricultural (rural) problem and . . . the failure of development is basically the failure of agriculture. This is not to say that the basic causes of rural poverty lie solely or even mainly in the countryside, only that the condition of the rural population must be the major focus of our concern.

By 'structural' poverty I mean poverty that is the result of the man-made political and economic framework in which the poor exist. This framework consists of those arrangements and institutions that give rise to and help maintain the present distribution of political and economic power. It includes, for example, the patterns of land ownership, of access to credit, capital, and modern technology, and the form of the relationships between poor and rich nations. The term structural also implies that poverty is *not* the result of poor soils, poor climate, inadequate natural resources, or other physical or biological conditions. . . .

A Theory of Fertility Control
Persistent high fertility in poor nations is the driving force of population growth. Therefore, the crucial task is to understand the fertility behavior of parents: why do they have large families in some circumstances and small families in others? In particular, we need to understand rural parents, for these not only constitute the great majority of parents in poor nations, but they also have larger families than their urban counterparts.

There is a well-developed body of theory attempting to explain the fertility behavior of parents; it has emerged since Notestein proposed the demographic transition theory in 1945.[10] It was known that fertility in the rich nations had declined over the past three-quarters of a century. The demographic transition theory developed in the 1940s and early 1950s explained that decline as a response to an earlier fall in the death rates and to improved economic conditions. Various changes in social structure, including the effects of urbanization and industrialization, were also thought to be important.

The fundamental notion is that family size is largely determined by parents' *motivation*, and that this motivation reflects rational, and broadly economic, decisions (Table 3). Family size is not seen as an accident, as the expression of religious beliefs, or as a result of the availability of birth control technology, although family planning can certainly affect family size.

The crux of the theory is that parents balance economic benefits against economic costs in deciding whether to have another child, especially a fourth or later child (The first two or three births do not cause population growth, and our concern is therefore with the extra children that characterize families in the developing nations.) The theory assumes that the benefit/cost ratio for extra children is high for poor families in poor societies and that this motivates poor parents to have large families. It assumes that as circumstances change and the economic welfare of families improves, the balance of costs and benefits also changes; costs come to exceed benefits and parents become motivated against having these extra children. Thus, as the level of economic well-being increases, the rationale and motivation for large families disappear.

The theory assumes three types of benefits:

1. 'Consumption benefit.' The child is wanted for itself, for the pleasure and emotional satisfaction it brings. This benefit is assumed not to vary with the level of the parents' economic welfare (though, clearly, it may vary with the number of children already in the family.

2. Work and/or income benefits. It may be difficult for those who live in an industrial society to appreciate that in poor countries children can be an important source of labor and income. But from a very early age children in poor countries, especially in rural areas, carry out crucial work: gathering firewood, collecting water, moving livestock around the countryside, helping with household chores, and providing extra labor in the fields, especially at critical periods such as harvesting

   The labor and income benefits from children increase with their age and are reaped as long as they are associated with the parents' household. In extended families this may be well into adulthood. For example, older children who have left the household and migrated to the city often send home cash.

3. Security benefit. In the absence of a social security system, children are the main source of security in old age. This security may take the form of cash or of food and shelter. Recently this idea has been extended to include security against emergencies that occur before old age.

Some economic benefits are hard to measure and do not fit neatly into any one category. For example, when extended families are the rule, children establish extensive ties when they marry. These ties can be a source of additional work and security benefits, but they can also provide a more general sort of economic benefit that derives from the size of the family. Caldwell describes this situation in Nigeria where 'in rural Yoruba society it is still taken as one of the immutable

Table 3. Factors affecting motivation to have a large family as economic well-being increases

	Motivation of poor parents	Motivation of richer parents
Benefits		
1. Consumption benefit	does not change	
2. Labour and/or income benefit	high	low
3. Security benefit (old age)	high	low
Costs	low	high
Competition from 'other consumption'	low	high

facts of existence that [extended] family numbers, political strength, and affluence are not only interrelated but are one and the same thing.' More generally, he notes that 'in traditional societies nearly all parents have social and usually economic gains which increase almost indefinitely with the size of the family.'[11]

Against these benefits must be balanced the costs of raising a child. There are two types: maintenance costs and 'opportunity' costs. In poor societies food is the major maintenance cost. As economic development proceeds, work for women becomes available and child rearing then imposes an opportunity cost equal to the income the mother could earn doing other work.

The economic motivation for having an extra child is that the benefits accrued from the child exceed the costs when both are calculated over the years that the child is attached to the household or is sending help to the parents. The theory does not claim that parents in poor countries actually make such detailed calculations explicitly. Indeed, they would be very difficult to make in any straightforward way. First, food and shelter or a few dollars sent to parents in a year when they are too old to support themselves would need to be weighted in the calculation much more heavily than the same help given them in their mid-life; such old-age support might well make the difference between life and death and the benefit would be essentially incalculable.

Secondly, peasants are not western businessmen: their desire to increase production or profits is strongly tempered by the need to avoid catastrophe, which is ever-threatening. They are, in economic jargon, 'risk-averse.' In the general absence of access to modern means of saving, the peasant can prepare to avert catastrophe mainly by accumulating children. Sometimes this can also be done by accumulating land, but usually this also requires a large amount of family labor. Such risk avoidance is certainly an economic benefit, but for parents facing a highly uncertain future, it is extremely difficult to calculate the likelihood of such risks, or the benefits. In these circumstances, we might expect risk to affect family size through the accumulated experience of the community as embodied in its 'folk wisdom.' Parental motivation can thus have a deep economic rationality even though parents may not be able to draw up a balance sheet of projected costs and benefits.

It is important to realize that the 'level of economic welfare' that influences motivation encompasses more than current income level, though current income obviously is an important aspect of economic well-being. People's motivations and attitudes arise out of their backgrounds, which for the bulk of reproductive parents covers a previous period of twenty to thirty years. Furthermore, it is not mere income but the goods and services income can buy, or those provided in some other way, that constitute economic welfare. So the theory in Table 3 is concerned not only with current income but with a broadly defined concept of welfare, or economic well-being, averaged over a period of at least a decade.

The theory postulates that changes in the level of well-being change people's behavior. In particular, parents at different socio-economic levels have different *backgrounds, desires,* and *preferences.* These profoundly affect both the likely benefits they can derive from children and how they view expenditures, including those for children. Parents at different levels of economic development thus have very different views of the economic utility of children.

It is easy to see how the value of children changes as families and societies in general become richer. As income rises it is possible to replace child labor by using some labor-saving machinery and by employing seasonal labor. As family income rises the child's contribution is likely to be less significant in the total family income. In addition, the child's income is likely to decline because, as the society becomes richer, it becomes more difficult for the child to gain employment, partly because of the changing types of jobs available and partly because economic development is generally accompanied by compulsory education and by child labor laws. Similarly, the need for children, especially male children, to provide economic security to the parents in old age also declines as the parents' economic welfare increases.

The cost of raising a child will clearly rise with income because the child will share a better house, diet, and general standard of living. The child will attend school rather than work. As development proceeds, women are able to join the labour force but a mother may have to forego income to stay home and care for her child. Within a society undergoing economic development, increasing education generally leads to the individual's receiving more income, and there is pressure to concentrate educational expenditure on fewer children. It is not clear that such costs per child necessarily increase faster than income, though they may well do so. However, even if they merely increase proportionately, the decreasing benefits will ensure that, as income increases, the balance will move toward fewer children.

Perhaps as important as the increasing cost of rearing children is the increasing competition provided by rising consumption standards during development. Economic development provides an increasing flow of new goods and new ways to spend money, which can substitute for expenditures on extra children.

Leibenstein has also suggested that the higher the socio-economic status of the parents, the higher the expenditure on 'status goods.' These goods involve services disproportionately, and their costs rise disproportionately as development proceeds.

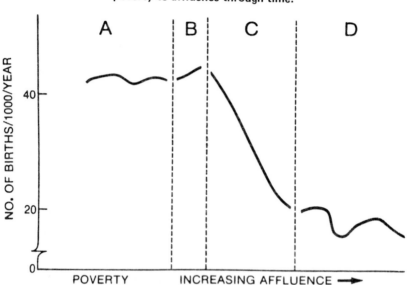

Figure 1. Changes in fertility as populations move from poverty to affluence through time.

We need to add three more components to make a complete framework for understanding fertility. First, parents desire *surviving* children, not births. Thus, when childhood mortality is lower, fewer births are needed to produce a given number of survivors. Second, Easterlin and others have pointed out that when fertility is depressed for medical reasons, the parents' 'demand' for births can exceed the 'supply.' For example, lowered fertility owing to ill health was common in poor countries before incomes started to increase and is still common in parts of sub-Saharan and West Africa. This is partly caused by disease-induced sterility and by poor parental health, which lowers the chances of conception and of successfully carrying the fetus to term. Thus, in a poor society increased income and associated better health can be expected initially to *raise* the birth rate. This is the general explanation for segment B in Figure 1.

Finally, family size is strongly influenced by the age at which parents, especially women, marry. In high-fertility countries family size is smaller where the age at marriage is older, for the obvious reason that the woman is exposed to pregnancy for fewer years. A reasonable estimate is that family size would be reduced by about two children if women married at age twenty rather than at fifteen.[12]

An increase in the age at marriage has been one of the first signs of fertility decline in LDCs and has accounted for roughly 35 to 40 per cent of the fertility decline observed there in the period from the early 1960s to around 1975.[13] Two recent and striking examples are in Tunisia, where the average age at marriage rose from nineteen in 1956 to over twenty-three in 1975, and in West Malaysia, where the age rose from nineteen to twenty-two in fifteen years. In Sri Lanka the age in 1975 reached 25.1 years. These ages should be compared with those in high-fertility countries such as Bangladesh (fifteen years), Nepal (fifteen years), and Pakistan (sixteen years), and with the US in 1975 (21.1 years).[14]

Age at first marriage and motivation for family size are affected by economic development in a similar way.[15] Marriage is likely to be postponed as both family and national income increase, as the importance of education (especially women's education) grows, and as opportunity for women's employment increases.

Costs and Benefits

There are two questions to be asked about the costs and benefits of children: in poor countries do the benefits that poor parents derive from children exceed the cost? Second, do the costs increase relative to the benefits as development proceeds and as the level of economic welfare of families increases?

Most students of poor societies agree that children there are a net economic asset to their parents over the long run. A highly detailed study in Bangladesh has substantiated these ideas.[16] It demonstrated that male children begin to provide labor and/or income at about age six. The value of their production exceeds that of their consumption from the time they are twelve (at the latest); their cumulative production exceeds their cumulative consumption by the time they are fifteen, and it exceeds their own and one sister's cumulative consumption by the time they are twenty-two. By age thirteen, boys are working more than nine hours a day and during almost four of these hours they are either earning wages or are engaged in trading.

Turning to our second question, there is no doubt that the costs of raising children increasingly outweigh the benefits as the level of economic welfare increases. Parents in developed countries gain almost no economic benefits from their children and the costs of rearing them are very high. In the United States in 1977 the direct maintenance cost of raising a child to age eighteen ranged from $31,675 to $58,255. In 1975 it cost an additional $18,416, on the average, to send the child through four years of college. This will have increased to about $50,000 by the 1990s. There is also an opportunity cost represented by income lost during child rearing. If the mother rears the child, the lost earnings are $26,562 to $54,347 at 1977 pay rates.[17]

Mellor shows, for Indian villages, how the value of child labor and income is lower, and the costs of child rearing are greater for parents with higher incomes. The children of poor parents are needed at home for work and, especially at harvesting time, they are out earning income. The fraction of these children that goes to school is therefore very small. In addition, the labor they do requires no formal education. By contrast, the children of richer parents are not needed to work on the farm or to earn outside income, and a high proportion attends school, which costs money.

However, as rural development proceeded in the study areas, and average income increased, so too did the types of employment that were available. In particular, there was an increased demand for educated labor. But in order to get such employment, the costs of education had to be borne, and these were quite sizeable. So the farmer, as he and his community rose from poverty, had to begin to spend more on raising each child in order to participate in development, and at the same time lost the child's labor and income. It is worth noting as an aside that these costs were sometimes so high that the peasants' children were excluded from the development process:

> In the outlying areas, in order to obtain economic rewards, further schooling must follow primary education. For additional education, a large proportion of rural people would have to move their children to an urban area. In 1971, according to Shortlidge's survey in Badaun district, the total of direct and indirect costs to send a child to primary school was Rs. 168 per year, or approximately three-quarters of the average landless laborer's annual per capita income; for attending middle school, the total cost rose to Rs. 343 – more than the average laborer's annual income.[18]

In summary, large families are an economic advantage to poor parents in poor countries. This advantage disappears as economic welfare increases. Formal studies and the general experience of scholars in the field confirm that parents consider the economic costs and benefits in arriving at a desired family size. Further, the actual and perceived ratio of benefits to costs declines as we move from the poorest rural populations to the richest urban populations. Childhood deaths in poor families also influence the desire for large numbers of births. Thus, as far as we can find by exploring stated attitudes and actual costs and benefits, the assumptions of the theory are confirmed.

Evidence on Predictions of the Theory
The theory set forth here predicts that family size will decline as the economic welfare of the family increases, although we expect a lag between increased welfare and the parents' perception that conditions have really improved permanently. On a larger scale, the theory predicts that the birth rate of the nation will decline as national economic development occurs.

Differences among countries and states
The simplest indicator of a nation's level of economic development is its annual per capita income. Figure 2 presents data for 116 countries and shows that the birth rate in 1970 was 40 or more in almost all of the poorest nations, less than 25 in almost all of the richer nations, and decreased to less than 40 somewhere between $250 and $500 annual income per head. Yotopoulos has made a similar

point and has also demonstrated that the total fertility rate . . . falls with increasing per capita income.[19]

The overall trend of fertility with income is clear. However, we will always get a negative correlation between fertility and income, or some other indicator of development, if we include the rich nations, since they all have low fertility. So a more powerful test of our theory is to compare fertility and income among only the developing nations. Even when we restrict the analysis in this way we still find that, on a global scale, birth rate is strongly and negatively correlated with average per capita income.[20]

Figure 2. Declines in birth rate as per capita income increases

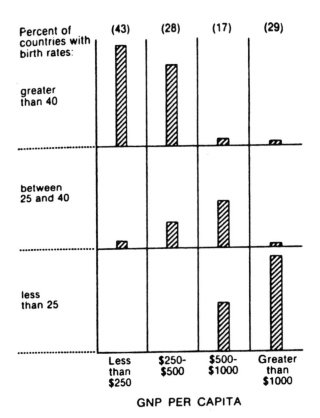

GNP PER CAPITA

Source: Dudley Kirk, 'A New Demographic Transition?' in National Academy of Sciences, *Rapid Population Growth: Consequences and Policy Implications* (Baltimore: Johns Hopkins University Press, 1971).

Note: Each column is the percentage of countries in a given class with birth rates of greater than 40, between 25 and 40, or fewer than 25 births per thousand per year. The number of countries in each income class is shown above the columns.

Conclusions

Our theory claims that the number of children desired by parents is greatly influenced by rational decision making, based on the balance between expected economic costs and benefits. The major benefits to be expected by poor parents in a poor nation are the labor, earnings, and future security the child will provide. Costs include both direct costs and opportunity costs, such as the income that might be foregone by a working mother.

The theory assumes, therefore, that parental decisions about children are largely economic and are determined by the parents' long-term average level of economic welfare. The level of welfare determines the parents' background, desires, preferences, and motivations. As income increases during economic development, these motivations change in favor of smaller families; the costs of children increase and the benefits decline; children begin to compete with other goods and services; and old age becomes economically more secure. Various structural changes also accompany development – in education, job opportunities, etc. – and these also make children less desirable. These processes, occurring during the shift from great poverty to relative affluence, are responsible for the major transition in birth rates during development, from around 40 per 1,000 per year to around 20 per 1,000 per year.

The economic costs and benefits can be shown to change with economic well-being, as the theory assumes. The evidence available from varied cultures throughout the developing world also substantiates the assumptions about parental motivation.

The major prediction of the theory, that fertility should fall with increasing economic welfare, is also borne out by all the various types of evidence that it is possible to bring to bear on it. This is true throughout the developing world, within countries over time, among socio-economic classes within countries, among regions within countries, and among countries at different stages of economic development. The best single estimator of welfare seems to be the level of education of the parents, especially of the mother.

Cultural values seem to be of minor significance, except that the culture, especially through family structure, may help determine when it becomes economically sensible to reduce family size.

Family planning programs can accelerate the rate of fertility decline, but they cannot, by themselves, cause the onset of such a decline.

NOTES

1. Paul Bairoch, *The Economic Development of the Third World since 1900* (Berkeley and Los Angeles: University of California Press, 1975); John W. Mellor, *The New Economics of Growth: A Strategy for India and the Developing World* (Ithaca, N.Y.: Cornell University Press, 1976), p. 6.

2. Selwyn Enzer, Richard Drobnick, and Steven Alter, 'Neither Feast nor Famine,' *Food Policy* 3 (1978): 3-17.

3. The first quote is from Paul R. Ehrlich, 'Human Population and Environmental Problems,' *Environmental Conservation* 1 (1974): 15. For a more recent and detailed presentation of Ehrlich's

views see Paul R. Ehrlich, Anne H. Ehrlich, and John P. Holdren, *Ecoscience: Population, Resources, Environment* (San Francisco: W. H. Freeman and Co., 1977). The second quote is from the Environmental Fund, in the *Wall Street Journal* of October 30, 1975.

4. The first quote is from the Environmental Fund, ibid., the second from the National Academy of Sciences, *Population and Food: Crucial Issues* (Washington, D.C.: National Academy of Sciences, 1975), p. v.

5. James R. Echols, 'Population vs. the Environment: A Crisis of Too Many People,' *American Scientist* 64 (1976): 165.

6. Lester R. Brown, *In the Human Interest: A Strategy to Stabilize World Population* (New York: W. W. Norton and Co., 1974), p. 53. A similar analysis is presented in Sterling Wortman and Ralph W. Cummings, Jr., *To Feed This World: The Challenge and the Strategy* (Baltimore: Johns Hopkins University Press, 1978), pp. 4, 203.

7. Environmental Fund (see note 3).

8. Garrett Hardin, 'Living on a Lifeboat,' *Bioscience* 24 (1974): 561-68; William C. Paddock and Paul Paddock, *Famine '75* (Boston: Little, Brown and Co., 1967).

9. Garrett Hardin, 'Not Peace, but Ecology,' in *Diversity and Stability in Ecological Systems, Brookhaven Symposium in Biology*, no. 22 (1969), pp. 151-61.

10. Frank W. Notestein, 'Population: The Long View,' in Theodore W. Schultz, ed., *Food for the World* (Chicago: University of Chicago Press, 1945).

11. John C. Caldwell, 'Towards a Restatement of Demographic Transition Theory,' *Population and Development Review* 2 (1976): 340; John C. Caldwell, 'The Economic Rationality of High Fertility: An Investigation Illustrated with Nigerian Survey Data,' *Population Studies* 31 (1977): 9.

12. Pan A. Yotopoulos, 'Population and Agricultural Development: Selected Relationships and Possible Planning Uses,' no. 2, 'The Population Problem and the Development Solution' (Rome: Food and Agriculture Organization, 1978), ES:DP/INT/73/P02, Technical Paper no. 2.

13. Judith Bannister, 'Implementing Fertility and Mortality Decline in the People's Republic of China: Recent Official Data,' from *The Current Vital Rates and Population Size of the People's Republic of China and its Provinces*, Ph.D. dissertation, Stanford University, 1977. Paper presented at the annual meeting of the Population Association of America, St. Louis, April 1977; Lee-Jay Cho and R. D. Retherford, 'Comparative Analysis of Recent Fertility Trends in East Asia,' International Population Conference, Liege (1973), vol. 2, pp. 163-81; Yotopoulos, 'Population and Agricultural Development'; W. Parker Mauldin and Bernard Berelson, 'Conditions of Fertility Decline in Developing Countries, 1965-75,' *Studies in Family Planning* 9 (1978): 89-147.

14. C. Stephen Baldwin, 'Policies and Realities of Delayed Marriage: The Cases of Tunisia, Sri Lanka, Malaysia, and Bangladesh,' *PRB Report* 4 (1977): 1-11; World Fertility Survey, 'The Nepal Fertility Survey, 1976: A Summary of Findings' (The Hague: International Statistical Institute, 1978); World Fertility Survey, 'The Pakistan Fertility Survey, 1975; A Summary of Findings' (1977); World Fertility Survey, 'The Sri Lanka Fertility Survey, 1976: A Summary of Findings' (1978).

15. Julian L. Simon, *The Economics of Population Growth* (Princeton, N.J.: Princeton University Press, 1977).

16. Some examples, in addition to references given earlier, include Alain de Janvry and Carlos Garramón, 'The Dynamics of Rural Poverty in Latin America,' *Journal of Peasant Studies* 4 (1977): 206-16; Mahmood Mamdani, *The Myth of Population Control* (New York: Monthly Review Press, 1972); John W. Mellor, *The New Economics of Growth: A Strategy for India and the Developing World* (Ithaca, N.Y.: Cornell University Press, 1976); Moni Nag et al., 'Economic Value of Children in Two Peasant Societies' (Mexico City: Paper Prepared for General Conference of the International Union for the Scientific Study of Population, August 8-13, 1977), data presented in Thomas J. Espenshade, 'The Value and Cost of Children,' *Population Bulletin*, vol. 32

(Washington, D.C.: Population Reference Bureau, 1977). On Bangladesh specifically, see M. T. Cain, 'The Economic Activities of Children in a Village in Bangladesh,' *Population and Development Review* 3 (1977): 201-28.

17. Epsenshade, 'The Value and Cost of Children.'

18. Mellor, *New Economics,* p. 258.

19. Yotopoulos, 'Population and Agricultural Development.'

20. See also William Rich, *Smaller Families Through Social and Economic Progress* (Washington, D.C.: Overseas Development Council, 1973), monograph no. 7.

Women and Agriculture

This paper comes from the Report of the United Nations Decade for Women Review Conference, State of the World's Women 1985 *(1985).*

Who grows the world's food?

Women have always known who weeds the sorghum, transplants the rice seedlings, picks the beans and tends the chickens. In fact it has been estimated that their labour produces almost half of the world's food.[1] But it has taken a long time for the rest of the world to discover these facts. In Africa, for example, three-quarters of agricultural work is done by women.[2] They are half of the agricultural labour force in Asia.[3] In Latin America and the Middle East, too, though official estimates are low, closer investigation reveals that women are doing a substantial amount of the farming as well.

In Egypt, for instance, the 1970 census identified only 3.6 per cent of women doing agricultural work. But local investigations revealed that, in the South, half of wives plough and level the land, and between 35 and 70 per cent are involved in planting, tilling and harvesting.[4] In Peru the 1972 census indicated only 2.6 per cent of women working in agriculture. A local survey corrected that figure to 16 per cent. And a carefully worded questionnaire, designed to account for people's tendency to under-report women's work, revealed that smallholding should properly be considered a woman's farming system because it occupied women from 86 per cent of households almost to the exclusion of men.[5]

As with their domestic work, much of women's agricultural work tends to be overlooked because it is unpaid. In Malawi and Botswana, for example, over three quarters of women work unpaid on the land. And there are far more women than men doing unpaid agricultural work in many countries. In Mali and Ghana the ratio is over two to one; in Cameroon it is more than three to one.[6]

Even when unpaid work is taken into account, however, women's agricultural workload still tends to be underestimated. This is largely because so much of it takes place away from the fields and the pastures. One study in Pakistan found that women's 'invisible' agricultural activities – like their vegetable garden by the house – took just as much time as the 'visible' ones.[7] Another area of activity rarely included is work with livestock – again partly because much of the work involved takes place in or around the house.

It is not only in developing countries that women's farm work is underestimated. Surveys in Turkey and Spain found farmers' wives working up to 70 hours a week out on the farm itself.[8]

Modernization for men

That women farmers in the developing world have been made invisible is only too visible from the statistics for agricultural innovations and projects. Information collected from 46 African countries showed that only 3.4 per cent

151

of trained government workers providing agricultural advice to people in rural areas were women.[9] Other research puts the figure still lower, at just 2.9 per cent.[10] In other parts of the world the situation is the same. In Nepal, for instance, studies show that women provide between 66 and 100 per cent of the labour in many agricultural activities and make 42 per cent of agricultural decisions – choosing which seeds to plant, deciding how much and what kind of fertilizer to apply.[11] But a review of government projects in 1983 discovered that, of all the agricultural advisors trained to help villagers, only one was a woman – and she had been trained in 'home economics', not agriculture.[12]

As the Food and Agriculture Organization (FAO) comments: 'Throughout the Decade developing countries revealed rather discouraging information about women's access to agricultural education, training and extension services'.[13]

Tools for change
It is not only training and advice about agriculture that has been directed more at men. When new technology is introduced it usually helps men with their traditional tasks of ploughing, irrigation and harvesting, but leaves women to continue their work of weeding, thinning and transplanting, by hand or with primitive knives and hoes. The rain-watered rice grown by women in Gambia, for example – which makes up 84 per cent of the country's entire rice harvest – covers 26 times as much land as the irrigated rice grown by men, but receives only one 26th of government spending on rice projects.[14]

Even when technology is introduced for tasks traditionally done by women, the machines tend to replace women completely rather than easing their work. Oil presses in Nigeria, tortilla-making machines in Mexico, sago-processing machines in Sarawak, are all owned and operated by men.[15] And in Bangladesh rice mills, employing only men, have been introduced, so depriving many local women – who used to husk rice for better-off families – of one of their main sources of income.[16]

FAO sums up the situation: 'In all regions the introduction of modern agricultural technology is primarily aimed at male tasks and used almost exclusively by men'.[17]

Costs and benefits of development
Agricultural development has advanced at a different pace and in different ways through the various regions of the world. Two major global trends – towards large scale commercialization and the growing of cash crops for export – have superimposed themselves on landscapes already eroded and shaped by history. These global trends have seldom benefitted men and women equally. But the picture in each major area of the world is slightly different.

Latin America
In Latin America where land ownership is often concentrated in just a few hands, this pattern has begun to be reshaped by a mixture of incomplete land redistribution and increasing control by multinational corporations of large

tracts of prime agricultural land. Here the tradition is to employ men as farm labourers and they far outnumber women in paid agricultural work in this region. In Costa Rica, Guatemala, Honduras, Panama, Chile and Colombia, for example, the ratio is ten to one.[18] Women tend only to be hired when extra hands are needed at harvest time. For the most part they work unpaid on their family's land or migrate to the town in search of paid employment.

But even where limited land redistribution has been introduced to cushion some of Latin America's rural poor against the impact of these changes, these policies have still tended to leave women in a vulnerable position. In Chile, for instance, land was only allocated to people who had been in continuous employment on an estate for at least three out of the previous four years. Since most women were only hired at harvest time, the majority did not qualify for land.[19]

Asia

In Asia – with the exception of China – a general pattern of 'development packages' (including high-yielding varieties or rice and wheat seed, fertilizers, pesticides, irrigation and tractors) have been superimposed on an existing picture of land scarcity and increasing landlessness. Between a quarter and a half of the rural population in Pakistan, India and Bangladesh are without land – and their numbers are growing.[20]

The result of these changes for Asia's women are mixed. The high-yielding seeds require more work – more weeding, more spraying, more planting and transplanting – and it is women who tend to be employed on the big farms to do these jobs. Though their average earnings are less than men's – with 56 per cent of women in rural Java earning under 3,000 *rupiahs* per month compared with just 14 per cent of men[21] – these increased job opportunities are some consolation. On the other hand, if the seeds are grown on her own family's land, the chances are a woman will have to do all the extra work herself – without pay.

Africa

In sub-Saharan Africa poor soil, low population density and traditional or communal rights to land, have been overlaid by a general move towards replacing subsistence crops like yam and sorghum with export crops like cotton and coffee.

Here, as in all regions, it is men who have been encouraged and helped to grow the new crops – despite the fact that in Africa, more than any other part of the world, it is women who do most of the agricultural work and despite the fact that large numbers of men have migrated to the cities in search of work leaving many households run entirely by women.

Unlike most other parts of the world, traditional land rights in parts of Africa have guaranteed women's independent access to land. But these rights have tended to be undermined – first by colonial land policies, and then by development projects, which have allocated land ownership to men. In Burkina

Faso for instance all new tenancies — for both food and cash crops — were given to men, despite women's tradition of growing all her family's subsistence food.[22] And in Kenya a women now only has access to land if she has a husband or a son alive.[23]

Land, loans and the law

The sweeping changes in agriculture in recent years have — with the exception of just a few countries — worsened the situation for the poorest and least powerful of the world's people. It is estimated that over half a billion people living in the rural areas of the developing world have no land.[24]

In many parts of the world it is new laws and competition with big commercial farms that have caused many millions of men to lose their land and, therefore, the ability to benefit directly from the fruits of their labour. But women regularly lose their land rights under some of the oldest laws in history: the laws of marriage and inheritance. Laws giving women the right to own land are, in the vast majority of cases, superseded by the laws of marriage and inheritance, which steal those rights back again. So complete is this disinheritance of women, that it has been estimated that they own less than one hundredth of the world's property.[25]

Under Islamic law — which operates in much of North Africa, the Middle East and parts of Asia — daughters inherit only half of what a son inherits and a widow gets just one eighth of her husband's estate if she has children, one quarter if she is childless.[26] In Peru, Bolivia and Brazil, too, married women are legally restricted in their ability to administer property without their husband's consent. And it has already been explained how land reform has tended to exclude women. Even when one group of Honduran women formed their own farmers' group and applied — as a group — to the authorities for land, their request was denied simply because they were women.[27]

In Asia almost all women are landless because of inheritance and divorce laws which prevent women gaining access to a man's land. Even where women can inherit — under the customary laws of the Hindu Mitakshara, Parsee and Christian sects in India, for example, or under Sawlawi law in Sri Lanka — they receive smaller shares than male heirs. And in the Philippines laws prevent a woman acquiring land at all without her husband's consent.[28]

Even in Africa, that one region where women have had traditional rights to land on a large scale, the customary laws still tend to discriminate against women. In a number of countries in Africa women's access to land is often more restricted than men's and may be conditioned by a woman's marital status.

Without land, property or a substantial regular income — collateral in banking terms — it is almost impossible for women to get loans.[29] Only five per cent of the money lent by African commercial banks goes into agriculture at all. And almost all of that goes to men.[30] Without help from the banks women are forced to turn to relatives or money lenders, the latter charging exorbitant interest rates — around 50 per cent a year in Ghana,[31] for instance, and up to 240 per cent in Nicaragua.[32]

The FAO puts it like this: 'In the Third World agricultural productivity cannot be substantially increased, nor can rural poverty be alleviated, unless women's access to key productive resources and services is substantially improved. The consequences of patriarchy for agricultural productivity are very expensive. Developing countries cannot bear their heavy cost'.[33]

Famine in Africa

The heaviest of the costs to which FAO is referrring is famine. It is now becoming clear that a factor contributing to Africa's acute food shortages is the way women have been systematically excluded from access to land and from control of modern agriculture in that region.

The processes are subtle but are beginning to prove devastating. And the devastation is greatest in Africa because this is the region where women do a greater proportion of agricultural work – between 60 and 80 per cent[34] – than in any other continent.

Even in 1980 – before the current drought hit – Africa was only 86 per cent self-sufficient in food. In the 1930s the continent was a net exporter of food. But by the 1960s self-sufficiency had dropped to 90 per cent.[35] Part of the problem is the sheer amount of work African women are expected to do. In Malawi, for example, women do twice as much work as men on the staple maize crop, equal amounts in the cotton fields, *plus* their domestic chores at home.[36] A survey in Burkina Faso found families lost weight during the rainy season – not because there was no food available, but because their long days in the fields left women too exhausted to cook.[37] And in Zambia another study found that the amount that was harvested depended, not on what the land could yield, but on the amount of work women could fit into the daylight hours.[38]

In Ghana when cocoa prices plummetted and large numbers of men migrated to the city, leaving women to shoulder all the agricultural work alone, many women decided to replace the traditional yam crop with less nutritious cassava because it takes so much less time to cultivate.[39] And it was in Ghana that acute malnutrition – called by its Ghanian name of *kwashiorkor* – was first identified, having been brought to doctors' attention by its appearance in huge numbers of small children being fed cassava as a weaning food.

Migration of men often leaves women with too much work to handle alone. In Botswana tradition forbids women to handle cattle and they are forced to pay neighbours to plough their fields, often finding themselves at the end of a long queue so that their land is not ready when the first of the rains arrive.[40]

Another reason for declining food production in Africa is the introduction of cash crops – to men. In the Ivory Coast a shortage of food staples resulted when the government encouraged men to grow cash crops. Some of the best land – where women had previously been growing food – was claimed by their husbands for the new cash crop and wives had to spend most of their time working on their husbands' fields instead of growing food.[41] Malawi's ground-nut harvest – grown chiefly by women – was down too, and for the same reasons, after a World Bank project encouraged men to expand staple maize production for export.[42]

And the failure of plans for Gambia to become self-sufficient in rice in 1980 has led to an *increase* of nearly 300 per cent in rice imports between 1966 and 1979. The reason? Because, though Gambian women grow 84 per cent of the country's rice, the agricultural advice and investment was given to men alone.[43]

Factors like these have contributed to a reduction in per capita food production in Africa over the last two decades. As FAO points out: 'Despite the well-documented, crucial role that women play in food production in this region, agricultural modernization efforts have excluded them, leading to negative consequences for food production and the perpetuation of rural poverty'.[44]

Passive resistance

Women in Africa have not always submitted lightly to their loss of land and livelihood, however. Some are objecting in the only way they can.

When government pricing policies sent men's maize profits soaring in Zambia and led to more land being put under maize, women kept working doggedly in their own groundnut fields and refused to turn them over to the more lucrative maize: because they – and not their husbands – kept the money from sales of groundnuts.[45]

In Tanzania, too, when the new hybrid maize seeds, plus fertilizer and pesticides, were given to men, their wives – who do most of the work in the fields – neglected the new crop because, while it increased their workload, the profits went only to their husbands.[46] The exact opposite happened in Zimbabwe, however, and yields rose dramatically when the same hybrid maize package was introduced. Why? Because the new seeds were given to women.[47]

Investing in women

It is a tragedy that women are forced into conflicts like these. Because the evidence points to the fact that, given the same kind of help, encouragement and incentives as men, women's agricultural productivity at least equals that of men.

In Africa there is evidence that women can become more productive farmers than men. In Kenya, for instance, where 38 per cent of the farms are run by women, those women manage to harvest the same amount per hectare as men, despite men's greater access to loans, advice, fertilizers, hybrid seeds and insecticide. And when women were given the same level of help, they were found to be more efficient than men, and produced bigger harvests.[48]

The key, says FAO, is to ensure that women can acquire and hang onto independent access to land and loans – independent, that is, of men. All-women cooperative farms and rural credit schemes appear to be the most promising way forward. And these have been tried with some success in countries such as Vietnam, Bangladesh and India.[49] But, laments FAO, 'Policy-makers and international experts have persistently resisted the idea of all women's co-operatives'[50] – even in West Africa where such co-operatives are traditional. And country-wide agricultural projects aimed specifically at women have not yet been implemented in any country, forcing FAO to conclude that: 'It is virtually impossible to identify any country in which national strategies have generally benefitted women's role in agriculture', adding that: 'No successes at the national level can be reported at this time'.[51]

Yet when women are able to profit directly from their work in the fields, they are not the only ones to benefit. Studies in Burkina Faso and Bangladesh have indicated that, when women do have time or money to spare, they use it to improve the health and well-being of their children.[52]

REFERENCES

1. J. Aronoff, W.D. Crano, 'A Re-examination of the Cross-Cultural Principles of Task Segregation and Sex Role Differentiation in the Family', *American Sociological Review*, Vol. 40, 1975.

2. 'The Data Base for Discussion of the Interrelations Between the Integration of Women in Development, their Situation, and Population Factors in Africa', UN Economic Commission for Africa, 1974.

3. World Survey on the Role of Women in Development, World Conference to Review and Appraise the Achievements of the United Nations Decade for Women: Equality, Development and Peace, Nairobi, Kenya, July 1985, A/CONF.116/4.

4. ibid.

5. ibid.

6. Women of the World: Sub-Saharan Africa, op. cit.

7. R. Dixon, op. cit.

8. Women in Statistics, op. cit.

9. World Survey on the Role of Women in Development, op. cit.

10. 'Women in Agricultural Production', FAO Women in Agriculture No. 1, Rome 1984.

11. World Survey on the Role of Women in Development, op. cit.

12. ibid.

13. ibid.

14. ibid.

15. B. Ward, 'Women and Technology in Developing Countries', in *Impact of Science on Society*, Vol. 20. No. 1, 1970.

16. World Survey on the Role of Women in Development, op. cit.

17. ibid.

18. Economic Commission for Latin America and the Carribean, Rural Women in Latin America. A Social Actor in the Past Decade (1975–1984).

19. World Survey on the Role of Women in Development, op. cit.

20. P. Harrison, *Inside the Third World*, Penguin Books, 1981; *Nutrition Intervention — Assessment and Guidelines*, Harvard Institute for International Development, US, 1978. R. Chambers, L. Longhurst, A. Pacey, *Seasonal Dimensions to Rural Poverty*, Frances Pinter Ltd., 1981; F. Moore Lappe, J. Collins, *Food First*, Abacus, UK, 1980.

21. R. Daroesman, *Optimum Participation of Women in Economic and Social Development*, ILO Jakarta 1978.

22. World Survey on the Role of Women in Development, op. cit.
23. ibid.
24. See references listed in footnote 20.
25. Report of the World Conference of the United Nations Decade for Women, Copenhagen 1980, op. cit.
26. *The Situation of Women in Rural Areas*, United Nations, awb/SEM/1984/BPI, Vienna.
27. World Survey on the Role of Women in Development, op. cit.
28. *The Situation of Women in Rural Areas*, op. cit.
29. World Survey on the Role of Women in Development, op. cit.
30. ibid.
31. 'The Role of Women in the Solution of the Food Crisis in Africa' (Implementation of the Lagos Plan of Action), Arusha, Tanzania, October 1984.
32. NFE Exchange, NFE Information Centre, Michigan State University, No. 22, 1981.
33. World Survey on the Role of Women in Development, op. cit.
34. UN Economic Commission for Africa, 1974, op. cit.
35. 'The Role of Women in the Solution of the Food Crisis in Africa', op. cit.
36. World Survey on the Role of Women in Development, op. cit.
37. Mitchnik, *The Role of Women in Rural Zaire and Upper Volta*, ILO.
38. M. Moore, Institute of Development Studies Discussion Report No. 43, Sussex, UK, 1974.
39. 'Women in Food Production and Food Security' – Government Consultation on the Role of Women in Food Production and Food Security, Harare, Zimbabwe, FAO, July 1984.
40. 'The Role of Women in the Solution of the Food Crisis in Africa', op. cit.
41. World Survey on the Role of Women in Development, op. cit.
42. ibid.
43. ibid.
44. ibid.
45. ibid.
46. 'Women in Food Production and Food Security', op. cit.
47. ibid.
48. World Survey on the Role of Women in Development, op. cit.
49. ibid.
50. ibid.
51. ibid.
52. ibid.

FURTHER READING
Angela Cheater, 'Women and their Participation in Commercial Agricultural Production: The Case for Medium Scale Freehold in Zimbabwe', *Development and Change*, 1981, Vol. 12, pp. 349-77, (London: Sage Publications).

The Food Problem:
Theory and Policy

Amartya Sen

This paper is from Altaf Gauhar (ed.), South-South Strategy *(1982).*

The various approaches to the food problem that can be found in the literature fall broadly into two groups. One group emphasises the natural sciences and engineering, and relates the food problem to technological issues of various kinds. The other group concentrates on social issues, including political economy, and sees the food problem primarily in social terms. At the risk of oversimplification, the two classes of approach may be called 'nature-focused' and 'society-focused', respectively. These are not, of course, pure, unmixed categories; the classification reflects the relative emphasis that is placed on the different factors. It is really a question of focus rather than of coverage.

It is fair to say that the nature-focused view has been traditionally the dominant one. Scepticism about the contribution that the social sciences can make to the food problem is not new. In fact, the antiquity of the nature-focused view of the food problem is brought out by an interesting conversation in Plato's *Statesman*, one of his celebrated dialogues involving Socrates. The so-called Stranger says the following:

> We come lastly to the getting of food and of all the substances the parts of which are capable of combining with the parts of the body to promote its health. This will make a seventh class and call it 'nourishment' unless we can find some better name for it. Provision of it is rightly to be assigned to the arts of farming, hunting, gymnastics, medicine, or butchering rather than to political science.[1]

To this Young Socrates replies: 'of course.'. . . . It is with that 'of course' that much of this [article] will be concerned . . . .

Malthusian Pessimism

Robert Malthus's *Essay on the Principle of Population*, published in 1798, falls fairly on the nature-focused side as far as his analysis of the origin of the food problem is concerned, though he also happened to think rather little of the ability of the natural sciences to expand the possibilities of food production. Malthus saw the food problem in terms of the growth of food supply falling behind the expansion of population, and saw both these growths as being primarily determined by nature. This is, of course, the context in which Malthus used his famous argument about food production growing in arithmetic progression, while population grew in geometric progression, soon overtaking the former. Malthus's particular fascination with the AP and the GP is not really crucial to his argument, and reflects – I suppose – an attempt to get profound insights from elementary mathematics – a tendency not altogether unknown in modern economics as well. What is important is his belief that : (1) the crucial variable is the ratio of aggregate food supply to population, and (2) there is a natural tendency for that ratio to fall, leading to starvation and other calamities until the ratio goes up again as a result of increased mortality. I shall refer to the former (i.e. the concentration on the ratio of aggregate food supply to population) as the 'Malthusian focus', and the latter (i.e., the natural tendency for that variable to fall) as 'Malthusian pessimism'.

While Malthus did suggest checking population growth through 'moral restraint' to combat what he called 'the excessive and irregular gratification of the human passions',[2] his scepticism of the actual possibility of achieving such a 'moral' solution is also abundantly clear. Malthusian pessimism reflects his view of a natural conflict, but more importantly, the Malthusian focus itself represents a far-reaching abstraction from various social influences on hunger, starvation and mortality, making the food problem turn on the ratio of two physical magnitudes.

Malthusian pessimism has not been well vindicated by history. His fears have proved to be not merely ill-founded but fundamentally misconceived, as the enormity of technical progress and the vast expansion of food production – far in excess of the growth of population which has itself been very rapid – have shown in the span of nearly two centuries since the publication of Malthus's well-known *Essay*. However, Malthusian pessimism has survived this bit of empirical failure, as indeed economic theories often do (witness the performance of so-called 'monetarism' and its nine lives). But there is a belief – backed by some quite respectable reasoning – that, while Malthus's fears did not come true in the first two hundred years, the stage is now set for his pessimistic predictions to be realised. The natural constraints on food production, it is argued, will now begin to bite in a way they have not in the past, and signs of decadence, it is alleged, can already be seen around us.

Indeed, this pessimism has been extended from food supply to other influences on the standard of living. Various studies commissioned by the Club of Rome and other organisations have tried to estimate the potentials of future economic growth in comparison with the growth of population.[3] Various types of crises with different timings have been read into the results that have emerged from such studies. While some models have not predicted disaster, others have, and some have indeed sounded screeching alarms, e.g.: 'Basically the prediction is that mankind has perhaps 40 or 50 years left. . . . The human race will be wiped out – mostly or completely – by the year 2100.'[4]

The assumptions underlying these pessimistic models have received a great deal of scrutiny recently, and there is little doubt that the shrill announcements of disaster and doom are not easy to justify in terms of rigorous economic reasoning. There are a great many arbitrary assumptions in the calculation and the results happen to be quite sensitive to the precise values assumed.[5] Further, gloomier assumptions have often been fed into the models that could be justified in terms of the available evidence. The more recent studies give far less pessimistic pictures. These studies include a variety of methodologies used respectively in the United Nations World Model,[6] the so-called Latin American World Model,[7] the extensive study by Interfutures,[8] the Global 2000 report commissioned by Jimmy Carter,[9] and even the later study done for the Club of Rome itself, called MOIRA (Model of International Relations in Agriculture).[10] They also leave much more room for policy response. It does not look as if the human race is about to be wiped out. (At least not for these reasons, though I believe it might be easy to underestimate our capacity and propensity to blow ourselves – literally – out of existence through devices precisely aimed to do that.)

Malthusian pessimism has typically been presented so forcefully that the impression has often been created that the world population has already been growing faster than the world food supply. That is most certainly not the case – indeed there has been a steady increase in the amount of food output per head even in recent decades. In fact, except for a part of Africa there is no substantial region in the world in which the food supply trend has fallen behind population growth. Some countries with well-known food problems, e.g. India, have moved from being consistent big importers of food to being typically self-sufficient and often more than that. While the future of the world food supply cannot be predicted with any confidence, there is really little reason to expect that food supply will presently start falling behind the growth of population.

I would now like to argue that the real problem is not Malthusian pessimism, but what – for want of a better term – I would like to call Malthusian optimism. If the Malthusian focus is retained, concentrating on the ratio of food supply to population and ignoring everything else, and that ratio is seen to be rising rather than falling, a sense of optimism about the food problem can be generated that would be both unjustified and dangerous. It is this question of Malthusian optimism that I would like to take up next.

Malthusian Optimism

If one were, to start with, worried about food supply falling behind population, and then were to find out that the converse happened to be the case – with food supply outrunning population – one might well end up being quite unworried, even smug. But that optimism, based on the Malthusian focus, can be quite unfounded if the Malthusian method of analysis is itself wrong. Is the causation of starvation and malnutrition best seen in terms of the relation between the physical magnitudes of food supply and population? Are famines caused by the decline of food availability per head? Are the Malthusian categories the right ones to use in studying the food problem?

I have argued elsewhere – in a book called *Poverty and Famines*[11] – that food availability per head is a very poor indicator of starvation. Major famines have taken place without any significant reduction in the ratio of food to population, and indeed some famines have occurred during years of peak food availability. Furthermore, the Malthusian focus has contributed to some of these famines not being anticipated, thereby causing a great many more deaths. The focus on food per head and Malthusian optimism have literally killed millions.

The problem may be illustrated with an example. The Bengal Famine of 1943, which killed about three million people,[12] was arguably the largest famine of this century, though there are also other claimants to that distinction. In terms of food availability per head, 1943 was not an exceptionally bad year, and indeed just two years earlier in 1941 the availability of food per person in Bengal had been a great deal less. One reason for the lack of government efforts to save the population from the famine was the absence of any recognition by the government that such a famine was developing. There were other reasons, of course, including the deeply unsympathetic nature of the British government then in power in India (of this the nationalist critics made a great deal, with good reason), and the priorities of fighting the war (of this the apologists of the regime made a great deal, again with good reason). But in addition to these general problems, the Malthusian focus on food output per head powerfully contributed to the absence of public policy to counter the famine.

The British Indian government went on calculating food availability in aggregate terms and saw no real reason for alarm.[13] Indeed, even when the famine erupted in Bengal with people dying in the streets, the government evidently had some difficulty in believing what was happening. The government's data about food availability in Bengal was fairly accurate, but its theory of starvation – based on the Malthusian focus – was totally wrong. Given the choice between the theory and facts, the government stuck to its theory – a phenomenon that is not unknown to us in Britain today. When eventually the government did concede the existence of a large famine in Bengal, more than a million had already died, and it was difficult to turn the forces of mortality back. The epidemic diseases including malaria and other fevers, cholera, smallpox, dysentry, etc., were already in full swing – as they typically are in these famines – and could not be made to stop before millions more were to perish. Interestingly enough, when the government did eventually concede the existence of the famine, it still stuck to its theory including the Malthusian focus, and simply revised the facts, by claiming the existence of an unobserved decline in the stocks of food carried over from previous years. There was no direct evidence whatever to back this claim, and there was little indirect reason to expect such a decline.[14] The Malthusian focus proved hardier than the contrary hard facts.

But why did food availability per head prove to be such a bad indicator of starvation possibilities? What is really wrong with the Malthusian focus? Does not commonsense suggest that starvation must be closely related to the availability per head of the commodity food, the absence of which leads to starvation? I don't think commonsense suggests any such thing, nor does economic reasoning, but it is an issue that requires a closer examination, and this is what I take up next.

Ownership and Entitlement

If we live in a society in which food is equally distributed among all the members of the society, quite clearly it will be the case that the command over food that each person has will be simply given by the aggregate food availability per head. We don't live in such a society, and indeed there is no such society. In every society that exists, the amount of food that a person or a family can command is governed by one set of rules or another, combined with the contingent circumstances in which that person or that family happens to be placed *vis-à-vis* those rules. For example, in a private ownership market economy, how much food a person can command will depend on (1) what he owns, and (2) what he can get in exchange for what he owns either through trade, or through production, or some combination of the two. Obviously, in such an economy a person may suddenly face starvation, either because his ownership bundle collapses (e.g., through alienation of land to the money lenders), or because the 'exchange entitlement' of his ownership (i.e. the command of what he owns) collapses (e.g. through his becoming unemployed and not being able to sell his labour power, or through a decline in his terms of trade *vis-à-vis* food).

A person starves when he cannot establish his entitlement to the food that he needs. This is not directly related to the aggregate food availability per head in the area, and in so far as aggregate availability has any effect at all, it must work through some variable or other that affects the person's legal entitlement to food. Such links, of course, do exist. A general shortage of food could raise the price of food *vis-à-vis* other goods and make it more difficult for a person to buy food in the market. But that is only one influence among many, and it is quite possible for food prices to rise even without any decline in food availability per head, e.g., due to an increase in the demand from others competing for the same volume – or indeed an increased volume – of food. This is basically what happened in the Bengal Famine of 1943, with a war-based boom leading to a food price inflation related primarily to an expanded demand.[15]

Furthermore, starvation can take place with little or no rise in food prices, and may be caused by factors such as loss of employment, or a decline in the output of goods that people make and sell to buy food, or a fall in the relative price of these goods. In the big Ethiopian famine of 1973, centred on the province of Wollo, hundreds of thousands died without any sustained rice in food prices.[16] In the 1974 famine in Bangladesh, while food prices did rise, the mortality of rural labourers – the most affected occupation group – was also directly linked with the loss of employment. The employment loss was due to the floods which destroyed the work opportunities immediately. As it happens, this occurred in a year of peak food availability, and the famine was, in fact, over before the food output fell after the appropriate gestation lag, many months after the floods.[17]

If starvation is seen in terms of a failure of entitlement rather than within the Malthusian focus of food supply per head, much of the mysteries of modern famines disappear. Rather than concentration on the crude variable of food output per head, which is just one influence among many affecting the entitlement of different groups to food, the focus of analysis has to be on the ownership patterns of different classes and occupation groups and on the exchange possibilities – through production and trade – that these groups face. The forces leading to famines affect different occupation groups quite differently, and famine analysis has to be sensitive to these differences rather than submerging all this in an allegedly homogeneous story of aggregate food supply per head affecting everyone's food consumption. The world isn't like that.

It is important to see the divisive nature of famines and starvation. There probably has never been a famine in which every group has suffered. There are, of course, many stories to the contrary, but they don't stand up to examination. The authoritative *Encyclopaedia Britannica*, in its vintage Eleventh Edition, does support the view – often asserted – that the Indian famine of 1344-5 was one such famine in which everyone suffered. The *Encyclopaedia* states firmly that even 'the Mogul emperor was unable to obtain the necessaries for his household'. This remarkable story does not bear scrutiny. This is not merely because the Mogul empire was not founded until 1526, that is, nearly two centuries after the famine in question! The Tughlak king who did rule much of India then – Mohammad Bin Tughlak, to be exact – not only had no difficulties with his own household necessities, he too succeeded in organising one of the most extensive famine relief programmes in history.[18]

As a matter of fact, Robert Malthus himself had the occasion to comment on the different impacts of food shortage on different sections of the society. In his *Investigation of the Cause of the High Price of Provisions*, published in 1800 – two years after his essay on population – Malthus discussed the question of distribution between the rich and the poor. While the shortages typically affect the poor, Malthus considered the possibility that redistributive relief through the Poor Laws, pursued too vigorously, could lead to a situation in which 'all the people would starve together' – a prospect which Malthus evidently relished rather little compared with the usual unequal sharing of the shortage. He went on to reassure the presumably nervous reader that 'there is no kind of fear, that any such tragic event should ever happen in any country.'[19]

Despite being interested in the distribution between the poor and the rich, Malthus did not pursue the distributional question sufficiently to recognise the limitation of his focus on aggregate food availability per head. In fact, famines divide the poor themselves just as they divide the poor from the rich, and depending on the position of different occupation groups *vis-à-vis* entitlement relations, groups that are normally equally poor end up in quite different boats in a famine situation. I shall have to come back to this question again presently when I go into policy issues, but here I just note that Malthus's categories are much too broad and crude. This crudeness also prevents him from seeing that some occupation groups can suffer from deep starvation even when food availability per head is unchanged or increased.

Policy: Anticipation and Relief

While understanding the causes of starvation and famines is of some interest on its own, its main interest must lie ultimately in the policy implictions that can be derived from this understanding. Food policy does, of course, have different facets, which require different types of analysis. At the risk of oversimplification, the policy issues connected with starvation and famines may be divided into three broad categories, namely (1) anticipation, (2) relief, and (3) prevention.

I have already discussed how and why the Malthusian focus on food availability per head can lead to failures of anticipation, delaying preventive and curative action. The entitlement approach points towards the variables that have to be watched to anticipate any growing food crisis whether or not it is accompanied by a decline in food availability per person. While the Malthusian focus is aggregative, the entitlement focus – by its very nature – is group specific. The ownership positions as well as exchange entitlement possibilities of different occupation groups can differ radically from each other, and correspondingly economic changes of one kind may affect one group while changes of a different kind will affect quite a different group. People who normally share the same level of poverty may be torn asunder by the dynamics of economic change.

For example, in the Bengal famine of 1943, the rural wage-labourers were among the hardest-hit group and provided the largest number of famine victims, whereas peasants and share-croppers, who are typically not much richer, were among the least hit. A rise in the price of foodgrains *vis-à-vis* rural wages ruined the rural labourers, but the peasants and share-croppers were to a great extent shielded from the effects of price change by the simple fact that their incomes typically take the form of a quantity of foodgrains itself. Similarly, urban labourers, particularly in Calcutta, who are normally not very much better off than the rural labourers were helped both by the war boom and by a system of rationing to survive the famine in good shape, while the unprotected rural labourers took the full impact of the rise in food prices – without a boom in incomes and without rationing – and went to the wall.[20] While the focus on food supply per head would not have – and indeed did not – give any clue to the coming doom of vast sections of the rural population, a more discriminating analysis focusing on entitlements could have led to early identification and possibly even vital anticipation before the event, providing scope for remedial public policy.

The approach of entitlements also provides guidance regarding relief of famines should it occur or threaten to occur. Moving food into famine areas will not in itself do much to cure starvation, since what needs to be created is food entitlement and not just food availability. Indeed, people have perished in famines in sight of much food in shops. This was widely noted in the Bengal famine of 1943. There was no run on food in the markets in Dessie, the capital of Wollo in Ethiopia, during the famine in Wollo in 1973. During the Irish famines in the 1840s, this was also a noted feature, and in late 1846 when people were dying in vast numbers from starvation, the local Relief Inspector, Major Parker, sent the following report from Skibbereen on 21 December: 'On Saturday, notwithstanding all this distress, there was a market plentifully supplied with meat, bread, fish, in short, everything.'[21] Since famines reflect a collapse of entitlement, famine relief has to take the form of generating entitlements through other channels.

There are many obvious ways of generating entitlements. The simplest, of course, is to provide free food in relief centres. It is an expensive form of relief since it is difficult to discriminate between famine victims and others who might not be averse to having some free food. A somewhat more organised form of relief is to set up work centres and pay food in exchange for employment. One side benefit of this is to get some useful things done through the work of the relief centre workers, e.g., digging wells or canals, but also the necessity of work can make, if the system is well organised, the abuse of the facilities that much more difficult. When a famine is caused by the loss of employment of rural labourers – as many famines in India or Bangladesh have been – creating alternative employment is an obviously sensible response. There is little doubt that the extensive floods in West Bengal in October 1978, in which about 3.5 million people lost their livelihood would have led to quite a large famine but for quick and effective relief operations. In fact, as a result of public policy there was no real famine, even though the incidence of malnutrition certainly did go up.[22]

Both direct food relief as well as food-for-work programmes require adequate stocks of food in the public distribution system. Sometimes such reliefs cannot be organised because that condition is not met. For example, even when the existence of the Bengal famine of 1943 was belatedly acknowledged by the government, the famine was not officially 'declared', since such a declaration would have created the obligation on the part of the government to offer relief in requisite quantities, as specified by the Famine Code of 1883. Sir T. Rutherford, the Governor of Bengal, wrote to the Viceroy: 'The Famine Code has not been applied as we simply have not the food to give the prescribed ration.'[23] The relief operations in the Bangladesh famine of 1974 were similarly delayed because of the lowness of the stock of food-grains in the public distribution system. That problem was, incidentally, vastly worsened by the decision of the United States government to cut off food aid to Bangladesh just at the peak of the famine because of Bangladesh's temporary refusal to accept the US demand that exports of Bangladeshi jute to Cuba be stopped. US food aid was resumed only when Bangladesh cancelled further exports of jute to Cuba, by which time the famine was largely over.[24]

The importance of having a sizeable stock of food in the public distribution system in famine-prone economies cannot be overemphasised. The most effective way of immediately creating entitlements for a famine-affected population is through public relief, and this is certainly a great deal easier if the relief can directly take the form of food distribution. The question, however, is worth asking whether the second-best policy in the absence of enough food in the public distribution system is to do nothing, or whether cash relief, say, through work programmes can help. It should be obvious that it could help if the additional purchasing power would lead to more food being drawn into the famine affected area. Very rarely would this condition not be fulfilled. While transport difficulties are often emphasised and can in some relatively rare cases be decisive, they very often are not so. Indeed, some of the cases that are typically cited as examples of food not moving into the famine area because of transport failure have turned out – on closer examination – to be not such cases at all, the non-movement being primarily due to the absence of effective demand for food in the famine area.[25] Cash reliefs can indeed help in creating this effective demand, i.e., in translating human needs into market demand, to which traders will respond.

There is an interesting 'classical' issue here that may be worth clearing up. The authority of Adam Smith has often been quoted by non-interventionists in famine situations. The role of market mechanism in moving food to distress areas has been emphasised in that context, e.g., by the Governor of Bombay in 1812 in justifying his refusal to intervene in a famine that was developing in Gujerat, referring to 'the digression of the celebrated author of the *Wealth of Nations* concerning Corn-trade' as being 'irresistibly applicable to every state of society where merchants or dealers in grain may be established'.[26] Such a non-interventionist policy has almost always led to disastrous results, since private merchants and traders will not move food to famine victims when their needs are not translated into money demands. Indeed, frequently food does move out of famine areas when the loss of entitlements is more powerful than the decline – if any – of food supply, and such food 'counter-movement' has been observed in famines as diverse as the Irish famines of the 1840s, the Ethiopian famine in Wollo of 1973, and the Bangladesh famine of 1974.

The failure of the market mechanism to help famine victims has puzzled non-interventionist public servants. During the Orissa famine of 1865-6, Commissioner Ravenshaw expressed astonishment at the lack of food movement into the famine area despite what he understood to be 'the ordinary rules of political economy', under which 'the urgent demand for grain ought to have created a supply from other and more favoured parts.'[27] Of course, political economy says no such thing, since there is no incentive for the traders to move food to famine victims as they lack purchasing power. (Poor Adam Smith must have grown very used to turning in his grave.)

So far, so bad. But when cash relief is given to famine victims, that does, of course, provide the missing link, creating effective demand for food. Even in the absence of food in the public distribution system, it is most plausible that food will move in response to the increased market demand. It is most unlikely that doing nothing could be even the second best policy – to be chosen when there is an inadequate public stock of food – since adding purchasing power itself contributes to the entitlement of the famine victims and would make the food supply respond. The case for public sector trading would also have to be considered in that context, especially if private trade has elements of monopoly or oligopoly.

Policy: Prevention and Security

The entitlement approach also suggests lines of analysis for preventing famines and avoiding starvation. It is a question not just of providing relief but of creating circumstances in which failures of entitlements will not occur. The reason why starvation is typically absent in the richer countries is not just the high level of the average income or average wealth in these countries but the arrangements for social security that provide a minimum entitlement to everyone. Even in a rich country widespread unemployment would lead to starvation and possibly even to a famine but for social security in the form of unemployment insurance, supplementary benefits, et cetera.

Can a poor country afford to provide security to everyone in these ways? It is common to argue that it cannot since this would prove much too expensive. I doubt this. I am not arguing that social security of this kind would be cheap; but then large costs might well be justified if the benefits are great, and what is at stake is the most elementary issue of life and death. Some poor countries have, of course, done much in this direction. China is an example, even though data problems make it difficult to assess its exact achievements, and there are big disputes that are currently going on within China as to what was or was not achieved. Sri Lanka is a country which has tried a system of free rice distribution, treating it as a general right of all those below a certain level of income. The costs have been substantial but evidently not unbearable.

It is sometimes argued that by spending money in providing free rice to all those who need it, Sri Lanka has starved capital formation and reduced its economic growth. While Sri Lanka's growth rate has not been exceptionally low – no lower than the average performance of South Asia – it has certainly not been very high either. On the other hand, Sri Lanka's concern with social services and social security – the rice policy is only part of this – has certainly contributed to the high expectation of life in that country, which comes close to European standards, and this is quite astounding for a country as poor as Sri Lanka. There is obviously some trade-off here. It is interesting to ask how long would it have taken Sri Lanka to reach its present level of longevity at birth if instead of trying to do it through social services it did it through faster economic growth, following the pattern of other developing countries. There is obviously much uncertainty in calculations of this kind, and it is necessary to try out alternative assumptions regarding the effect of transferring social service expenditures to capital formation of the usual kind.

Sri Lanka's longevity level is, of course, very much higher than what would correspond to its income per head in cross-country comparisons. What is calculated first is the income level at which Sri Lanka would have achieved its present level of longevity in that international fit. Then it is calculated, with alternative assumptions, how many years it would take Sri Lanka to raise its income per head from what it is now to what it would need to be for it to achieve the same level of longevity as it already actually has if Sri Lanka were just another country in the cross-country international comparison. The answer depends on the exact effects of transferring its social service expenditure to straightforward capital formation, and it turns out that the answer lies somewhere between 58 to 152 years[28] – a very long haul indeed no matter which figure we choose. To replicate what Sri Lanka has got from its social service-oriented public policy through the more traditional means of capital formation and growth would take a terribly long time. Paying direct attention to people's needs rather than doing it through economic growth is not such an expensive strategy after all in terms of human life. Social security may be expensive, but the rewards are high too.

How easy it might be for other countries to emulate Sri Lanka's social service-oriented policy is a difficult question to answer. The government of Sri Lanka itself has recently tended to underplay these remarkable aspects of its public policy. Certainly, the fact that Sri Lanka has so far avoided getting into heavy military expenditure and has indeed shunned so-called 'defence' makes it rather unique among the developing countries – indeed in the world. It might look as if this makes Sri Lanka's achievements hard to emulate, but I believe Sri Lanka's experience also helps to bring out the real social costs and sacrifices induced by defence expenditure.

I turn now to aspects of prevention other than social security. Failures of entitlement – as I have already discussed – might originate either in a fall in ownership bundles (e.g. through the alienation of land, or loss of grazing grounds for animals), or in a fall in the 'exchange entitlement' (e.g. through unemployment, or worsening of terms of trade).[29] While everyone might be ultimately vulnerable to these fluctuations, some groups are a great deal more vulnerable than others. In fact, two groups stand out in terms of special vulnerability judging from empirical studies of modern famines. They are respectively landless rural labourers, especially in South Asia, and pastoralist nomads, especially in sub-Saharan Africa.

Landless rural labourers have to live by selling the only substantial thing they own, namely, their own labour power. If they can't sell it, i.e., not find employment, they must starve. If they do find employment but food prices rise to make the market command of their wages decline sharply, then again they may have to start starving. Even their normal wage rates earned over periods of high agricultural activity typically leave them no option but to starve in less busy seasons – often called 'the hungry months'. While vagaries of weather have always produced uncertainty in the lives of the agriculturalist, the early stages of capitalist development in agriculture make the rural labourers particularly vulnerable. Historically, as the landless rural proletariat emerges in a peasant economy, the security of ownership of land – no matter how small – characteristic of a peasant economy is lost, and at the same time social security arrangements, which are characteristic of more advanced capitalist economies, are yet to come. This produces exceptional vulnerability for the class of rural landless labourers in this intermediate period, and, indeed, famine after famine have brought home how terribly vulnerable this class actually happens to be.

The pastoralist in sub-Saharan Africa has also been made more vulnerable by economic development, in this case by the development of capitalist agriculture, encroaching on grazing land – often the very best grazing land, e.g., in the Awash river valley in Ethiopia. This has made the pastoralist even more prone to disaster in drought situations.[30] But on top of that the dependence of the pastoralist on the market mechanism adds sharply to his vulnerability. The pastoralists typically sell animal products to buy cheaper calories in the form of foodgrains, which in the Sahel and in the Horn of Africa accounts for about half the calories they consume. A rise in the price of foodgrains *vis-à-vis* animal products can ruin the pastoralist. And, indeed, it did just that in the Ethiopian famines of 1973-4. The drought reduced both the agricultural output and the animal stock, but the economic impoverishment led to a general shift in demand away from richer food, namely, animal products, to relatively less expensive food, namely, foodgrains. There was as a consequence a sharp fall in the terms of trade of animal products *vis-à-vis* foodgrains, making it hard for the pastoralist to get enough to eat.[31]

---

*. . . with the present political system in India, it is almost impossible for a famine to take place. The pressure of newspapers and diverse political parties make it imperative for the government in power to organize swift relief . . . . On the other hand, there is no such relief for the third of the Indian rural population who go to bed hungry every night and who lead a life ravaged by regular deprivation. The quiet presence of non-acute, endemic hunger leads to no newspaper turmoil, no political agitation, no riots in the Indian parliaments. The system takes it in its stride.

The position in China is almost exactly the opposite of this. On the one hand, the political commitment of the system ensures a general concern with eradicating regular malnutrition and hunger . . . . In a normal year, the Chinese poor are much better fed than the Indian poor . . . . On the other hand, if there is a political and economic crisis that confuses the regime and makes it pursue disastrous policies with confident dogmatism, then it cannot be forced to change its policies by crusading newspapers or by effective pressure from opposing political groups . . . . It is, in fact, now quite clear that in China during 1959-61 there were deaths on a very large scale due to famine conditions . . . .

The Indian political system may prevent famines but, unlike the Chinese system, it seems unable to deal effectively with endemic malnutrition. In a normal year when things are running smoothly both in India and China, the Indian poor is in a much more deprived general state than his or her Chinese counterpart.

Amartya Sen, *Resources, Values and Development*
(Oxford: Basil Blackwell, 1984), pp. 500-03.

In the prevention of starvation and famines, particular importance has to be attached to monitoring the position of specially vulnerable groups. The entitlement approach helps not merely to identify which groups are vulnerable, but also precisely why they are vulnerable. Food security cannot be built without public policy being geared to countering the sources of these different types of vulnerability.

This quotation has been added by the Editors.

Food and Society

I began with the contrast between the nature-focused and the society-focused approaches to the food problem. I have tried to show why food is a social problem and it is not just a question of raising food production *vis-à-vis* population. It is not my intention to deny, in any way, the importance of technological issues in the production of food, or those related to its storage and transportation – they are indeed important. But, ultimately, the food problem is not concerned just with the availability of food but with the disposition of food. That involves economics, politics and even law.[32] Starvation and malnutrition relate ultimately to ownership and exchange in addition to production possibilities.[33]

I believe Young Socrates was much too rash in agreeing so readily that the problem of nourishment did not belong to political science. It does, in fact, belong to political economy and to political science. There is, indeed, no such thing as an apolitical food problem.

NOTES AND REFERENCES

1. Plato, *Statesman*, 288e in the 1578 edition by Henri Estienne (Stephanus); English translation in E. Hamilton and H. Cairns (eds), *Plato: The Collected Dialogues*, Princeton University Press, 10th printing, 1980, p. 1057.

2. Robert Malthus, 'A Summary View of the Principle of Population,' 1830 (revised version of his piece for the *Encyclopaedia Britannica*, 1824); reprinted in T. Malthus, J. Huxley and F. Osborn, *Three Essays on Population*, Calcutta: Oxford & IBH, 1969, p. 59.

3. See particularly D. H. Meadows, D. L. Meadows, J. Randers, and W. W. Behrens III, *The Limits to Growth*, Washington DC: Potomac Associates, 1972; J. W. Forrester, *World Dynamics*, Cambridge, Mass.: Wright-Allen, 1971; M. D. Mesarovic and E. Pestel, *Mankind at the Turning Point*, New York: Dutton, 1974; A. Peccei, *The Human Quality*, Oxford: Pergamon, 1977.

4. T. H. Nelson, *Computer Lib*, Chicago: Hugo's Book Service, 1974; quoted in Council on Environmental Quality and the Department of State, *The Global 2000 Report to the President*, Harmondsworth: Penguin Books, 1982, p. 612.

5. See, for example, H. S. D. Cole, (ed), *Models of Doom*, New York: Universe, 1973; Interfutures, *Facing the Future*, Paris: OECD, 1979.

6. W. Leontief *et. al.*, *The Future of the World Economy*, New York: Oxford University Press, 1977.

7. A. O. Herrera *et. al.*, *Catastrophe or New Society? a Latin American world model*, Ottawa: International Development Research Centre, 1976; *Handbook of the Latin American World Model*, Paris: UNESCO, 1977.

8. Interfutures, *Facing the Future*, 1979.

9. Council on Environment Quality and the Department of State, *The Global Report to the President*, 1982.

10. H. Linnemann, *MOIRA: a model of international relations in agriculture*, Amsterdam: North-Holland, 1981.

11. *Poverty and Famines: an essay on entitlement and deprivation*, Oxford: Clarendon Press, 1981.

12. See *Poverty and Famines*, Appendix D.

13. See *Poverty and Famines*, chapter 6.

14. See *Poverty and Famines*, pp.62-3, 78-83.

15. See *Poverty and Famines*, chapter 6, and also my 'Starvation and Exchange Entitlements: a general approach and its application to the Great Bengal Famine,' *Cambridge Journal of Economics* (1) 1977.

16. See *Poverty and Famines*, chapter 7.

17. See *Poverty and Famines*, chapter 9. See also M. Alamgir, *Famine in South Asia — political economy of mass starvation in Bangladesh*, Cambridge, Mass.: Oelgeschlager, Gunn and Hain, 1980.

18. See *Poverty and Famines*, p. 43.

19. T. R. Malthus, *An Investigation of the Cause of the Present High Price of Provisions*, London, 1800, p. 18.

20. See *Poverty and Famines*, chapter 6, and Appendix B.

21. See C. Woodham-Smith, *The Great Hunger: Ireland 1845-9*, London: Hamish Hamilton, 1962; New English Library edition, 1975, p. 159.

22. See my 'Family and Food: sex bias in poverty,' in P. Bardhan and T. N. Srinivasan, (eds), *Rural Poverty in South Asia*, (forthcoming) to be published by Columbia University Press. (Reproduced in this volume pp. 173-91).

23. See N. Mansergh, (ed), *The Transfer of Power 1942-7*, vol. IV, London: HMSO, 1973, p. 363, Document No. 158.

24. See D. F. McHenry and K. Bird, 'Food Bungle in Bangladesh,' *Foreign Policy* 27 (Summer) 1977; R. Sobhan, 'Politics of Food and Famine in Bangladesh,' *Economic and Political Weekly*, (14) 1979.

25. See *Poverty and Famines*, chapters 7 and 10.

26. See S. Ambirajan, *Classical Political Economy and British Policy in India*, Cambridge University Press, 1978, p. 71.

27. See Ambirajan, p. 76. On this general question, see S. Rashid, 'The Policy of *laissez-faire* during Scarcities,' *Economic Journal*, (90) 1980, and my *Poverty and Famines*, chapter 10.

28. See my 'Public Action and the Quality of Life in Developing Countries,' *Oxford Bulletin of Economics and Statistics*, (43) 1981, pp. 301-6.

29. See also K. Griffin, *International Inequality and National Poverty*, London: Macmillan, 1978.

30. See L. Bondestam, 'People and Capitalism in North-East Lowlands of Ethiopia,' *Journal of Modern African Studies*, (12) 1974; G. Flood, 'Nomadism and Its Future: the Afar,' *Royal Anthropological Institute News* (RAIN), (6) 1975; also my *Poverty and Famines*, chapters 7 and 8.

31. See *Poverty and Famines*, pp. 104-11.

32. See my 'Ingredients of Famine Analysis: availability and entitlements,' *Quarterly Journal of Economics*, (95) 1981.

33. In this article I have not gone into the question of distribution of food within the family. There is much evidence for an age bias (against the children) and a sex bias (against women) in the division of food within the family in developing countries and even in some developed ones in periods of economic crisis. On this question see my 'Family and Food: Sex-Bias in Poverty,' referred to earlier [note 22]. This issue adds a further social dimension to the food problem.

Family and Food:
Sex Bias in Poverty

Amartya Sen

This reading is from the author's Resources, Values and Development *(1984).*

The food consumption of a person depends among other things, on (1) the power of the family to command food, and (2) the division of food within the family. The former variable I have tried to examine in an earlier series of studies (Sen, 1976, 1977a, 1981a, 1981b), concentrating particularly – though not exclusively – on famines and acute starvation. The studies used what was called 'the entitlement approach', focusing on ways and means through which a family can acquire bundles of commodities, making use of the legal, economic, social and political opportunities faced by the family. Starvation was seen in this context as resulting from a failure of entitlement.

Entitlements of families do not, however, determine what a particular member of the family can eat. The division of food within the family can be a variable of importance of its own. Governed by mores, conventions and other factors, there may be various patterns of distribution within the family. It is with this problem of division of food within the family that this paper is concerned. It concentrates on the elementary question of the presence or absence of sex-bias in the distribution of food within the family. There is no attempt at causal analysis here, though I have tried to go into that question elsewhere.[1]

The regional concentration of this paper is on Bengal, more specifically on West Bengal in India, even though I shall have some things to say also about the other part of Bengal, viz. Bangladesh. But despite this relatively narrow regional focus, the main analysis may possibly be of some relevance in understanding poverty and malnutrition in the Third World in general. It also has implications for economic theory related to welfare economics, normative statistics, household economics and planning.

Intra-family Disparities

There is a good deal of evidence from all over the world that food is often distributed very unequally within the family – with a distinct sex bias (against the female) and also an age bias (against the children). Such biases have been observed even in the richer countries,[2] but the picture of discrimination is, of course, much sharper and more widespread in the poorer Third World economies. Evidences of sex bias and age bias in the distribution of food within the family are indeed plentiful (see the survey of den Hartog, 1973, and Schofield, 1975), and come from different parts of the world, including Africa,[3] Asia[4] and Latin America.[5]

However, many of the more striking case studies are of the anecdotal variety, so that it is difficult to decide how much weight to attach to them. Also, the information is very often 'directional' (e.g. noting that women get less) rather than quantitative (e.g. how much less?). Given the nature of the comparison, hard, quantitative information is indeed difficult to get. Who eats how much in a family is a part of the private life of a family, and there is little possibility of an observer coming and measuring precisely what is happening, without affecting the phenomenon to be observed.

Nevertheless, there have been several careful studies, and two in particular related to Bangladesh deserve special attention. The Institute of Nutrition and Food Science of the University of Dacca did a sample survey during 1975-76 of 60 households each from 12 locations in rural Bangladesh.[6] Chen, Huq and D'Souza (1980) also did a study, in 1978, of intra-family food allocation in 135 families residing in four villages in Matlab Thana in Bangladesh.[7]

Table 1. Calorie and protein intake by age and sex in Matlab, Bangladesh (June-August 1978)

Age (years)	Calories			Protein (grams)		
	Male	Female	Female shortfall (−) (percentage)	Male	Female	Female shortfall (−) (percentage)
0-4	809	694	−14	23.0	20.2	−12
5-14	1590	1430	−10	50.9	41.6	−18
15-44	2700	2099	−22	73.6	58.8	−20
45+	2630	1634	−38	71.8	46.9	−35
Total	1927	1599	−17	55.0	45.5	−17

Source: Chen, Huq and D'Souza (1980).

Table 1 presents the results of the Chen, Huq and D'Souza study. In every age group the female members seem to consume less calories and less protein than the male members, with an overall shortfall of 17 per cent in each of these two nutrients. The disparity is particularly large for later age groups with the 45+ having a 38 per cent calorie shortfall and a 35 per cent protein shortfall.

Table 2 presents the results of the survey by the Institute of Nutrition and Food Science of Dacca University. The age classification is finer, even though there is no sex classification for children (under 10). The sex bias is seen in every age group for both calories and proteins, with the disparity reaching its peak for the oldest group, viz. 70+. The next highest contrast comes in the adolescent years of 16-19. It is not, of course, possible to compare the exact age patterns of disparity in the reported results of the two surveys, since the age classifications are quite different in the two studies.

These tables are, however, far from compelling in establishing that there exists any clear sex bias in Bangladesh rural consumption of food. The difficulty rests not just in possible doubts about the representative nature of the two samples, but also in the fact that the so-called 'requirements' of food may be different for males and females. Indeed, the Institute study postulates food requirements that have the effect of showing that typically men are *more* deprived compared with women in terms of the relation of food intake vis-à-vis 'requirements'. This is shown in Table 3. The female intake shortfall is, in every case other than that for children between 10 and 12 years of age, less than the 'requirement' gap.[8] Indeed, from these Institute figures it would look as if the females have no deficit compared with requirements after the age of 15, and even before 15 their deficits – substantial as they are – are equal to or less than that of males. In fact, throughout the age range between 20 and 69 the women seem to have intakes greatly in excess of their 'requirements'. Men do far less well, and the tables seem to be turned.

Table 2. Calorie and protein intake by age and sex in rural Bangladesh (1975-76)

Age (years)	Calories			Protein (grams)		
	Male	Female	Female shortfall (−) (percentage)	Male	Female	Female shortfall (−) (percentage)
10-12	1989	1780	−11	56.6	52.7	−7
13-15	2239	1919	−14	61.2	53.9	−12
16-19	3049	2110	−31	83.3	55.8	−33
20-39	2962	2437	−18	82.0	66.6	−19
40-49	2866	2272	−21	79.8	65.3	−18
50-59	2702	2193	−19	78.2	60.3	−23
60-69	2564	2088	−19	72.7	58.1	−20
70+	2617	1463	−44	72.4	40.9	−44

Source: Institute of Nutrition and Food Science, Dacca (1977).

The nutritional requirement figures used in these Institute estimates have distinguished lineage, viz. the recommendations of FAO/WHO Expert Committee (1973).[9] But distinction is a different virtue from accuracy, and there are by now a great many doubts about the whole basis of nutritional requirement calculations.[10] There seems to be a substantial amount of interpersonal variability, and even for a given person much variation over time. Also possibilities of 'multiple equilibria' of energy intake and use – at various levels of consumption – seem to exist. Furthermore, there are good reasons to dispute the assumptions about the energy use of activities performed by women, which are not as 'sedentary' as calorie calculations tend to assume.[11] Also the extra nutrition requirements of the pregnant women and lactating mothers require fuller acknowledgement.

Finally, there is a great danger of circular reasoning in linking calorie 'requirements' to physical characteristics, since energy 'requirements' are calculated by multiplying the body weight by 'energy requirement per kg body

Table 3. Calorie intake vis-à-vis alleged requirement by age and sex in rural Bangladesh (1975-76)

	Male			*Female*				
Age (years)	*Intake*	*'Requirement'*	*Percentage 'deficit' (–) or 'excess' (+)*	*Intake*	*'Requirement'*	*Percentage 'deficit' (–) or 'excess' (+)*	*Female 'requirement' gap (–) (percentage)*	*Female intake shortfall (–) (percentage)*
10-12	1989	2600	–24	1780	2350	–24	–10	–11
13-15	2239	2753	–19	1919	2224	–14	–19	–14
16-19	3049	3040	0	2110	2066	+2	–32	–31
20-39	2962	3122	–5	2437	1988	+23	–36	–18
40-49	2866	2831	+1	2272	1870	+21	–34	–21
50-59	2702	2554	+6	2193	1771	+24	–31	–19
60-69	2569	2270	+13	2088	1574	+33	–31	–19
70+	2617	1987	+32	1463	1378	+6	–31	–44

Source: Institute of Nutrition and Food Science, Dacca (1977).

Table 4. Extent of 1979 malnutrition among children in five rural blocks affected by 1978 floods in West Bangal (percentage of respective age and sex group)

	Age in months													
	0-12		*13-24*		*25-36*		*37-48*		*49-60*		*61-72*		*Total*	
Grades of malnutrition	*male*	*female*	*male*	*female*	*male*	*female*	*male*	*female*	*male*	*female*	*male*	*female*	*male*	*female*
Grade III	7.1	11.3	18.2	26.2	9.4	16.6	6.0	10.5	6.5	7.6	4.1	10.3	9.2	14.6
Grades III and II	21.4	27.8	42.2	56.5	35.7	48.2	29.6	47.4	30.8	37.2	18.9	41.0	31.8	44.6
Grades III, II and I	59.5	75.2	87.0	89.3	79.0	84.6	70.8	74.2	69.8	73.1	67.6	66.7	73.9	79.4
Normal	40.5	24.8	13.0	10.7	21.0	15.4	29.2	25.8	30.2	26.9	32.4	33.3	26.1	20.6
Total (number)	126	133	192	168	224	247	216	190	169	145	74	39	1001	922

Source: Based on data presented in UNICEF (1980) sample Survey Report.

weight',[12] related to the activity level, while the person's body weight as well as his or her activity level does depend crucially on the energy intake of the person.[13] Calorie deficiency can, up to a point, justify itself!

Chen, Huq and D'Souza (1980) carry out rather different corrections – though also based on body weight and activity level – and come to the general conclusion that 'for all age groups, male:female intake to requirement ratios are at near parity, although marked male predominance persists among the young children', though they also warn that 'these adjustments are illustrative rather than precise' (p. 10). In fact, it is very doubtful that given the theoretical problems and practical obscurities, the comparison of intake-requirement ratios throws much light on the relative positions of men and women in the division of food within the family.

It may be more useful to look at the actual consequences of food disparity rather than trying to compare the intake disparity with the 'requirement' disparity. This pushes us in the direction of anthropometric comparisons and also towards contrasting morbidity and mortality related to nutritional deficiency. There is indeed some evidence of greater incidence of malnutrition among female children than male children in rural Bangladesh.[14] There is some evidence also of excess female mortality among children, and a suggestion that ' "excess" female mortality was consistently higher during the food shortage years 1974-75 vis-à-vis 1975-77'.[15]

Floods and Undernutrition: Rural West Bengal 1978-79

There were damaging floods in West Bengal during August-October 1978, affecting 30,000 square kilometres, with a population of 15 million, of whom – it is estimated – that 3.5 million lost their livelihood because of crop destruction and reduction of employment.[16] There was quite an extensive and efficient flood relief programme carried out by the state government. In connection with that work an extensive survey was carried out in 1979 of all the children registered in four child-care centres – selected at random – in each 'block', choosing five blocks out of 30,[17] also by random method.

Undernutrition of the children was studied in terms of 'weight for age', following the conventional standard adopted by the Indian Academy of Pediatrics, classifying the children into four groups, viz. 'normal', and suffering respectively from Grades I, II and III undernutrition.[18] Using these data, Table 4 has been constructed, partitioning the children into three groups: (1) Grade III (severe undernutrition), (2) Grades III and II (substantial to severe undernutrition), (3) Grades III, II and I (moderate, substantial or severe undernutrition), and (4) normal. The children are classified into these categories for each 12-month age group (i.e. 0-12, 13-24, etc.). Total number of observations in each age group is also recorded in Table 4.

The picture that emerges from this is one of uniformly larger incidence of undernutrition among female children compared with the male. There is only one exception to it, viz. age group 61-72 months, in the aggregate category of Grades III, II and I undernutrition, and the gap there is slight (67.6 per cent for

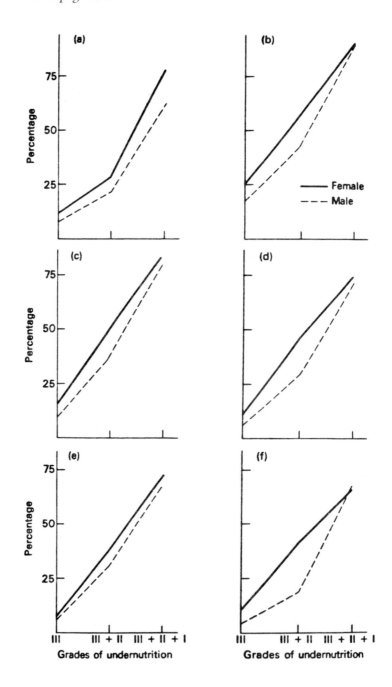

Figure 1. Incidence of different grades of undernutrition among rural children in flood-affected West Bengal, 1979, by age (see Table 4): (a) 0-12 months, (b) 13-24 months, (c) 25-36 months, (d) 37-48 months, (e) 49-60 months, (f) 61-72 months

males vis-à-vis 66.7 per cent for females). In every other comparison — 17 in all — the level of undernutrition of girls exceeds — often by far — that of boys of comparable age. Indeed, even for the age group 61-72 months the incidence of severe (Grade III) undernutrition is much greater for females (10.3 per cent vis-à-vis 18.9 per cent for males). The figures are also represented in diagrammatic form in Figure 1 for visual comparison.

It should be remarked that these comparisons do not suffer from some of the difficulties noted in the last section concerning food-intake studies. They deal with *results* of food-intake rather than with the quantities of food-intake itself, and the doubtful concept of 'food requirement' does not have to be invoked. In Section 4 the contrast between the two approaches will be taken up at a more general level.

On the other hand, it should be noted that the comparisons refer to a distress situation — one following severe flooding and coinciding with unusual economic deprivation. In fact, a relatively small survey of rural households from *all parts* of West Bengal, carried out earlier in 1978, indicated a markedly greater incidence of undernutrition (in terms of weight for age) among boys vis-à-vis girls in the 1-5 year age group.[19] Indeed, in terms of the alleged normally superior performance of girls, the substantially greater incidence of undernutrition among girls in a situation of economic distress is particularly striking.

Differential Morbidity: Calcutta 1976-78

The Calcutta Metropolitan Development Authority carried out surveys of health and socioeconomic conditions in greater Calcutta during 1976-78. The findings can be used for comparison of male and female morbidity in Calcutta and its immediate vicinity. This is a large settlement, with 3.31 million people living in Calcutta proper, 1.28 million in the adjacent town of Howrah, 1.01 million people in the town of Hooghly and 4.72 million in other adjacent towns and villages, forming a total urban complex of 10.33 million people (in early 1978). Greater Calcutta has the reputation of being noticeably the poorest large city in the world.

The survey, which was conducted in collaboration with the Indian Statistical Institute and the Department of Health of the Government of West Bengal, was based on a stratified multi-stage sampling scheme. Altogether 4728 households were surveyed out of an estimated total of 2.19 million households, representing 0.22 per cent coverage.

While undernutrition data were not directly covered, morbidity information was gathered and analysed. Table 5 presents comparative morbidity incidence of males and females in different parts of greater Calcutta, classified according to age groups. Three general categories were used, viz. 'well', 'indifferent' and 'ill'. Table 5 (and Figure 2) present percentages of people who were either ill or in indifferent health.

Table 5. Incidence of poor health conditions of usual male and female residents of the CMDA area
(percentage of each age-sex group)

	Health	Age in years last birthday										All ages	
		14 and below		15-25		26-45		46-60		61 and above			
		male	female	male	female	male	female	male	female	male	female	male	female
(a)	North Calcutta												
	ill	1	1	1	1	0	1	2	8	9	9	1.0	1.7
	ill and indifferent	37	35	16	25	15	38	38	56	63	68	25.9	37.3
(b)	Central Calcutta												
	ill	2	3	2	4	1	3	5	6	4	14	2.0	3.8
	ill and indifferent	31	29	15	33	23	39	39	50	67	68	27.1	36.7
(c)	South Calcutta												
	ill	2	3	1	1	2	3	1	2	4	7	1.6	2.7
	ill and indifferent	20	21	5	13	13	31	15	44	50	62	14.8	27.0
(d)	Total Calcutta												
	ill	1	3	2	2	1	2	3	4	4	8	1.6	2.8
	ill and indifferent	30	30	13	25	37	32	47	47	58	67	23.6	34.4
(e)	Howrah and municipal towns												
	ill	3	2	2	1	1	2	3	6	6	5	2.0	2.0
	ill and indifferent	35	34	23	33	23	47	47	57	78	73	31.4	41.0
(f)	Other towns and villages												
	ill	2	1	1	0	1	2	2	0	15	8	1.9	1.5
	ill and indifferent	20	20	13	15	14	35	32	47	65	64	19.9	27.0
(g)	Total CMDA area												
	ill	2	2	2	1	1	2	3	2	5	9	1.9	2.2
	ill and indifferent	29	28	18	26	19	40	39	49	64	70	26.1	34.7

Source: CMDA (1980). The columns for 'all ages' are based on Table 71 of the general report, while the other columns are derived from Table 202 of Part III of 'Tables with Notes'. The latter are reconstructed from an overall percentage breakdown, and to avoid spurious precision, are recorded only as percentage whole numbers.

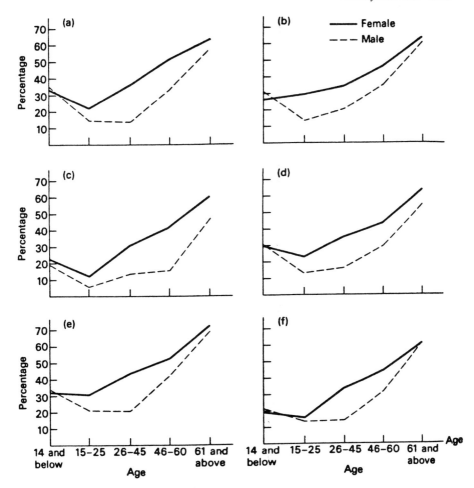

Figure 2. Incidence of poor health conditions (ill and indifferent health) in the CMDA area by district: (a) North Calcutta, (b) Central Calcutta, (c) South Calcutta, (d) Calcutta (total), (e) Howrah and municipal towns, (f) Other towns and villages in the CMDA area

These categorized data – based on interviewing – have some obvious defects, but the survey was carefully done, and it is interesting to see the picture that emerges from them for the poorest city of the world. The pattern is a mixed one, but there is a higher level of female morbidity compared with male morbidity in most regions except for the very young (14 and below).[20]

There are also data for the slum-dwellers in Calcutta. Table 6 presents the figures for two types of 'bustees' – the 'unimproved' and the 'improved' (with certain amenities provided). With very few exceptions, female morbidity in terms of both categories (viz. 'ill' and 'ill or indifferent') emerge as being appreciably higher than male morbidity in each age group.

Table 6. Incidence of poor health conditions of usual male and female residents in the improved and unimproved bustees in CMDA (percentage of each age-sex group)

Health	Age in years last birthday											
	14 and below		15-25		26-45		46-60		61 and above		All ages	
	male	female	male	female	male	female	male	female	male	female	male	female
Improved bustees ill	3	5	—	—	1	3	—	3	—	18	1.4	4.0
ill and indifferent	22	27	17	18	24	56	40	67	44	53	24.4	38.6
Unimproved bustees ill	1	1	2	1	—	4	6	3	—	—	1.1	1.6
ill and indifferent	36	38	13	21	21	52	37	61	65	80	27.5	41.1

Source: The columns for 'all ages' are based on Table LI of Seal *et al.* (1981). The other columns are derived from Table 202 of Part III of 'Tables with Notes' of CMDA (1980), and being reconstructed from an over-all percentage breakdown, are recorded only as percentage whole numbers, to avoid spurious precision. Dash (—) stand for zero or negligible.

It is not, of course, by any means obvious that morbidity is primarily the result of malnutrition. But malnutrition is one of the factors in morbidity, and the pattern of deprivation in food may well go together with other types of deprivation. In any case, for what it is worth, the morbidity picture – possibly providing some indirect evidence of nutritional disparity – gives some reason to expect discrimination against the female, though the pattern here is not at all as clear as the pattern of malnutrition among the children in the flood-affected regions of rural West Bengal (Section 2 above).

Finally, the figures relating to the slums have the advantage of concentrating on an economically deprived group. The over-all figures for the normal residents of greater Calcutta, presented in Table 5, aggregate over a very wide range of income groups. This is a source of some possible bias, since sex distribution might well be related to the income level, particularly in view of the large number of migrant (often out-of-state) male labourers who work in Calcutta and have their families back in the village. The CMDA data do, however, cover monthly household expenditures per capita of the households surveyed. Table 7 presents the picture for the different expenditure groups (see also Figure 3). As is to be expected, the incidence of illness typically goes down with rise in household per capita expenditure – a rough index of economic prosperity – but the females have consistently greater morbidity in *each* expenditure group.

Table 7. Incidence of poor health conditions of usual male and female residents of the CMDA area by per capita household expenditure groups (percentage of each sex-expenditure group)

	Per capita monthly expenditure group (Rupees per month)							
	0-54		55-128		129 and above		Total	
	male	female	male	female	male	female	male	female
III	2.4	2.5	1.8	2.2	1.6	2.0	1.9	2.2
III and indifferent	30.6	34.6	26.5	37.1	21.7	28.4	26.0	34.7

Source: Table 73 of the general report of CMDA (1980).

Implications for Economic Analysis and Policy

The existence of substantial intra-family disparities would have serious implication on economic analyses of many different types. The family is often the decision-making unit for work and consumption. If these decisions are based on systematic discrimination between different members of the family it becomes difficult to relate these decisions to individual welfare.[21]

This particular problem is typically avoided in traditional economic theory by one of three possible devices. One is simply to abstract from the family, and carry on the analysis as if each individual takes decisions on 'his' own, and this is the typical structure of, say, the theoretical literature on 'general equilibrium'.

The model works neatly enough, but that is not the way the world is, in fact, organized.

The second approach is to ignore the individual altogether, and to take the family as the unit of analysis – of decisions, of actions, and even of welfare. In terms of economic behaviour this may or may not be close to the reality, but even if it is, it raises the deep question as to whether the well-being of individuals can be ignored in making social welfare judgements or in comparing standards of living, and whether economic policy should be geared only to the conception of family well-being that the decision-takers in the family could be seen as pursuing. If that family-based conception permits disparities (e.g. putting lower weight on the undernourishment of the children or of women), should that be the basis of social assessment and public policy? I believe to ask this question is to answer it. It would be very odd indeed if the family head's view of family welfare were all that mattered for public judgement and social policy.

The third approach is to *assume* complete harmony within the family, with the well-being of every member of the family being equally served by the family decisions. In this approach everyone shares the same level of well-being, and it does not matter whether we look at the average level (in the Benthamite way), or at the minimal level (in a Rawlsian way), since they give the same answer. This is an empirical assumption, and if true, it avoids many practical difficulties. The trouble is that as an empirical assumption, it is very difficult to justify. Indeed, the evidence on the sharp disparities within the family, discussed in this paper, would seem to militate against the assumption.

While these are the traditional assumptions – though usually made implicitly – there is a fourth approach that is worth considering, and which has received some support recently. It can be argued that the notion of 'individual welfare' itself is a non-viable concept in societies in which the family is dominant. There might be, it is argued, no way of specifying the welfare of the individual in contrast with that of the family.[22] This fourth view has some similarity with the second, except that individual welfare is not so much *ignored* as taken to be a *non-sustainable* concept in this context.

It is important to distinguish between two different views that may be associated with this approach. First, it may be argued that individual welfare cannot be taken to be independent of the welfare of the rest of the family.[23] This is convincing enough, but it need not really make the concept of individual welfare non-sustainable, since it only rejects the *independent* conception of that welfare. *Separateness* of individual welfare has to be distinguished from the *independence* of the individual welfare. Individual welfares may be interdependent but distinct.

Second, it might be argued that the *introspective* notion of individual welfare may be itself unsustainable, since that is not how members of the family do introspect. Certainly, for some members of the family – such as infants and children – the introspective notion is problematic or useless; but for others it seems a bit difficult to claim that a member of the family would not be able to attach any meaning to the notion of his or her individual welfare as it appears to him or her. The issue is not whether the person poses this question to himself or herself as a regular introspective activity, but whether he or she is able to understand and answer such a question if it were posed. The traditional acceptance of deep inequalities within the family – against women in particular – does indeed thrive on not asking some of these questions that appear to be 'divisive', but that is *not* because such questions cannot, *if posed*, be understood or answered.

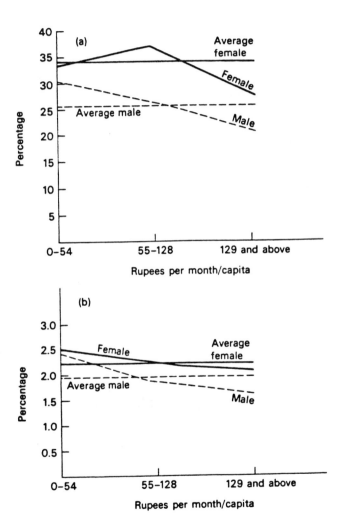

Figure 3.   Incidence of poor health conditions in the CMDA area by expenditure group (see Table 7): (a) Ill and in indifferent health, (b) Ill only

It is, of course, possible to argue that the introspective concept of individual welfare – while perfectly sustainable – is not an adequate basis for discussions on social welfare, standard of living and economic policy. Indeed, I have tried to argue in that direction elsewhere, showing the limitation of the traditional notion of 'utility' as a basis of judgement and action.[24] In particular, there are good grounds for arguing that a person's capability failure may well be judged not on the metric of how upset he is about it, but by the *extent* of the capability failure itself. If a person is unable to get the nourishment he or she needs, or unable to lead a normal life due to some handicap, that failure – on this view – is itself important, and not made important only because he or she incurs dissatisfaction or disutility from that failure.

If the focus is on the deprivation of *personal capabilities*, then inequalities within the family have an importance of their own, no matter what view we take of the sustainability of the notion of individual welfare in cultures in which the family plays a dominant role. There is no escape from the grave tragedy of the disproportionate undernourishment of children (or sharper undernourishment of the *female* children in distress situations, as discussed in Section 2), or the unusual morbidity of women (as discussed in Section 3). The problem has to be distinguished from the deprivation of goods as such since the 'capability approach' is concerned with what goods can do to human beings.[25] Thus, undernourishment and morbidity – not to mention mortality – provide a better focus than food-intake itself (see Section 1).

If disparities within the family are not ruled out of court with one assumption or another, the implications for economic analysis and policy are truly monumental. This is not the occasion to go into a full-fledged analysis of the different implications, but some may be briefly referred to as examples.

First, in terms of policy, the problem of malnutrition and hunger can no longer be seen only as a matter of entitlement of the family, depending on the family's earning power and market command, and requires analysis of the division of entitlements *within* the family.[26] The issue of social values, including what 'divisive' questions are or are not posed (as discussed earlier), becomes a central one, in this context.

Second, the gap between decisions of family heads and the well-being – introspective or not – of individual members of the family makes market data that much more difficult to interpret in terms of need satisfaction. The market demands would, at least, reflect the relative importance of different items as seen by the decision-takers ('revealed preference' cannot go beyond that, even if it can go so far as that).[27] This calls into question not merely the traditional efficiency or optimality results related to the market mechanism (for market socialism[28] as well as for competitive capitalism),[29] it also has far-reaching implications for public policy and planning using market information.[30]

Third, the evaluation of standard of living is usually done on the basis of market data. While the problems arising from different sizes and compositions of families are often neglected, there have been a number of important contributions recently to correct for variations of size and composition through the use of 'equivalence scales'.[31] But these scales operate on a notion of 'family welfare' that is reflected by the maximand of the family's market behaviour. For reasons already discussed the procedure is not easy to justify.

Much of economic analysis proceeds on the basis of linking decision-taking with individual well-being. Disparities within the family strike at the root of this relationship.

NOTES

1. Sen (1983a, 1983b), Kynch and Sen (1983) and Sen and Sengupta (1983). These studies have followed up some issues raised in this paper.

2. See, for example, Ritchie (1963) on the food consumption behaviour of Scottish mining families during the last World War, and that of US mining families during the depression of the thirties. See also Spring Rice (1939).

3. See, for example, Thomson (1954), Nicol (1959), Davey (1962a, 1962b), McFie (1967), Bohdal, Gibbs and Simmons (1968), University of Ibadan (1970), Crawford and Thorbecke (1980).

4. Postmus and Van Veen (1949), Mathur, Wahi, Shrivastava and Gahlaut (1961), Blankhart (1967), Government of Pakistan (1970), Institute of Nutrition and Food Science, Dacca (1977), D'Souza and Chen (1980) and Chen, Huq and D'Souza (1980).

5. Flores, Garcia, Florez and Lara (1964), Foster (1966), Flores, Menchu, Lara and Guzman (1970).

6. From a total of about 5,000 'census circles' in the 1974 Bangladesh census, 160 were selected at random. These 160 circles, each containing 10-14 villages, were then arranged into four groups 'according to the four major administrative divisions of the country' (Chittagong, Dacca, Rajshahi and Khulna). Then three census circles were selected in each of these divisions by a sampling method based on the total population of the census circles. Then from each of these census circles a single village was selected at random. A total of 12 'locations' was thus obtained, and 60 households were studied in each location.

7. The families were selected 'purposefully' using the criteria of households (a) having one or more children under 5 years, (b) being accessible for practical organization of dietary observation, and (c) grouped according to landownership ('landless', 'marginal' and 'surplus').

8. The nutritional 'deficit' of the children is marked. The average calorie intakes of children of age groups 1-3, 4-6 and 7-9 years are respectively 630 ('requirement' 1360), 1172 ('requirement' 1830) and 1497 ('requirement' 2190). The disproportionately high mortality rates of children in Bangladesh has been analysed by McIntosh, Nasim and Satchell (1981).

9. See also WHO (1974).

10. See, for example, Sukhatme (1977, 1978), Scrimshaw (1977), Srinivasan (1977, 1979); also Davidson, Passmore, Brock and Truswell (1979).

11. Chen, Huq and D'Souza (1980) blame 'faulty national statistics on women's work and lack of quantitative information on the energy demands of household and home-based work' (p. 10). See also Farouk and Ali (1977).

12. Institute of Nutrition and Food Science, Dacca (1977, p. 31).

13. On the complex relationships between work and food, see Bliss and Stern (1978).

14. See Table 7.7 in Institute of Nutrition and Food Science, Dacca (1977).

15. Chen, Huq and D'Souza (1980, p.9).

16. See UNICEF (1981).

17. The combined population of the 30 blocks is 4.2 million.

18. These standards were determined in the Hyderabad meeting of the Nutrition Subcommittee of the Indian Academy of Pediatrics in 1972.

19. See National Institute of Nutrition, Hyderabad (1979, Tables 24 and 25). The better performance of girls holds for every one of the ten Indian States that were covered, except for Madhya Pradesh, for one category ('severe') malnutrition. However, the samples are small, e.g. in West Bengal only 518 children were surveyed from the whole state (in contrast with 1923 children from only 30 blocks in flood-affected districts in West Bengal in the 1979 UNICEF survey).

20. It is worth noting here that there is very often a tendency towards under-reporting of female morbidity. See Sen (1982).

21. This adds to the dichotomy between choice and welfare that exists even without considering the problem of intra-family distribution. On that general dichotomy, see Sen (1977b).

22. Cf. Das and Nicholas (1981).

23. Cf. '. . .in the important area of food, nutrition and health, it would be a gross oversimplification to define an individual's welfare as his state of satisfaction from the goods and services that he receives from his environment' (Das and Nicholas, 1981, p. 26).

24. Sen (1977c, 1979, 1980).

25. The 'capability approach' (Sen, 1980) can be seen as an extension of Rawls's (1971) focus on 'primary goods'. Rawls motivates his concern with primary goods by showing their relevance to what people are able to do. While he postpones the question of interpersonal variation in the transformation of primary goods into capabilities, the capability approach takes explicit note of that. For nutrition and health such variations are, of course, inescapable.

26. This is not to deny the importance of entitlement of families in the causal analysis of starvation and undernourishment, both in famine and non-famine situations (see Sen, 1981a, 1981b). But the analysis has to be carried beyond that, especially in catching the specific pattern of deprivation. In Sen (1984) there is an attempt to extend the entitlement analysis to divisions *within* the family interconnected with entitlements *of* families.

27. See Samuelson (1947).

28. See Lange (1936, 1938) and Lerner (1944).

29. See Arrow (1951), Debreu (1959) and Arrow and Hahn (1971).

30. It is, of course, quite possible that the favouring of the male children (see Section 2) reflects hard-headed calculation by the family heads regarding the greater future earning power of the male children. Devotees of the 'invisible hand' would no doubt see its benign presence in these distressing facts. But even if this were the only reason for the disparity, which I doubt, it would still be legitimate to distinguish between the returns to the family heads (e.g. through support in old age) and the return to *all* members of the family (*including*, of course, the family heads).

31. See especially Deaton and Muellbauer (1980, Chapter 8), who also discuss the earlier literature.

REFERENCES

Arrow, K. J. (1951): 'An Extension of the Basic Theorems of Classical Welfare Economics', in J. Neyman (ed.), *Proceedings of the Second Berkeley Symposium on Mathematical Statistics and Probability* (Berkeley: University of California Press).

_____ and F. H. Hahn, (1971): *General Competitive Analysis* (Edinburgh: Oliver & Boyd; reprinted by North-Holland: Amsterdam).

Bardhan, P. (1974): 'On Life and Death Questions', *Economic and Political Weekly*, **9**, Special Number.

Blankhart, D. N. (1967): 'Individual Intake of Food in Young Children in Relation to Malnutrition and Night Blindness', *Tropical and Geographical Medicine*, **19**.

Bliss, C. and N. H. Stern (1978): 'Productivity, Wages and Nutrition', Parts I and II, *Journal of Development Economics*, **5**, **4**.

Bohdal, M., N. E. Gibbs and W. K. Simmons (1968): 'Nutrition Survey and Campaign Against Malnutrition in Kenya', mimeographed, report to the Ministry of Health of Kenya on the WHO/FAO UNICEF 1964-1968 assisted project.

CMDA (1980): 'Health and Socio-Economic Survey of Calcutta Metropolitan Development Area', Calcutta: I.S.I. and Calcutta Metropolitan Development Authority.

Chen, L. C., E. Huq and S. D'Souza (1980): 'A Study of Sex-Biased Behaviour in the Intra-Family Allocation of Food and the Utilization of Health Care Services in Rural Bangladesh', International Centre for Diarrhoeal Disease Research, Bangladesh and Department of Population Sciences, Harvard School of Public Health.

Crawford, L. and E. Thorbecke (1980): 'The Analysis of Food Poverty: An Illustration from Kenya', *Pakistan Development Review*, **19**.

Das, V. and R. Nicholas (1981): ' "Welfare" and "Well-Being" in South Asian Societies', mimeographed, ACLS-SSRC Joint Committee on South Asia, SSRC, New York.

Davey, P. L. H. (1962a): 'Report on the National Nutrition Survey', mimeographed, Food and Nutrition Board, Accra.

_____(1962b): 'A Summary of Conclusions and Recommendations of the National Surveys of 1961 and 1962', mimeographed, Food and Nutrition Board, Accra.

Davidson, S., R. Passmore, J. F. Brock and A. S. Truswell (1979): *Human Nutrition and Dietetics*, 7th edn (Edinburgh: Churchill Livingstone).

Deaton, A. and J. Muellbauer (1980): *Economic and Consumer Behaviour* (Cambridge: Cambridge University Press).

Debreu, G. (1959): *The Theory of Value* (New York: Wiley).

den Hartog, A. P. (1973): 'Unequal Distribution of Food Within the Household', *FAO Newsletter*, **10**, 4 (October-December).

D'Souza, S. and L. C. Chen (1980): 'Sex Bias of Mortality Differentials in Rural Bangladesh', mimeographed, International Centre for Diarrhoeal Disease Research, Dacca, Bangladesh.

FAO/WHO Expert Committee (1973): *Energy and Protein Requirements* (Rome: Food and Agriculture Organization of the United Nations).

Farouk and N. Ali (1977): *The Hardworking Poor (A survey of how people use their time in Bangladesh)* (Dacca: Bureau of Economic Research, University of Dacca).

Flores, M., B. Garcia, Z. Florez and M. Y. Lara (1964): 'Annual Patterns of Family and Children's Diet in Three Guatemalan Indian Communities', *British Journal of Nutrition*, **18**, 281-93.

_____ M. T. Menchu, M. Y. Lara and M. A. Guzman (1970): 'Relación entre la ingesta de calorías y nutrientes en preescolares y la disponibilidad de alimentos en la familia', *Archivos Latino-Americanos de Nutricion*, **20** (1), 41-58.

Foster, G. M. (1966): *Social Anthropology and Nutrition of the preschool child, especially as related to Latin America* (Washington, DC: National Academy of Sciences, National Research Council, Publication 1282).

Government of Pakistan (1970): *Nutrition Survey of West Pakistan — Ministry of Health, Labour and Family Planning February 1965-November 1966* (Islamabad: Government of Pakistan).

Institute of Nutrition and Food Science, Dacca (1977): *Nutrition Survey of Rural Bangladesh 1975-76* (Dacca: University of Dacca).

Kynch, J. and A. K. Sen (1983): 'Indian Women: Well-being and Survival', *Cambridge Journal of Economics*, 7.

Lange, O. (1936): 'On the Economic Theory of Socialism', *Review of Economic Studies*, 4 (1936-37).

_____ (1938): 'The Foundations of Welfare Economics', *Econometrica*, 10.

Lerner, A. P. (1944): *The Economics of Control* (London: Macmillan).

Mathur, K. S., P. N. Wahi, S. K. Shrivastava and D. S. Gahlaut (1961): 'Diet in Western Uttar Pradesh', *Journal of Indian Medical Association*, 37 (2), 58-63.

McFie, I. (1967): 'Nutrient Intakes of Urban Dwellers in Lagos, Nigeria', *British Journal of Nutrition*, 21, 257-68.

McIntosh, J., A. Nasim and S. Satchell (1981): 'Differential Mortality in Rural Bangladesh', mimeographed, University of Essex. Presented at the Development Studies Association 1981 Annual Conference.

Miller, B. (1981): *The Endangered Sex: Neglect of Female Children in Rural North India* (Ithaca, NY: Cornell University Press).

Mitra, A. (1980): *Implications of Declining Sex Ratio in India's Population* (Bombay: Allied Publishers).

National Institute of Nutrition, Hyderabad (1979): 'National Nutrition Monitoring Bureau Report for the Year 1978', mimeographed.

Nicol, B. M. (1959): 'The Calorie Requirements of Nigerian Peasant Farmers', *British Journal of Nutrition*, 13, 293-306.

Postmus, S. and A. G. Van Veen (1949): 'Dietary Surveys in Java and East Indonesia (II)', *Chron. Nat.*, 105 (11), 261-8.

Rawls, J. (1971): *A Theory of Justice* (Cambridge, Mass.: Harvard University Press).

Registrar General of India (1980): *Survey of Infant and Child Mortality, 1979: A Preliminary Report* (New Delhi: Office of the Registrar General of India).

Ritchie, J. A. S. (1963): *Teaching Better Nutrition*, FAO Nutritional Studies, 6 (Rome: FAO).

Samuelson, P. A. (1947): *Foundations of Economic Analysis* (Cambridge, Mass.: Harvard University Press).

Schofield, S. (1975)": *Village Nutrition Studies: An Annotated Bibliography*, Institute of Development Studies, University of Sussex.

Scrimshaw, N. S. (1977): 'Effect of Infection on Nutrient Requirements', *American Journal of Clinical Nutrition*, 30, 1536-44.

Seal, S. C., B. Bhattacharjee, J. Roy and R. Rao (1981): 'Comparative Study of Improved and Unimproved Bustees', mimeographed, Calcutta Metropolitan Development Authority.

Sen, A. K. (1976): 'Females as Failures of Exchange Entitlements', *Economic and Political Weekly*, 11, 31-33, Special Number.

_____ (1977a): 'Starvation and Exchange Entitlements: A General Approach and its Application to the Great Bengal Famine', *Cambridge Journal of Economics*, 1, 33-59.

_____ (1977b): 'Rational Fools: A Critique of the Behavioural Foundations of Economic Theory', *Philosophy and Public Affairs*, 6, 317-44; reprinted in F. Hahn and M. Hollis (eds), *Philosophy and Economic Theory* (Oxford: Oxford University Press), and my *Choice, Welfare and Measurement* (Oxford: Blackwell, 1982).

_____ (1977c): 'On Weights and Measures: Informational Constraints in Social Welfare Analysis', *Econometrica*, **45**, 1539-72, reprinted in *Choice, Welfare and Measurement*.

_____ (1979): 'Personal Utilities and Public Judgments: Or What's Wrong with Welfare Economics?', *Economic Journal*, **89**, 537-58; reprinted in *Choice, Welfare and Measurement*.

_____ (1980): 'Equality of What?', in S. McMurrin (ed.), *Tanner Lectures on Human Values* (Cambridge: Cambridge University Press); reprinted in *Choice, Welfare and Measurement*.

_____ (1981a): *Poverty and Famines: An Essay on Entitlements and Deprivation* (Oxford: Clarendon Press).

_____ (1981b): 'Ingredients of Famine Analysis: Availability and Entitlements', *Quarterly Journal of Economics*, **95**, 433-64.

_____ (1982): 'Food Battles: Conflicts in the Access to Food', Coromandel Lecture, 12 December 1982, New Delhi.

_____ (1983): 'Economics and the Family', *Asian Development Review*, 1.

_____ (1984): 'Women, Technology and Sexual Divisions', Working Paper, Technology Division, UNCTAD, Geneva.

_____ and S. Sengupta, (1983): 'Malnutrition of Rural Children and the Sex Bias', *Economic and Political Weekly*, **18**, Annual Number.

Spring, Rice, M. (1939): *Working-Class Wives: Their Health and Condition* (Harmondsworth: Penguin).

Srinivasan, T. N. (1977): 'Development, Poverty and Basic Human Needs: Some Issues', *Food Research Institute Studies*, **16**.

_____ (1979): 'Malnutrition: Some Measurement and Policy Issues', mimeographed, World Bank, Washington, D.C.

Sukhatme, P. V. (1977): *Nutrition and Poverty* (New Delhi: Indian Agricultural Research Institute).

_____ (1978): 'Assessment of Adequacy of Diets at Different Income Levels', *Economic and Political Weekly*, **13**, Special Number.

Thomson, B. P. (1954): 'Two Studies in African Nutrition', Lusaka: Rhodes Livingstone papers, No. 24.

UNICEF (1981): *A Sample Survey Report on the Health and Nutrition Status of Children Covered by the Mother and Child Care Programme under the UNICEF Assisted Food Rehabilitation Programme in West Bengal (First Assessment 1979)* (Calcutta: UNICEF).

University of Ibadan (1970): *Technical Report on the Nutrition Survey, Oje District, Ibadan Town* (Nigeria: Food Science and Applied Nutrition Unit, University of Ibadan).

Visaria, P. (1961): *The Sex Ratio of the Population of India*, Monograph 10, Census of India 1961 (New Delhi: Office of the Registrar General of India).

WHO (1974): *Handbook of Human Nutrition Requirement* (Geneva: World Health Organisation).

FURTHER READING *(suggested by the Editors)*.

Vaughan, Megan (1987) *The Story of an African Famine: Gender and Family in 20th Century Malawi*, (Cambridge: Cambridge University Press).

Jiggins, Janice (1986) 'Women and Seasonality: Coping with Crisis and Calamity', *IDS Bulletin*, July, Vol. 17, No. 3, pp. 9-18.

Longhurst, Richard (1986): 'Household Food Strategies in Response to Seasonality and Famine', *IDS Bulletin*, July, Vol. 17, No. 3., pp. 27-35.

Section III
The Changing World Economy

The Changing World Economy

The economies of the Third World are integrated in various ways into the international economic system, otherwise known as world capitalism. The form and extent of this integration are a matter of disagreement among theorists, but that every economy in the world is affected by the operation of the system as a whole is not in doubt. This section is concerned with three aspects of international economic exchange: trade, the role played by multinational corporations (MNCs), and the debt crisis.

In the first reading, 'The Third World in the International Division of Labour', Green and Sutcliffe look at the shifting patterns of world trade since World War II. The volume of trade has expanded enormously, but trade between industrialised countries still dominates, with roughly two-thirds of the total. Manufactured products now form a greater proportion of Third World exports than primary commodities. But this is almost entirely accounted for by the success of what are known as 'newly industrialising countries' (NICs) – Hong Kong, Singapore *et al* – and, when they are excluded, the pattern of Third World trade shows the expected heavy reliance on a few primary commodities. Some countries rely on just one commodity for more than half their export earnings – Ghana on cocoa, Uganda, Ethiopia and Columbia on coffee, and so on.

Trade figures provide only part of the picture of international economic activity. Ankie Hoogvelt, in 'From World Market to World Factory', points out that there has been 'a qualitative change in the organisation of the world economy' away from trade between nations towards international production organised by multinational corporations. 'The combined production of all MNCs abroad . . . is now greater than the total value of goods and services that enter the trade between countries.'[1] 'It may be that the export success of the NICs is due less to industrial transformation than to their being used as sites for multinational production: '. . . what we are witnessing is not so much the rapid industrialisation of certain successfully developing countries, but rather the selection of certain *sites* in the Third World for the purpose of relocation of industrial activity from the advanced countries.'

Those sites are often chosen because of the availability of cheap, docile labour – mainly young women. In 'The Subordination of Women and the Internationalisation of Factory Production', Diane Elson and Ruth Pearson ask 'Why is it young women who overwhelmingly constitute the labour force of world market factories?' To say that the jobs they do are 'women's work' does not explain why jobs are sex-stereotyped in the first place. Elson and Pearson agree that there is a difference between women and men as potential factory workers, but they argue that this difference is not natural. Women have 'nimble fingers' because of their domestic training, and the jobs they do are classed as unskilled because it is women who do them; 'technically similar jobs identified as "men's work" tend to be classified as "skilled".' This is part of 'a process of the *subordination* of women as a gender.'

Multinationals are often cast as villains in the theatre of economics. The paper by Benjamin Higgins and Jean D. Higgins, 'Multinationals and Foreign Investment', takes a cool look at the arguments for and against the MNCs as agents of development. Ireland, with its heavy reliance on foreign investment, is an interesting case study. It is still one of the richest countries in the world, but as a small, peripheral economy it faces particular problems in attempting to industrialise further. Since the 1950s, outward-looking, free market strategies have been adopted with a measure of success. Eoin O'Malley, in 'The Problem of Late Industrialisation and the Experience of the Republic of Ireland', argues, however, that this success is due less to these strategies than to the exceptional circumstances of attracting a high proportion of mobile foreign industry.

The debt problem is part of the crisis affecting the economic system as a whole, but its effects are crippling many countries. How this international crisis arose is recounted by Harold Lever and Christopher Huhne in 'Debt and Danger'. They place responsibility both for the crisis and for its resolution firmly at the doors of the industrialised nations. It was long understood, they argue, that there should be a net transfer of resources to the Third World for the foreseeable future, and up until 1973 it was also understood that commercial banks were not a suitable vehicle for such lending. What led to the crisis was the need to keep up the level of demand in the world economy, by recycling the dollars earned by the oil-exporting countries after the OPEC countries raised the price of oil in 1973, allied to the delusion that sovereign borrowing was risk-free.

In 'The Debt Crisis and the Poor', Keith Griffin argues that the 'so-called debt crisis is essentially the financial counterpart to the current prolonged recession.' If the world economy were to recover, and growth rates to increase, the debt problem would shrink and probably disappear. But the crisis exists and it is the debtor countries that are paying the price. Griffin, too, places responsibility with the developed countries who dominate world financial institutions, especially the International Monetary Fund. Only the international financial authorities have the power to resolve the issue.

In the final reading, 'The End of the Third World', Nigel Harris reflects on the decline of Third Worldism as an ideology, 'a type of national reformism dedicated to the creation of new societies and a new world'. The view of the world it represented was over-simplified, Harris argues. The reality is more complex. The 'great unfinished question of world history' remains: 'the freedom not of minorities, nor of states, but of the majority'.

The Third World in the International Division of Labour

Francis Green and Bob Sutcliffe

This extract is from the authors' The Profit System *(1987).*

In one sense international commodity trade is only a special case of a more general phenomenon, the social division of labour. Whether exchange involves international trade depends upon the partly arbitrary fact of where national borders have been drawn. The sale of Californian wine in New York is not international trade but involves much greater geographical separation of producers and consumers than the sale of Dutch cheese in Belgium. The laws which determine international trade, therefore, are partly a subcategory of the laws which determine the division of labour in a more general sense.

But international trade is different from internal trade in the sense that it is governed by an extra set of rules and regulations. Within countries there are usually not many restrictions on the free movement of goods; whereas across national borders trade can be restricted by customs tariffs and duties, quantitative restrictions and regulations relating to hygiene, standards and so on. And international trade involves the exchange of different currencies; the regulations governing this can be at least as involved as trade regulations.

The history of the study of international trade has been dominated for one and a half centuries by a famous theory – the theory of comparative advantage as outlined by the renowned English nineteenth-century economist and politician, David Ricardo. It argues that those who live in different countries can gain if in each country production is concentrated on those commodities with the greatest comparative advantage: that is, where costs are lowest compared to other commodities, so that both countries should specialize and then trade with each other. Consumers can then buy the whole range of goods and services through trade. Thus, trade restrictions should be removed to enable maximum benefits to be gained from exchange. If the model is generalized to the whole world then the productive capacity of the world's labour force would be maximized and each country would be better off than with national self-sufficiency.

The theory makes no explicit reference to capitalism. Indeed as a principle it has been applied to individuals and to many kinds of economic system. But traditionally it has been closely associated with capitalism. It carries the assumption that the division of labour which it recommends will be best achieved by the unfettered working of the market system. Businesses in each country will specialize in the commodities in which they have comparative advantage because it will be more profitable to do so.

But since profits in international trade are partly determined by exchange rates between currencies, the model makes an assumption also about the determination of exchange rates. There are two possibilities.

(a) It could assume that exchange rates are settled by means of competitive financial markets for currencies. Thus when one country has a surplus in its balance of trade there will be an excess demand for its currency. This will tend to drive up the price of its currency, thereby reducing the competitiveness of that country's products. In this way exports are brought into balance with imports; and international specialization based on comparative advantage will be automatically assured by the operating of free markets and the pursuit of profit by producers, traders and currency speculators.

(b) Alternatively, exchange rates may be fixed by governments intervening in the currency markets. If one country has a deficit in its trade, its government will continually have to support its currency by buying it up, using its stocks of gold and other international reserves. It is assumed that this would so drain away the gold in the country that prices would generally fall, and continue to do so until its commodities became more competitive and its trade deficit eliminated. So the comparative advantage theory could equally work, on these assumptions, when there are fixed exchange rates, as long as in each country prices are free to move up and down with ease.

Since Ricardo's time, the model of comparative advantage has been elaborated and modified. The Hecksher-Ohlin theory (named after its founders) argues that the basis of comparative advantage is the factor-intensity of production. A country will therefore have comparative advantage in producing those goods which use a relatively large amount of those factors of production (labour, machinery and land) which it possesses in relative abundance.

In this slightly more complicated version the theory still sounds reasonable enough, almost commonsensical. But empirical studies have shown that the world does not work, or so it seems, as the theory predicts. For instance, the exports of the USA, contrary to expectations, turn out to be more labour-intensive than its imports – the oddity is known as Leontief's paradox after its discoverer. It may be less paradoxical if the model is made even more complicated by the addition of more differentiated factors of production.

Studies which have produced these kinds of conclusion still basically maintain the comparative advantage notion. But there is another tradition which rejects it, completely or in part. Comparative advantage was used by Ricardo and his followers in the nineteenth century to justify Britain's policy of free trade. Other countries, however, saw the matter very differently. In Germany and the USA economists and politicians regarded the free trade policy not as a way of maximizing mutual benefit through international trade but as a way for British manufacturers to maintain their superiority in world trade. The most famous advocates of protectionist policies were Friedrich List in Germany and Alexander Hamilton in the USA. Ideas such as theirs have been followed by states wishing to industrialize.

Nowadays protectionism in relatively less developed economies is normally justified by a partial or complete denial of the validity of the comparative advantage principle. Orthodox economists have occasionally accepted minor doctrinal modifications of this kind. They accept that efficiency can sometimes change as a result of gaining experience, so tariff protection for 'infant' industries may be justified for short periods for specific industries. But the opponents of comparative advantage go much further than this and economists usually condemn them for heresy.

They say that comparative advantage is invalid as a principle for organizing world trade under capitalism because it tends to freeze the existing structure of world production to the disadvantage of the underdeveloped countries. The doctrine is used, it is argued, to lock the underdeveloped countries into a world division of labour in which they remain primary producers while the richer countries maintain their industrial prevalence. In this way the international trade system is seen as a mechanism which exploits the underdeveloped countries and which helps to perpetuate underdevelopment. Trade is thus held under certain circumstances to be not an instrument of enrichment, as Ricardo had claimed, but rather an instrument of immiserization.

In other words, the comparative advantage principle may be logical and valid in a hypothetical *static* unchanging world of acts of exchange, but in a real dynamic capitalist world market its prescriptions are often perverse. . . .

Growth of trade

The growth of world trade has been erratic and far from universal. In some periods, its value grew substantially, as in the four decades from 1840 to 1879 when it rose by about 336 per cent, far outstripping the 165 per cent growth of industrial production. Throughout the nineteenth century, trade grew so much that by one estimate it was as much as a third of output by the eve of the First World War.

In other periods, as during the Great Depression in the 1930s, capitalist countries became inward-looking and protectionist, and world trade fell. Overall, by 1948 world industrial production was about 2.7 times its 1913 level, but trade was virtually the same as in 1913.

The post-war period has seen a renewed trend towards internationalization. The volume of trade grew on average by just under 7 per cent per annum from 1948 to 1979, which was roughly half as fast again as the growth of output. In the latter years trade was beginning to slow down, and in the world recession of the early 1980s it began to fall again. But the amounts remain enormous: $1,700 billion worth of goods and services were exchanged across national borders in 1983, just under one-fifth of the total value of commodities produced in the world.

A closer examination shows also a substantial change in the geographical patterns of trade. The post-war period has been the era for expanded trade between the advanced capitalist countries. In 1935 in the aftermath of the tariff protection, trade controls and restrictive currency areas which the major capitalist countries imposed in response to the Great Depression, trade between the advanced industrial countries was only about 26 per cent of total world trade. Partly as a result of tariff-reducing exercises like the EEC and the 'Kennedy' and 'Tokyo' rounds of tariff-reduction, the markets of the advanced industrial countries became more open to each others' products after the Second World War. So by 1970 they had cornered as much as 66 per cent of the world trade.

So from the point of view of the advanced capitalist countries the market is much more of a global arena than it was fifty or even a hundred years ago. In 1870 their trade was on average about 14 per cent of their national products, by 1938 it had dropped to 8 per cent; but in 1983 it was as much as 23 per cent. When account is taken of the fact that some commodities, such as accommodation or haircuts, have to be consumed on the spot, the overall significance of their trade appears even greater.

But many parts of the Third World, such as most of Africa, India and China, failed to participate in the trade boom and now account for a much lower share of world trade than they did before. They have a much smaller place in the international division of labour . . . .

The Third World in the International Division of Labour

In recent times the underdeveloped countries, even after achieving formal political independence, have continued to be profoundly affected by the development of the advanced capitalist countries. Most Third World countries reaped some rewards from the post-war boom, but many suffered badly with the onset of crises in the 1970s.

But the variations were very significant (see Table 1). A number of Third World countries had higher than average growth rates and made some headway towards closing the gap in income levels. Among these were some of the oil-producing countries though their major gains occurred after 1973. The other

Table 1. Annual growth in GNP per capita, 1960-84

	1960-73	1973-80	1980-84
All underdeveloped countries	3.6	3.3	0.5
India	1.3	1.9	2.5
Low-income Africa	0.9	−0.1	−2.1
Major exporters of manufactures	4.3	3.7	0.1
Middle-income oil exporters	3.5	3.1	−0.8
Industrial capitalist countries	3.9	2.1	1.4

Source: World Bank, *World Development Report, 1985,* New York: Oxford University Press for the World Bank, 1985.

major gainers during the boom were the so-called NICs (Newly Industrializing Counties) which successfully broke into the export markets for certain manufactured goods as diverse as basketball shoes and computers. By contrast the boom scarcely reached Africa. In most parts of that continent growth in average income was barely perceptible.

This gulf in economic growth was sharply accentuated by the onset of crises in the world economy. In Africa, 1973 initiated a period of first slow and then rapid decline of its already tragically low incomes. Yet NICs like South Korea, Taiwan, Singapore and Hong Kong continued to boom, even if at times their success seemed a little more precarious.

There is a remarkably close correspondence between a country's average income and the way in which its productive activity is divided up between agriculture and industry. In the low-income countries the typical situation is for three-quarters of the labour force to work in agriculture and produce a little more than one-third of the value of national production. In what the World Bank calls 'middle income economies' 44 per cent of the labour force on average produce 15 per cent of national output. By contrast in the developed countries a mere 6 per cent of the workforce remain in agriculture, producing only 3 per cent of national output.

Moreover, the industrial workforces of the Third World have only been expanding slowly, with the exception of the NICs. The typical picture is one of only very slow change from the traditional, overwhelmingly agricultural productive structure.

Generally, productivity in agriculture is much lower than it is in industry. But in the most advanced countries agricultural productivity has caught up with overall productivity. This means that the small number of farmworkers in the most developed countries are immensely more productive than the relatively numerous farmworkers in underdeveloped countries. The value of output produced by a farmworker in the USA is about a hundred times that produced by a farmworker in India.

The division of international trade to some extent reflects these differences in economic structure between underdeveloped and developed countries, but with some exceptions. As expected, the great majority (86 per cent) of world manufactured exports come from the developed industrialized countries and only 14 per cent from the underdeveloped countries (see Table 2).

Many underdeveloped countries, especially the poorest ones, export almost exclusively raw materials (agricultural or mineral) which have been little, if at all, processed. Taken as a whole, more than three-quarters of the Third World's exports are raw materials. But this figure is misleading. It includes oil, which is a very special commodity, many of whose producers, if geographically part of the Third World, are by no means poor. It may seem surprising that, excluding oil, the other primary products exported by Third World countries are now smaller in value than their manufactured exports. But these come from a tiny handful of countries. If these NICs are also excluded, then other Third World countries, especially in Africa, do indeed display the traditional expected pattern of exports

Table 2. Capitalist world exports by commodity and area, 1980 (in $ billion)

		Developed countries	Underdeveloped countries	Total
Primary commodities:	oil	84	348	432
	others	237	118	355
Total		321	466	787
Manufactures and others		885	142	1027
Total		1206	608	1814

Source: Chris Edwards, *The Fragmented World: Competing Perspectives on Trade, Money and Crisis,* London and New York: Methuen, 1985, p.56.

almost exclusively of primary products. For some, more than half their exports are of one commodity: Uganda, Ethiopia and Colombia (coffee), Sudan (cotton), Zambia and Chile (copper), Ghana (cocoa), Guinea (bauxite), Bolivia (tin) and Malawi (tobacco).

It may also come as a surprise that the Third World's exports of primary products, other than oil, are smaller in value than the primary product exports of the advanced countries. This fact shows that in addition to the difference between rich and poor nations in the *structure* of trade there is also a difference in the *amount* of trade. Developed countries account for about two-thirds of all world exports and about the same proportion of primary commodity exports other than oil. While their share of manufactured exports dropped a little in the twenty years from 1960 to 1980, their share of primary exports actually increased during that time.

The comparative failure of underdeveloped countries even in primary products was provoked by three factors. One was the disruption of production by the great variety of economic, political and physical problems which have beset Third World countries, including natural disasters, planning and policy errors, lack of internal and external investment, famine, wars, invasions and political upheavals. A second was the fact that many of the primary products which the Third World produces are products for which demand has not expanded very fast in the long run, or fell very sharply in the short run after the crisis of 1973. As a result of this, the average prices of the Third World's primary products have, apart from a sudden and temporary upward lurch in 1973, declined continuously since 1965, while the prices of the manufactured imports have continued to rise. Third World countries have suffered, in other words, a worsening in their terms of trade. This has exacerbated balance of payments deficits and led to indebtedness. . .

A third, and associated, reason why underdeveloped countries have been losing their share of primary product exports is agricultural protectionism in the advanced capitalist countries. Because of the disproportionate political weight of farming communities in North America and western Europe, they have been systematically assisted by deficiency payments schemes or by protective import-prevention and surplus-buying schemes such as the EEC's Common Agricultural Policy. The most frequently condemned feature of this policy has been the obscene coexistence of vast surplus food stocks in rich western Europe and widespread famine and hunger in Africa, Asia and Latin America. The EEC's 'defence' of its refusal to distribute the food stocks to those who need them is that this would ruin the market and so undermine the protective effect of the policy.

A less generally appreciated consequence is that the agricultural protectionism of the advanced countries closes off potential markets for Third World agricultural producers. It has been estimated by the World Bank that in 1983 the revenues lost to the Third World as a result of trade barriers against sugar and beef and veal exporters amounted in total to about $12.5 billion, at 1980 prices, which was about 10 per cent of the Third World's total exports of primary products.

It is a frequent complaint of Third World governments and capitalists that protectionism is also a major obstacle in the way of increasing their exports of manufactured goods to the markets of the developed countries, which try artificially to extend the life of dying industries whose products could be produced more competitively in the Third World. There is a lot of justice in this complaint. The tariff structures of the advanced countries are typically graded so that goods with a higher degree of processing pay a higher rate of duty. And in recent years there has been an upsurge of non-tariff restrictions on imports to the advanced countries (known as 'the new protectionism') which have been aimed specifically against the exports of Japan and the NICs. About one-fifth of all exports from underdeveloped countries are affected by such measures.

Typical of what can happen is the case of the Bangladeshi shirts. In the early 1980s a group of capitalists in Bangladesh (a country which according to World Bank statistics is exceeded in poverty only by Ethiopia) started exporting cotton shirts to Europe. They found a loophole through which to enter the market and had an extraordinary success. Sales in the UK alone jumped from 200,000 in 1983 to over 1 million in 1984. Similar amounts were sold in France and Germany. The industry accounted for nearly a tenth of Bangladesh's export earnings though it represented only one-thousandth of Europe's garment imports. But the UK and France took steps in 1985 to impose quotas against it. In the face of such policies it is hard not to be cynical about the possibilities of any real transformation of the world division of labour in favour of the underdeveloped countries.

None the less the NICs have succeeded where others have failed. No simple explanation is possible. The NICs differ and in all cases there have been multiple reasons for their success. But one reason has clearly been that the developed countries have been prepared to allow their industrial growth by granting them special privileges. They have been given more generous import quotas than other countries, though even so they have sometimes had to exhibit some very deft footwork to dodge the effect of the advanced countries' protectionism. They have also had some special privileges with regard to finance. Undoubtedly such special consideration had political motives. The desirability of supporting countries on the borders of Asian communism (South Korea, Hong Kong, Taiwan and Singapore) or with strong anti-socialist regimes (the Brazilian military dictatorship after the 1964 coup) were no doubt important considerations.

Orthodox economists have broadcast a fable that the NICs confirm the rewards given to the traditional virtues of free competition and the market. This is hardly supported by the evidence. South Korea, to quote an example, is extremely protectionist of its home market; its government has rigidly controlled the activities of foreign capital; its own capitalist sector is dominated by a group of huge conglomerate monopolies known as *chaebols* (of which one collapsed in 1985); and the state interferes in most aspects of the economy. Politial opposition and in particular the free organization of labour have been ruthlessly suppressed, as in Singapore and other NICs.

While the real experience of the NICs can give little comfort to the proponents of orthodox free market economics, they also cannot be regarded, as many dependency theorists have regarded them, as insignificant exceptions to the general rule of underdevelopment as a polar opposite of development. The NICs are authentic examples of capitalist development taking place in the modern world.

The profit system has worked in a significant group of countries to produce industrialization at a much faster rate than in any of the developed countries except for Japan. Yet it has also produced, as it did in Europe and the USA in the nineteenth century, a relatively low-paid industrial proletariat, often predominantly of women, who to avoid starvation must endure sweatshop working conditions, which irreversibly damage their health, and who are usually prevented from organizing to defend themselves. It would be hard to evaluate their lives in comparison with the rural poverty of the billions who do not live in one of the NICs.

SOURCES

Crow, Ben and Alan Thomas, with Robin Jenkins and Judy Kimble, *The Third World Atlas*, Milton Keynes: Open University Press, 1983.

Edwards, Chris, *The Fragmented World: Competing Perspectives on Trade, Money and Crisis*, London and New York: Methuen, 1985.

Hayter, Teresa and Catharine Watson, *Aid: Rhetoric and Reality*, London: Pluto Press, 1985.

International Monetary Fund, *International Financial Statistics*, Washington DC: IMF, various issues.

Kaplinsky, Raphael (ed.), *Third World Industrialization in the 1980s; Open Economies in a Closing World*, London, Frank Cass, 1984.

Kenwood, A.G. and A.L. Lougheed, *The Growth of the International Economy, 1820-1980*, London: Allen & Unwin, 1983.

OECD Economic Outlook, *Historical Statistics, 1960-1983*, Paris: OECD, 1985.

Sen, Amartya, *Poverty and Famines: An Essay on Entitlement and Deprivation*, Oxford: Oxford University Press, 1982.

Sivard, Ruth Leger, *World Military and Social Expenditures, 1983*, Washington DC: World Priorities, 1983.

US Department of Commerce, Bureau of the Census, *Statistical Abstract of the United States*, Washington DC, various years.

Versluysen, E.L., *The Political Economy of International Finance*, Farnborough: Gower Press, 1981.

World Bank, *World Development Report, 1985*, New York: Oxford University Press for the World Bank, 1985; and previous years.

From World Market to World Factory

Ankie M.M. Hoogvelt

This paper is taken from the author's study,
The Third World in Global Development *(1982)*

Multinational corporations (i.e. economic enterprises with production facilities in more than one country)[1] have existed for a very long time. But what has made them a dominant feature of the recently evolved world economic order is certain cumulative changes in their size, in their number, and in the scope and nature of their activities. These cumulative changes together have added up to a qualitative change in the organisation of the world economy itself, namely one involving a shift away from international trade and towards international production. What we are witnessing is a change from 'world market' to 'world factory' . . . .[2]

The world economy is conventionally seen as consisting of a number of independently producing countries. These countries meet in the world market where they exchange their goods and services at prices determined 'neutrally' by the market forces of supply and demand. The proceeds of these sales are distributed amongst the producing individuals of each country concerned. The success of a nation's performance in the international hierarchy, and hence the *per capita* income of its people, is seen largely as a function of a nation's industriousness at home and its competitiveness abroad. Governments are thought able to affect the national economic performance by adopting and implementing policies designed to encourage industriousness at home and improving the competitive position abroad.

Things, however, are never as they seem. Today, for instance, the four largest *transnational* corporations together have an annual turnover greater than the total GNP of the whole continent of Africa. The top thirty-four companies, with turnovers over 10 billion dollars per year, outdistance the GNPs of some seventy countries normally ranked in the 'world economic hierarchy'. Together these companies have a global production in excess of the total product of some eighty poor countries in which over half of the world population live.[3] All MNCs together employ some 13-14 million people, of which an estimated 3-4 million are in the developing countries.[4] Some of the larger ones with up to 400,000 employees effectively affect[5] the lives of at least as many people as a one-million population nation.

Yet, when reporting on the world economic situation, the World Bank, the IMF, the Bank for International Settlements, the OECD and the UN Economic and Social Council will ignore these global economic enterprises with grim determination. The latter, apparently, are to be considered as 'epiphenomena', best examined and reported on by separate, *ad hoc*, groups of experts, by a specially set up commission of the United Nations. Despite an abundance of

206

information available on the subject, collected moreover by these same eminent groups of experts (from which I shall quote below), the official annual recording of the world economic situation will simply not mention it.

This is really a most intriguing phenomenon . . . . [The] *World Bank Development Report* (glowingly described by *The Guardian* as the nearest thing to having an annual report on the present state of the planet and the people who live on it)[6] puts a premium on a country's participation in world trade. Indeed, in its view, the rise and fall of nations in the world economic hierarchy is ultimately attested by their participation in international trade. And much of the World Bank's current optimism regarding the middle-income countries' future stems from the observation that they have increased their percentage share of world exports of manufactures from 6 to 10 per cent. Yet as early as 1973 an *ad hoc* group of experts from the United Nations concluded that 'international production defined as production subject to foreign control or decision and measured by the sales of foreign affiliates of multinational corporations has surpassed trade as the main vehicle of international economic exchange'.[7] In that year there were some 10,000 enterprises identifiable as 'multinational' (i.e. firms with at least one foreign affiliate link, even though the link itself can include more than one outlet per host country). It was estimated by UN experts that in 1971 international production reached approximately 330 billion dollars, somewhat larger than the total exports of all market economies. Using the same measures of estimation a second group of experts some five years later put the figure for 1976 at 830 billion dollars.[8]

This is what is meant by 'international production surpassing international trade'. We can appreciate the metaphor of international production being a *vehicle* for international exchanges even better if we consider that national and world trade figures always include, and hence conceal, so-called intra-firm sales, that is, sales between various affiliates of the same multinational group and between these and the parent company. It is estimated that in 1974 nearly half of all imports to the USA and just half of all exports from the USA consisted of such intra-firm transactions. Comparable figures for other OECD countries were, however, lower, putting the figure at one-third of the trade of these countries.[9]

The discrepancy between international production data and international trade data bears out with special penalty for precisely those countries which are most deeply involved in international production, both as 'home' countries and as 'host' countries.

The USA, for example, remains the most important domicile for the headquarters of multinational corporations, particularly if measured by size of firms. In 1976 the foreign affiliates of US companies sold 212 billion dollars worth of goods. This is the equivalent of about one-quarter of total US domestic industrial production.[10] Of the total of affiliate sales 161 billion dollars worth was sold in the foreign countries hosting the affiliates, while 14.1 billion dollars, or 6.6 per cent, was exported to the USA, and 37.7 billion dollars, or 17.7 per cent, was exported to third countries.[11] The latter figure represents, as it were,

US 'foreign' exports as opposed to US domestic exports. It is no wonder that when we look at the list of the fifty leading US 'domestic' exporters, we find the real giants of the US business world poorly represented (thirteen out of fifty).[12] After all they are doing their 'exporting' from foreign lands. What this points to, of course, is that there are two American economies in the world: one domestic, one foreign; one the largest, the other about the fifth largest; one officially recorded and statistically represented, the other invisible and statistically absent. The divergence between the USA's domestic economy and its 'foreign' economy has consequences for its position as a 'super power' as well as for the general organisation of the world capitalist economy. This is a central focus of debate among Marxist writers on imperialism . . . .

As for the hosts of international production, here – contrary to popular myth – the Third World *as a group* is not of very great importance. In fact, the role of the Third World (again, as a group) as receiver of foreign direct investment has been steadily declining. In 1960 the Third World accounted for one-half of total direct overseas investments. This percentage had declined to one-third in 1966 and to one-quarter in 1974.[13] Instead, international production has been more and more concentrated in the already advanced market economies, and much of the growth of this international production has been due to the rapid expansion of cross-Atlantic penetration, particularly since the creation of the EEC. This geographical redirection of direct foreign investment has accompanied a reorientation of investments by branch of economic activity. As the investing countries became more industrially developed, so they switched their investments away from raw-material production (and cost-reducing profit strategies) into manufacturing industries (and market-orientated strategies). (See Table 1.) This, note, is a *relative* change in investment pattern and not an absolute one, just as the implied decline of the advanced world's dependence on the Third World is also relative and not absolute.

While it is true that the advanced countries have become less dependent on the procurement of agricultural commodities from the Third World, and while technological development has helped them also to reduce their dependence on a variety of raw materials traditionally supplied by the Third World, their vulnerability in respect of a limited range of 'critical' minerals of which certain

Table 1. Accumulated stock of direct investment in developing countries by major industrial sector (1966 and 1974)

	1966	1974
Mining and petroleum	49%	18.6%
Manufacturing	27%	44.0%
Utilities plus services	24%	37.3%

Sources: For the 1966 data see Lester B. Pearson, *Partners in Development* (London: Pall Mall Press, 1970) p. 100; for the 1974 data see *Transnational Corporations in World Development* (New York: United Nations, 1978) table III, 38 (this table excludes data on Japanese overseas investment).

Third World countries are significant suppliers has increased.[14] In descending order of import dependence, these critical minerals are chromium, tin, cobalt, nickel, petroleum, manganese and bauxite. Of these, the developing countries can be said to control only four major commodity markets at present: again in descending order, tin, bauxite, petroleum and copper (Tables 2 and 3).[15] Precisely because the number of Third World countries that possess these resources is limited, direct foreign investment in extractive industries generally is concentrated in a limited number of countries. On the other hand, and simultaneously, the relative shift away from investments in extractive industries into manufacturing industries has meant that private capital, when penetrating into developing countries, has become selective in respect of the host countries' potential either as market or as supplier of cheap labour.

Table 2. Dependence on selected imported industrial raw materials, 1975 (imports as a percentage of consumption)

	USA	European Community	Japan
Aluminium (ore and metal)	84	75	100
Chromium	91	98	98
Cobalt	98	98	98
Copper	*	98	90
Iron (ore and metal)	29	55	99
Lead	11	85	73
Manganese	98	99	88
Nickel	72	100	100
Petroleum	37	93	100
Tin	84	93	97
Tungsten	55	100	100
Zinc	61	70	53

*Net exporter.

Source: Council on International Economic Policy, *International Economic Report of the President,* Washington, D.C., January 1977, quoted in W. Arad and Uzi B. Arad, *Sharing Global Resources* (New York: McGraw-Hill, 1979) p.43.

Table 3. LDC share in world trade for selected commodities (in percentages)

Tin	86
Bauxite	79
Petroleum	73
Manganese	56
Copper	54
Iron ore	39

Source: Ronald J. Redker (ed.), *Changing Resource Problems of the Fourth World* (Johns Hopkins University Press for Resources for the Future, 1976).

Table 4. Stock of private overseas direct investments in developing countries, 1977 (principal hosts)

Total of all developing countries = $84,996 m.

	$m.	% of total	Classification
Antibes (Neth.)	2,000	2.3	Mineral exporter
Argentina	2,850	3.3	NIC/mineral exporter
Bahamas	1,470	1.7	Tax haven
Bermuda	4,068	4.7	Tax haven
Brazil	10,700	12.5	NIC/mineral exporter
Chile	1,215	1.4	Mineral exporter
Colombia	1,410	1.6	Mineral exporter
Hong Kong	1,730	2.0	NIC
India	2,450	2.8	Low-income/industrialising
Indonesia	5,160	6.0	Low-income/mineral exporter
Iran	1,000	1.2	Capital surplus oil exporter
South Korea	1,280	1.5	NIC
Liberia	1,035	1.2	Mineral exporter
Malaysia	2,700	3.1	Mineral exporter/NIC
Mexico	5,070	5.9	Mineral exporter/NIC
Nigeria	1,040	1.2	Mineral exporter
Panama	2,750	3.2	Mineral exporter
Peru	1,930	2.3	Mineral exporter
Philippines	1,620	1.9	NIC
Singapore	1,500	1.7	NIC
Spain	5,114	6.0	NIC
Taiwan	1,720	2.0	NIC
Trinidad and Tobago	1,260	1.5	Mineral exporter
Venezuela	3,300	3.8	Mineral exporter
Zaire	1,110	1.3	Mineral exporter
Sub-total	$65,482 m.	77%	

Source: *OECD 1979 DAC Review* (Paris, 1979) table E.1, pp. 255-6.

Along with the scarce mineral exporters, we find the newly industrialising countries the most favoured recipients of direct foreign investment. Table 4 lists those developing countries that at the end of 1977 played host to the largest stock of accumulated private foreign investment. Besides the Bermudas and the Bahamas (which are tax havens) all the countries in the list are either mineral exporters or newly industrialising countries, including India. Between them they accounted for 77 per cent of all outstanding direct foreign investment in 1977. This marks a degree of concentration of direct foreign investment greater than in the preceding decade.[16]

It was observed before that the success of the development performance of the rapidly developing countries was associated with their success in participation in world trade, either as producers of vital resources or as industrialising markets. . . .[17]

It is now becoming obvious that to a not insignificant extent this participation in world trade in its turn is a matter of being 'co-opted' into an expanding system of international production. For example, recalling the data on manufacturing exports from developing countries, four NIC countries (South Korea, Taiwan, Spain and Hong Kong) are known to contribute 45 per cent of all manufacturing exports from developing countries, while the NIC as a group plus India are responsible for no less than 80 per cent. Looking at these same countries (in so far as data are available) we discover that the percentage share of multinational companies in the exports of manufactures of these same countries varies from 20 per cent in Taiwan in 1971 to 90 per cent in Singapore in 1976 (see Table 5). This leads one to estimate that probably the larger part of Third World export-orientated industrialisation is controlled by multinational corporations with headquarters in the West.[18]

Table 5. Share of multinational companies in the exports of manufactures from selected developing countries

Country	Year	MNC share in the exports of manufactures (%)
South Korea	1974	27.8
Taiwan	1971	20.0
Singapore	1976	90.0
Colombia	1970	35.0
Argentina	1969	30.0
Mexico	1969	25.0
Brazil	1969	43.0

Source: P. K. M. Tharakan, *The International Division of Labour and Multinational Companies* (European Centre for Study and Information on Multinational Corporations, in co-operation with Saxon House, 1979) table 3.3. Tharakan's own sources are as follows: B. I. Cohen, *Multinational Firms and Asian Exports* (Yale University Press, 1975); data on Mexico and Brazil were supplied by G. K. Helleiner; the 1976 figures for Singapore are from the *Singapore Bulletin*, vol. 5, no. 9, May 1977, p. 5.

When one transposes such facts of international production on to a picture of Third World differentiation and development . . . one may well conclude that what we are witnessing is not so much the rapid industrialisation of certain successfully developing countries, but rather the selection of certain *sites* in the Third World for the purpose of relocation of industrial activity from the advanced countries. What appears from one point of view to be the rapid development of independent countries appears from another angle to be but a new phase in the development of one single world economy. This, for example, is the view taken by Fröbel *et al.* in what is to date the most comprehensive and detailed survey of multinational manufacturing operations in developing countries. One of the more marked aspects of multinational corporate development over the past fifteen years, they argue, has been the setting up of so-called 'world market factories' in certain selected Third World countries. The locations designated for such factories are variously referred to as 'export-processing zones', or 'free producing zones', or 'industrial parks'. On these sites the MNCs have relocated the more labour-intensive parts of their globally fragmented production process in order to benefit from the availability of free and unorganised labour. Fröbel *et al.*, in their extensive investigation into the origins, the pattern of development and the consequences of such industrial relocation, observe that 'whereas scarcely any industrial production for the world market existed in Asia, Africa and Latin America in the mid-1960s, by the middle of the 1970s world market factories were in operation in seventy-nine free production zones in thirty-nine countries and in many sites outside the zones, employing in all 725,000 workers'.[19] To the extent that production in these world market factories is integrated into the MNCs' global production and distribution flows, they accuse it of being next to useless from the point of view of the establishment of an integrated industrial complex in the host countries themselves.[20] Indeed, as if to underscore the disarticulation from the domestic economy, the majority of such export-processing zones are physically separated and fenced off from their surrounding environment.

Not only do industrial relocation plants not contribute to a country's economic development, their initial selection as preferred sites seems also unconnected to the level of economic development already obtained or even the availability of skills and/or other natural endowments. All that matters is whether a country has a cheap and abundant labour force and a government willing to suppress it as well as offer generous tax allowances and profit-remittance legislation.[21]

The Changing Organisation of International Production

It is risky to say anything definitive about trends in international production, because quite apart from the run of the mill problems of reliability inherent in all statistical data collection, we encounter additional problems when studying multinational corporations. For multinational corporations are 'invisible empires' because they are not by convention, or by law, subject to the kind of detailed systematic information-gathering that national account data are. Furthermore, multinational enterprises are like chameleons, adapting their outward appearance and organisational form remarkably swiftly to changes in their respective environments. A good example of this is the way in which multinational corporations in recent years have acquiesced to demands for nationalisation by their Third World hosts. Already, long before the *Charter of Economic Rights and Duties of States* was adopted by the UN General Assembly in 1974, and gave the practice of nationalisation of foreign enterprises legal status in international law, the mad rush of nationalisations had receded and MNCs were rapidly diversifying into a great many different non-equity or part-equity 'cross-border' arrangements. These novel arrangements included: joint ventures, management agreements and service contracts, licensing and franchise agreements, production-sharing agreements, and sub-contracting. While in 1951 only about one-fifth of 1,276 manufacturing affiliates of 391 MNCs had been established as co-owned or minority-owned affiliates, by 1970 this proportion had risen to over one-half.[22] And in the extractive industries (especially petroleum) the phenomenon of wholly owned or majority-owned subsidiaries has by now become, if not entirely extinct, distinctly rare.

The relative decline of the wholly owned and majority-owned subsidiaries and the emergence of many novel forms of cross-border arrangements between independently owned economic enterprises of course greatly distorts our perception of the size and development of international production. For, when measured by the conventional criterion of 'direct overseas investments' and of 'sales of wholly owned or majority-owned affiliates', it does appear, first, that the rate of growth of international production has stabilised since its meteoric expansion in the 1960s,[23] and that, second, intra-firm trade constitutes a declining phenomenon in trade between rich and poor countries. Since it is the Third World countries and not the advanced countries who are sensitive about the degree of foreign ownership of their domestic economic activities, and demand novel arrangements, we should not be surprised if the statistics tell us that developing countries are increasingly being left out of the process of 'multinational corporatisation' of world trade. Helleiner reckons that between 1967 and 1975 the share of total US imports which originated with US majority-owned affiliates had risen markedly in Europe and Canada, yet had actually fallen in Latin America, Asia and Africa. He, too, puts the blame for this distortion almost entirely on the diversification of the organisational forms of international production.[24]

The crucial issue when contrasting international production data with national development and trade figures is the extent to which nationally owned economic enterprises are *subject to control and decision* by (foreign) multinational enterprises. The question is ultimately who decides what is to be produced, how much of it is to be produced, how it is to be produced, where it shall be sold, at what price, and what shall be done with the proceeds. Earlier estimates of international production had correctly linked this concept of control to ownership of *capital*, as indeed there used to be a close correspondence between the two. But in the course of the last twenty years two developments – one political, the other technological – have interacted upon one another in such a manner as to permit a far greater separation of ownership and control. In a bid for national economic liberation and acting upon the belief, correct at the time, that ownership of capital conveys control, host governments of Third World countries demanded an *equity* stake in the foreign companies operating on their soil. Multinational corporations, for their part, responded by developing novel forms of organisation that did not require formal ownership of the capital of the subsidiary operations but instead hinged upon the parent company's *formal ownership of the product* as this is protected by international patent law. This product could be either an end-product or a technological operation, a piece of 'know-how' or a producer good. Contractual agreements (licence and franchise agreements as well as management and service contracts) between the parent company and the ex-affiliate would specify in minute detail all manner of plant operations, production and sales. The agreements would cover anything ranging from production volume and product range to tied purchase clauses, transfer prices, sale and export markets, use of personnel, etc.[25]

It did not take long before host governments realised that economic control over their enterprises remained as elusive as ever, and soon the corridors of the international organisations and conferences were chanting the calls for international codes of conduct for MNCs and even for radical changes in the Paris Convention on International Patent Rights.[26] To date several such draft Codes have been prepared by international groups of experts for UNCTAD, for the ILO, for the OECD and for the UN Department of Economic and Social Affairs . . . . . Although the chances for international ratification remain slim, that is not really important. The drafting exercise itself has been very enlightening and educational for host governments. Equipped with a growing arsenal of documents on the nature and scope of 'restrictive' practices, many Third World hosts are now operating a sophisticated screening process of all contracts with MNCs.[27]

However, what is enlightening to some is, of course, equally enlightening to others. As host governments scrutinised contractual agreements, so MNCs began to prepare to abandon them. There is now some evidence of yet a new practice by parent companies involving the *relocation* of control over their foreign operations away from the 'legal' ownership of the product, and towards the *technological properties* of that product. By making the physical characteristics of their plant and machinery, of their technical operations, and of their end-product, critically different from other similar machinery, processes and products that are available in the world markets, MNCs can establish and preserve future supply, servicing and maintenance links quite independently of any written agreement or any form of legal ownership. In other words, con-tractual restrictions are being replaced by 'technology-embodied' restrictions, as (for example) when the MNC plans the technological indivisibility of the 'package' it sells to its subsidiaries.[28]

In this way technological dependence has begun to take over where first political dependence, and then economic dependence, have left off. Ironically it is the very ownership of the equity capital of foreign operations that make Third World hosts (be they governments or individual entrepreneurs) unable and unwilling to resist this technological dependence. It would indeed be the height of financial folly if they were to buy up a foreign establishment and next strip it of all its physical apparatus and equipment so as to shop around for 'alternative' technology on a world-wide basis.

For the MNCs the ultimate purpose of effective control is the ability to appropriate the surplus produced by the subsidiaries. Whether this is for purposes of enhancing the growth and viability of the corporation or in order to pay handsome dividends to the parent firms' stockholders is beside the point here.

With the shifting location of control just described have come different methods of appropriation of surplus by the parent firm from its subsidiaries. In the days when control was firmly rooted in the parent company's ownership of the affiliate's capital, surplus appropriation took the familiar route of payments of dividends to the shareholders (e.g. the parent firm) requiring the remittance of profits overseas to wherever the MNC's headquarters were located. With the divestment of equity to bodies or persons outside the MNC's corporate circuit came new methods of surplus appropriation. The traditional profit and loss account lost its status as a financial record of the affiliate's performance and the concept of 'profit' became meaningless. Profits could be arbitrarily adjusted downwards depending on the degree to which cost items consisting of a variety of financial payments to the parent (e.g. royalties, interests on loans from the parent, loans *to* the parent, 'transfer prices' for tied purchases from the parent or any of its other subsidiaries, management costs, service and maintenance payments, etc.) were increased. The discovery of these 'hidden' transfers occasioned vigorous research activity, especially on the part of scholars from Latin America, where 54 per cent of all Third World foreign investments are located. An epoch-making study by Vaitsos in 1970 set the scene.[29] He discovered that, for example, in the pharmaceutical industry in Colombia as little as 3.4 per cent of the effective returns to the parent company consisted of 'declared profits'. Another 14 per cent was accounted for by royalty payments and 82.6 per cent was contributed by the parent company's 'over-pricing' of its sales to the affiliates. Clearly, then, an important conclusion from this is that *trade earnings are rapidly replacing traditional 'invisible' earnings* such as declared profits and royalty payments as method of surplus appropriation by parent companies of their affiliates. To the extent, furthermore, that defensive legislation on the part of host governments in order to counter the abuses of 'over-pricing' in intra-company trade and in order generally to dismantle the contractual purchasing links between affiliates and parents have been successful, it is now encouraging a degree of 'technological overspecification' or products and producer goods that completes the process of replacement of invisible earnings by trade earnings.[30]

Considerations of a similar kind apply to primary production. International extractive industries are typically small in number and consist of vertically integrated firms. They direct their output according to the global requirements of the parent firm or of major customers linked by long-term contract. Because they control market outlets, it has proved often hard for a country which has nationalised its raw-material production to sell large quantities of the material even disregarding the question of a collective boycott by potential purchasers.[31]

In conclusion, it is useful to compare the recent developments in international production, notably the apparent decline of overseas investments in Third World countries, its concentration in the rapidly growing Third World countries, the separation of ownership and control and the new methods of surplus appropriation, with the fact on international borrowing presented earlier in this chapter. For, as the 1977 World Bank report notes in a remarkably perceptive passage, there is a connection between declining direct overseas investments in the Third World on the one hand, and the phenomenal expansion of *bank lending* to the Third World (or rather, the rapidly growing countries of the Third World) on the other:

> With the steady growth of direct foreign investment in developing countries, the larger banks also became active in developing countries, firstly on behalf of their corporate clients who were investing in these countries and then directly on their own account. For large projects *syndicated loans became increasingly common, replacing, at least in part, equity investment.* The principal transformation came in lending for mineral exploitation. There were at least two reasons. Firstly, mineral and associated processing projects were becoming larger. But more importantly, investors wanted to reduce their equity exposure. As developing countries began to increase the share of resource rents they wished to appropriate, returns to equity were regarded as profits and were therefore taxable, whereas interest on loans was a cost and therefore deductible from taxable income. Countries which nationalized their mineral resources were only interested in loans, not in equity participation. Mineral-rich countries thus became heavy borrowers in private markets, where previously they had accepted equity capital. But whereas returns to equity capital fluctuated with changes in mineral prices, service obligations on loans were fixed, creating liquidity problems in price downswings [my emphasis].[32]

Instead of viewing third World governments' nationalisation programmes with dismay, the MNCs were smart enough to realise that local participation in their overseas affiliates opened up still greater opportunities for making super-profits, and (what is more) without carrying any additional risk. When viewed in this context there are two more developments in the 1970s worth noting: (i) the phenomenal increase in direct overseas investments in developing countries by the *banking* sector (see Table 1, under 'utilities and services', 50 per cent of which represents banking),[33] and (ii) the intensification of the process of integration of bank capital with industrial capital, again more particularly noteworthy inside the Third World.[34] As one observer put it, 'the dyke which separates the land of banking from the sea of commerce has sprung a leak'.[35] Swollen with recycled petro-dollars, banks have increasingly ventured into non-banking activities overseas, while conversely multinational industrial companies have acquired banking interests.

NOTES

1. Recently the nomenclature *transnational corporation* has gained currency as an alternative term for the *multinational corporation.* The term 'transnational' is favoured in some circles, notably that of international organisations, because it carries the impression that multinational companies truly

transcend national boundaries, including that of the home countries. In this book I use the terms interchangeably.

2. The term 'world market factory' is coined by Folker Fröbel, Jüngen Heinrichs and Otto Kreye, *The New International Division of Labour* (Cambridge University Press, 1980), p. 6.

3. These figures are arrived at by comparing the 'sales' column in *Fortune*'s list of the 500 largest industrial US companies and their list of the 500 largest non-US companies (1978) with the gross national product data per country and region presented in the *World Bank Atlas 1977*.

4. H. Schwamm and D. Germidis, *Codes of Conduct for Multinational Companies: Issues and Positions* (Brussels: ECSIM, 1977) p. 25.

5. On the assumption that individual employees support an average-sized family of three to four persons.

6. A letter from the Director of Information and Public Affairs of the World Bank which was inserted in the *World Bank Development Report 1980*, quoting *The Guardian* without proper reference.

7. UN ECOSOC, *Multinational Companies in World Development* (New York: United Nations, 1973) p. 14. See the footnote to that page for an explanation of how estimates of international production are obtained.

8. UN ECOSOC, *Transnational Corporations in World Development: A Re-examination* (New York: United Nations, 1978) p. 35. See footnote to that page for an explanation of the variations in calculations of 'international production' between the 1973 and the 1978 reports.

9. Ibid, p. 43; but note that most of these intra-firm transactions concern non-manufacturing goods, and that especially the international *oil* trade greatly exaggerates the picture of intra-firm transactions. According to Paul Streeten, intra-firm trade constitutes only 25 per cent of all international trade in *manufacturing*: Paul Streeten, 'Multinationals Revisited', *Finance and Development*, June 1979, p. 40.

10. 'Industrial' includes mining and construction as well as manufacturing activities.

11. These figures are taken from H. Magdoff, 'The US Dollar, Petrodollars and US Imperialism', *Monthly Review*, January 1979, p. 12. Magdoff appears to suggest here that these figures refer to sales of manufactures. This, however, cannot be the case. For, when we compare his data with those presented in the United Nations ECOSOC Report, *Transnational Corporations in World Development*, it is obvious that what Magdoff is talking about must refer to all US affiliate *industrial* production (manufacturing plus mining and smelting, and construction, but excluding services and banking).

12. *Fortune*, 22 September 1980, p. 114.

13. For the 1960 figure (United Kingdom plus the USA) see M. Barratt Brown, *The Economics of Imperialism* (Harmondsworth: Penguin, 1974), pp. 206, 207. For 1967, see Lester B. Pearson, *Partners in Development* (London: Pall Mall Press, 1970) p. 100. For 1974, see *Transnational Corporations in World Development*, table III, 38, p. 242.

14. See H. Magdoff, *The Age of Imperialism* (New York: Monthly Review Press, 1966) pp. 50-1. Magdoff makes the point that with the advent of the jet engine, the gas turbine and nuclear reactors, the USA had become more dependent than before on imports of critical materials. A similar position is taken by Pierre Jalee, *Imperialism in the Seventies* (New York: The Third Press, 1972). Lester Brown, *World Without Borders* (New York: Random House, 1973), estimates that by the end of the century the USA would be dependent on imports for half or more of its supplies of *all* basic industrial raw materials except phosphate, as compared with a similar import dependence only for aluminium, manganese, nickel and tin in 1950, and these four and zinc and chromium in 1970 (quoted in Fishlow *et al.*, *Rich and Poor Nations in the World Economy*, p. 33).

15. W. Arad and U. B. Arad, *Sharing Global Resources* (New York: McGraw-Hill, 1979) p. 42.

16. *Transnational Corporations in World Development: A Re-examination*, p. 56.

17. See also ibid.

18. G. Adams, 'New Trends in International Business', *Acta Oeconomica*, vol. 7, nos 3-4, 1971, pp. 349-67. Adams says that it is something of a 'truism' that competitive exports from less developed countries in manufactured goods are already to a 'significant' extent accounted for by the international companies. And Werner J. Feld, *Multinational Corporations and UN Politics: the Quest for Codes of Conduct* (Oxford: Pergamon Press, 1980), comments that while Brazil, Mexico, India, Malaysia and the tax havens increased their share of foreign investments appreciably in the period 1967-71, that of other less developed countries, including OPEC, declined (cf. p. 10).

19. Fröbel *et al.*, *The New International Division of Labour*, ch. 2. See also Adams, 'New Trends in International Business', who argues that world-wide sourcing is now part and parcel of international business planning and is resulting in a mass exodus of labour-intensive (and production-intensive) industries from the developed to the low-wage developing countries.

20. Fröbel *et al.*, *The New International Division of Labour*, p. 6.

21. Ibid, p. 313.

22. This figure is derived from data presented in *Transnational Corporations in World Development: A Re-examination*, table III, 25.

23. Cf. ibid, pp. 35-6, where a comparison is made between present international production statistics and those collected in 1971 by the previous groups of experts (*Multinational Corporations in World Development*, 1973). Indeed, it must be said that in relation to total world trade international production has slightly *declined* over the period in question. This is in contrast to an earlier period (1967-71) when it had not only just outgrown international trade but when direct overseas investment stock also grew slightly faster than the GDI of the advanced nations.

24. Helleiner, 'Structural Aspects of Third World Trade: Some Trends and Some Prospects'.

25. For a 'minimal' list of such practices, see Schwamm and Germidis, *Codes of Conduct for Multinational Companies*, pp. 18-19.

26. The 1974 UN programme of action on the establishment of a New International Economic Order . . . includes the desirability of such a code of conduct as one of its main programme points. On the various draft codes, see Dieter Ernst, 'A Code of Conduct for the Transfer of Technology: Establishing New Rules or Codifying the Status Quo?', in K. Sauvant and H. Hasenpflug, *The New International Economic Order* (Boulder, Col.: Westview Press, 1977) pp. 297-314. The need to review and revise the *international patent system* is the subject of UNCTAD Resolution *TAD/RES/88/(IV)*, 30 May 1976. For a discussion see Constantine V. Vaitsos, 'The Revision of the International Patent System: Legal Considerations for a Third World Position', *World Development*, vol. 4, no. 2, 1976, pp. 85-102.

27. Cf., for instance, the progress made in this respect by the Andean pact countries which have already passed novel industrial property legislation. See Commission of the Acuerdo de Cartagena, 'Common Treatment of Foreign Capital, Trademarks, Patents, Licensing Agreements and Royalties in the Andean Common Market', *Journal of Common Market Studies*, vol. 10, 1972, pp. 339-59.

28. See Ernst, 'A Code of Conduct for the Transfer of Technology'. Some empirical evidence of the development of technology-embodied restrictions in response to progressive host government legislation was collected by this author in Nigeria: see Ankie Hoogvelt, 'Indigenisation and Technological Dependency', *Development and Change*, vol. 11, 1980, pp. 257-72.

29. C. V. Vaitsos, 'Bargaining and the Distribution of Returns in the Purchase of Technology by Developing Countries', *Bulletin of the Institute of Development Studies*, vol. 3, no. 1, 1970, pp. 16-23.

30. See Hoogvelt, 'Indigenization and Technological Dependency'.

31. Cf. R. Murray, 'Underdevelopment, International Firms and the International Division of Labour', in *Towards a New World Economy*, Papers and Proceedings of the Fifth European Conference of the Society for International Development, The Hague (Rotterdam University Press, 1972) esp. pp. 226-7, which list the monopolistic restrictions that might apply in this area. See also S. Sideri and S. Johns, *Mining for Development in the Third World* (Oxford: Pergamon Press, 1980).

32. *Prospects for the Developing Countries 1978-85*, p. 100.

33. *Transnational Corporations in World Development*, p. 46.

34. Ibid., p. 49.

35. J. D'Arista, 'US Banks Abroad', in United States Congress, House Committee on Banking, Currency and Housing, *FINE: Financial Institutions and the Economy* (Washington, US Government Printing Office, 1976) book II, p. 850, quoted in *Transnational Corporations in the World Economy*, p. 49.

The Subordination of Women and the Internationalisation of Factory Production

Diane Elson and Ruth Pearson

*This reading is from Kate Young, Carol Wolkowitz
and Roslyn McCullagh (eds),* Of Marriage and the Market *(1981).*

Since the late 1960s a new type of wage employment has become available to women in many Third World countries: work in 'world market factories' producing manufactures exclusively for export to the rich countries (Hancock, 1980b). In these factories the vast majority of employees are usually young women between the age of fourteen and twenty-four or five. While these women are only a small proportion of all young women in the Third World, and a minute proportion of all Third World women, theirs is an important case to study, because the provision of jobs for women is often seen as an important way of 'integrating women into the development process', a demand which emerged from the United Nations Conference of International Women's Year in 1975, under the tutelage of various international development agencies.

The idea that women's subordinate position stems from a lack of job opportunities, and can be ended by the provision of sufficient job opportunities, is deeply rooted and held by a wide spectrum of opinion, from international development agencies, government bureaux, mainstream Marxists to many women's organisations. Our work in the Workshop on the Subordination of Women in the process of development has lead us to reject this perspective as a starting point. We do not accept that the problem is one of women being left out of the development process. Rather, it is precisely the relations through which women are 'integrated' into the development process which need to be problematised and investigated. For such relations may well be part of the *problem,* rather than part of the *solution.* Our starting point, therefore, is the need to evaluate world market factories from the point of view of the new possibilities *and* the new problems which they raise for Third World women who work in them.

World Market Factories: The Latest Phase of the Internationalisation of Capital

World market factories represent a re-location of production of certain kinds of manufactured product from the developed countries, where they continue to be consumed, to the Third World.[1] These products are often classified into two groups, those using old established (or 'traditional') technologies, such as garments, textiles, sporting equipment, toys, soft goods, furniture, etc; and those using modern technologies, such as the electrical goods and electronics industries.

The stress on the modernity (or otherwise) of the technological base can, however, be misleading. For the sophisticated, highly knowledge-intensive processes which produce the technological base for something like the electronics industry remain located in a few developed countries, in particular Japan and USA. The parts of such an industry which are relocated to the Third World share many characteristics with world market factories based on old-established technologies: their production processes are standardised, repetitious, call for very little modern knowledge, and are highly labour intensive. In many cases the reason for the high labour-intensity is that the production processes are assembly-type operations which have proved difficult and/or costly to mechanise further.

Subcontracting from Large Corporations

World market factories typically produce on subcontract to the order of a particular overseas customer, and the customer arranges the marketing of the product. The world market factory may be owned by indigenous capitalists, or may be a wholly owned subsidiary of its overseas customer, or may be a joint venture of some kind between Third World businessmen and the overseas customer (Tang, 1980). World market factories producing components for the electronics industry are typically wholly or partially owned subsidiaries of Japanese, North American, or European, multinationals (Hancock, 1980a). Large multinational trading and retailing firms based in developed countries have been very important in the development of trade in final consumer goods from world market factories. Large US and European retailing firms, like Sears Roebuck, Marks and Spencer and C & A Modes, now place very large contracts with world market factories. In South East Asia the huge Japanese trading firms (such as Mitsubishi, Mitsui, Sumitomo), are very important customers of world market factories.

Some world market factories producing final consumer goods do no more than assemble together parts supplied by their customers. Typical cases are the sewing together of products like garments, gloves, and leather luggage, the design and cutting of the parts having been carried out in the developed country by the customer. For instance, trousers are cut out in Germany, then flown in air-containers to Tunisia, where they are sewn together, packed and flown back for sale in Germany. In such cases, the world market factory is fully integrated into the production process of the customer firm, even though in formal even though in formal terms it may be independent. Through the provision of material inputs, or design capacity, or working capital, the customer may control the production process to the extent that though the supplier has formal autonomy, in practice the customer is operating a new and more sophisticated version of the 'putting-out' system. The transfer of the goods across national boundaries, though ostensibly organised through market sales and purchases, may in substance be a transfer between two departments of an integrated production process.

In some cases there is some scope for local initiative, a certain relative autonomy. The case of Hong Kong is a good example of the form that such relative autonomy might take: faced with import controls Hong Kong businessmen in the garment industry have successfully switched to new product lines, catering for the higher quality, rather than the cheaper end of the market. But in general the degree of autonomy enjoyed by world market factories is very limited. The fundamental reason for this is that they lack the means to develop new technologies.

Labour Force Requirements of World Market Factories

A critical factor in the location of world market factories is the availability of a suitable labour force. It must be a labour force which provides a ratio of output to costs of employment superior to that which prevails at existing centres of capital accumulation in the developed countries. And this superior ratio must be achieved *without* superior technology. It is by now well documented that this has been achieved in world market factories by a combination of much lower costs of employment, and matching of even higher productivity than that achieved in developed countries. Wages in world market factories are often ten times lower than in comparable factories in developed countries, while working hours per year are up to 50 per cent higher. Additional costs, such as social security payments, fringe benefits and work clothing are also much lower. The US Tariff Commission found that productivity of workers in foreign establishments assembling or processing products of US origin generally approximates that of workers with the same job classification in the USA. Several other studies have reported instances of productivity substantially higher than in the USA. This is not being achieved through superior technology: it is the result of greater intensity of work, greater continuity of production; in short, greater control over the performance of the labour force.

This greater degree of control is facilitated by the measures which have been taken by Third World governments to suspend workers' rights in world market factories. Many Third World countries which in the past had enacted progressive labour legislation, often as a result of the contribution of trade union struggles to the fight against imperialism, have by now incorporated the official trade union organisation into the state apparatus; and either suspended, or failed to enforce, major provisions of that legislation. Workers in world market factories have been left exposed by the abrogation of their rights on such matters as minimum wage payments, contributions to insurance funds, limitations on the length of the working day and week, security of employment, redundancy conditions and payments, and the right to strike. Free Trade Zones[2] have particularly stringent controls on the activity of workers' organisations. But in some countries, particularly in South East Asia, the whole country is covered by such controls, and the power of the state is vigorously used to enforce them. It is ironic that in the name of improving the lives of the poorer groups in the Third World by creating more employment opportunities for them, many Third World governments have actively reduced the ability of the poor to protect themselves against the most blatant forms of exploitation. The situation of workers in world market factories cannot, however, be analysed simply in terms of class struggle and national struggle. It has also to be analysed in terms of gender struggle.

The Employment of Women in World Market Factories

Why is it young women who overwhelmingly constitute the labour force of world market factories? This question is more conspicuous by its absence in most of the studies done by economists (Lim, 1978, is a notable exception). Perhaps this is because the type of jobs done by women in world market factories in the Third World are also done by women in the First World. It might seem to follow that the labour force of world market factories is inevitably predominantly female because the jobs to be done are 'women's work'. But to note that jobs are sex-stereotyped is not to explain why this is so.

The reproduction in world market factories of the sexual division of labour typical in labour-intensive assembly operations in developed countries rests upon some differentiation of the labour force which makes it more profitable to employ female labour than male labour in these jobs. Female labour must either be cheaper to employ than comparable male labour; or have higher productivity; or some combination of both; the net result being that unit costs of production are lower with female labour. In general, the money costs of employing female labour in world market factories do seem to be lower than would be the money costs of employing men. Kreye found that women's wages in world market factories are in general 20 per cent -50 per cent lower than wages paid for men in comparable jobs (Fröbel, Heinrich, Kreye, 1980). Direct productivity comparisons between male and female workers are hard to make, since so few men are employed in comparable labour intensive assembly operations. In the few documented cases where men have been employed – in Malaysian electronics factories and Malawi textile factories – their productivity was in fact lower than that of women employed in the same plants. Firms running world market factories seem firmly convinced that this would generally be the case.

What produces this differentiation? The answers that companies give when asked why they employ women, as well as the statements made by governments trying to attract world market factories, show that there is a widespread belief that it is a 'natural' differentiation, produced by innate capacities and personality traits of women and men, and by an objective differentiation of their income needs, in that men need an income to support a family, while women do not. A good example is the following passage in a Malaysian investment brochure, designed to attract foreign firms:

> The manual dexterity of the oriental female is famous the world over. Her hands are small and she works fast with extreme care. Who, therefore, could be better qualified *by nature and inheritance* to contribute to the efficiency of a bench-assembly production line than the oriental girl (emphasis added).

Women are considered not only to have naturally nimble fingers, but also to be naturally more docile and willing to accept tough work discipline, and naturally more suited to tedious, repetitive, monotonous work. Their lower wages are attributed to their secondary status in the labour market which is seen as a natural consequence of their capacity to bear children. The fact that only young women work in world market factories is also rationalised as an effect of their capacity to bear children – this naturally means they will be either unwilling or unable to continue in employment much beyond their early twenties. Indeed the phenomenon of women leaving employment in the factory when they get married or pregnant is known as 'natural wastage', and can be highly advantageous to firms which periodically need to vary the size of their labour force so as to adjust to fluctuating demand for their output in the world market. While we agree that there is a real differentiation between the characteristics of women and men as potential workers in world market factories, in our view it is far from being natural.

Where do Women get their Skills?
The famous 'nimble fingers' of young women are not an inheritance from their mothers, in the same way that they may inherit the colour of her skin or eyes. They are the result of the *training* they have received from their mothers and other female kin since early infancy in the tasks socially appropriate to woman's role. For instance, since industrial sewing of clothing closely resembles sewing with a domestic sewing machine, girls who have learnt such sewing at home already have the manual dexterity and capacity for spatial assessment required. Training in needlework and sewing also produces skills transferable to other assembly operations:

> . . . manual dexterity of a high order may be required in typical
> subcontracted operations, but nevertheless the operation is usually one
> that can be learned quickly on the basis of traditional skills. Thus in
> Morocco, in six weeks, girls (who may not be literate) are taught the
> assembly under magnification of memory planes for computers – this is
> virtually darning with copper wire, and sewing is a traditional Moroccan
> skill. In the electrical field the equivalent of sewing is putting together
> wiring harnesses; and in metal-working, one finds parallels in some forms
> of soldering and welding (Sharpston, 1976, p. 334).

It is partly because this training, like so many other female activities coming under the heading of domestic labour, is socially invisible, privatised, that the skills it produces are attributable to nature, and the jobs that make use of it are classified as 'unskilled' or 'semi-skilled'. Given that 'manual dexterity of a high order' is an admitted requirement for many of the assembly jobs done by women in world market factories, and that women working in the electronics industry have to pass aptitude tests with high scores, it is clear that the categorisation of these jobs as 'unskilled' does not derive from the purely *technical* characteristics of the job. The fact that the training period required within the factory is short, and that once this period is over workers do not take long to become highly proficient, does not detract from this conclusion. Little training and 'on the job' learning is required because the women are already trained:

> It takes six weeks to teach industrial garment making *to girls who already know how to sew* (Sharpston, 1975, p. 105, emphasis added).

In objective terms, it is more accurate to speak of the jobs making a demand for easily trained labour, than for unskilled labour. But of course, skill categories are not determined in a purely objective way (Braverman, 1974). In particular, jobs which are identified as 'women's work' tend to be classified as 'unskilled' or 'semi-skilled', whereas technically similar jobs identified as 'men's work' tend to be classified as 'skilled' (Phillips and Taylor, 1980). To a large extent, women do not do 'unskilled' jobs because they are the bearers of inferior labour; rather, the jobs they do are 'unskilled' because women enter them already determined as inferior bearers of labour.

Women's Subordination as a Gender

The social invisibility of the training that produces these skills of manual dexterity and the lack of social recognition for these skills is not accidental. It is intrinsic to the process of gender construction in the world today. For this is not simply a process of gender differentiation, producing two 'separate but equal' gender roles for women and men, any more than *apartheid* produces two 'separate but equal' roles for blacks and whites in South Africa. Rather it is a process of the *subordination* of women as a gender (Whitehead, 1979). This is not only an ideological process, taking place in the realm of attitudes and values. It is not just a matter of people ascribing lesser value to women's gender roles; of simply failing to see the contribution that women make; or of believing that it is only right and proper for women to accept a second place to men. Though ideology plays a role, we would argue that the subordination of women as a gender cannot be understood simply as a matter of 'patriarchal attitudes'. Rather it is a material process which goes on not just in our heads, but in our practices.

In claiming that it is a material process we do not intend to reduce it to an economic process, to be analysed only in terms of labour, but rather to emphasise that it cannot be changed simply through propaganda for more 'enlightened' views, but requires practical changes in daily living. We would suggest that this process of subordination of women as a gender can be understood in terms of the exclusion of women as a gender from certain activities, and their confinement to others; where the activities from which women as a gender are excluded are some of those which are constituted as public, overtly social activities, and the activities to which women as a gender are confined are some of those which are constituted as private, seemingly purely individual activities.

The constitution of activities as public or private, social or individual, of course differs over time, and between different kinds of society, and is itself a matter of struggle, not a pre-determined 'given'. The importance of activities in which the social aspect is dominant, which are overtly represented as social, is that these confer social power. This is not to say that *no* power is conferred by activities in which the private aspect is dominant: but in our view it is a mistake to see private power as co-equal with social power. Social power is collective power, reproducible through social processes, relatively autonomous from the characteristics of particular individuals. But private power is purely individual power, contingent as the specific characteristics of particular individuals, reproducible only by chance.

A distinction can usefully be made between relations which are *gender ascriptive,* that is, relations which are constructed intrinsically in terms of the gender of the persons concerned; and relations which are not gender ascriptive, but which can nevertheless be *bearers of gender* (Whitehead, 1979, p.11). An example of the first is the conjugal relation: marriage is a relation necessarily involving the unions of persons of definite and opposite gender; unions between persons of the same gender are not marriage. An example of the second is the sexual division of labour in the capitalist labour process. Though the capital-labour relation is not gender ascriptive, it is nevertheless a bearer of gender (Phillips and Taylor, 1980).

Gender ascriptive relations are clearly the fundamental sites of the subordination of women as a gender, and in them women's subordination may take a literally patriarchal form, with women directly subject to the authority of the father, their own or their children's. But male hegemony in gender ascriptive relations does not always assume a patriarchal form. Rather it is a matter of the extent to which women's social being can only be satisfactorily established through the mediation of a gender ascriptive relation, whereas the same is not true for men. This kind of gender subordination is not something which an individual woman can escape by virtue of choosing to avoid certain kinds of personal relation with men. For instance, it means that the *absence* of a husband is as significant as his presence for the establishment of a woman's social identity. As Elizabeth Phillips of the Jamaica Women's Bureau has pointed out: 'the apparent independence of women from men can be misleading: while women may not be directly subordinate to a particular member of their male kin, they are nonetheless subject to an overall culture of male dominance'. For women, unlike men, the question of gender is never absent.

Behind the Mirage of Docility
It is in the context of the subordination of women as a gender that we must analyse the supposed docility, subservience and consequent suitability for tedious, monotonous work of young women in the Third World. In the conditions of their subordination as a gender, this is the appearance that women often present to men, particularly men in some definite relation of authority to them, such as father, husband, boss. A similar appearance, presented by colonised peoples to their colonisers, was brilliantly dissected by Fanon, who showed how the public passivity and fatalism which the colonised peoples

displayed towards the colonisers for long periods concealed an inner, private, rebellion and subversion. But this passivity is not a natural and original state: to achieve it requires enormous efforts of self-repression. The 'native' is in a state of permanent tension, so that when he does resist it tends to be with a spontaneity and intensity all the stronger for having been so long pent-up and hidden. Action, not negotiation, is the characteristic response (Fanon, 1969, p. 48).

That self-repression is required for women to achieve an adequate level of docility and subservience can be demonstrated on an every day level by differences in their behaviour when authority figures are present and absent. An example is the behaviour observed by Heyzer (1978) in a world market factory producing textiles in Singapore. Here the women workers were always on guard when the supervisors were around, and displayed a characteristic subservience; but in the absence of supervisors behaviour changed. Far from displaying respectful subservience, workers mocked the supervisors and ridiculed them. Another indication that the 'private' behaviour of women workers in their peer group differs from their behaviour when outsiders are present, comes from the fact that some electronics factories on the Mexican border have introduced a few men on to production lines formerly exclusively the province of women, in the belief that this will improve the discipline and productivity of the women. The stress that such self-repression can impose and the 'non-rational' forms its relief may take is exemplified in the well-documented occurrence of outbreaks of mass hysteria among young women factory workers in South East Asia.

It is interesting that governments and companies are unwilling to trust completely the personal docility of women workers and feel a need to reinforce it with that suspension of a wide variety of workers' rights which is such a selling point of Free Trade Zones. Nevertheless, in spite of being faced with extensive use of state power to control labour unions and prevent strikes, women workers in world market factories have at times publicly thrown off their docility and subservience and taken direct action, though their level of participation in trade unions is reported to be very low. There are indications that these struggles tend to erupt outside the official trade union framework, taking for instance, the form of 'wild cat' sitdowns or walk-outs, rather than being organised around official negotiations (Tang, 1980).

Secondary Status in the Labour Market

A major aspect of the gender differentiation of the labour force available for employment in world market factories is what is generally referred to in the literature as women's 'secondary status' in the labour market (Lim, 1978, p. 11). The main aspects of this secondary status are that women's rates of pay tend to be lower than those of men doing similar or comparable jobs: and that women tend to form a 'reserve army' of labour, easily fired when firms want to cut back on their labour force, easily re-hired when firms want to expand again. This tends to be explained in terms of 'women's role in the family' or 'women's reproductive role'. In a sense this is true, but it is an ambiguous explanation, in that for many people 'women's role in the family', 'women's reproductive role' is an historical fact, given by biology. What has to be stressed is that women's role in the family is socially constructed as a subordinated role – even if she is a 'female head of household'. For it is the female role to do the work which nurtures children and men, work which appears to be purely private and personal, while it is the male role to represent women and children in the wider society. And it is the representative role which confers social power.

This kind of gender subordination means that when a labour market develops, women, unlike men, are unable to take on fully the classic attributes of free wage labour. A man can become a free wage labourer

> in the double sense that as a free individual he can dispose his labour-power as his own commodity and that, on the other hand, he has no other commodity for sale . . . he is free of all the objects needed for the realisation of his labour-power (Marx, 1976, p.273).

A woman is never 'free' in this way. She has obligations of domestic labour, difficulties in establishing control over her own body, and an inability to be fully a member of society in her own right. She may also obtain her subsistence from men in exchange for personal services of a sexual or nurturing kind, thus realising her labour-power outside the capitalist labour process. It is this gender difference which gives women a 'secondary status' in the labour market. Our purpose is not to deny the social reality of this secondary status. But it is to take up a critical stance towards it, rather than view it as 'natural': nature does not compel the tasks of bringing up children to be the privatised responsibility of their mother while depriving her of the social power to secure, in her own right, access to the resources required for this, thus forcing her into a dependent position.

This secondary status arising from women's subordination as a gender, means that women workers are peculiarly vulnerable to super-exploitation, in the sense that their wages may not cover the full money costs of the reproduction of their labour-power, either on a daily or a generational basis. It also means that women tend to get lower wages than men, even when those wages contribute to the support of several other people, as do the wages of many of the young women who work in world market factories (or indeed of many women workers in developed countries). Sending a daughter to work in such a factory is in some cases the only remaining strategy for acquiring an income for the rest of the family.

The Interplay of Capital and Gender:
The Limits to Liberation through Factory Work

Ever since large numbers of women were drawn into factory work in the industrial revolution in 19th century England there has been a strong belief that wage work can liberate women from gender subordination. The fact that the social relations of factory work are not intrinsically gender ascriptive, but are rooted in an impersonal cash nexus, gives some plausibility to such views. For instance, it seems plausible that competition between women and men for jobs would tend to undermine any material basis for gender differentiation of the labour force in world market factories. If initially capitalists prefer to employ women because they can be paid low wages, can be trained quickly, and appear to accept easily the discipline of factory life, then surely high male unemployment will tend to undermine this preference as men are induced to accept the same wages and working conditions, to acquire the same attributes that make women employable, in order to get a job. The end result of such a process would be a labour force undifferentiated by gender, with women and men doing the same jobs, in the same conditions, for the same wages, modified only by personal preferences or prejudices for this or that kind of employment or employee. There would be no objective basis for gender differentiation.

But this argument fails to consider *how it is* women have acquired the characteristics that make them initially the preferred labour force. If men are to compete successfully, they also need to acquire the 'nimble fingers' and 'docile dispositions' for which women workers are prized. But for this, they would require to undergo the same social experience as women. In order to compete successfully, men would need to experience gender subordination. But since men and women cannot *both* simultaneously experience gender subordination, this could only happen if women were to be freed from gender subordination; i.e. a reversal, rather than an elimination of gender differentiation. Competition between women and men in the labour market can tend to produce, in certain circumstances, signs of such a reversal (Engels, 1976, pp. 173-174), provoking the traditionalist critique of women's participation in wage work as an overturning of the natural order of things. But these signs of the reversal of gender roles are themselves a demonstration of the fundamental interdependence of the labour force characteristics of women and men. Though, as competitors in the labour market, women and men may at first appear as atomised individuals, they are never so completely separated. They are always linked through gender ascriptive relations, and their labour market relations become bearers of gender. The important point about the development of capitalism is that it does offer a form of interdependence – the cash nexus – which is not gender ascriptive. But though capitalist production is dominated by the cash nexus, in the sense that it must be organised to make a profit, it cannot be organised solely through cash relations (through wages and prices) but requires a specific hierarchical managerial organisation: the capitalist labour process. It has to be organised through the giving of orders, as well as the making of payments. It is because of this that capitalist production may be a bearer of gender, though it is not intrinsically gender ascriptive (Phillips and Taylor, 1980; Whitehead, 1979). Typically, the giving of orders in the capitalist labour process is defined as a male prerogative, while the role of women is defined as the carrying out of orders.

Another intrinsic limit is that the socialisation of the reproduction of labour-power cannot be accomplished completely through the cash nexus. A great deal of the labour required to provide the goods and services needed for the reproduction of labour power quite clearly can be socialised through the cash nexus. The monetisation of labour processes formerly carried out domestically, and socialised through the gender ascriptive relations of marriage, is one of the hallmarks of capital accumulation (Braverman, 1974, chapter 13). But the establishment of the social identity of children, their social integration, cannot be accomplished solely through the cash nexus. One implication of this is that the *de facto* position of women workers as major contributors to the family incomes does not automatically mean that they will become socially recognised as 'breadwinners', their secondary status in the labour market ended. For the position of breadwinner is not constituted purely at the economic level: it is also constituted in the process of establishing the connection of the family with the wider society. The breadwinner must be also the public representative of the family. Whitehead (1978) suggests that the wage itself, though clearly not a gender ascriptive form, tends to become a bearer of gender, in the sense that wages of male and female family members are not treated as interchangeable, but are earmarked for different things.

The recognition of this limitation does not mean that we must therefore deny capitalism *any* liberating potential: the alternative, cash-based, forms of socialisation it entails do tend to undermine and disrupt other forms of socialisation, including the gender ascriptive relations which are fundamental to the subordination of women as a gender. In this way they provide a material basis for struggle against the subordination of women as a gender. But there is no way that capitalist exploitation of women as wage workers can simply *replace* gender subordination of women. Indeed, the capitalist exploitation of women as wage workers is parasitic upon their subordination as a gender.

The Dialectic of Capital and Gender

We would like to distinguish three tendencies in the relation between factory work and the subordination of women as a gender: a tendency to *intensify* the existing forms of gender subordination; a tendency to *decompose* existing forms of gender subordination; and a tendency to *recompose* new forms of gender subordination. We are not suggesting that these are mutually exclusive tendencies – any specific situation might well show signs of all three. They are, moreover, not categories which can be aggregated to produce a uni-dimensional conclusion that the position of women is getting worse or better. Rather, they are suggested as ways of analysing particular conjunctions of forces shaping women's lives, in the hope that this will help clarify the strategic possibilities facing women in those situations.

There is evidence of all three tendencies at work in the case of women employed in world market factories. One example of the way existing forms of gender subordination may be *intensified* is the case of a multi-national corporation operating in Malaysia which believes in deliberately trying to preserve and utilise traditional forms of patriarchal power. Instead of undermining the father's authority over the daughter by encouraging 'modern', 'Western' behaviour, it pursues a policy of reinforcement:

the company has installed prayer rooms in the factory itself, does not have modern uniforms but lets the girls wear their traditional attire, and enforces a strict and rigid discipline in the work place (Lim, 1978, p. 37).

The enhanced economic value of daughters certainly provides a motive for fathers to exert more control, including sending them to work in the factories whether they wish to or not. On the other hand, the ability to earn a wage may be an important factor in undermining certain forms of control of fathers and brothers over young women, an advantage which has been mentioned frequently by Malaysian women working in world market factories. However, this does not mean that there is a reversal of the authority structure of the family. There is considerable empirical evidence that their wages do not confer greater status or decision-making power on the women, even though they may be the chief source of family income.

As an example of the way existing forms of gender subordination may be *decomposed*, we can cite Blake's observation (1979) of the importance of factory work as a way of escaping an early arranged marriage in some Asian countries. But the ability to resist arranged marriage and opt for 'free-choice' marriage is two-edged. In the conditions of a society dominated by the capitalist mode of production, 'free-choice' marriage tends to take on the characteristics of the dominant form of choice in such societies, a *market* choice from among competing commodities. And it is women themselves who take on many of the attributes of the competing commodities, while it is men who exercise the choice. This tendency towards the recomposition of a specifically capitalist, 'commoditised' form of making marriages is actively encouraged by the management styles of some of the large American multi-national electronics companies which provide lessons in fashion and 'beauty care' and organise beauty contests and Western-style dances and social functions for their employees. This is rationalised as the provision of fringe benefits which naturally appeal to the 'feminine interests' of the young women workers. Such interests are indeed 'feminine' in a situation where many young women are competing in a marriage market hoping to attract a husband. But they stem not from the eternal structure of the feminine psyche, but from concrete material conditions in which a young woman's face may be quite literally her fortune.

Though one form of gender subordination, the subordination of daughters to their fathers, may visibly crumble, another form of gender subordination, that of women employees to male factory bosses, just as visibly is built up. Work in world market factories is organised through a formal hierarchy with ordinary operators at the bottom controlled by varying levels of supervisors and managers. In study after study the same pattern is revealed: the young female employees are almost exclusively at the bottom of this hierarchy; the upper levels of the hierarchy are almost invariably male. Only in the lowest level of supervisors is it at all common to find women. The relationship of female employees to male bosses is qualitatively different from the relationship of male employees to male bosses. One important feature is that the sexual element in the relation between female employee and male boss is not contained and shaped by kin relations. This is one of the reasons why factory girls are often regarded as not quite 'respectable'. In some cases sexual exploitation is quite widespread – in the Masan Free Export Zone in South Korea, for example, numerous instances have occurred of sexual abuse of women employees by Japanese supervisors.

This *recomposition* of a new form of gender subordination in which young women are subject to the authority of men who are not in any family relation to them can also have the effect of intensifying more traditional forms of gender subordination of wives to husbands. The fact that if his wife works in a factory she will be subject to the authority of other men may be a powerful reason for a husband wishing to confine his wife to the home. Husbands' dislike of their wives working in factories is mentioned by Lim (1978) as one of the reasons why so few married women are employed in world markets factories in Malaysia.

Instability of Employment

But the problem is not simply that young women may, through factory work, escape the domination of fathers and brothers only to become subordinate to male managers and suprvisors, or escape the domination of managers and supervisors only to become subordinate to husbands or lovers. There is also the problem that the domination of managers and supervisors may be withdrawn – the woman may be sacked from her job – while the woman is without the 'protection' of subordination to father, brother, husband.[3] She may be left dependent on the cash nexus for survival, but unable to realise her labour power in cash terms through working in the factory.

This problem is particularly acute for women who work in world market factories. Some change in some distant, unknown part of the world may at any moment undercut their position, leaving their product and their labour power without a market. The recession in world demand in 1974 provoked massive cut-backs in employment in many world market factories: for instance about one-third of all electronics workers in Singapore lost their jobs (Grossman, 1979, p. 10). Moreover, there is still a possibility of a resurgence of competition from firms located in developed countries. The very success of world market factories has made them vulnerable to retaliation. So far this has mainly taken the form of the growth of restrictions on imports of manufactures, particularly of consumer goods like textiles, garments and shoes. More recently there have been signs of fresh attempts to revolutionise the production process in developed countries, to eliminate the advantage which cheap labour gives to world market factories in the production of labour intensive goods. At the request of the European Clothing Manufactures Federation, the Commission of the EEC is to fund a research programme on ways of automating garment making. The fact that the mass of capital continues to be accumulated in developed countries means that market demand, and technical know-how and finance continue to be concentrated there, so that world market factories, representing relatively small dispersions of capital accumulation, are inherently vulnerable to changes in the conditions of accumulation in developed countries.

The hiring and firing practices of particular firms do, however, add to the inherent precariousness and instability of employment in world market factories. The preference of firms for young workers means that workers in their early twenties who have not yet left voluntarily are the first to be dismissed if it is necessary to retrench the labour force. Pregnancy is often grounds for dismissal. Or women are dismissed on the grounds that they can no longer meet productivity or time-keeping norms. A deterioration in performance is, in fact, often the result of some disability caused by the work itself. Women employed in the garment industry on the Mexican Border tend to suffer from kidney complaints and varicose veins. Women using microscopes every day in the electronics industry suffer eye-strain and their eyesight deteriorates. The shift work which is common in electronics and textile factories can produce continual fatigue, headaches, and general deterioration of health. The net result is that it is quite often workers who have already acquired new consumption patterns, responsibilities, and in many cases, debts, who lose their jobs, rather than those who have just entered factory life.

If a woman loses her job in a world market factory after she has reshaped her life on the basis of a wage income, the only way she may have of surviving is by selling her body. There are reports from South Korea, for instance, that many former electronics workers have no alternative but to become prostitutes (Grossman, 1979, p. 16). A growing market for such services is provided by the way in which the tourist industry has been developed, especially in South East Asia.

Our conclusions may be summarised as follows: there are inherent limits to the extent to which the provision of wage work for women through capitalist accumulation can dissolve the subordination of women as a gender. Rather than ending such subordination, entry into wage work tends to transform it. While there is a tendency for the decomposition of some existing forms of gender subordination, such as the control of fathers and brothers over the life-styles of young women, there is also a tendency to the recomposition of new forms of gender subordination, both through the recomposition of gender ascriptive relations in new forms, and through relations which are not intrinsically gendered becoming bearers of gender. Indeed the decomposition tendency itself helps to strength the recomposition tendency. For the former, while it brings independence, of a sort, also brings vulnerability. This is particularly true when, as is the case with world market factory employees, this tendency affects only a small proportion of the relevant age cohort, and an even smaller proportion of the total female population of the society concerned. As an insurance against this vulnerability, individual women may often have little choice but to actively accept, indeed seek, the 'protection' of new forms of gender subordination . . . .

NOTES

For their helpful comments in the preparation of this paper, we should like to thank: the members of the Workshop on the Subordination of Women, Institute of Development Studies, University of Sussex; the participants in the international conference on the Continuing Subordination of Women in the Development Process, IDS, September 1978; the participants in the IDS Study on Women and Social Production in the Caribbean, held in Puerto Rico, June-July 1980; and members of the Editorial Collective of *Feminist Review*.

1. The forces underlying the process of relocation are discussed in greater detail in Elson and Pearson, 1980, and Elson and Pearson, 1981.

2. Free Trade Zones are special areas which are exempt from normal import and export regulations, and also from many other kinds of regulation, such as protective labour legislation and tax laws.

3. It may seem paradoxical to talk of the protection afforded by subordination, but the paradox lies in the social relations themselves. When the social identity of women has to be established through their relation with men, the absence of father, brother, or husband, is also disadvantageous.

REFERENCES

Blake, M. (1979): 'Asian Women in Formal and Non-Formal Sectors – Review and Proposals for Research – Education-Mobilisation', *Occasional Paper*, No. 2, United Nations Asian and Pacific Centre for Women and Development.

Blake, M. and C. Moonstan (1981): 'Women and Transnational Corporations (The Electronics Industry) Thailand', Honolulu, Working Paper of East-West Culture Learning Institute.

Braverman, H. (1974): *Labour and Monopoly Capital*, London and New York: Monthly Review Press.

Elson, D. and R. Pearson (1980), 'The Latest Phase of the Internationalisation of Capital and its Implications for Women in the Third World', *Discussion Paper* No. 150, Institute of Development Studies, University of Sussex.

Elson, D. and R. Pearson (1981), 'Nimble Fingers Make Cheap Workers: An Analysis of Women's Employment in Third World Export Manufacturing', *Feminist Review*, No. 7.

Engels, F. (1976): *The Condition of the Working Class in England*, St. Albans: Panther.

Fanon, F. (1967): *The Wretched of the Earth*, Harmondsworth: Penguin.

Fröbel, F., J. Heinrichs and O. Kreye (1980): *The New International Division of Labour*, Cambridge: Cambridge University Press.

Grossman, R. (1979): 'Women's Place in the Integrated Circuit', *South East Asia Chronicle*, No. 66 (Joint issue with *Pacific Research*, Vol. 9, No. 5-6).

Hancock, M. A. (1980a): 'Electronics: The International Industry. An Examination of US Electronics Off-Shore Production Involving a Female Workforce in Southeast Asia', Honolulu, Working Paper of East-West Culture Learning Institute.

Hancock, M. A. (1980b): 'Women and Transnational Corporations: A Bibliography', Honolulu, Working Paper of East-West Culture Learning Institute.

Heyzer, N. (1978): 'Young Women and Migrant Workers in Singapore's Labour Intensive Industries'. Paper presented to Conference on the Continuing Subordination of Women in the Development Process, Institute of Development Studies, University of Sussex.

Lim, L. (1978): 'Women Workers in Multinational Corporations in Developing Countries – The Case of the Electronics Industry in Malaysia and Singapore', *Women's Studies Program Occasional Paper*, No. 9, University of Michigan.

Marx, K. (1976): *Capital*, Vol. 1, Harmondsworth: Penguin Books.

Phillips, A. and B. Taylor (1980): 'Sex and Skill: Notes towards a Feminist Economics', *Feminist Review*, No. 6.

Sharpston, M. (1975): 'International Subcontracting', *Oxford Economic Papers*, March.

Sharpston, M. (1976): 'International Subcontracting', *World Development*, Vol. 4, No. 4.

Tang, S. L. (1980): 'Global Reach and its Limits: Women Workers and their Responses to Work in a Multinational Electronics Plant', Mimeo, Department of Sociology, Chinese University of Hong Kong.

Whitehead, A. (1979): 'Some Preliminary Notes on the Subordination of Women', *IDS Bulletin*, Vol. 10, No. 3.

Multinationals and Foreign Investment

Benjamin Higgins and Jean Downing Higgins

This extract is from the authors' Economic Development
of a Small Planet *(1979).*

The multinational enterprises (MNEs) have aroused a highly emotional debate. 'For some,'[1] Wilfred Jenks comments (at the time Director General of the International Labor Office) 'the multinational corporations are an invaluable dynamic force and instrument for the wider distribution of capital, technology and employment; for others, they are monsters which our present institutions, national and international, cannot adequately control, a law unto themselves which no reasonable concept of the public interest or social policy can accept.'

The essential nature of the multinational or global enterprise lies in the fact that its managerial headquarters are located in one country (referred to as the 'home country') while operations are carried out in a number of 'host countries' as well. Not that MNEs are a new phenomenon. Multinational and multiproduct enterprises existed already in the seventeenth century: the British East India Company and the Netherland East India company were among the largest, most far-flung, and most spectacular; many of the plantation and mining companies were mainly concerned with exploitation of natural resources, international trade, and international finance. Some of today's MNEs are similarly engaged. However, what characterizes today's version of the MNEs is a sharp shift away from such colonial patterns of investment, in favor of establishing *manufacturing* enterprise in the Third World.

The basic argument in favor of the MNEs is their efficiency. The multinational firms collect in their head offices, and quite often in their field operations and branch plants as well, the best entrepreneurial, managerial, scientific and engineering skills available. The battery of brains is then available for solving all manner of production, marketing and financing problems in any country, and in any line of economic activity, that offers interesting prospects. The highly skilled top management is backed up by large and high-quality research and development staffs. Together, these teams of highly qualified personnel produce a steady stream of innovations. When branch plants are opened, these technologies are transferred and, according to a study made by the International Labor Office (ILO), lead to a lively interaction of ideas, stimulating a two-way flow between home and host countries:

> The multinational corporations can usually set an example of enlightened and effective management in a developing host country. It can also have a direct impact on the development of national management cadres in the host country, by training national managers in the firm, who later go into local firms or government service.[2]

236

Growth of the Multinational

At first glance, then, the concept of the 'global factory' seems logical. The idea of at last pursuing true comparative advantage on a global scale by pulling the vast labor force of the Third World into manufacturing would seem to set right the economic distortions of the past, and provide a means of spreading world wealth.

The move toward freer trade after World War II did, in accordance with neoclassical principles, stimulate a movement of capital and modern technologies into the Third World. High-cost producers in advanced countries, threatened with competition from cheaply produced industrial products (particularly from Japan) began to expand their production facilities into Asia, Africa, and Latin America. 'Export platforms' were established in low-wage areas such as Hongkong, Taiwan, Singapore, and the United States-Mexican border area, where TV units, cameras, calculators, stereo sets, and computers could be produced and then sold in advanced countries. Meanwhile, Japanese capital and technology was moving into Asia. Environmental considerations, the tightening supply of raw materials, combined with Japan's shift from standard manufacturing to knowledge-intensive industries, and increasing reluctance of the Japanese to do factory work has been initiating what may prove to be a massive movement of Japanese capital into industry in neighboring countries such as South Korea, Taiwan, some of the Southeast Asian countries, and even into China. Meanwhile western producers have also established factories within the Soviet Bloc. Everyone was supposed to profit by this great new experiment. Bringing technologies that had already been developed at considerable expense at home, Western producers could apply them abroad with relatively little extra cost. On the other hand, the host countries would receive modern technologies, managerial expertise, jobs, finance capital, increase in earning from exports, and taxes from the global firm. Critics however deny these latter claims.

Current Criticisms

Far from being a source of capital, the argument goes, the MNEs earn little foreign exchange, and by one device or another repatriate their profits. The MNEs, it is claimed, do not in fact provide significant amounts of capital to developing countries, and may even generate a net drain of capital and of foreign exchange. There is little doubt that the latter situation can occur. In the early 1950s a Brazilian Minister of Finance was heard to remark 'If Brazil gets any more foreign investments, we are going to go broke.' What he meant was that foreign enterprises were borrowing from Brazilian banks in cruzeiros in order to establish manufacturing and mining enterprises, making profits both in the domestic market and abroad, and then transferring these profits in foreign exchange. Moreover, large foreign enterprises like Exxon or General Motors are likely to be regarded by local investors and banks as better and safer investments than small local enterprises. (About 78 percent of the manufacturing operations of US based global corporations in Latin America during the sixties were financed with local capital). Thus the presence of the MNEs in a developing country may attract local savings away from the investment in domestic enterprises.

It is also pointed out that the vertical integration which is characteristic of many MNEs permits swollen profit transfers and tax evasion. Vertical integration of the product from the extraction of raw materials through to the end product, opens the door to the creation of artificial 'transfer prices.' Profits can be transferred by overpricing imports from the parent firm for resale in domestic markets of the host country, or by overinvoicing raw materials and equipment obtained directly from the parent firm or another branch, so as to show a narrower profit margin in the host country. Thus, not only can profits be transferred beyond the agreed level, but taxes are reduced by the lower apparent profit. A study of US based global corporations in Latin America found that 75 per cent conduct all export transactions with other subsidiaries of the same parent, and control prices to suit. They consistently charged on an average of 40 per cent less for their exports than prices charged by local firms.[3] Guatemalan economist Gert Rosenthal, calculating the 'financial contribution' of global corporation to the Central American Common Market countries found that while net inflows increased during 1960-71 by 344 per cent, outflows rose by 982 per cent.[4]

Critics insist that globals also like to maintain maximum control of their processes, marketing, and management. A study of 409 'transfer of technology' contracts, in Ecuador, Bolivia, Peru, Chile, and Colombia, shows that in almost 80 per cent of them, the parent company totally prohibited the use of the transferred technology for producing exports. UN studies in India, Pakistan, the Philippines, Mexico, and Iran indicate a similar widespread use of 'restrictive business practices.' In some cases, the local subsidiary was permitted to export to nearby markets too small to be of interest to the parent company, or to distant markets beyond its reach. Nor have they transferred key managerial responsibility. The International Labor Office study points out that while multinational corporations run courses for middle and junior management, relatively few of the local managers are promoted from the subsidiaries to top positions in the head offices in the home country.[5]

One of the most frequently voiced accusations against the MNEs is that they do not adapt their technology to the factor endowment of the developing countries. Despite the scarcity of capital and the redundance of labour, it is argued, they still use capital-intensive labor-saving techniques. That such techniques aggravate unemployment problems is well illustrated by agricultural modernization. Huge farms produce an average of four hundred times what small farms can produce, but they employ only fifteen times as many workers. Moreover, agricultural business is accused of affecting foodstuff distribution through its increasing control of land use. Agribusiness prefers to grow high-profit crops such as strawberries and asparagus for export rather than low-profit grains for local consumption. In Colombia, a hectare devoted to carnation cultivation reaps a million pesos a year, while wheat or corn brings only 12,500 pesos. Meanwhile local populations find local fruits and vegetables priced beyond their reach.

Multinationals are also blamed for introducing inappropriate life styles. Marshall Wolfe, Director of the Social Development Division of the UN Economic Commission for Latin America, maintains that the MNEs contribute to internal instability of developing countries, by accelerating the 'revolution of rising expectation' to a point where no government of a developing country can hope to keep up with the demands of all the politically powerful groups within a society. In his view, this situation is particularly severe in Latin America:

> At prevailing per capita income levels, satisfactions of these taste for minorities that are much larger than the previous élites implies patterns of income distribution, patterns of distribution of public expenditure on services and urban infrastructure, and patterns of saving, investment and production that are just as remote from conventional conceptions of developmental priorities as they are from the publicly endorsed principles of social justice. The initiative for implantation of the new life styles has come mainly from the world center through the transnational corporations' mass media content . . . .[6]

Finally, imported life styles threaten to stifle indigenous cultural creativity.

Appraisal

It is probably true, as the global managers claim, that the global corporations are the first in history with the organization, technology, and money to manage the world as a unit by integrating production on a worldwidescale. It is estimated that global corporations already have more than $200 billion in physical assets under their control, and that by 1985, two hundred to three hundred of them will control 80 per cent of all productive assets of the non-Communist world. A comparison of the annual sales of corporations with the gross national product of countries for 1973 reveals that in these terms, General Motors is bigger than Switzerland, or Pakistan; Royal Dutch Shell is bigger than Iran, Venezuela, or Turkey; and that Goodyear Tyre is bigger than Saudi Arabia. Moreover, by 1973, US and Western European companies had already entered into more than twelve-hundred cooperative agreements with socialist governments. Finally, the average growth rate of the most successful global corporations is two to three times that of most advanced industrial countries.[7]

There can be little doubt that the introduction of the multinationals into the Third World has tended to aggravate the technological dualism inherited from the colonial regime, and that multinationals can be elusive of government control. In appraising the behavior of the MNEs, however, it is necessary to separate the responsibility of the multinationals from those of government, and to discern problems that have their roots in basic economic dilemmas. The problem of the Colombian carnations, for example, involves dilemmas of modernization often requiring government action to make necessary adjustments within the economy. Modernization, by displacing labor with capital, leads to a higher degree of specialization and thereby creates greater *dependence*. A shift from self-sufficient agriculture to producing crops for export is a case in point. If wheat and corn do not flow automatically through the market process to replace the wheat and corn which would have been grown in the carnation fields, the government must insure that they are imported and distributed. Furthermore, displaced workers do not have the purchasing power to create a market for wheat and corn. If they do not find jobs through the employment market it is up to the government to devise alternative occupations for them. Through job creation the government can take care of a crucial responsibility for redistribution; it captures a fair share of the profits from the sale of carnations and channels them back into the economy. Wherever possible, however, the multinationals have a clear responsibility to adapt their technology to local conditions.

Certainly, rapid changes in technology can have adverse effects on local producers in a developing country. Replacement of artisan workshops and cottage industries by mass-production techniques can lead to unemployment and the squelching of potential indigenous entrepreneurial material. The question then arises as to whether or not there exists a *high productivity*, labor-intensive technology which can be applied over a wide range of manufacturing activities.

At first glance, the picture seems mixed. Two studies made in Indonesia suggest that the MNEs tend to transfer their technology to their subsidiaries intact.[8] On the other hand, a study made for the United Nations Institute for Training and Research (UNITAR) states that foreign firms operating in the Third World have investigated possibilities of employing more labor-intensive methods with reasonable care:

> Such successful modifications as have been made have resulted from disaggregating the production function and seeking out those operations that may be effectively modified, notably in the plant and in construction operations as well as in the simpler repetitive operations in technologically unsophisticated forms of food processing, pharmaceutical packaging and the like.[9]

A Japanese glass company, for example, operated a subsidiary in India which was about half the size of the company's plant in the home country, but employed three times as many workers, using manual methods for cutting sheet glass, materials handling, and crushing coal.[10] Years ago at the brand new, fully automated Standard Vacuum Company refinery in Bombay, more workers were observed outside, cutting the lawns with knives, than in the plant itself. But beyond such devices, which do not alter the total employment picture very much, UNITAR found little scope for replacement of capital-intensive with labor-intensive methods. One of the most thorough studies of choice of technology found substantial adaptations by MNEs to local conditions in

Brazil.[11] Fixed capital per employee is markedly lower in the Brazilian plants than in the United States (as is value added per worker). The same firms use much more nonautomatic, general purpose machinery in Brazil than in the United States. For example, in the US, painting is highly automated in both the automobile and consumer durable goods industries; in Brazil only hand-held spray guns were found. However, the study makes the point that the adaptations were in response to the small size of the market rather than the abundance of cheap labor, and that the most important factor in choice of technology is scale of production, not the relative cost of labor and capital. While these studies suggest some flexibility, it seems that in general, technical coefficients (proportions in which factors of production are combined) are more or less fixed for most industries and for each scale of production.

. . . governments are beginning to find ways to curb and guide multinationals. In some cases, the host government is completely excluding foreign firms whose operations are deemed detrimental to the country. Guatemala, for example, decided to keep Sears Roebuck out of the country, because of its threat to small indigenous retailers. (This decision will be applauded by anyone who has searched in vain for an item, then looked vainly for a sales clerk in Sears' vast environs; or by anyone who has had the extraordinary good fortune to find a sales clerk, only to be told that the desired item is out of stock.)

When governments choose to accept the multinational, the objective is to curb and guide the multinationals through planning, legislation, regulation, and international codes of good behavior, in such a way as to dovetail the operation to the needs of the country – encouraging labor-intensive enterprises being a prime example. The ILO suggests that the right kind of contract is the key:

> Since the establishment, by a multinational corporation, of a subsidiary in
> a developing host country is preceded by months or even years of
> negotiation with the host government there is ample opportunity to plan,
> in direct collaboration with the government, for management development
> and training that will be of benefit both to the firm and to the host
> country, provided that such collaboration and planning are based on
> fairness and reciprocal respect for the aims of each party.[12]

But according to dependency theory, at least in its pure neo-Marxist form, such care in designing the contract would avail nothing because the multinationals exercise power on local governments and the local elite, and at the same time multinationals themselves form an exceedingly powerful club.

There can be little doubt that in today's world (as in the past) control of advanced technology is a source of power. If the management of MNEs, or at least the larger of them, are regarded as members of a species of 'international club,' and if, as Adam Smith maintained, such people cannot assemble together 'even for merriment and diversion' without joining together in some new conspiracy in restraint of trade, the aggregation of the power of the MNEs can be awesome indeed. There is also no doubt that a meshing of interest among local governments, the local élites, and multinationals can exist – Cuba was a case in point.

On the other hand, the fact that the MNEs are scaling down their investments in the Third World (particularly in Latin America) suggests that they have *not* had the power to arrange things as they would like.

Present Trends in International Investment
While a great deal has been said concerning the misdoings of the multinationals, their managers in turn face a 'hostile' climate in the Third World. Difficulties attending investment in the Third World include such problems as unrealistic profit limitations (hence the transfer prices), chronic uncertainty concerning tax laws, foreign exchange regulations, and possibilities of expropriation – not to mention being required in some cases to put money into the enterprises of ambitious generals or government officials. Multinational managers who really want to contribute to the development of the country (and there are many of these) do not relish it when the royalties and taxes which they do pay find their way into the Swiss bank accounts of politicians rather than being spent on development. Moreover, the climate has been deteriorating in *advanced* countries with regard to investment in the Third World.

It would appear that the amount of employment provided by MNEs in developing countries must be significant, if only because of the deep concern expressed by representatives of trade unions in advanced countries. According to the AFL-CIO, the US Division of the Global Factory lost 900,000 jobs during the sixties. These losses were deemed largely due to industrial plants moving to Canada, Japan, Taiwan, Hongkong, and Mexico, reducing the United States to 'a nation of hamburger stands.' According to union spokesmen, this transfer not only reduced jobs, but exerted a downward pressure on wages by the demonstrated freedom of choice of location.

Whether from domestic pressure, or as a result of the hostile climate in some developing countries, patterns of investment are changing. Today the activities of the MNEs do not reflect primarily a transfer of capital from advanced countries, in order to exploit natural resources and cheap labour in the developing countries. Table 1 shows the changes in geographic distribution of American foreign investment in the fifties and sixties. Most striking is the relative decline in importance of Latin America for United States direct foreign investment, and the relative growth of investment in Europe. (Some of the strongest attacks on MNEs, and on foreign investment in general, have come from Latin America). Asia also shows a slight decline in importance, Africa an increase. Table 2 indicates that the role of American direct investment in developing countries has declined substantially as a proportion of total activity, in favor of a significant increase in the relative importance of American investment in other highly developed market economies. Table 3 indicates that the United Kingdom as well as the United States is reducing the share of its direct investment abroad which is allocated to Latin America and the former

Table 1. Percentage distribution of United States direct investments abroad, by area, in selected years, 1950-70

Area	1950	1960	1965	1970
Africa	2.4	2.8	3.9	4.4
Asia	8.5	7.0	7.2	7.2
Canada	30.4	34.2	31.0	29.2
Western Europe	14.7	20.4	28.3	31.3
of which: EEC	(5.4)	(8.1)	(12.7)	(15.0)
Latin America	38.8	28.3	22.0	18.8
Rest of world	4.3	7.3	7.7	9.0

Source: Survey of Current Business (Washington, DC, US Department of Commerce), Aug. 1963, pp.18-19, Sept. 1967, p.42, Oct. 1970, p.31, and Oct. 1971, p.32.

Table 2. Percentage distribution of United States direct investments abroad as between developed and developing countries in selected years, 1950-70

	1950	1955	1960	1965	1970
Developed market economies	48.3	54.0	60.6	65.2	68.0
Developing countries	48.7	42.9	35.1	30.8	27.5
International, unallocated	3.0	3.1	4.3	4.0	4.5

Source: Survey of Current Business, Aug. 1957, p.24, Aug. 1959, p.30, Aug. 1963, pp.18-19, Sept. 1967, p.42, Oct. 1970, p.31, and Oct. 1971, p.32.

Table 3. United Kingdom net direct investments abroad[a] in selected years, 1960-66

Area	*(Millions of US$)*			
	1960	1962	1964	1966
North America	124.6	51.5	97.4	171.1
Western Europe[b]	71.1	134.7	116.5	172.2
of which: EEC	(60.2)	(81.8)	(102.8)	(141.4)
Latin America[c]	40.9	38.9	50.7	31.4
Overseas Sterling Area	477.7	342.4	450.8	332.6
Rest of world	15.7	17.6	21.0	65.5
All areas	730.0	585.1	736.4	772.8

Source: European Free Trade Association: *EFTA Foreign Investment: Changes in the Pattern of EFTA Foreign Direct Investment* (Geneva, March 1969), p.32.

a Excluding oil and, for 1960 and 1962, insurance.
b Comprises members of the European Free Trade Association and the European Economic Community only.
c Listed as 'South and Central America' in the source.

244 *The Developing World*

British colonies (overseas sterling area) and increasing the relative importance of investment in Western Europe, North America, and the rest of the world. United States investment in Europe and European investment in the US are growing simultaneously. Japan too is investing mostly in Europe, North America, and Australia.

Will this new trend in investment liberate the developing world from the advanced world at last? Once again the picture blurs. In comparing the multinational to the colonial investors of old, there is one more significant difference: the volume of investment.

Table 4. Net flow of resources received by developing countries

	(Billions of Dollars)			
	1970-72 Average	1973	1974	1975
1. *Bilateral flows (total net)*	16.9	23.5	29.1	39.1
—DAC countries	15.3	21.7	25.0	33.8
of which: ODA	6.2	7.1	8.3	9.8
other official flows + private	9.1	14.6	16.7	24.0
—OPEC countries	0.4	0.6	2.9	4.4
—Centrally Planned Economies	1.1	1.2	1.2	0.9
2. *Flows from multilateral institutions, net*[a]	2.1	3.3	4.6	5.8
3. *Estimated Euro-currency, borrowing, net*	2.1	8.5	8.0	9.5
4. *Total I to III*	21.1	35.3	41.7	54.4
IMF Oil Facility	—	—	1.1	2.4
Grand Total	21.1	35.3	42.8	56.8

Source: Organisation for Economic Cooperation and Development, *Development Cooperation, Efforts and Policies of the Members of the Development Assistance Committee, 1976 Review,* Pans (UECO) November 1976.

a DAC Members provided $3.8 billion to multilateral agencies as ODA in 1975.

The astronomical statistics connected with the multinationals are somewhat misleading. It is seldom appreciated that in relation to the world economy, the flow of capital to the developing countries today is a trickle in comparison with the flood of capital to the developing countries in the nineteenth century, a torrent which helps to explain the takeoffs of the United States, Canada, Australia, New Zealand, and Argentina after heavy initial British investment. A. K. Cairncross estimated in 1953 that if the United States were to lend abroad on a scale equivalent in terms of per capita real income to that of the United Kingdom during the nineteenth century, the United States would have $600 billion of foreign investments.[13]

Today the figure would be closer to $2,000 billion. To match the *flow* of capital from the United Kingdom in the nineteenth century, relative to its per capita real income, the United States would have to carry out the entire Marshall Plan three times every year, which today would mean spending some $200 billion annually. Instead, there is only $50 billion of US foreign investment at present in developing countries; and net transfers of capital, including foreign aid from all sources, run at some $57 billion per year (see Table 4). The predominant financial problem today in most underdeveloped countries is still the lack of foreign exchange. Developing countries lack equipment and expertise within the country to develop and do not have the foreign exchange to import them. Except for the few lucky countries with strong exports, imports have had to be curtailed, reducing development efforts. In sum the retreat of the colonial powers has left a gap which has not been filled either by foreign investment or by foreign aid.

NOTES

1. International Labor Office, *Multinational Enterprises and Social Policy* (Geneva, 1973), p. ix.

2. ILO, *Multinational Enterprises*, p. 62.

3. Richard J. Barnet and Ronald E. Muller, *Global Reach* (New York: Simon and Schuster, 1974), p. 158.

4. Gert Rosenthal, *The Role of Foreign Private Investment in the Development of the Central American Common Market*, Guatemala, 1973 (a study prepared under auspices of the Adlai Stevenson Institute of International Affairs, Chicago, and the Permanent Secretary of the Central American Common Market).

5. ILO, *Multinational Enterprises*, p. 60.

6. Marshall Wolfe, 'Approaches to Development: Who Is Approaching What?' *CEPAL-Review*, first semester 1976, pp. 151-152.

7. Barnet and Muller, *Global Reach*, p. 15.

8. Grant L. Reuber, *Private Foreign Investment in Development* (Oxford: Oxford University Press, 1973); Louis T. Wells Jr., 'Economic Man and Engineering Man!' Choice of Technology in a Low Wage Country', *Public Policy* 21, no. 3, 1973, pp. 319-42.

9. Walter A. Chudson, *The International Transfer of Commercial Technology to Developing Countries* UNITAR Research Reports No. 13 (New York, UNITAR, 1971), p. 25-26.

10. Terulomo Ozawa, *Transfer of Technology from Japan to Developing Countries*, UNITAR Research Reports No. 7 (New York, UNITAR, 1971), p. 13.

11. Samuel A. Morley and Gordon W. Smith, 'The Choice of Technology: Multinational Firms in Brazil,' *Economic Development and Cultural Change* 25, No. 2 (January 1977), pp. 239-64.

12. International Labor Office, *Multinational Enterprises and Social Policy*, p. 53.

13. A. K. Cairncross, *Home and Foreign Investment 1870–1913* (Cambridge: Cambridge University Press, 1953), p. 3.

FURTHER READING

Frank, A. G., 'Global Crisis and Transformation' in *Development and Change*, 1983, Vol. 14.

Halfani, M. and J. Barker, 'Agribusiness and Agrarian Change' in *Politics of Agriculture in Tropical Africa*, Sage Publications Inc, 1984.

Heyzer, Noeleen, *Working Women in South East Asia: Development Subordination and Emancipation*, Milton Keynes: Open University Press, 1986.

Kaplinsky, Raphael, 'Foreign Capital, Employment and Accumulation in Kenya', *Development and Change*, July 1981, Vol. 12, No. 3.

Kirk C. *et. al.*, 'Contracting Out: Plantations, Small Holders and Transnational Enterprises', *IDS Bulletin*, 1987, Vol. 18, No. 2.

The Problem of Late Industrialisation and the Experience of the Republic of Ireland

Eoin O'Malley

This article appeared in Cambridge Journal of Economics
(1985, 9).

The literature on industrialisation in developing countries has become strongly influenced by the view, derived from neoclassical economic theory, that outward-looking policies with reliance on free market forces and minimal State intervention are the key to success.[1] Reference to the experience of Japan, some Far Eastern NICs and Puerto Rico, and the supposedly free-market policies followed there, has increasingly been made in support of this view. The Republic of Ireland, which has experienced rapid industrial growth since adopting neoclassical-type policies in the 1950s, has also been referred to as a successful example (e.g., Farley, 1973).

There must, however, be considerable doubt about the validity of this view in respect of some of these countries, particularly Japan, South Korea and Taiwan. It is not at all clear that these countries relied on the pure outward-looking free-market strategy for industrial development. Rather their success may well be attributable to departing significantly from this strategy – by using protection against imports combined with selective state intervention and guidance to develop targeted industries to internationally competitive standards.[2]

This article examines the record of industrial growth in the Republic of Ireland and argues that it too offers no convincing support for a general recommendation of outward-looking free-market policies for late-industrialising countries. The reason for this conclusion, however, is different for Ireland than for the countries mentioned above. Ireland has undoubtedly followed a free market strategy more closely than these other countries, but arguably the success achieved by following this strategy has occurred only because of *exceptional* circumstances. Hence Ireland's experience does not offer general support for outward-looking free-market policies. Furthermore, future prospects for Ireland look less than favourable if the country persists with this strategy.

Barriers to Entry for Latecomers

The neoclassical prescription of an 'outward-looking' strategy consists of three specific policies – free international trade, the favouring of export industries (or at least non-discrimination against them), and freedom for foreign investors. The reliance on market forces which is also recommended would allow, at most, state intervention in the form of generalised, automatic incentives, such as tax concessions or investment grants. But it would not allow more active, selective intervention, such as the use of state enterprises to develop targeted industries or measures to encourage private firms to pursue objectives set by the state.

It may be seriously doubted whether such openness to international market forces can best serve to promote industrial development, given the competitive disadvantages faced by countries making a relatively *late start* to industrialisation. In various strands of the development literature it is recognised that the long-established industries of advanced industrial countries have built up competitive advantages so strong as to create serious barriers to entry into many manufacturing sectors. Such entry barriers take many forms, their nature and scale varying from industry to industry.

Significant barriers to entry into international markets can be created for late-industrialisers as a result of factors such as economies of scale in production, advantages of large established firms in marketing and raising capital, and the established technological strength of existing industries in advanced industrial countries. In industries where economies of scale are important, newcomers would have to produce and sell on a large scale to be competitive but may have great difficulty in capturing quickly the necessary market share. The marketing strength of established firms compounds such difficulties, while technological disadvantages can be even harder to overcome. Thus in many industries newcomers would have to go through a period of initial losses, which they may not be able to survive. [3]

For these reasons indigenous private firms in a late-industrialising country with outward-looking, free-market policies would generally tend to be deterred from trying to enter many internationally traded industries where entry barriers are important. This would leave them largely confined to investing in sheltered or non-traded industries, internationally traded industries with relatively insignificant barriers to entry, or simple, low value-added processing of local primary products. Since there is a good deal of evidence to suggest that imperfect competition and barriers to entry are prevalent in many important branches of manufacturing, this confinement to the accessible, 'easily-entered' sectors would present strictly limited opportunities for industrial development. [4] These limitations are all the more significant in view of the degree of competition between so many latecomers in the same limited range of industries.

These considerations are relevant to *indigenous* industries, but there is also the possibility of attracting direct investment from established firms in advanced countries, not subject to the constraints on newcomers. Foreign investment, however, can scarcely provide a general solution to the problem of late industrialisation since it tends to occur on a relatively small scale. Most firms are attracted to advanced industrial areas and relatively few are sufficiently mobile or footloose to move to less developed locations. Thus, in 1977, less than 15 per cent of the assets of foreign subsidiaries of US manufacturing companies were located in developing countries. Nevertheless, the Republic of Ireland has attracted a very substantial share of the foreign manufacturing investment going to late-industrialising countries – a share greatly disproportionate to the country's own small size. [5] But even with this major concentration of foreign investment, industry in Ireland still accounts for a significantly smaller proportion of output and employment than in the rest of Western Europe.

Although the overall impact of foreign investment in developing countries is limited, a few small late-industrialising countries, which are *exceptionally* attractive sites for mobile foreign investment, can achieve quite rapid industrial growth, sufficient to have a significant impact on their economies for some time, by attracting a greatly disproportionate share of such investment. This can occur even though their indigenous industrial development is seriously constrained. This article aims to show that, to the extent that Ireland has had some success with the outward-looking free-market strategy, it has been an exceptional case of this type (rather like Puerto Rico or Singapore). Rather than supporting the neo-classical view, the weak performance of Irish indigenous industry illustrates the serious difficulties faced by latecomers and suggests a need for different policies.

Irish Industry before the 1950s

The early history of Irish industry is relevant here. For over a century up until the 1930s, Ireland was in a position analogous to that of present-day latecomers following outward-looking policies and relying on market forces. For most of this period, Ireland was part of the UK (then the world's most advanced industrial country) and had free trade with other parts and followed classic *laissez-faire*, free market policies; and for nearly ten years after the establishment of the Irish Free State in 1922 this did not change greatly. The consequences for most of Irish industry, except in the Belfast region in the north-east, were quite devastating.

Industry had developed to substantial proportions in Ireland by the early nineteenth century, suggesting that local conditions were not markedly unfavourable for industrialisation. But the decline in most areas thereafter indicates that the attainment of suitable local conditions, and reliance on market forces, are not sufficient to generate sustained industrialisation in a country making a late start on a small scale in developing mechanised industry (in relation to Great Britain's pioneering industrial revolution). As the development of mechanised industry proceeded, the growing importance of economies of scale, the external economies of large industrial agglomerations, and technological capabilities created ever stronger concentrated industrial centres in those areas of the UK (including the Belfast region) which began mechanised development on a large scale first, while those starting relatively late and/or on a smaller scale (including most of Ireland outside Belfast) were gradually eliminated by competition.[6]

When the Irish government introduced strong protectionist policies in the early 1930s, rapid growth of industrial employment followed for two decades, apart from during the Second World War when it was difficult to import inputs. Starting from only 62,000 in 1931, employment in manufacturing grew to 140,000 in 1951, an average growth rate of 4.2 per cent per year. But labour productivity growth was sluggish and the volume of output per worker grew by only 1.4 per cent a year in 1931-51.[7]

If the labour productivity trend suggests that the protected industries were inefficient, this impression is strengthened by the fact that sales were concentrated on the small protected domestic market and few industries were able to compete effectively in export markets. Leaving aside Food, Drink, and Tobacco, which had been the only substantial export industries in the 1920s, the rest of manufacturing exported only 6 per cent of its output in 1951. Further evidence comes from the reports of the Committee on Industrial Organisation, established in 1961, which noted that old equipment, small scale, short production runs and wide ranges of products (resulting from the prevailing orientation towards the small protected domestic market) commonly resulted in high production costs.[8]

The lack of export growth was important because economic growth depended on importing the many capital goods, components and materials still not available domestically. In these circumstances, a chronic balance of payments crisis emerged in the 1950s and the deflationary measures taken to reduce imports resulted in prolonged recession, rapid decline in employment and massive emigration.

It may be concluded that the industrial structure generated by protection was rather inefficient, largely unable to export and thus ultimately causing growth to be constrained by a lack of foreign exchange., This is not to say, however, that the introduction of protection was the *original* cause of industrial stagnation. Seen in a longer-term perspective, it is evident that free trade and reliance on market forces had already produced industrial decline or stagnation for more than 100 years before the 1930s when protection was introduced. Protection, for a time, probably generated greater industrial growth than would have occurred under continuing free trade and reliance on market forces. But it seems that protection alone was ultimately *inadequate* to overcome the entry barriers into international competition which had been raised to a high level by the mid twentieth century.

Seen in this longer-term perspective, it might have been appropriate to use stronger systematic and selective state initiatives to supplement protection as a means of building industries capable of overcoming international entry barriers. But the prevailing view favoured a return to the outward-looking free-market approach. General incentives to promote export industries and to attract foreign investment were introduced in the 1950s and the removal of protection began in the mid 1960s.[9]

Indigenous Industry under the New Policies
Roughly coinciding with this policy change, economic recovery began in the late 1950s, and industrial output in the 1960s and 1970s grew at over three times the rate of the 1950s. Manufactured exports grew particularly rapidly as Ireland's share of foreign markets increased and diversification occurred into a wider range of goods, including technically advanced products such as computers, and fine chemicals and pharmaceuticals. Irish industrial wages rose almost to equal UK levels by 1979. This experience of industrial growth since the 1950s has been widely regarded as a fundamental breakthrough, and Ireland is now conventionally classified as an advanced industrial country. As suggested

above, however, these developments are largely attributable to Ireland's exceptional success in attracting a greatly disproportionate share of mobile foreign industry. Indigenous industry has shown signs of relative decline since the removal of protection began.

Table 1 shows that employment in industries other than new foreign ones grew by almost 20,000 in 1960-66 while protection still remained, but then declined slightly under freer trade after the mid 1960s. Output in these industries has grown since the mid 1960s, but they have experienced declining market shares – a trend which may be described as one of relative decline. Relative decline occurred in the domestic market, as shown by the growth of competing imports, which had gained only an extra 0.2 per cent a year of the Irish market in 1960-67, but then gained an extra 1.5 per cent a year in 1967-73, and 1.0 per cent a year in 1973-79.[10] Since the new foreign industries are very highly export-oriented, they have always accounted for less than 5 per cent of domestic market sales, so the rise in import penetration has taken market shares almost exclusively from other industries.

Table 1. Manufacturing employment in new foreign industry and the rest of industry, 1960-80 (thousands)

	1960	1966	1973	1980
New foreign industry	3	10	36	61
Rest of industry	169	188	186	182
Total	172	198	222	243

Sources: Trend in Employment and Unemployment series for Total; *IDA Employment Survey* for New foreign in 1973 and 1980; New foreign in 1960 and 1966 estimated from *Survey of Grant-Aided Industry* (1967); Rest of industry by subtracting New foreign from Total.

Note: New foreign industry is defined to be majority foreign-owned firms grant-aided under the Industrial Development Authority's (IDA) New Industry scheme for projects started since the 1950s or their Small Industry scheme begun in 1967.

It might be thought, of course, that while a rise in import penetration was predictable under freer trade, the accompanying gain in export market shares would compensate (or more than compensate) for this. In fact, however, Irish industries other than new foreign industry showed no overall gain in export market shares. They accounted for an estimated 0.26 per cent of the manufactured exports of all market economies in 1966 and the same percentage in 1976.[11] In the same period, the share of *total* Irish manufactured exports, including new foreign firms, rose from 0.33 per cent to 0.48 per cent.

It may be concluded from these aggregate trends that Irish indigenous industry suffered a net loss in market share as it lost out in the home market without a compensating increase abroad. It may be concluded, too, that rather little progress has been made in industrial development under outward-looking free-market policies, apart from the development of the country as a site for mobile foreign industries. The more detailed analysis which follows tends to support the view that the basic problem confronting indigenous industry is the existence of barriers to entry in many internationally traded industries which confine latecomers to a limited range of activities.

Certain types of Irish indigenous industry have, in fact, fared quite well under outward-looking free-market policies, while others have tended to decline rapidly. Table 2 illustrates this variation in experience. As columns 1 and 2 of

Table 2. Performance indicators for indigenous industry, by sector

	Increase in competing imports' Irish market share 1967-79 (% p.a.)	Employment change (%) 1973-80 in firms existing before 1973	Total Employment change (%) 1973-80
Clay, Glass and cement	0.2	6.5	16.4
Drink and tobacco	0.3	1.1	1.6
Food	0.5	−2.1	4.9
Paper and printing	1.4	−2.0	16.0
'Other' manufacturing	1.4	−14.2	5.2
Wood and furniture	2.0	−16.0	6.8
Metals and engineering	2.3	−8.7	23.9
Chemicals	2.3	−27.1	−9.1
Textiles	2.8	−39.9	−33.4
Clothing and footwear	4.6	−36.3	−24.6
All sectors	1.2	−12.8	−3.0

Sources: Competing imports derived from *Review of 1973 and Outlook for 1974* for 1966-73, from *Trade Statistics of Ireland* for 1973-77 and from data supplied by the Department of Industry, Commerce and Tourism for 1977-79. Employment data, which refer to Irish-owned industries, are obtained from *IDA Employment Survey*.

Notes: Column 1 shows the average gain per annum in competing imports' percentage share of the Irish market (e.g. an increase from a 30% share held by competing imports in 1967 to 54% in 1979 would appear in column 1 as a 2% gain per annum). Column 2 shows the percentage change, in 1973-80, in employment by firms which already existed in 1973, while column 3 shows total employment change in 1973-80 including new firms set up *during* that period.

Table 2 show, Clay, Glass and cement, Drink and tobacco, Food, and Paper and printing performed relatively well, resisting import penetration and suffering little or no loss of employment between 1973 and 1980 in firms established before 1973, while recording an increase in the total numbers of jobs in the industry. Chemicals, Textiles, and Clothing and footwear have the weakest record on these three indicators and show signs of significant decline. The performance of the remaining three sectors – Metals and engineering, Wood and furniture, and 'Other' manufacturing – was relatively weak in terms of the first two indicators, but total employment increased.

The strongest performances have generally occurred in industries which are *not* subject to the constraints imposed on latecomers by barriers to entry. These industries are characterised by either (a) low valued-added processing of local primary products, or (b) being long established in Ireland, or (c) being the 'non-traded' sectors enjoying a degree of natural protection because of transport or logistical costs.

Thus the Irish Food industry consists mostly of very basic processing of local primary products: value-added in the main subdivisions ranges from 13 to 21 per cent of gross output compared with 44 per cent in non-food manufacturing. The Drink and tobacco sector, which has higher value-added, is largely composed of a few big firms which date back at least 160 years and which have not, therefore, had to face barriers-to-entry problems. Clay, Glass and cement and Paper and printing consist largely of virtually non-traded activities, as is demonstrated by their success in resisting import penetration without at the same time achieving success in exporting.[12]

Small-scale firms in Metals and engineering, Wood and furniture, and Other manufacturing have also fared quite well where they have been engaged in small non-traded activities such as carpentry, simple metal fabrication, structural steel, plastic moulding and tyre remoulding. However, these three sectors also include larger scale, internationally traded industries, which have lost ground to competing imports, so that the overall increase in import penetration in each of these sectors is in the intermediate range in Table 2. Overall employment growth was almost entirely due to small firms setting up (employment in plants with under 200 workers increasing by 32 per cent in 1973-80) employment in large firms declining significantly (by 30 per cent in plants with over 200 workers).

The sectors with the weakest overall performance, Chemicals, Textiles, and Clothing and footwear, enjoy little or no natural protection and were fully exposed to competition under free trade. Within Textiles and Clothing and footwear, however, there are activities with relatively low barriers to entry, as witnessed by their growth in many NICs. It might be expected that Ireland, as a latecomer, ought to have had some success in competing internationally in these areas. There have, in fact, been some successes in developing exports, with all of the eight largest Textiles and Clothing firms exporting exceptionally large proportions of output – ranging from 31 per cent to over 90 per cent in 1978.[13] But many Irish firms have not succeeded in developing the scale, degree of specialisation and marketing sophistication required for international competition even in these low-entry-barrier industries. Competition from low-wage NICs has also been a problem in certain areas, though the overall impact has been limited (Fitzpatrick, 1981).

To sum up, although growth occurred in certain indigenous industries which enjoyed natural advantages, there was a substantial decline in employment in most internationally traded sectors. By the early 1980s, there were few private indigenous firms in large-scale, traded industries except for basic processing and long-established companies which had not had to overcome entry barriers. Among the 100 largest private indigenous manufacturing firms, in terms of sales in 1981/82, 76 (accounting for 89 per cent of sales and 86 per cent of employment) were mainly engaged in Clay, Glass and cement, Drink and tobacco, Food, and Paper and printing, and the relatively easily-entered Textiles and Clothing and footwear sectors.[14] Virtually none of the largest indigenous firms was mainly engaged in Metals and engineering, Chemicals, or Other manufacturing, which tend to be dominant among the activities of the biggest firms in advanced industrial countries (in branches such as transport equipment, metals, consumer durables, industrial chemicals, and so on, characterised by barriers to entry). Only one of the 23 Irish private indigenous manufacturing companies employing over 1,000 people is in this sector, and it is more involved in construction and services than in large-scale manufacturing.

Rather than gradually developing larger-scale, more technically demanding, traded industries, the trend among Irish indigenous firms has been more in the opposite direction. Expenditure on R & D actually declined in relation to industrial output between 1971 and 1979.[15]

Irish indigenous industry has made little progress, if any, under outward-looking free market policies, in overcoming barriers to entry. Moreover, far from being hostile to industrial development, the rapid expansion of foreign industry in Ireland in the 1960s and 1970s demonstrates that local economic and social 'supply-side' conditions – in the form of the infrastructure, the political and bureaucratic environment, financial and professional services, and the attitudes and commitment of the labour force – have been reasonably favourable. (Foreign companies have enjoyed no exclusive qualification for state support or assistance in Ireland, and grant assistance and advisory services have become more intensive, if anything, for indigenous firms since the early 1970s – see O'Malley, 1980).

Nor does an absence of entrepreneurial initiative seem to be a sufficient explanation for the problems of Irish industry. New Irish entrepreneurial activity has, in fact, been quite considerable, but this does not necessarily lead to satisfactory industrial development involving the growth of internationally traded industries. Thus many new indigenous manufacturing firms were established in the period 1973-80, accounting for as much as 37 per cent of all Irish manufacturing firms operating by 1980, the rate of formation per 1000 employees being more than double that of the East Midlands of England in 1968-75, which then had a rate 50 per cent above the UK average (O'Farrell and Crouchley, 1984). But the new Irish manufacturing firms are mostly small and (despite tax incentives to export up until 1981) in largely non-traded activities. The decline in older large firms has, therefore, meant a decline in employment in indigenous manufacturing and little export development.

It could be argued, however, that Irish entrepreneurship is deficient in the sense of lacking the *specialised skills and experience* required in specific traded industries. Such 'entrepreneurial' deficiencies could be seen as a form of entry barrier, rather than as a social-psychological deficiency, since specialised business competence based on experience is not easily acquired in an economy where the industries concerned do not already exist. Thus the fact that Irish firms have not attempted to develop in many traded industries with substantial entry barriers could reasonably be interpreted as rational and realistic behaviour for profit-seeking private entrepreneurs, who may be conscious both of conventional entry barriers and the need for some familiarity with a complex area of business before setting up a new enterprise.

Foreign industries in Ireland

It is clear from the discussion above that industrial growth in the Republic of Ireland over the past two decades has been due largely to success in attracting mobile foreign industry. By 1982, foreign-owned firms accounted for more than one-third of manufacturing employment and over 70 per cent of manufactured exports.

Some foreign firms had been set up before the 1950s, motivated mainly by Ireland's former protectionist policies to establish plants in Ireland to serve the local market, and these tended to decline at much the same rate (in terms of employment) as Irish-owned firms under the freer trade of the 1970s. But the new export-oriented foreign sector has expanded rapidly. Studies of new foreign industries in Ireland suggest that they are mostly similar to those established in low-wage LDCs or NICs during the 1960s and 1970s, in so far as they fall within the following two categories. First, there are technically mature, labour-intensive products (such as clothing, footwear, textiles, plastic products and toys) which, as Vernon (1966) has suggested, are capable of locating in industrially undeveloped countries because they have no great dependence on close contact with the specialised skills, knowledge, suppliers and services of advanced industrial centres. Second, there are newer and more sophisticated products (such as machinery, electronic products, chemicals, etc.) but typically only those *stages* of their production which make few demands on technical skills or local high-quality suppliers. These activities are roughly comparable to those which Helleiner (1973) regarded as the emerging growth area for foreign manufacturing investment in LDCs, again because of little dependence on the skills and external economies of advanced industrial centres.[16] However, in some cases (such as electronics) Ireland has more highly-skilled activities than most NICs, though still generally lacking key R & D functions or significant local linkages.

Consistent with these suggestions, a recent detailed assessment of new foreign firms in Ireland includes the following:

(On electrical and electronic firms)

> Of the 60 companies surveyed, none have a truly stand-alone operation in Ireland, and only three have operations in Ireland which embody the key competitive elements of the company's business. All others are currently manufacturing satellites, performing partial steps in the manufacturing process. Skill development and linkages in Ireland have been limited. The electronics industry is a high-skilled industry worldwide, but the activities in Ireland's electronics industry do not now reflect this.

(On mechanical engineering firms)

Ireland's foreign-owned mechanical engineering companies consist mainly of sub-assembly and assembly shops of the sort commonly found in newly-industrialising countries . . . Of the 34 shops surveyed, about half had only one or two skilled blue-collar workers and one or two engineers.

(On foreign-owned firms in general)

Foreign-owned industrial operations in Ireland with few exceptions do not embody the key competitive activities of the businesses in which they participate; do not employ significant numbers of skilled workers; and are not significantly integrated into traded and skilled sub-supply industries in Ireland (Telesis Report, 1982).

Although foreign firms have made a major contribution to industrial growth in Ireland, the nature of their activities means that their impact in encouraging indigenous development is minimal. Future industrial growth remains heavily dependent, therefore, on the continuing growth of new foreign industry.

This point has been made by earlier studies which have shown that the new foreign firms set up in Ireland have not developed close linkages with indigenous industry and have contributed rather little in the way of skill development, technology transfer, or the generation of 'spin-offs'. New foreign industries (excluding Food) purchased only 11.2 per cent of their inputs of materials and components from Irish sources in 1974 (McAleese, 1977, Table 5.4), which means that their purchases amounted to less than 3 per cent of the sales of indigenous industry. McAleese and McDonald (1978) found that the proportion of purchases by foreign firms from Irish sources has been increasing, but only by about two or three percentage points per decade up to 1974, and O'Loughlin and O'Farrell (1980) found no evidence of this increase continuing. With such low levels of local purchasing, foreign firms can have done little to stimulate development of an indigenous plant and machinery industry, which is one significant secondary benefit that might have been expected. The extracts from the Telesis Report (1982) quoted above suggest that new foreign firms have contributed little to the development of indigenous skills and technological capabilities.[17]

On the more positive side, McAleese (1977) has investigated and rejected the hypothesis that new foreign firms might have actually damaged indigenous industry by paying wages above the national norm, thus raising wage expectations generally and causing a worsening of cost competitiveness. And they have earned foreign exchange and thereby facilitated the growth of domestically-oriented indigenous industries (which need to import many inputs, quite apart from the spending on imports from the income generated by them). But this particular contribution to indigenous industrial growth itself implies a state of continuing dependence since (unlike technology transfer, skill development, or spin-offs) it is not a lasting benefit which could continue independently of developments in the foreign sector. The survival and growth of indigenous industries remain heavily dependent on the ability of other sectors – agriculture and foreign borrowing by the government as well as foreign firms – to push back the foreign exchange constraint.

The continuing viability of the country's current development strategy depends mainly on the prospects for future growth of the foreign-owned sector. An important factor tending to create increasing difficulties in securing a high rate of growth in the foreign-owned sector is the fact that new foreign firms in Ireland show a tendency eventually to decline, at least in terms of employment. Thus, according to the IDA Employment Survey, employment in new foreign firms fell by 2.4 per cent in 1973-80 in the case of those established before 1973 and by over 10 per cent in those established before 1969.

This decline probably reflects in part increasing difficulty in competing with producers of similar products in low-wage NICs. However, it probably also reflects the sectoral composition of the foreign industries concerned, many of which tend to be maturing industries which have experienced weak growth internationally. Both of these factors may well continue to apply with each succeeding generation of foreign investment, since industries generally only become sufficiently mobile to move to a less advanced industrial environment as they mature. When an industry reaches a stage where it can readily locate a plant in Ireland, it can soon do so in low-wage NICs as well. And it would also be drawing closer to the phase of slower growth commonly faced by mature industries.[18]

The declining trend in the longer-established foreign firms means that Ireland has depended on *new first-time* foreign investors for manufacturing employment growth. If the newcomers themselves tend eventually to go into decline, there will be a gradually increasing proportion of relatively old declining plants, necessitating continuous increases in new first-time investment to attain net employment increases of any given amount.

It looks very doubtful, at present, whether such continuous increases can be achieved. In the 1960s and 1970s, the Republic of Ireland was able to attract many mobile industries successfully, despite having much higher labour costs than most LDCs, because of a combination of advantages such as political 'reliability', proximity to the European market, free trade with the UK and later the EEC, tax and grant incentives, effective promotion work by the Industrial Development Authority, and other institutional and cultural factors which reduce information costs, uncertainty and perceptions of risk. And Ireland's attractions, as compared with other European locations, have lain mainly in tax and grant incentives and cheaper labour costs.

However, the development of a number of low wage NICs as 'reliable', relatively risk-free sites since about the mid 1960s, combined with rising labour costs in Ireland, have to some extent eroded the attractions which brought many of the labour-intensive mobile foreign investors to Ireland up to the late 1960s. But this appears to have been offset by Ireland's improved market access to the UK market since the mid 1960s and to the EEC market since 1973 –

which brought new foreign investors seeking secure access to those markets. This advantage, however, may now be diminishing as a result of stronger competition from other EEC members for foreign investment. An important factor here is the relative decline of the UK economy, which has led to increased efforts by the UK to attract foreign investment. The recent or imminent accession of Greece, Spain and Portugal to the EEC may also be creating new sources of stronger competition for the type of mobile foreign investment for which Ireland had special attractions in the 1970s.

Coupled with this increasing competition, relatively slow growth in European markets in the 1980s has led to greater difficulties in attracting new foreign firms to Ireland. New US manufacturing investment in Ireland peaked in 1979-81 and then declined until 1983, with only a small recovery in 1984. Furthermore, Ireland's *share* of new US manufacturing investment in Western Europe also declined after 1979-81 (after rising almost continuously since 1972).[19] Although there may be some recovery, it is still very doubtful whether it will be possible to achieve continuous increases in new foreign investment.

Conclusion

It has been argued above that industrial growth in the Republic of Ireland under outward-looking, free-market policies offers no general support for such policies. The growth of industry in Ireland has been mainly due to the attraction of an *exceptionally* large share of a globally limited amount of mobile foreign industry, while indigenous industry was in relative decline. Furthermore, the continuation of the relatively high overall industrial growth rates of the 1960s and 1970s under these policies is now in some doubt, because of the difficulties of securing a continuous high rate of expansion of foreign industry, while the fundamental problem of overcoming barriers to entry facing indigenous industry remains to be addressed effectively.

Singapore and Puerto Rico are two other late-industrialising countries which are often referred to as examples of the success of the neoclassical strategy, but the validity of these two cases can be doubted on much the same grounds as in the case of Ireland. Both of these countries appear to have depended even more heavily than Ireland on attracting *exceptionally* large shares of mobile foreign industry, which was sufficient to have a major impact on industrial growth. By 1980, 52 per cent of industrial employment, 71 per cent of industrial output and 90-95 per cent of industrial exports were accounted for by foreign firms in Singapore (Cheah, 1980; Telesis, 1982, p. 367). In Puerto Rico, foreign firms accounted for 73 per cent of industrial employment and 90-95% of industrial exports (Villamil, 1979; Telesis, 1982, p. 367).

By contrast, indigenous industry in South Korea, Taiwan and especially Japan has made significant progress in overcoming the barriers to entry faced by latecomers in international markets, but it is very doubtful whether this has been achieved (as is sometimes claimed) through relying on a pure outward-looking, free-market strategy. Rather, success may be attributable to significant departures from this strategy.

The type of policy adopted by these countries is summed up by a Japanese policy-maker (quoted by Allen, 1981) who said the policy was to (a) select industries carefully, (b) prevent ruinous competition at the infancy stage, (c) nurse them to competitive stature and then expose them to outside competition. All three stages of such a strategy involve departures from fully outward-looking, free-market policies. At the same time, the element of selectivity and the measures taken to develop a fully competitive stature distinguish this strategy from the simple, indiscriminate protectionism which has ultimately failed in many countries, including Ireland in the 1950s.

If the analysis of Ireland's experience in this article shows that an outward-looking, free-market strategy has proved inadequate to overcome barriers to entry for late-developing indigenous industry, the experience of countries such as Japan and South Korea seems to indicate that an efficient selective and directive state policy can help to achieve better results. Protection, however, would obviously be of less value as a means of ultimately developing internationally competitive industries in Ireland, in view of the small domestic market of only a few million people. There are, of course, many reasons why the Japanese or Korean approach might not be fully transferable to a different culture. But it seems reasonable to conclude that Irish policy makers should develop some variant of a more active, directive approach, aiming to build up selected industries (along the lines, for example, proposed in the Telesis report, 1982).

It would be essential for Ireland to focus mainly on developing traded *export* industries in adopting such a strategy, since such a small economy will inevitably continue to depend heavily on imports of many kinds for further growth. The development of exports to pay for the necessary imports is thus the key constraint to be tackled in promoting economic development, and industry should play a major role in exporting since many non-industrial activities are largely oriented to local markets. The target export industries would have to be selected on the basis of careful analysis of the specific requirements for international competitive success in the industries concerned, together with a realistic assessment of the potential and constraints arising from Ireland's existing skills, resources and size. This would tend to mean that Ireland would have to select quite specialised industries, whether these are specialised by product, customer, geographical area, or a combination of these. Such specialised, or 'niche' industries, have the advantage of avoiding direct competition with very large firms, which are not interested in, or may not be flexible enough to compete in, these activities.[20] The actual development of the selected industries would then require active state initiatives and concentrated support to sustain them, while policies and resources would need to be focussed on building up the necessary characteristics for competitive success – such as scale, skills, technology and marketing.

Addendum: Irish Industry in the 1980s
This article was concerned with industrial development in Ireland up to the start

of the 1980s. More recent trends indicate that a significant turning point was reached at about that time, particularly with respect to employment. Manufacturing employment peaked at 243,000 in 1980 and then fell continuously to 201,000 by 1986, which was the greatest and longest sustained decline since the foundation of the State.

The causes of this decline can be linked to the above analysis of the earlier period. First, Ireland's heavy reliance on new first-time foreign investors for manufacturing growth, which was evident in the 1970s, has proved to be a real weakness. New overseas capital investment approved by the IDA fell from an average of £270.5 million per annum in the peak years 1979-81 to an average of £132.9 million per annum in 1982-86 (in constant 1980 prices). This was a reflection of a generally lower rate of US investment in Europe and stronger competition within Europe for mobile investment. Largely as a result of this trend, employment in foreign-owned manufacturing fell by 10.5 per cent between 1981 and 1986, in marked contrast to the continuous growth seen in the foreign-owned sector in the previous two decades.

In the same period, employment in Irish indigenous industry declined by 19.5 per cent. In this case the basic problem was a weakening in domestic demand. Indigeneous industry had for long been dependent on strong demand in the home market to sustain its employment, given that it was selling very largely to the domestic market and was losing market shares. But domestic demand weakened significantly in the 1980s as a result of a weaker stimulus from foreign investment, difficulties in the agricultural sector, and the growing burden of public debt which led to growing debt service payments abroad, higher taxes and cuts in public spending.

Despite the sharp deterioration in manufacturing employment trends, industrial output continued to grow quite rapidly. But this growth was largely confined to a few of the predominantly foreign-owned sectors, mainly electronics and pharmaceuticals, which import most of their inputs and repatriate substantial amounts of profits (O'Malley, 1986). Thus most of the wealth generated by such industries leaks abroad rather than being retained in the Irish economy.

In these circumstances, and in the context of a sharp rise in unemployment, there has been some evidence of serious reconsideration of industrial development policy, with the emphasis shifting to greater efforts to develop indigenous industry. This new emphasis was reflected, for example, in a reorganisation of the Industrial Development Authority along lines which give formal recognition to the distinction between Irish-owned and foreign-owned firms. The IDA has stated that the proportion of its resources devoted to domestic industry is now to increase significantly.

A number of new policy measures have been introduced specifically to cope with perceived general weaknesses of indigenous firms, particularly with respect to management, export marketing and acquisition of technology. These are areas in which indigeneous firms frequently have weakenesses which are not so commonly found among the multinationals. In addition, industrial policy towards indigeneous industry is becoming more selective in certain respects, in the sense of aiming to build on selected companies and sectors. This more selective approach was articulated in the *Programme for National Recovery* (1987). It could not be claimed, as yet, that the expressed change in approach has led to very dramatic new policy actions, but a more selective and active policy may be emerging.

NOTES

1. Little, Scitovsky and Scott (1970) and Balassa (1980) are good representatives of this neoclassical view.

2. See, for example, Allen (1981) and Adams and Ichimura (1983) on Japan; Luedde-Neurath (1980 and 1984) on Korea; Wade (1984) on Taiwan.

3. For more detailed discussions of barriers to entry see Bain (1956) and Porter (1980, ch. 1). In the development literature, the 'Dependency' school is particularly conscious of the problems caused for late-industrialisers by barriers to entry.

4. The view that imperfect competition and barriers to entry are widespread is commonly held by Marxist writers, such as Baran (1973), and Bienefeld and Innes (1976). It also features, however, in basic textbooks on industrial or business economics.

5. The Republic of Ireland, with a population of little over three million or about 0.1 of that of the less-developed countries, had 4.8% of the assets of US manufacturing companies in developing countries in 1977 (US Department of Commerce, *Survey of Current Business*, October 1981); in addition, non-US foreign companies together account for more manufacturing employment in Ireland than US firms.

6. A full discussion of the causes of the nineteenth-century decline of most of Irish industry, in contrast to the Belfast area, is beyond the scope of this article (see O'Malley, 1981).

7. These data are from the Census of Industrial Production. The output per worker data for 1931-51 refer to 'Transportable Goods' industries, which include mining and peat as well as manufacturing, but manufacturing accounts for over 90% of the total.

8. See Committee on Industrial Organisation (1965).

9. Details of the steps by which these policies were introduced are contained in O'Malley (1980).

10. 'Competing' imports are imports of manufactured goods which are considered to be competing directly with existing producers of similar products in Ireland. Official data on competing imports for 1960-73 are published in the *Review of 1973 and Outlook for 1974*; for 1973-77 data were derived from the *Trade Statistics of Ireland* by summing up import items classified as 'competing' according to Matthews (1980); for 1977-79, data are as supplied by the Department of Industry, Commerce and Tourism for a study of industrial job losses by the National Economic and Social Council.

11. Exports of Irish industries other than new foreign industry are calculated by subtracting data on new foreign industry from national totals. Data on new foreign industry are derived from the *Survey of Grant-Aided Industry* (1967) and O'Farrell and O'Loughlin (1980). Exports of all market economies are derived from the UN *Yearbook of International Trade Statistics 1977*.

12. The percentage of output exported by firms other than new foreign firms was only 15 per cent in Clay, Glass and cement and 13 per cent in Paper and printing in 1973 – the last year for which data are available – slightly lower than in 1960 in both cases and well below the 1973 average of 26 per cent for all industries other than new foreign industry.

13. 'Irish Companies 1978', *The Irish Times,* 1 and 2 January 1979.

14. Derived from *Irish Business*, January 1983 list of top companies.

15. According to the National Board for Science and Technology statistics, real expenditure on R & D increased by 3.7 per cent a year as against a growth rate of industrial output of 5.5 per cent. These figures include foreign subsidiaries, but the fact that the many new foreign firms established in the 1970s had, on average, a higher R & D intensity than the Irish firms, means that R & D intensity in Irish firms must have declined significantly.

16. Studies of new foreign industries in Ireland which would suggest that they mostly fall into these categories include Cooper and Whelan (1973); Buckley (1975); Teeling (1975); and Stanton (1979).

17. See also Cooper and Whelan (1973) and Buckley (1975) on the question of transfer of skills and technology; and see Cogan and Onyenadum (1981) on the low level of 'spin-offs' from foreign electronic firms.

18. The decline in employment in longer-established firms in 1973-80 is at least consistent with this hypothesis of a recurring pattern of eventual decline, but the available data are limited to too short a period to establish this point firmly. However, data on employment in new overseas firms in Northern Ireland clearly show this pattern in every five-year cohort going back as far as the late 1940s (Northern Ireland Economic Council, 1983, Figure 5).

19. Ireland's share of new US manufacturing investment in the EEC (nine countries) fell from 2.5 per cent in 1979 to 1.7 per cent in 1983, whereas the UK's share rose from 26.4 per cent in 1977 to 29.2 per cent in 1983. Ireland's share of new US manufacturing investment in the 'EEC twelve' (including Spain, Greece and Portugal) fell from 2.4 per cent in 1979 to 1.6 per cent in 1983, whereas Spain's share rose from 2.4 per cent to 3.9 per cent, and Portugal's share from 0.2 per cent to 0.4 per cent, although Greece's share did not increase in 1979-83 (US Department of Commerce, *Survey of Current Business*, October 1981 and September 1984).

20. See National Board for Science and Technology (1983), for further discussion of this point.

BIBLIOGRAPHY

Adams, F. G. and S. Ichimura, 1983. 'Industrial Policy in Japan', in F. G. Adams and L. R. Klein (eds), *Industrial Policies for Growth and Competitiveness*, Lexington, Wharton Econometric Studies.

Allen, G. C., 1981. 'Industrial Policy and Innovation in Japan', in C. Carter (ed.), *Industrial Policy and Innovation*, London, Heinemann.

Bain J. S., 1956. *Barriers to New Competition*, Cambridge (Mass.), Harvard University Press.

Balassa, B., 1980. *The Process of Industrial Development and Alternative Development Strategies*, World Bank Staff Working Paper No. 438, October.

Baran, P. A., 1973. *The Political Economy of Growth*, Harmondsworth, Penguin.

Bienefeld, M. and D. Innes, 1976. 'Capital Accumulation and South Africa', *Review of African Political Economy*, No. 7.

Buckley, P. J., 1975. 'The Effects of Foreign Direct Investment on the Economy of the Irish Republic', Ph.D. thesis, University of Lancaster.

Cheah Hock Beng, 1980. 'Export-oriented Industrialisation and Dependent Development: The Experience of Singapore', *IDS Bulletin*, Sussex, vol. 12, no. 1, December.

Cogan, J. and E. Onyenadum, 1981. 'Spin-off Companies in the Irish Electronics Industry', *Journal of Irish Business and Administrative Research*, vol. 3, no. 2, October.

Committee on Industrial Organisation 1965. *Final Report*, Dublin, Stationery Office.

Cooper, C. and N. Whelan, 1973. *Science, Technology and Industry in Ireland*, Report to the National Science Council, Dublin, Stationery Office.

Farley, N., 1973. 'Outward-looking Policies and Industrialisation in a Small Economy: Some Notes on the Irish Case', *Economic Development and Cultural Change*, vol. 21, no. 4, pt 1, July.

Fitzpatrick, J., 1981. *Industrialisation, Trade and Ireland's Development Co-operation Policy*, Dublin, Advisory Council on Development Co-operation.

Helleiner, G. K., 1973. 'Manufactured Exports from Less Developed Countries and Multinational Firms', *Economic Journal*, vol. 83, no. 329, March.

Industrial Policy, 1984. Irish Government White Paper, Dublin, Stationery Office.

Little, I., T. Scitovsky and M. Scott, 1970. *Industry and Trade in Some Developing Countries — A Comparative Study*, London, New York and Toronto, OUP.

Luedde-Neurath, R., 1980. 'Export Orientation in South Korea: How Helpful is Dependency Thinking to its Analysis?' *IDS Bulletin*, Sussex, vol. 12, no. 1, December.

Luedde-Neurath, R., 1984. 'State Intervention and Foreign Direct Investment in South Korea', *IDS Bulletin*, Sussex, vol. 15, no. 2, April.

McAleese, D. and D. McDonald, 1978. 'Employment Growth and the Development of Linkages in Foreign-owned and Domestic Manufacturing Enterprises', *Oxford Bulletin of Economics and Statistics*, vol. 40, no. 4, November.

Matthews, A., 1980. *EEC External Trade Policy: Its Relevance to Ireland*, Dublin, Irish Council of the European Movement.

National Board for Science and Technology, 1983, *Technology and Irish Industrial Policy*, Dublin, NBST.

Northern Ireland Economic Council, 1983. *The Duration of Industrial Development Assisted Employment*, Belfast, Northern Ireland Economic Development Office.

O'Farrell, P. N. and R. Crouchley, 1984. 'An Industrial and Spatial Analysis of New Firm Formation in Ireland', *Regional Studies*, vol. 18, no. 3, June.

O'Farrell, P. N. and B. O'Loughlin, 1980. *An Analysis of New Industry Linkages in Ireland*, Dublin, Industrial Development Authority.

O'Loughlin, B. and P. N. O'Farrell, 1980. 'Foreign Direct Investment in Ireland: Empirical Evidence and Theoretical Implications', *Economic and Social Review*, vol. 11, no. 3, April.

O'Malley, E., 1980. *Industrial Policy and Development: A Survey of Literature from the Early 1960s to the Present*, National Economic and Social Council, Paper No. 56, Dublin, Stationery Office.

O'Malley, E., 1981. 'The Decline of Irish Industry in the Nineteenth Century', *Economic and Social Review*, vol. 13, no. 1, October.

O'Malley, E., 1986. 'Foreign Owned Industry in Ireland: Performance and Prospects', in Peter Bacon (Ed.) *Medium Term Outlook: 1986-1990*. Dublin: Economic and Social Research Institute.

Porter, M., 1980. *Competitive Strategy — Techniques for Analyzing Industries and Competitors*, New York, Free Press.

Stanton, R., 1979. 'Foreign Investment and Host-country Politics: The Irish Case', in D. Seers, B. Schaffer, and M. Kiljunen (eds), *Underdeveloped Europe: Studies in Core-Periphery Relations*, Hassocks, Harvester Press.

Survey of Grant-Aided Industry, 1967. Survey team's report to the Industrial Development Authority, Dublin, Stationery Office.

Teeling, J., 1975. 'The Evolution of Offshore Investment', DBA thesis, Harvard University.

Telesis Consultancy Group, 1982. *A Review of Industrial Policy*, National Economic and Social Council, Paper No. 64, Dublin, Stationery Office.

Vernon, R., (1966). 'International Investment and International Trade in the Product Cycle', *Quarterly Journal of Economics*, vol. LXXX, no. 2, May.

Villamil, J. J., 1979. 'Puerto Rico 1948–1976: The Limits of Dependent Growth', in J. J. Villamil (ed.), *Transnational Capitalism and National Development*, Hassocks, Harvester Press.

Wade, R., 1984. 'Dirigisme Taiwan-style', *IDS Bulletin*, Sussex, vol. 15, no. 2, April.

Debt and Danger

Harold Lever and Christopher Huhne

This extract is from the authors' book,
Debt and Danger *(1985).*

We have made a labyrinth and have got lost in it.
We must find our way again.
Denis Diderot

The flows of finance between the advanced and the developing worlds, which have in the past done so much to promote economic stability, employment and the progress of living standards, are now characterized by a perverse and dangerous anomaly. Until 1982 it was understood that there had to be, for a prolonged period, a one-way flow of resources from the advanced countries to the Third World to promote its development. The view went unchallenged in either official or private-sector circles and was supported by every school of economic thought, albeit for differing reasons. Since the debt crisis which broke in 1982, those flows have been reversed for each important group of countries in the Third World. IMF estimates imply that in 1985 there was a resource flow from the fifteen largest Third World borrowers to their more prosperous creditors worth $37 billion, or one quarter of their entire earnings from the sales of their exports of goods and services.[1]

This reverse or negative flow is a perversion of common sense and of sound economics. On a classical view, the developing contries should attract capital from the industrial world because they are able to increase output by more than rich countries for a given increase in investment. On an alternative view, the debtors need balance-of-payments finance because their domestic economies are capable of expanding more rapidly than they are able to increase their foreign-exchange earnings and imports, due mainly to their reliance on export commodities whose demand grows less rapidly than world income. To our knowledge, no economist has yet advocated a large flow of resources from the poorer countries as a way of stimulating their economic progress.

Nor was this ever the intention of those who encouraged or undertook the original lending to the debtors, the interest payments on which are the main cause of the reverse transfer. It was always implicitly assumed that the financial markets would continue to refinance old debt and extend new credit so that the flow of resources to the developing world would continue, at least until some far-distant future in which the debtors would reach a level of development where it was feasible and desirable for them to export rather than import capital. This unplanned reverse flow of resources is made all the more extraordinary because it has been elevated into a necessary symptom of 'adjustment' by the official policy of the industrial countries, which are as unwilling today to take

263

their proper responsibility for the healthy functioning of the world's economy as they were after the first oil shock of 1973, which laid the foundations for this anomaly.

Yet such abdication of responsibility is singularly misplaced. The world's financial safety and economic health is balanced on a knife-edge. If defaults halt the reverse flows, many of the largest banks in the advanced countries will become insolvent. A crisis of the kind which we have thankfully not experienced since the Great Crash of 1929 would once again be a terrible reality. But if the Third World's debtors continue to generate the large trade surpluses required to make payment to the advanced countries, their economic development, already manifestly inadequate, will be hobbled for a generation. The effort to sustain the large trade surpluses required imposes enormous strains on the world's trading system, as industries in the advanced countries have to make way for Third World exports and resist the adjustment by means of ever more strident appeals for protectionism. Moreover, the very uncertainty of continued payments in these circumstances of rising political pressures in both debtor and creditor countries causes the banks themselves to slow down their lending, adding a further depressive influence to world trade.

The debtors can do no more to resolve their predicament. All the pressures on them are to expand their economies more rapidly, which would inevitably entail smaller rather than larger trading surpluses and would quite possibly result in creeping defaults on debt. The bankers cannot realistically lend more money to offset the interest payments coming back to them on the outstanding debt without a further loss of credibility. As it is, their outstanding lending to the Third World outstrips their own capital by a factor of two or more. Only the governments and monetary authorities of the advanced countries have the resources and the standing to reconcile the interests of both debtors and bankers – and to safeguard the world economy.

It is not, though, their unique financial power which alone casts the advanced-country governments in the natural role of managers of the debt crisis. They also bear a heavy responsibility for the events which led up to its occurrence. Until 1973 it was widely understood that commercial lending was not a safe or sure vehicle for development finance. Banks could neither impose conditions to ensure the fruitful use of the funds they lent, nor could they, when the need arose, postpone debt servicing and provide new funds without undermining the confidence of those who deposit money with them. After 1973 it was absolutely right for the advanced countries to seek to ensure that the developing world had the funds to continue to import the material they needed for development, despite the sharp rise in the price of oil. Without those funds, Third World imports would have collapsed and, with them, the jobs of millions in the advanced countries who sell to them. What was wrong was for the advanced-country governments to push the commercial banking systems of their countries into a role which should have been supported and regulated by the authorities whose public purposes it rightly fulfilled.

In the years after the first oil-crisis of 1973-4 the banks took the unspent cash surpluses of the oil-rich countries and lent them to the oil-dependent Third World. Reinforced by the approval and encouragement of their governments, the banks happily developed the conviction that there was no risk in this lending to foreign governments. They came to believe that they had hit upon the most profitable area in banking history. Nowhere else could such huge sums be placed at an assured profit and with minimal administrative cost. The banks that lent in this field soon found that the profits from what they had convinced themselves was risk-free lending greatly exceeded those from the rest of their much more complicated and onerous activities.

In the years after 1974 the borrowing countries financed the trade deficits of their imports over their exports increasingly by borrowing from the banks. The borrowing was originally prompted by the need to cover the cartel's oil price rises. It was soon extended to cover virtually any borrowing that the developing countries' governments saw fit to make. Indeed, countries like Mexico, Venezuela and Nigeria, which were beneficiaries of the oil price rises, were among the heaviest borrowers. There was no thought of servicing the debt by generating trade surpluses and reverse transfers. The service of interest and repayments was expected to be met, and was in fact met year after year, by new borrowing in addition to loans to cover current needs.

The happy-go-lucky assumption by governments and banks that the debts could be serviced indefinitely by new borrowing on the financial markets went virtually unchallenged. All the agreements with debtor countries for service of interest and capital were manifestly on terms which could not be met by the debtors' export earnings but only by new borrowing, as one of the present authors repeatedly warned both within the government between 1974 and 1979 and thereafter.

Yet uncritical self-congratulation over the advantages of these arrangements was the order of the day. The bankers liked them because apparently never were propriety and profit so happily conjoined. The borrowers liked them because they placed little restraint on the volume or the purposes of their borrowing. The Organization of Petroleum Exporting Countries (OPEC) liked them because they enlisted the banking system of the West in support of the ability of their poorest customers to meet the cartel's oil price rises. The aid lobby liked them because they provided a novel transfer of resources to the poorer countries on a scale greater than ever before. Santa Claus had appeared in the guise of sound commercial activity, and nobody wanted to shoot him. Western governments liked these arrangements because they appeared to support their belief that this lending was urgently needed in the world interest and could be dealt with indefinitely by unassisted bank intermediation rather than by recourse to public budgets.

The inexorable result, however, was the crisis of debt and growth which we suffer today. The period between borrowing and servicing of debt by a real flow of foreign currency back to the lender can be bridged by further commercial borrowing – but only as long as that real flow is a credible prospect. Nobody could claim that this prospect grew to match the ever-growing mountain of private debt, and this was bound to bring into question the credibility of most of the debtors and the lending system itself. The build-up to crisis was inevitable. Prolonged recession and the move to higher real interest rates after 1979 speeded up the disintegration of confidence, but they were not its fundamental cause. . . .

The pyramid of debt has proved sustainable since the Mexican crisis of 1982 only because of extraordinary sacrifices on the part of debtors and considerable effort by creditors and official institutions alike.* But most of the factors which have encouraged a 'co-operative' handling of the debt crisis will be hard to sustain.

Reschedulings, whereby certain interest and principal repayments which come due are postponed when the banks put up some new lending partially to offset them, will become more and more difficult. As it is, the banks are increasing their outstanding loans to most of the debtors only under official duress. The structure of the banking market is such that each creditor has an individual interest in reducing its exposure to the debtor countries, though if all creditors followed their individual interest and reduced their exposure (and hence met even fewer of the interest and principal payments coming back to them), the debtor countries would be put in an impossible position very rapidly.

Even if such a crisis could be averted, the situation from the point of view of the debtors looks no happier. Negative transfers and their associated trade surpluses are enormous and growing, despite some new bank lending and funds from the IMF. They have been achieved largely by drastic cuts in imports engineered by a depression of demand, output and employment. The recent increases in exports from the debtor countries, which alleviate the import-cutting effects of the negative transfers, are nevertheless woefully dependent on the buoyancy of the American marketplace. They cannot be sustained as American growth slows down and the United States' trade deficit is reduced.

Moreover, several of the reasons why the debtors have so far been prepared to accept the enormous sacrifices demanded of them rather than to default on their obligations in the face of domestic pressures, may also be waning. The threat of vanishing trade credit if a country defaults is less potent when foreign-exchange reserves are building up and barter trade is growing. They have also hoped that eventually Western governments will come to see the difficulty of their situation and intervene with debt relief. If that prospect is not kept alive, defaults could follow swiftly.

[Why did countries incur debt?] Money – and particularly foreign exchange – is 'fungible' in the sense that it is not always easy to track down its true end use because a loan can easily be transferred to purposes other than those for which it was contracted. Lending is thus general lending to the country concerned to

---

*In August 1982, Mexico announced an immediate moratorium on its foreign-currency debt: it had been unable to raise new loans big enough to repay the debts which were becoming due. Within months, the markets which had lavished funds on the debtor countries were closed to them. (Lever and Huhne, *Debt and Danger*, 1985), p. 39.

maintain a higher level of imports than would otherwise be the case and in the hope that it will be able to repay. With these caveats, it is clear that the increased oil bill of the non-oil Third World countries was the main cause of the debt build-up from the debtors' point of view, though rising interest rates and mistaken exchange-rate policies also played a role. . . .

A further oil price rise and the rise in real interest rates were only part of the shock delivered to the debtors between 1978 and 1982. Once again, the effect of Western policy aimed at countering renewed inflation by depressing demand was to cause a sharp drop in the value of Third World exports. Even the upper-middle-income countries of Latin America remain strongly dependent on commodity exports. In Brazil soya beans, coffee and iron ore accounted for 83 per cent of merchandise exports in 1981-2.[2] In Argentina wheat, corn and beef provide one-third of exports. In Chile copper alone accounts for nearly half. As the industrial world went into recession, commodity prices fell by one-quarter between 1980 and 1982.[3] Rising oil prices, higher nominal and real interest rates, sluggish developed-country markets, a rise in the dollar in which most of the debt was denominated and falling export prices added up to a formidable shock, diminishing the sources of foreign exchange while increasing demand for it.

It is clear, however, that the attempt to compensate for external shocks to debtor economies was not the only use for foreign-currency finance and that some of the other explanations are decidedly less flattering to the Third World's policy-makers. Two classes of policy decision added unnecessarily to outstanding debt by the time of the 1982 crisis. (Alternatively, they can be seen as having reduced potential economic growth for the given increase in debt.) The first was the clear instances of political decisions to increase arms imports, which could not produce domestic investment, still less provide capacity which would increase the foreign-exchange earning power needed to service debt. The second were macro-economic policy errors which encouraged imports, discouraged exports and stimulated the build-up of private capital abroad by Third World residents. . . .

An unsupported and insufficiently regulated banking system was revealed, in the period 1979-82, to be an inherently unstable source of balance-of-payments funding for the developing world. When times were good, the banks thrust tempting loans on to favoured Third World governments, though they were in no position to ensure that good economic policies would be pursued. When times were bad, the banks were no longer prepared to fund mounting deficits.

The irony is that, with some clear exceptions, the private financing of Third World current-account deficits over the decade to 1982 was a considerable success story from the point of view of world growth and public policy. Neither the level of the debt nor its results need have caused alarm: the problem lay not so much in the amounts of money which were extended but in the nature of the lending. The debt, after all, did allow the non-oil developing countries to maintain far higher growth rates than they would otherwise have been able to do. Comparing the pre-1973 and post-1973 period, we know that industrial-country growth slowed down markedly: the surprise is that the non-oil developing countries managed to compensate for this slow-down to a large degree in their main markets and the rise in the cost of their main imports by making up their import capacity with debt. Indeeed, the average annual rate of growth of the non-oil Third World between 1973 and 1981 was 5.1 per cent, compared with 5.8 per cent in the period 1967-72.[4] In retrospect this was a quite remarkable performance. The industrial countries, by contrast, slowed down from an annual average growth of 4.4 per cent in 1967-72 to one of 2.8 per cent. If the developing world had slowed down still more, it would have cut its imports from the industrial countries and hence their growth. From the world's point of view, it was better for the lending to have taken place clumsily than not at all.

One cost, of course, was a rising debt burden for the debtors, though on conventional measures it looked far from unsustainable even at the end of the decade. The real value of total debt for the non-oil developing countries, expressed in constant 1975 dollars, rose from $169 billion in 1973 to $294.7 billion in 1979.[5] But even this rise went side by side with a substantial expansion in the Third World's foreign-currency earnings. The total debt to export ratio was 115.4 per cent in 1973 and rose to 130.2 per cent in 1978. But the following year it was back to 119.2 per cent, scarcely higher than at the beginning of the decade. The debt service to export ratio – the amount of interest payments and repayments of principal due in a year relative to exports – indicated a slightly graver problem: it rose from 15.9 per cent in 1973 to 19 per cent in 1979. If, however, the debt had been contracted at maturities longer than the typical eight-year loan, even this ratio could have been contained at more or less its level at the beginning of the decade. Clearly, the conventional debt ratios tell us little about the likelihood of crisis.

The truth is that neither conventional creditworthiness indicators nor the results of Third World policies suggest that the build-up of debt, at least to the end of the 1970s, was misplaced. What *was* unsustainable was the system and nature of that debt. The similarity of the conventional creditworthiness ratios at the beginning and the end of the period merely disguise a much more funda-mental change in the structure of the outstanding debt.

The advanced countries had thrown a single vulnerable section of their economies, the banking system, into a task which it could not bear without official support. The key difference between the position of the Third World debtors in 1973 and at the end of the 1970s was that their debt was no longer largely official debt: it was commercial debt to the banks. Governments can afford to roll over interest and capital obligations as circumstances require. Banks cannot without embroiling themselves in a dynamic of increasing incredibility. The share of outstanding commercial debt in total loans rose from 11.6 per cent in 1973 to 37.5 per cent in 1982.[6] In the case of the richer debtors in Latin America the proportion rose from 23.8 per cent to 62 per cent. The debtors inevitably became vulnerable to the disintegration of market confidence. The sharp rise in bank debt would itself have eventually been enough to cause the lending to stop. External shocks such as the rise in interest rates merely accelerated the process. Unsupported private banks could never have provided enough time for the debtors to repay by generating export surpluses. There was no contemplation of this until the smooth, automatic new lending which had been expected failed to arrive.

The banks were simply unable to maintain their own confidence in the commercial nature of the loans they were making, with the result that the mechanism of the commercial banks' balance-of-payments financing became in 1982 the very opposite of what had been intended. The international credit market had been justified on the grounds that countries should have time to 'put their own houses in order', but it instead became a burden on developing countries already facing, in the commodity markets, a magnified impact of the industrial world's gathering recession. It acted to exacerbate the depressive forces in the world economy rather than to alleviate them. The unregulated international credit market had failed.

NOTES AND REFERENCES

1. This figure is derived from IMF, *World Economic Outlook*, Washington DC, October 1986.

2. Inter-American Development Bank, *Annual Report 1984*, Washington DC, 1985, Table 12, p. 126.

3. IMF, *International Financial Statistics Yearbook 1984*, All Commodities Index, p. 133.

4. IMF, *World Economic Outlook*, Washington DC, June 1981, Table 2, p. 112.

5. William R. Cline, *International Debt: Systemic Risk and Policy Response*, Institute for International Economics, Washington DC, 1984, Table 1.1, p. 2.

6. 'Overview Paper on Debt'. Mimeo background papers for the Commonwealth Expert Group on Debt, CDG/1/Com.Sec., April 1984.

FURTHER READING *(suggested by the Editors)*.

Susan George, *A Fate worse than Debt*, (Harmondsworth: Penguin, 1988).

Helen O'Neill, 'Debts, Deficits and Development: Some Elements in Interdependence of Monetary and Trade Issues in the Global Economy' in *EADI Bulletin* No. 2, 1987.

The Debt Crisis and the Poor

Keith Griffin

This paper is from the author's World Hunger
and the World Economy *(1987).*

The current economic crisis is global in nature and is not to be explained simply by mistakes made by borrowing countries or by lending institutions. That is not to say that some governments were not imprudent or that some banks did not make foolish loans, but the essence of the problem arises from the unsatisfactory performance of the world economy rather than from excessive international lending and borrowing. It is deplorable that part of the foreign debt has been used to finance a boom in imported consumer goods (as in Chile), or to pay armaments (as in Argentina) or to facilitate capital flight (as in Mexico), but borrowing for such purposes was not the cause of the crisis. The cause lies elsewhere. Indeed, had the commercial banks been incapable of lending the surpluses generated by the major oil-exporting countries and had other countries been unwilling to borrow abroad in order to maintain their capacity to import, there would have been a sharp decline in aggregate demand at the global level and the worldwide recession would have been even worse than it is.

This is especially true of the 1970s and the origins of the current massive imbalance of international payments. Since 1981, however, the OPEC countries as a group have been in balance of payments deficit. Moreover, there is a statistical discrepancy in global balance of payments figures so that the total for the world is not zero but a very large deficit.

None the less, it remains true that the massive borrowing by Third World countries in the last decade arose from the need of the international system as a whole to recycle the balance of payments surpluses of a small number of Arab petroleum-producing countries. The net transfer of savings from lenders to borrowers via the commercial banking system was mutually advantageous and is no cause for criticism. Indeed, by preventing further deflation, the recycling activities of the commercial banks were of general benefit, even to those countries which were neither lenders nor borrowers.

Again, it must be said that the above does not imply that the way the recycling was done was necessarily the best way to do it. It is a cause for regret that the structure, the resources and the politics of the IMF did not permit it to play a more constructive role, and in particular to lend more for longer periods on more generous terms. In retrospect it is a great pity that the liquidity of the international economy, as measured, say, by the ratio of liquid international reserves to the value of world trade, has been allowed to decline in recent decades. But given the reduced liquidity of the system as a whole, and given that there is no international lender-of-last-resort, recycling by the commercial banks has played a very positive role.

The so-called debt crisis is essentially the financial counterpart to the current prolonged recession. There is no financial crisis apart from the crisis in the real economy. That is, if the recession were to disappear, and sustained worldwide expansion were to be restored, the debt crisis would abate and perhaps disappear.

Whether one agrees with this view or not, the fact remains that a crisis exists and the burden of adjusting to the crisis has fallen disproportionately on the Third World. Different countries have been affected in different ways and in different degrees, but it may be helpful to list the more important ways in which Third World countries have been harmed.

The Effects on Poor Countries

First, the slowing down of growth in the world economy has led to slower growth of the volume of exports of Third World countries. For example, between 1960-70 and 1970-81, the rate of growth of the volume of exports from the 'low-income economies' fell from 4.9 per cent a year to minus 0.7 per cent a year. This has been accompanied, second, by a decline in the price of exports. For example, in 1981, the worst year, the export price of sugar fell by nearly 40 per cent, lumber by nearly 17 per cent, natural rubber by 24.5 per cent, tin by nearly 15 per cent and copper by over 20 per cent. The combination of a more slowly growing volume of exports and lower prices has resulted, third, in a marked reduction in the rate of growth of the value of exports. In several cases, fourth, these unfavourable tendencies produced by market forces have been exacerbated by rising protectionism in the advanced economies as a result of the imposition of higher tariff and non-tariff barriers to trade.

The prices of goods imported by Third World countries have not in general fallen, and in the case of oil, prices were raised sharply in 1973-4 and again in 1980. The result has been, fifth, a deterioration in the net barter terms of trade. The deterioration affected all groups of countries except for the oil-exporting ones and was particularly severe during the period 1978-81. Brazil's terms of trade, for instance, declined by 48 per cent during that period and that of the 'low-income economies' by just over 20 per cent. Sixth, in a great many cases the income terms of trade (or the capacity of a country to pay for imports out of exports) also declined.

Our seventh effect has received a great deal of attention, namely, the dramatic increase in the real rate of interest paid by debtor countries. Nominal prime rates of interest charged by US commerical banks rose from an average of 8.1 per cent in 1970-9 to 14.95 per cent in 1980-3; real rates of interest increased from 1.33 to 7.9 per cent between the two periods. That is, real rates increased six-fold. Most Latin American governments, however, must pay a premium over prime rates of 0.5−2.0 per cent and thus the real rate paid by them probably approaches 10 per cent (or even more) today.

Moreover, Latin America's foreign debt is denominated in dollars and since 1981 the US dollar has appreciated against other currencies. This, our eighth effect, has made it even more difficult for the debtor countries to service their loans and has greatly increased the domestic resource cost of interest payments.

That is, the borrowing countries have had inflicted upon them a nearly intolerable combination of a higher real rate of interest on dollar denominated debt and a higher price of the dollar.

Lastly, unable to import capital on acceptable terms, the Third World finds it increasingly difficult to export labour. Both in Europe and in North America the advanced economies are adopting more restrictive policies towards immigration in an attempt to reduce their own high rates of unemployment. The Third World thus is assailed from all directions: its trading environment has deteriorated; foreign borrowing has declined and become much more expensive, and the net movement of capital has in some cases become negative; and the possibility of the poor escaping economic hardship by emigration has become more difficult.

The Policies of Rich Countries

Viewed as a whole, the main problem of the world economy is that since 1974 the rate of growth of the seven major OECD countries (USA, Japan, Canada, France, Germany, Italy and the UK) has been very slow, although there was some acceleration in 1984. The weight of these economies in the world economy is so great that poor performance by these seven countries makes it very difficult indeed for the rest of the world to sustain an acceptable rate of growth.

Unfortunately, the seven major OECD countries have collectively deflated their economies since the mid-1970s and apart from 1978 the 'cyclically adjusted budget deficit' as a percentage of GNP has declined steadily. In fact since 1979 the rise in the budget deficit of the Group of Seven has been due entirely to the operation of automatic stabilisers, e.g. higher unemployment compensation and lower tax receipts because of a lower level of economic activity. That is, discretionary government policy has been strongly deflationary and the reduction in aggregate demand has plunged the world into a lengthy recession – the worst since the 1930s – which has created in its wake a nasty international debt crisis. The only positive outcome, possibly only temporary, has been a reduction in the international rates of inflation.

The balance of fiscal and monetary policy within the Group of Seven has varied from one country to another. Fiscal policy, i.e. tax and expenditure policy, has been restrictive in Japan and Europe, particularly in the United Kingdom. In the United States since 1982, however, a policy of high interest rates pursued by the autonomous Federal Reserve System has been combined with a cyclically adjusted budget deficit (largely caused by the decision of President Reagan to increase substantially expenditure on armaments). The United States is thus experiencing an armaments-led expansion of aggregate demand. This has re-ignited a worldwide arms race, but at the same time has provided a faint hope that the world recession may slowly be coming to an end.

The set of policies that ideally should be pursued by the Group of Seven are rather obvious. First the European nations should relax their fiscal policies, preferably by increasing public investment in labour-intensive construction activities. Second, the United States should relax its monetary policy (thereby lowering real rates of interest) while changing the balance of fiscal policy (switching from armaments to more productive activities). It is important, however, that the USA should not reduce interest rates through a large unilateral reduction in its budget deficit, for this would almost certainly lead to a contraction of aggregate demand which would threaten any hope there may be for an expansion of the world economy. Third, expansion would be more rapid and more certain if it were possible for the OECD countries, or any large sub-set of them, to coordinate their economic policies, but alas this seems to be politically impossible, at least for the time being.

The ultimate objective, however, should be an expansion of aggregate demand in Europe and a consequent balance of payments deficit there. This would permit an easing of monetary policy in the United States and lower real rates of interest combined with a slight reduction in the growth of aggregate demand, which probably is increasing at a pace which cannot be sustained much longer.

The Response of the Third World
The policy responses in the Third World to the problems that beset them have been: (i) devaluation, in an attempt to switch resources to exports and reduce the demand for imports; (ii) deflation of aggregate demand (higher taxes, tighter control over the money supply, lower levels of public investment and a reduction in welfare services) in an attempt to reduce domestic absorption and generate savings that can be transferred abroad to service the foreign debt; and (iii) renegotiation of the overseas commercial debt on an *ad hoc* basis in an attempt to ease the burden of adjustment while avoiding an outright default.

Narrowly viewed, the policies that have been adopted have enjoyed some success. Default has been avoided, domestic absorption has been reduced and Latin America as a whole has generated a large and rising trade surplus which has enabled at least part of the interest on the debts to be paid. Far from being a recipient of foreign capital, Latin America since 1982 has been a net exporter of capital, some of it in the form of capital flight. This raises three possible problems. First, Latin America's balance of trade surplus will have to be accommodated by the creditor countries in the form of a balance of payments deficit. This will create adjustment problems in the United States and Europe which may be difficult to overcome, particularly in the context of a depressed international economy. Indeed the rising protectionism to which we have already referred indicates that the problem may be a real one. Second, if the debtor countries deflate in an attempt to create larger export surpluses and the creditor countries pursue restrictive monetary and fiscal policies in order to avoid large trading deficits, there is a danger that the Third World's efforts to solve the debt crisis will give a further deflationary bias to the entire world economy. Finally, there is a danger that, in practice, the net transfer of resources from Latin America and other debtor countries may be too small to end the world banking crisis while being so large in relation to the debtor countries that their economies are severely damaged. Certainly the damage they have suffered so far has been considerable.

The consequences for the debtor countries of the current prolonged recession and the policies they have been forced to adopt have been the following:

(i) higher unemployment and disguised urban under-employment combined with an expansion of the low-productivity petty services sector;

(ii) a reduction in real wages and living standards, particularly of those employed or formerly employed on fixed wages in the organised urban sector;

(iii) a reduction in the rate of investment and in the growth of the potential productive capacity of the economy;

(iv) a reduction in the actual rate of growth of industrial output and domestic product;

(v) a fall in average income per head;

(vi) a rise in the tax burden or the ratio of taxes to GNP;

(vii) a sharp rise in political and social discontent which if continued could lead to grave instability in several countries.

Perhaps ironically, inequality in the distribution of income may not have increased and in some cases may have diminished. That is, it is possible that a smaller national income may be distributed more equally. The reason for this is that the effects of the economic contraction may have fallen most severely upon those who are relatively better off rather than upon the poor. The contraction in aggregate demand has been greater in the urban areas than in the rural, and greater in manufacturing and the public sector than in agriculture. In fact, agricultural exporters in some countries may have enjoyed absolute gains in income, and where peasant agriculture is important, the poor may have shared in the rise in income.

The largest losers are likely to include (i) urban entrepreneurs in construction and manufacturing; (ii) those in relatively highly paid urban wage employment, including civil servants; (iii) those receiving welfare payments and food subsidies, including members of the armed forces and the civil service; (iv) those forced to bear the burden of higher taxation, which could, of course, be the poor if the tax system on the margin is regressive; and (v) borrowers from the domestic banking system who have to pay higher real rates of interest. (Net savers with the commercial banking system would, of course, benefit from the present state of affairs.) Most of these losers are likely to have incomes above the median level and hence the decline in average incomes may well have been accompanied by an improvement in the distribution of income. I hasten to add that this is no consolation to those concerned with alleviating poverty, but it does suggest that political protest, where it occurs, will come not from the poorest members of society but from those who once were relatively prosperous.

Possible Solutions

A solution to the current problems of the world economy will require both financial and macro-economic measures. Let us begin with the financial measures.

It is possible that an *ad hoc*, case-by-case approach favoured by the governments of most creditor countries may be made to work, in the sense that the commercial banking system can avoid collapse. A 'cap' can be put on interest rates, repayments of interest can be 'postponed', the commercial banks can reduce the balance sheet value of some of their overseas 'assets', the banks can 'agree' to make further loans to the debtor countries to enable them to continue paying at least part of the interest owed, etc. All of these solutions are largely cosmetic, but they do entail a partial default and they might just provide a breathing space in which to design more fundamental policies.

The first thing that should be done is to strengthen international monetary institutions. The IMF should be enlarged substantially, preferably by the creation of SDRs, and should become an international lender-of-last-resort. That is, the Fund should be transformed into a world central bank. The Third World should have much greater representation on the executive board of the reformed IMF than it presently enjoys and the staffing arrangements within the Fund's bureaucracy should be overhauled. Further comments on the IMF are made below. Next, the global debt should be restructured or funded with a view to switching from variable interest rate loans to fixed interest rates, and from short-term commercial credit to long-term loans. This switch is likely to imply a reduction in private lending (particularly from the commercial banks) and an increase in public lending (not only from a greatly enlarged IMF, but also from the IBRD, IDB and other regional development banks). Finally, the governments of creditor countries should announce publicly that, should the need ever arise to protect the banking system as a whole, they stand prepared to bail out their own commercial banks on a case-by-case basis by acting as a domestic lender-of-last-resort.

These arrangements should ensure that the commercial banks are protected from the worst consequences of default, the debtor countries are given relief from a situation not of their own making and for which they are not responsible, and the international monetary system as a whole has a regulatory institution of a size and scope that is adequate for the tasks it confronts.

Even if all this is done, however, the problems of the world economy will persist unless there are changes in macro-economic policy. Real interest rates must be reduced, and this requires a change in US monetary policy. Effective demand must increase, and this requires a change in fiscal policy in Europe. World trade must be stimulated, and this requires lower protection in the Group of Seven. If dollar-denominated debts are to be repaid, the overvaluation of the US dollar must end, and this too requires changes in monetary, trade and fiscal policies in the United States. Finally, it would be advantageous to countries such as Mexico if the United States were to relax its restrictions on the immigration of labour from western hemisphere countries. The purpose of this set of policies thus is two-fold: to shift more of the burden of adjustment from debtor to creditor countries, from South to North; and to stimulate the overall growth of the world economy. It is possible, and perhaps even likely, that an expansion of aggregate demand at the global level would result in some increase in the rate of inflation, but this is a very small price to pay for a solution to problems that have seemed to be intractable for a decade or more.

What should the Third World do? To answer this question it is necessary to go back to the beginning, to the fundamental cause of the current crisis. There is no doubt that bankers, like any other businessman, can make mistakes or be less than prudent; equally, there is no doubt that borrowers can use the resources put at their disposal foolishly; but such actions do not account for the current recession, the worst recession in the world economy in the last half century.

The crisis – a crisis which now has lasted for over a decade – was caused by governments in the advanced industrial capitalist economies deliberately reducing aggregate demand in an attempt to control domestic inflation. It may appear to be even-handed to share responsibility for the resulting disaster among the banks, the borrowers and the governments of the major OECD countries, but this is a curiously wrong-headed view of our problems. The responsibility lies entirely with the advanced economies including, of course, the UK.

In the 1930s world expansion was limited by beggar-thy-neighbour protectionism. Later we saw countries engage in competitive devaluation in an attempt to reduce imports. Today we live in an era of competitive deflationary policies. The 'first world' deflates by choice and the Third World has no choice but to do the same. Indeed, of the major OECD countries, only the United States is running a discretionary, cyclically adjusted budget deficit – and this is due entirely to very rapid expansion of expenditure on military equipment. Keynes must be turning in his grave.

The effects, as we all know, of the macro-economic mismanagement of the world economy have been horrific and even optimistic forecasts of future prospects leave no hope that there will be a substantial fall in unemployment, a reduction in mass poverty or a rise in living standards for many millions of ordinary working people, in the rich countries as well as in the poor.

It must be emphasised that the author attaches strategic importance to a complete overhaul of world financial institutions and, in the struggle to create a New International Economic Order, this surely deserves high priority. Our present arrangements, centred on the IMF, impart a strong deflationary bias to the world economy. This institutionalised policy stance must be changed. And this implies a transformation of the IMF into a lender-of-last-resort, a massive expansion of its resources and a change in its *modus operandi*, the replacement of the US dollar as a reserve currency by an international financial instrument, and much increased representation of the Third World on the governing board of the transformed institution.

Let us now turn to policies that can be adopted by Third World countries acting unilaterally or, preferably, in cooperation. Two countries – Brazil and Mexico – have such large commercial debts that they are a genuine threat to the banks. Hence their bargaining position potentially is very strong. On the other hand, both have been able to respond quickly to the crisis and now have a negative net transfer of resources to the rich countries. This may reduce their incentive to use their strong bargaining position. (In the old days a transfer of savings from the poor countries to the rich would have been regarded as exploitation; today, ironically, it is regarded as successful economic policy. This author, being an old-fashioned person, considers the former view was the right one.)

Be that as it may, several other countries – Argentina, Chile, Bolivia, Peru – are in a weaker bargaining position but have gained less from their involvement in the international banking system: growth has been slow, poverty has increased, costs of adjustment have been exceptionally high. The same has been true of a number of African countries. Thus these countries in Latin America and Africa have a greater incentive to exploit whatever bargaining power they have.

Ideally, the debtor countries should get together and form a cartel. Their differing situations and interests, however, suggest that formation of a formal cartel is, alas, unlikely. It might be possible, on the other hand, to form an informal cartel and for a member of the group – acting in a similar way to a 'price leader' in an oligopolistically organised industry – to take on the role of 'default leadership'.

It is taken for granted here, as obvious and unnecessary for debate, that default – disguised, partial but more than marginal, done in a polite, quiet and gentlemanly way, but default none the less – is the name of the game. It is bound to play a strategic role in future economic policy in many Third World countries unless there is a radical improvement in the performance of the world economy. If the politicians will not default on the debt, then surely the people will.

The purpose of a debtors' cartel, of 'default leadership' and of creeping or disguised renunciation of the debt is twofold. First, to buy time, to bring short-term relief to the major debtor countries so that more of their resources can be devoted to raising the living standards of their people. Second, to increase pressure on the major OECD countries to transform international institutions and international economic policy. In short, the purpose is to force them to the bargaining table.

It might be thought that the massive foreign debt of the United States will some day encourage that country to seek a global solution to the world's financial difficulties. Unfortunately, however, that would be wishful thinking. The difference between the American debt and that of the Third World lies in the fact that the US dollar is a reserve currency – indeed it is still the dominant reserve currency – and there is almost nowhere else for savers to place their capital, especially if they wish to place large amounts of capital. The dollar, like sterling in the first two decades after the Second World War, is grossly overvalued and it is virtually certain that at some stage it will be devalued sharply. When that happens, those who hold dollar assets will find in effect that part of their assets have been expropriated. The US 'debt problem' will be solved by a transfer of the real purchasing power of assets – a capital transfer – from the Arabs and other creditors to the US economy.

There are enormous advantages to a country in being at the centre of the world's trading and financial system. The point just made illustrates one aspect of this, namely, that US banks can earn very large incomes lending other people's money at usurious interest rates. At the same time, the USA as a whole can borrow heavily from the rest of the world, and if the debt becomes inconveniently large, it can reduce the real burden on the country merely by changing the exchange rate.

How nice it would be if other debtor countries – the debtor countries of the Third World – could solve their problems so easily! The alternative open to them to reduce the burden of their debt is a partial default and probably, in one way or another, default is essential and hence inevitable.

The End of the Third World

Nigel Harris

This extract is from the author's The End of the Third World *(1986).*

The Third World is disappearing. Not the countries themselves, nor the inhabitants, much less the poor who so powerfully coloured the original definition of the concept, but the argument. Third Worldism began as a critique of an unequal world, a programme for economic development and justice, a type of national reformism dedicated to the creation of new societies and a new world. It ends with its leading protagonists either dead, defeated or satisfied to settle simply for national power rather than international equality; the rhetoric remains, now toothless, the decoration for squabbles over the pricing of commodities or flows of capital.

The conception of an interdependent, interacting, global manufacturing system cuts across the old view of a world consisting of nation-states as well as one of groups of countries, more and less developed and centrally planned – the First, the Third and the Second Worlds. Those notions bore some relationship to an older economy, one marked by the exchange of raw materials for manufactured goods. But the new world that has superseded it is far more complex and does not lend itself to the simple identification of First and Third, haves and have-nots, rich and poor, industrialized and non-industrialized.

Yet the world order is still dominated by the culture, politics and ideology of the old pattern, a world of national egotisms where states determine what is important. Indeed, the global manufacturing system can only be identified through the prism of national shares of output; the interests of states take priority over understanding the technical geography of production. The concepts of nationalism thus organize our perception and our consciousness, and so predetermine our view of what is reality. It will be a long time before the identification of the world catches up with the reality.

The simple dichotomies of the past, First and Third World, imposed their own gross distortion. Poor and rich were never properly defined by different countries. Even the so-called poorest country has its clutch of millionaires living in the same lifestyle as their peers in the richest country. Each so-called rich country has, trapped in the cruel interstices of its economy, thousands of hungry and poor. The division between rich and poor is represented in each microcosm of the system; poverty at the global level was never a territorial concept. The 'geopoliticization' of inequality illuminated in the first instance, but finally obfuscated. The poor of the United States were defined out of existence. The rich of India were carefully concealed from view.

The case deflected attention to geography. The stereotypes and the impassioned reformism attracted a generation of idealistic young people. Those on the left absorbed an enormous amount from Third Worldism and a version

279

of the experience of the less developed countries. It seemed for a long time the only part of the world where men and women still struggled to be free, still had the capacity to dream and strive for a different world. When the more developed countries seemed sunk in apathy, selfishness and materialism, the old aspirations seemed still to exist in a Third World – as well as the energy to achieve them, to leap the stages of what seemed bureaucratically defined history. States became the surrogate for all those unknown millions of poor, and the rhetoric of national politicians stood proxy for the yearnings of silent masses. It was a nonsense to conceal the emergence of new classes, relating to the majority in much the same way as they did everywhere else.

Capitalism remained the same. The market remained the market. Only for a short time did it seem that the state had conquered the economy – to guarantee full employment in one part of the world, to force perpetual growth in the other. The period was long enough to soak into popular consciousness and the social sciences on both left and right. Conscious reform by the state, it was supposed, now replaced the blind transformations of the market. It was a half hint of socialism, a human order determined by need, but without the precondition – power in the hands of the majority. In place of popular democratic control of the means of production, much of the Third World offered old-fashioned dictatorship, the one-party state or the revolutionary military junta. The majority could not be trusted to exercise power.

National reformist aspiration grew weak as the new orders settled more comfortably into power. The old issues became less urgent. But, also, the needs of accumulation limited the potential for social reform. Furthermore, an increasingly integrated world system lays down narrower and narrower limits to the possibility of local eccentricity, including reform. In a competitive system, holding down the price of labour takes precedence over protecting it, and the domestic economy becomes increasingly a spin-off of a wider order. Such a prospect causes understandable alarm. If the state cannot control domestic affairs, regulate and order the growth of incomes and employment, and propel self-sufficient economic growth, all, it seems, becomes dangerously random. It is little consolation to repeat that we can always perceive the losses in what is declining, rarely the gains in what is rising. Nor is it much comfort to observe that if the old aspiration was utopian, then to stop believing it is the precondition for identifying the grounds for real optimism. One of those sources of optimism is in the weakening of the drive to war; as capital and states become slightly dissociated, the pressures to world war are slightly weakened. Furthermore, there promises to be some decrease in the belief that killing foreigners is a good thing. The process of dispersal of manufacturing capacity brings enormous hope to areas where poverty has hitherto appeared immoveable, and makes possible new divisions of labour and specializations which will vastly enhance the capacity of the world to feed everyone. Above all, the realization of one world offers the promise of a rationally ordered system, determined by its inhabitants in the interests of need, not profit or war. Of course, it will not be won by waiting. The world of states will not wither away of its own accord; old orders cling to their power with increasing vigour as they grow obsolete, particularly when they continue to have privileged access to the surplus generated in the system. Great battles will be required against states to win the new world; but the possibilities of doing so are now much enhanced by the changes that are under way.

It is particularly painful for the left to detach itself from the fate of states. If trade unions needed national governments to curb the competition of workers and so limit the drive of capital, the left needed the state to introduce reforms, even if that meant overthrowing the old government by national revolution and creating a new state. In the last two great waves of the struggle for national independence – the first when empires in Europe broke up in the first twenty years of this century; and the second when the European empires in the rest of the world disintegrated after the Second World War – the cause of socialism became swamped by the politics of nationalism and national liberation. Indeed, straightforward revolutions that did not involve expelling a colonial power became none the less 'national liberation', symbolizing how far the interests of creating a new state had overcome any interest in abolishing states. Nation and state replaced class. And the world of states was thereby preserved from challenge, for the warriors against imperialism contributed to maintaining it. That issue is now nearly over. The world consists of independent states, threatened by revolts of national liberation movements – the Tamils of Sri Lanka, the Sikhs of India, the Mindanao Muslims. These issues are far removed from the great unfinished question of world history: the freedom not of minorities, nor of states, but of the majority.

Index

immigration restrictions, 272, 275
imperialism, 52, 208
  and modernisation theory, 68-9
  theories of, 5, 71-2
import substitution, 56
  in Africa, 110, 115-16
  failures of, 56, 75, 115-16
  and industrialisation, 9, 47, 52, 115-16
  in Latin America, 55, 74-5
income
  average, 19, 28, 201
  distribution, 75, 274
India, 9, 14, 55, 131, 200, 201, 279, 281
  agriculture, 8, 127-8, 134, 138, 161
  Bengal
    food distribution, 173, 176-83
  child labour, 145-6
  development economics, 50
  exports, 211
  famine, 161-2, 166, 167
  foreign investment in, 210
  GDP, 40
  import substitution, 9
  industrialisation, 19
  MNCs in, 238, 240
  role of women, 153, 154, 156
  socialism in, 48
  terms of trade, 128-30
  urban-rural relations, 128-9, 135
Indian Academy of Paediatrics, 177
Indian Statistical Institute, 179
Indonesia, 48, 131
Industrial Development Authority, 256, 259
industrialisation, 203-4
  average income, 201
  barriers to entry, 246-8, 251, 253, 257
  and donor agencies, 117-18
  gender relations, 66
  in Ireland, 245-60
  in Latin America, 47-8, 74-6
  and MNCs, 212
  in modernisation theory, 65
  problems of, 54-6
  and protectionism, 113, 116
  through import substitution, 9, 47, 52, 115-16
  women in, 195-6
Institute of Nutrition and Food Science, Dacca, 174
integration strategy, 78-82
Interfutures, 160
international agencies

  and integration of women, 80-81
International Comparison Project, 39-40
International Development Bank (IDB), 275
International Labour Organisation (ILO), 50, 56, 141, 236, 238
  and MNCs, 214, 238
International Monetary Fund (IMF), 110, 275
  conditionality, 121-2
  and debt crisis, 8, 263, 270
  lender of last resort, 275, 276
  and MNCs, 206-7
investment trends, 242-5
Iran, 13, 238, 239
Ireland, xvi, 248-9
  employment, 252-3, 259
  foreign investment, 196, 250, 254-7, 259
  Great Famine, 92, 165, 167
  indigenous industry, 249-54, 259-60
  niche industries, 258
  in the 1980s, 258-60
irrigation schemes, 95
Islam, 66, 154
Italy, 272
Ivory Coast, 8, 155
  export crops, 99, 104

J
Jamaica Women's Bureau, 226
Japan, 66, 125, 244, 272
  industrialisation, 201, 221, 246, 257-8
  MNCs, 221, 237, 240, 242
  modernisation theory, 16
Java, 131
Jenks, Wilfred, 236

K
Kenya, 14, 40, 103, 131
  export crops, 99
  women in agriculture, 153-4, 156
Keynes, John Maynard, 276
Keynesianism, 56
Kidron, Michael, 53
Kiernan, V G, 15
kinship
  effects of modernisation, 67-8
  and female factory workers, 231-2
  in traditional society, 60-1

L
labour, division of, 69, 74, 197-204